SUVAMADVIPA ANCIENT INDIA COLONIES IN THE EAST (2VOLS.)

SUVAMADVIPA ANCIENT INDIA COLONIES IN THE EAST (2VOLS.)

BY

R.C. MAJUMDAR

GYAN

ISBN : 978-81-212-0040-0(SET)

ISBN : 978-81-212-0178-0(VOL2)

First Published, 1986

Published by

Gyan Publishing House
5, Ansari Road
Daryaganj, New Delhi-110002
Phone: 011-47034999, 9811692060
www.gyanbooks.com
E-mail: books@gyanbooks.com

Printed at: G. Print Process, Delhi.

SUVARṆADVĪPA

ANCIENT INDIAN COLONIES IN THE FAR EAST

SUVARNADVĪPA

ANCIENT INDIAN COLONIES IN THE FAR EAST

R. C. MAJUMDAR

Volume Two

(CULTURAL HISTORY)

IN TWO VOLUMES

GIAN

GIAN PUBLISHING HOUSE

New Delhi-110002

GIAN PUBLISHING HOUSE
PUBLISHERS OF BOOKS ON HUMAN CIVILIZATION
4-C, Ansari Road, Daryaganj New Delhi-110 002

First Reprint in India, 1986

Published by Mrs. Gayatri Garg for Gian Publishing House, New Delhi-110002.
Printed at Goyal Offset Works, Delhi.

TABLE OF CONTENTS

PAGE

Book VI. Art in Suvarnadvipa

PREFACE

There has been some delay in bringing out this volume on account of the large number of plates which I found it necessary to insert for illustrating the chapter on Art. Where it has not been possible to add illustrations, I have given reference to texts which contain them, so that, with the help of these, even readers, unacquainted with Dutch, will be able to follow the description given in this book.

I take this opportunity of expressing my gratitude to the following for their kind permission to reproduce plates published by them.

1. Kern Institute, Leiden
2. Kirtya Liefrinck-van der Tuuk, Singaradja (Bali)
3. The India Society, London
4. Bruno Cassirer, Berlin
5. G. Kolff and Co. Batavia
6. Martinus Nijhoff, the Hague

As already announced in Preface to Part I, the next volume of this series, published in two parts, will deal with Kāmboja (Cambodia and Siam). But in view of my present administrative duties and other commitments I am unable to say when, if ever, they will see the light of the day.

Ramna, Dacca
August, 28, 1938.

R. C. Majumdar

ABBREVIATIONS

(In addition to those given in Part I)

A. S. R.=Report of the Archæological Survey of India published under the superintendence of Major-General Sir A. Cunningham, Vols. 1—XXIII. (1861 etc.). (Published by the Government of India).

Moojen-Bali=Kunst op Bali by P. A. J. Moojen, Adi Poestaka, The Hague (1926).

Stutterheim-Bali=Oudheden van Bali by Dr. W. F. Stutterheim, Published by Kirtya Liefrinck-van der Tuuk, Singaradja, 1930.

ADDITIONS AND CORRECTIONS

Part I

Page 197. f.n. 2. Cf. T. B. G. 1937, p. 251.

Page 204. The location of Zābag and connected problems have been discussed by J. L. Moens in an elaborate article in T. B. G. 1937, pp. 317-487.

Page 241 f.n. 7. Read 'Nos. 10 and 11' in place of 'Nos. 8 and 9'.

Page 354. About Bhre Daha, cf. T. B. G. 1936, p. 338.

Part II

Page 74. f.n. 1. The text of Koravāśrama has been edited with a translation by Dr. J. L. Swellengrebel (Thesis for Doctorate, Leiden University, 1936).

Page 86. l. 21. On Tantri Kāmandaka, cf. I. H. Q. Vol. XIII, p. 506.

Page 105. f.n. 2. Cf. also T. B. G. 1936, p. 471.

Page 225 for §7 read §8.

Page 296. l. 1. For Pl. XLVI, *read* Pl. XLII.

LIST OF PLATES

Book V

CULTURE AND CIVILISATION IN SUVARNADVIPA

SUVARṆADVĪPA

BOOK V

Chapter I.

LAW

The legal system of Java was mainly of Hindu origin, though modified by local conditions. There were written law-codes in Java and Bali, and these resembled the Indian Law-books—Dharmaśāstras or Smṛtis—to a large extent, both in form and substance. How far these Law-books were promulgated by constituted authorities and represented the actual conditions of society is a common problem both for India and her colonies. But the general picture afforded by these books may be taken in either case as a safe guide for obtaining a broad view of the state and society in the past. The variations of rules and principles noticed in different law-books must be attributed, as in the case of India, to varying indigenous customs in different localities and in different ages. To this we may perhaps add the influence of the different Indian Law-books introduced, perhaps at different times, in Java.

Among the more important Law-books of Java and Bali which are known to exist at the present time, the following deserve special mention.[1] :—

1. Sārasamuccaya[2]—It consists mostly of Sanskrit verses, followed by an Old-Javanese translation. It begins with an

1. The list is given on the authority of Juynboll (B.K.I., Vol. 71, pp. 568-569). It differs from that in Friederich-Bali, pp. 93 ff. See further fn. 3, p. 2, and fn. 1, 2, p. 3.

2. This is different from a Tutur work of the same name, though Friederich (op. cit) took the two to be identical. cf. Cat. II, pp. 275-6.

account of Viṣṇu who came to Mdang, ruled there as *rahyang tavkan dyāvan*, and had four sons.

2. Svara Jambu (probably corrupted from Svayambhu)[1] is mostly the translation of the eighth book of the Mānava-dharmaśāstra. Only the last part, written in later dialect, deviates from this source.

3. The Śivaśāsana, written in pure Old-Javanese, is referred to in an inscription of 991 A.D., and is associated with king Dharmavaṁśa teguh Anantavikramottuṅgadeva.[2]

4. The work generally known as Pūrvādhigama, and designated at the end as 'Śivaśāsana-sāroddhṛta' may be regarded as a later redaction of No. 3.

5. The Balinese work Pūrva-āgama is perhaps the modern form of No. 4.

6. The Devāgama, also known as Kṛtopapati, quotes many rules from Māṇava-dharmaśāstra.

7. The Kuṭāra-mānava is also largely influenced by Mānava-dharmaśāstra.

8. 'Gajah Mada'—a law book attributed to Gajah Mada, the famous Prime Minister of Majapahit. The existing text is undoubtedly more modern, but as Gajah Mada is credited with a knowledge of law in Nag. Kr. (12 : 4), it is not unlikely that he was the author of the original work.[3]

9. Ādigama—This is one of the Law-books now regarded as authentic in Buleleng (Bali). It is attributed to Kanaka, the Prime Minister of Majapahit from 1413 to 1430. The date given in the manuscript is 1401 A.D.

---

1. Jonker—Wetboek, p. 3,

2. See p. 264, Part I. For Nos, 3-5, cf. also Krom—Geschiedenis, pp. 230-231.

3. For Nos. 8 and 9, cf. Krom, op. cit., pp. 421-2, 445. No. 8 is not mentioned by Juynboll.

10-11. Kerta Sima and Kerta Sima Subak, showing strong Balinese influence.[1]

12. Pasvara—a comparatively recent Balinese Law-book[2] in the form of a collection of royal edicts. There are many collections of this kind.

Among the texts mentioned above, the Kuṭāra-mānava[3], No. 7, which is now held authentic in Bali, may form the basis of a detailed study of the Indo-Javanese law. The book was regarded as of the highest authority in the flourishing period of the Majapahit empire. This is indisputably proved by the Bendasari inscription[4] dating from the middle of the fourteenth century A.D. It is a record of a judgment in a civil case (dispute over the possession of land) and describes the way in which the judges came to a decision. There were six of them, referred to as '*Dharmapravakta Vyavahāra-vicchedaka*'. They heard the statements of both the parties, and in accordance with established practice, interrogated some impartial local people about it. Then they took into consideration the law, as enunciated in legal texts, the local usages and customs, the precedents, and the

1. For Nos. 10 and 11, cf. T.B.G., Vol. XXIII.

2. To this list we may add Agama, Duṣṭakalabaya, Devadaṇḍa and Yajña-Sadma mentioned by Friederich (op. cit, pp. 93-4) ; Drama Upapati (Dharmopapatti) and Uttara Mānava, mentioned by Van Eck ; and Śastra Pasobaya cited by Jonker (Wetboek, p. 3).

Among these Devadaṇḍa is described by Juynboll (Cat. II, pp. 182-184) and others, and there is a Dutch translation of it by Blokzijl (T.B.G., Vol. 18, pp. 295-309). But although the older writers describe it as written in very old language it is not borne out by the manuscripts catalogued by Juynboll. Of the other books I am not able to say much, not even whether they are all really different books from those mentioned above ; *e.g.* the 'Uttara-Mānava' may be the same as Kuṭāra-mānava.

3. Edited with a scholarly introduction and Dutch translation by J.B.G. Jonker (Leiden, 1885).

4. O.J.O., No. 85 ; Krom, op. cit., pp. 421-2.

opinions of religious teachers and old men, and ultimately decided according to the principles enunciated in Kuṭāra-mānava.

That the Kuṭāra-mānava was regarded as of the highest authority also follows from another inscription, dated 1358 A.D.,[1] in which the judges, seven in number, are described as '*Kuṭāra-mānavādi-śāstra-vivecana-tatpara*', *i.e.*, persons skilled in the knowledge of 'Kuṭāra-mānava and other Law-books.

The antiquity of the Law-book also follows from the total absence of fire-arms in the list of weapons, enumerated in section 59[2], by which a wound could be caused. The language of the existing text of the Kuṭāra-mānava, however, shows that it is a later redaction of that work, though it is not easy to determine the nature and extent of the modifications introduced in later times. That the book underwent some amount of Balinese influence is also clear from a study of the existing text.[3]

The text, as we have it now, is a compilation from various sources, some of which are named in the book itself, and others are referred to in general terms, such as 'so say the wise people,' *etc.* The arrangement is also somewhat irregular, the same topics even the same rules, recurring in different parts of the work, and sometimes there are different rules about the same topics, This is more particularly the case with regard to rules about slaves, pledge, the marriage-price, and adultery. The legal principles and detailed rules are mostly based on Hindu law-books, but slight modifications of these and addition of new rules betray clearly the influence of indigenous laws and customs. The influence of indigenous law and variations from or modifications of Indian law are clearly much greater in the earlier than in the later part, and this has given rise to the

1. O.V., 1918, pp. 108-112; Krom, op. cit., p. 422.
2. Jonker-Wetboek, p. 34.
3. Ibid, pp. 34-35.

question whether the whole of the present text formed part of the original work. The unity of the language is in favour of this view.[1] But Brandes thinks that it really consists of two parts, the Kuṭāra, inspired by Bhṛgu, and the Mānava, inspired by Manu. Brandes also refers to a Malay Chronicle according to which it was composed under Surya Alam, king of Demak.

About the indebtedness of Kuṭāra-mānava-śāstra to different Indian Law-books we find the following interesting passage in the book itself.

"A buffalo or a cow, given in pledge, is forfeited to the creditor, if it is not redeemed within three years. Thus says Kuṭārāgama. According to Mānavāgama, the period is five years. One of these two must be followed. It is wrong to suppose, however, that one of these Law-books is better than the other, both being authoritative. The Mānava-śāstra was communicated by Mahārāja Manu who was like god Viṣṇu. The Kuṭāra-śāstra was communicated by Bhṛgu in the Tretāyuga ; he was (also) like god Viṣṇu ; the Kuṭāra-śāstra is followed by Paraśurāma and by the whole world, it is not a product of the present time, but...........(121).[3]

In many other sections (*cf.* § 137, 143) also, the different rules of Mānava-śāstra and Kuṭāra-śāstra are placed side by side. There is no doubt that this circumstance explains the title of the Law-book. References to Manu or Mānava-śāstra are, however, more frequent.

What Indian Law-book is meant by Kuṭāra-śāstra, we do not know. The reference to Paraśurāma makes it plausible enough to derive Kuṭāra from Kuṭhāra,[4] but that does not help us much in tracing the original work.

---

1. Ibid, pp. 1-35.
2. Catalogue, sv. Kuṭāra-mānava.
3. The figures within bracket on this and the following pages indicate the section or paragraph of Kuṭāra-mānava-śāstra.
4. Jonker-Wetboek, p. 15.

As regards Mānava-śāstra there cannot, of course, be any doubt, that it refers to the famous Indian Law-book, Mānava-dharmaśāstra or Manu-saṁhitā. An analysis of the contents of the Javanese Law-book shows that this work formed its chief source. Not only numerous isolated verses, but sometimes a whole series of them, are reproduced, with slight variations and modifications in many cases. These variations are sometimes the results of the misunderstanding of the original text, but are also in some cases undoubtedly due to an effort to bring the law into line with Javanese conditions. But the parentage is unmistakable.

In the passages quoted from Manu-saṁhitā, the order of topics, and also, generally speaking, of the individual rules, closely follows that of the original. It is, therefore, exceedingly probable that there was an Old-Javanese translation of Manu-saṁhitā or parts of it (notably chaps. VIII-IX) as *e.g.*, Svara Jambu, from which our author largely borrowed. The high authority enjoyed by this Indian law-book is proved by other evidences also. It is mentioned in Bhomakāvya (1.5), and an Old-Javanese inscription [1] refers to it in such a way as to leave no doubt of its authoritative character. The Carita Parahyangan, from which so many interesting historical details have been quoted above, says of king Niskalavastu Kañcana, "that he did many good deeds for the holy persons, was dear unto the gods, and strictly followed the law-code of Manu".[2] The Ṛṣiśāsana also refers to Manu as law-giver,[3] while Pratasti Bhuvana and Puruṣadasanta refer to Manuśāsana[4]. All these references indicate the high honour in which Manu's Law-book was held in Java, and it is, therefore, quite natural that the Javanese law-book should take it as the chief guide.

---

1. K.O., No. 16.
2. Cf., Bk. III, Chs. I, VIII (pp. 230, 358).
3. Pigeaud—Tantu Panggelaran, p. 300.
4. Ibid, p. 294 : Juynboll, Cat. I, p. 211.

At the same time a close analysis of the Javanese text makes it abundantly clear that Indian law-books, other than Manu-saṁhitā, were consulted by the Javanese author.[1] For, in some cases more than one Hindu legal principle is given, while in others, such as the use of 'documentary evidence', '*Sāhasa*' (Assault), '*Śulka*' (marriage-price) *etc.*, the rules given differ from those of Manu. It is not always easy to trace the origin of these rules, but a strong presumption arises in certain cases. The rule, for example, that rights over land are barred by limitation after twenty years (268) is found in Yājñavalkya, Vyāsa, and Kauṭiliya alone, while the classification of interests for money (262) is given only in Bṛhaspati-saṁhitā. It is probable, therefore, that some of these law-books were known in Java, though the possibility is not excluded that the same rules occurred in other Indian law-books, or in different versions of existing law-books, not known to us at present. This possibility is strengthened by the fact that the Javanese law-book contains several Sanskrit terms which cannot be traced in existing Indian law-books *e.g.*, Pañcasādhāraṇa, Jīvadāna, Devāgama (for divya), *etc.*

While the Javanese law-book clearly shows that not only were Indian law-books known in general, but also the Indian legal system was transplanted in Java, it is equally clear at the same time that it was substantially modified by indigenous laws and customs. This is quite natural and inevitable, specially in view of the fact that in the Manu-saṁhitā the local manners and customs are recognised as possessing legal authority. These modifications are met with in other law-books of Java, such as Devadaṇḍa or Sāra-Samuccaya, and it is probable that legal texts like these served, in this respect, as the source of Kuṭāra-mānava-śāstra. These modifications will be noticed in course of explaining the detailed contents of the book, to which we may now turn.

---

1. Jonker—Wetboek, pp. 17 ff.

These detailed rules may be broadly divided into two classes, Civil and Criminal Law, and each is dealt with under several sub-heads or titles of law.

The very first section deals with murder. Eight classes of murderers are defined: (1) He who kills an innocent man; (2) he who incites another to kill an innocent man; (3) he who wounds an innocent man; (4) he who eats with a murderer; (5) he who keeps company with a murderer; (6) he who is on friendly terms with a murderer; (7) he who gives shelter to a murderer; and (8) he who renders any help to a murderer. The first three classes are liable to capital punishment, which however may be changed by the king to a fine of 40,000[1] The last five are liable to a fine of 20,000.

Similarly, thieves are divided into eight classes (21-28) on the above principle so as to include, in addition to actual thieves, those who instigate, help, or befriend him. The man who actually steals is not only liable to capital punishment, but his wives (lit. women) and children together with all his possessions become the property of the king. But a thief may purchase life by paying 40,000 to the king, and a compensation to the owner equivalent to double the value of the stolen goods. He who instigates another to commit theft is also liable to capital punishment. His wives and children may escape with a heavy fine, but if they are also guilty of joining him in instigating the crime, they are liable to capital punishment. Other abettors of the crime are fined according to the nature and gravity of the offence.

The next important headings of criminal law are defamation and assault described in the Indian Law-books by the technical terms Vākpāruṣya and Daṇḍapāruṣya. Here, for the first

---

1. While giving the amount of fines, the law-book never states the unit coin it has in view. For reasons explained below, the value of this unit may be regarded as one-twentieth of that (paṇa) used in Manu-saṁhitā.

time, we meet with that discrimination of treatment in law according to the caste of persons, which is a characteristic feature of Hindu law. In order to give an adequate idea of this, we may give in full the penalties for abuse or defamation. If the offender and the offended belong to the same class the fine is only 250. The following table shows the amount of fines when the two parties belong to different castes.

Offender	*Offended*	*Penalty (Figures denote Amount of fine)*
Brāhmaṇa	Kṣatriya	1,000
Do	Vaiśya	500
Do	Śūdra	250
Kṣatriya	Brāhmaṇa	2,000
Do	Vaiśya	1,000
Vaiśya	Brāhmaṇa	5,000
Do	Kṣatriya	2,000
Do	Śūdra	1,000
Śūdra	Brāhmaṇa	*Death*
Do	Kṣatriya	5,000
Do	Vaiśya	2,000

The regulations exactly follow Manu-saṁhitā (VIII. 267-269), if we regard the unit, to which the amount of fine refers, as one-twentieth of that used in Manu. The Javanese law-book, however, gives a complete statement, and further adds that a Caṇḍāla who defames a Brāhmaṇa should be put to death.

Similarly, the rules about the assault closely follow those of Manu. The famous dictum of Manu, that "with whatever limb a man of a low caste does hurt to (a man of the three) highest (castes), even that limb shall be cut off" (VIII. 279), is reproduced with the specification of the limbs. As a matter of fact many of the penal laws about assault, hurt, theft, robbery, plunder, cattle-lifting, damage or destruction of property, and adultery are taken directly from Manu, and the following passages from this law-book are reproduced with little or no modification : Manu-saṁhitā—Bk. VIII, verses 279-284, 286-288, 295-300, 320-23, 325, 328-330, 337, 350, 352, 356, 357, 361, and also probably 365 and 366. All these penal laws provide discrimination in punishment, according to castes, as in the case of defamation, and need not be described in detail. There are, of course, additional rules or illustrations in many cases, too numerous to mention in detail.

Penalties are also laid down for miscellaneous offences such as witchery (27, 173, 174, 178-182), quackery (274) etc.

Although the system of criminal law is evidently based on Hindu law and follows it closely, we may notice some striking differences which are presumably to be attributed to indigenous influence.

In the first place, the regulations about murder and theft are more comprehensive than what we find in the Hindu law. They also introduce two new principles, *viz.*, (1) that the crime is shared by the abettors and friends of the criminals, and (2) even the family members of the criminal (in case of theft) and persons who instigate the crime are liable to punishment.

Secondly, the penal law in Java shows that the old idea that offences were torts rather than crimes had not altogether died out. Although offences were usually regarded as crimes and punished by the king with fine and corporal punishment, the idea of paying compensation to the injured is more marked in the Javanese law than in the Hindu law-books. For example, in Manu VIII, 295-296, the death caused by rash driving is considered purely as a crime, but the corresponding rule in Javanese law-book (232) adds that a compensation should be paid to the blood-relations of the deceased, if he is a free man, and to his owner, if he is a slave. The same conclusions follow from the laws of adultery (134-8) in which the fine was chiefly a compensation to the injured husband, and the latter had the right to put the criminal to death if he were caught red-handed. Again, the penalties imposed by Manu for theft include only in two specific cases

(VIII—319-20) a compensation to the owner, equivalent to the value of the stolen goods. But the general rule in Java was to add to the fine a compensation equivalent to double the value of the goods stolen.

Thirdly, while both Javanese and Hindu laws make discrimination according to castes, in awarding punishments for various offences, the former make an exception in cases of murder and theft (1-2, 21-28). In other words, all criminals in Java, accused of these two offences, were dealt with in the same way, irrespective of the castes to which they belonged, while in India, the consideration of caste prevailed even in these two classes of crimes.

The Civil Law throws a great deal of light on the social conditions in Java, and, in particular, deals in great detail with two classes of persons, *viz* : (1) Women and (2) Slaves.

The marriage of a woman is preceded by the payment of *Sulka* or marriage-price by the bridegroom. The acceptance of this price by the bride's party creates the legal obligation to marry the girl to the bridegroom. If the father marries the girl to another or connives at the girl's marrying another, he has not only to return to the original suitor twice the amount given by him, but is also fined 40,000 by the king. The girl and her husband also are each fined the same amount (18.111). If the bridegroom, after the payment of the price, refuses, or fails to marry the bride within five months, the price remains with the bride as her own property (213-14). On the other hand if he violates the girl before the fixed date, he not only loses the price but is also fined 40,000 (192). If a bride dies after the payment of the price, the bridegroom cannot claim it back. On the other hand, if the bridegroom dies after paying the price, his younger brother (*devara*), if any, may, if he so desire, claim the bride as his own (215).

But a girl was legally entitled to refuse to marry anyone suffering from physical deformities or disabilities, bad diseases in hidden parts of the body, insanity, impotence, or epilepsy. In these cases she had simply to refund the marriage-price.

The law lays down no restriction regarding the prohibited degrees of marriage except that one should be punished if one marries his step-daughter (149)[1]. As regards legal formalities, a sort of registration by the village headman seems to be regarded as essential (191).

The grounds, stated above, on which a maid could refuse to marry a man, also entitled her to seek divorce even after the marriage were consummated. A wife could also seek divorce from her husband simply on the ground that she disliked him (19); and so could the father of the girl dissolve the marriage if he disliked his son-in-law (125); but in either case twice the marriage-price had to be refunded to him, and certain prescribed ceremonials had to be gone through before the marriage was legally dissolved. The relevant law runs as follows: "For a divorce four things are necessary: (1) Pronouncement of the divorce; (2) the breaking of a coin while the husband makes the pronouncement; (3) the giving of water to wash the face; (4) the giving of a rice. These serve as the evidences of the divorce. After all these four are performed the marriage is deemed to be legally dissolved, but not otherwise. If a woman re-marries without going through these formalities, then the new husband will be fined, 40,000" (5).

Further, a woman could divorce her husband, before the marriage was consummated, simply by repaying double the marriage-price, and evidently without any other formality (126).

This is clearly an indigenous custom which is not only without any parallel in Indian Law-books, but directly contrary to the spirit and provisions of Hindu law. But the influence of the latter is clearly visible in another set of regulations. These prescribe heavy penalties for the man who takes to wife a married woman with husband living (17). The former husband can either put the new pair to death or accept a fine of 40,000. Those who were witnesses of such a marriage are also liable to heavy fines.

---

1 According to Vratiśāsana, certain relatives could not be married (Pigeaud—Tantu Panggelaran, p. 296).

But in certain contingencies even a married woman, with husband alive, could take another husband after waiting for a prescribed period. These are described in a tabular form below (143, 254-256).

Conditions of the husband	Period of waiting.
1. Going abroad for performing sacred or religious duty, penance, or some other good work.	8 years.
2. Going abroad to learn the śāstras. ...	6 „
3. Going abroad for commerce, sea-voyage, or acquisition of wealth	10 „
4. Going abroad to marry a second wife. ...	3 „
5. Making journey to distant lands. ...	4 „
6. If the husband is absent but not on any ground mentioned in 2, 3, and 5 above	4 „
7. If the husband is mad, epileptic, impotent, or destitute of manly strength	3 „
8. If the husband is lost (*i.e.* missing), dies in course of journey, becomes a monk, or is impotent.	nil.

Nearly the whole of these regulations is based on Hindu legal principles as enunciated in Manu (IX. 76-78) and Nārada (XII. 97ff) and follow them closely. These are followed immediately by the single regulation which authorises a husband to discard a wife.

"If a wife dislikes her husband, he must wait for one year. After that, if the dislike still continues, she shall return double the marriage-price. This is named—rejection of sexual intercourse" (257).

This is obviously based on Manu IX. 77. But it is to be noted that while this and other Indian law-books authorise the husband to discard his wife on this and sundry other grounds (cf. Manu, IX. 80-81) the Javanese law-book ignores them altogether, save and except this one, *i.e.*, on ground of dislike. But, then, it is to be remembered that the Javanese law-book gives the same right to the wife, *viz.*, to divorce the husband if he dislikes her. Again, the Javanese laws that a wife could marry again, if the husband was mad, epileptic, or destitute of manly strength, or that a Javanese maid could refuse to marry or seek divorce from a husband suffering from diseases, physical deformities, or disabilities *etc.*, have no parallel in Indian Law-books. Rather, according to Manu (IX. 78), "she who shows disrespect to a husband who is addicted to (some evil) passion, is a drunkard, or diseased, shall be deserted for three months (and be) deprived of her ornaments and furniture," though the same Law-book permits a diseased wife to be superseded at any time by another wife" (IX-80). When we remember that the Javanese law-book so closely followed the Manusaṁhitā, the additions and the omissions leave no doubt that a woman enjoyed a far higher status in Java that in India in the age of Manu. In support of this view we may quote a curious provision of the law that a man shall be fined 20,000 if he quarrels with a woman, the amount to accrue to her husband, if the woman were married (142).

But while the Javanese law gave means to a wife to regain her independence, the husband seems to have complete domination over her so long as she remains in his family. The head of the family is to keep a strict vigilance on women, slaves, and children, and can even chastise them for doing wrong by a cane or a wooden stick. But he must not strike them on the head, otherwise he should be fined by the king (131). This is obviously a leaf taken out of Manu's book (cf. VIII. 299, 300). The dominance of the husband is also manifest from the following :—

"Father alone has the control of children, not the mother. If a mother arrange the marriage of her daughter without the consent of the father, the father may dissolve the match, and the marriage-price has to be returned to the rejected suitor by the mother and the girl" (193).

PLATE I

Fig. 1. Candi Bima (Dieng) (Krom, Pl. 2).

Fig. 2. Candi Kalasan (Krom. Pl. 11).

PLATE II

Fig. 1. Candi Sari (Krom, Pl. 15).

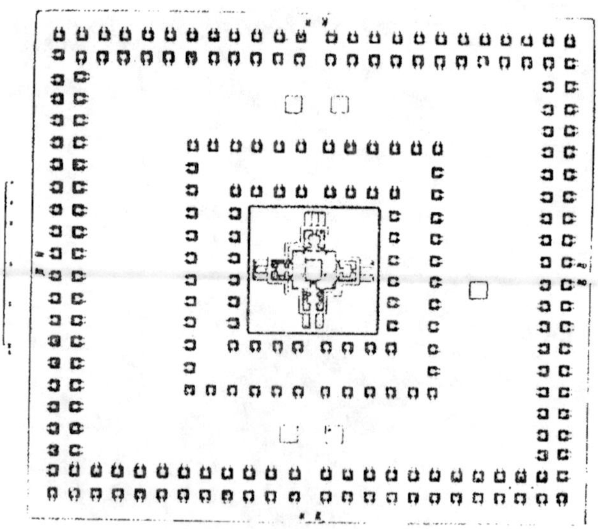

Fig. 2. General Plan of Candi Sevu (Krom, Pl. 15).

PLATE III

Candi Mendut (restored) (Krom, Pl. 20).

PLATE IV

Candi Pavon (Krom, Pl. 24).

PLATE V

General Plate of Barabodur (Krom, Pl. 25).

PLATE VI

General View of Barabudur (Krom, Pl. 27).

PLATE VII

Fig. 1. Gallery, Barabudur. (Krom, Pl. 28).

Fig. 2. Staircase and Gateway, Barabudur. (Krom, Pl. 29).

PLATE VIII

Fig. 1. Upper three Terraces and the Main Stupa, Barabudur. (Krom, Pl. 10).

Fig. 2. Monument of Cupuvata. (Krom, Pl. 10).

PLATE IX

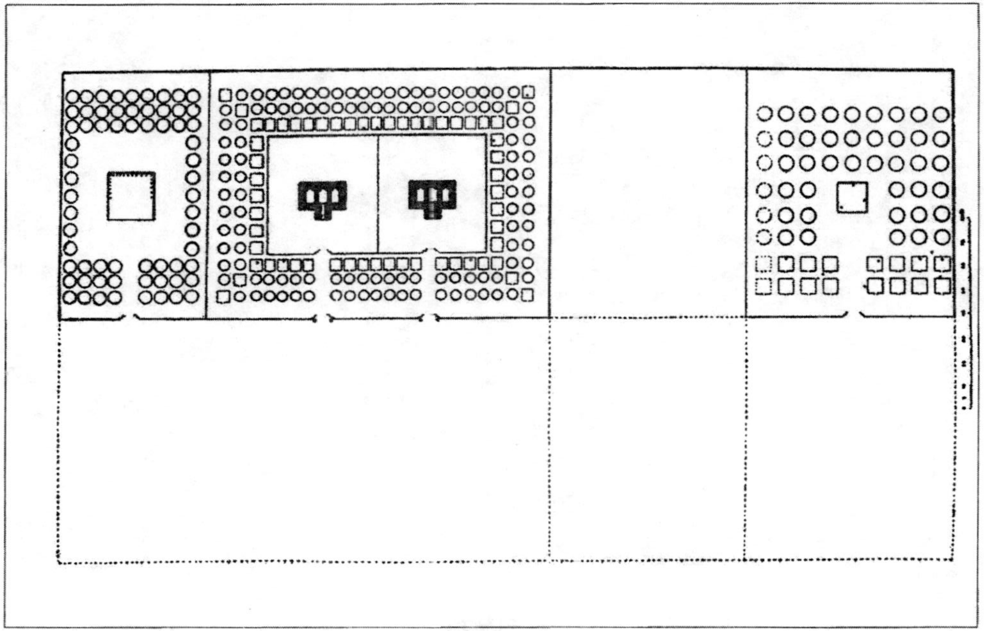

General Plan, Plaosan (Krom, Pl 41).

PLATE X

Siva Temple, Lara Jongrang (Krom, Pl. 36).

PLATE XI

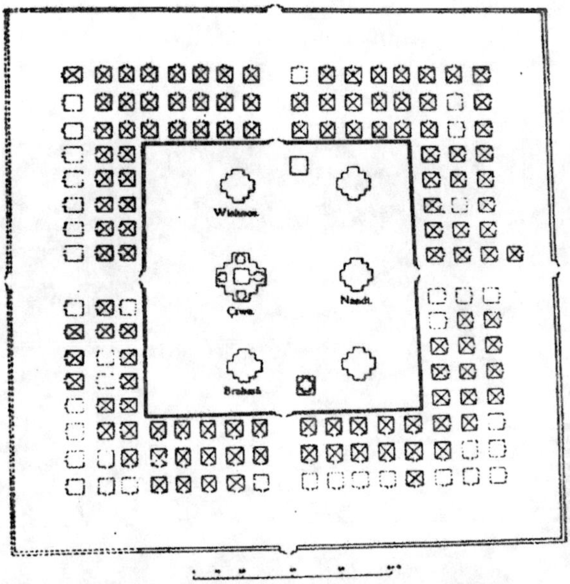

Fig. 1. General Plan of Lara-Jongrang. (Krom, Pl. 35).

Fig. 2. Candi Merak–Doorway of the Gopuram.

PLATE XII

Fig. 1. Bagelen Image of Siva (?) (Cohn-Ind., Fig. 157)

Fig. 2. Human Bust, Candi Bima. (Cohn-Ind., Fig. 158)

PLATE XIII

Buddha, Barabudur (Krom, Pl. 32).

PLATE XIV

Avalokitesvara of Candi Mendut.(Krom, Pl. 21).

PLATE XV

Fig. 1. Descent of Bodhisatva.(Krom–Barabudur).

Fig. 2. Selection of Gopa.(Krom– Barabudur).

PLATE XVI

Fig. 1. Buddha and the Sick.(Krom–Barabudur).

Fig. 2. Buddha and the Sleeping Dancing Girls.(Krom – Barabudur).

PLATE XVII

Fig. 1. Visit of Bimbisara. (Krom–Barabudur).

Fig. 2. Buddha and his Five Disciples. (Krom–Barabudur).

PLATE XVIII

Fig. 1. Buddha and the Gods. (Krom–Barabudur).

Fig. 2. Buddha Washing the Cloth. (Krom–Barabudur).

PLATE XIX

Fig. 1. Story of Sudhanakumara. (Krom–Barabudur).

Fig. 2. Barabudur Panel–Dancing Scene (Cohn, Pl. 155).

Fig. 3. Barabudur Panel–Court Scene (Cohn, Pl. 154).

PLATE XX

Fig. 1. Anantarayana of Visnu (Panel I).(Kats-Ramayana).

Fig. 2. Visvamitra Visits king Dasaratha (Panel II).(Kats-Ramayana).

Fig. 3. Coronation of Bharata (Panel X).

Fig. 4. Dasaratha and Kausalya (Panel XI).

Fig. 5. Rama and Sita driving to the Forest (Pane XII) (Kats-Ramayana).

PLATE XXI

Fig. 1. Rejection of Surpanakha (Panels XVII-XVIII).

Fig. 2. Death of Marici (Panels XIX, XX) (Kats-Ramayana).

Fig. 3. Hanuman Recites the Story of Sita and Rama (Panels XXXIX) (Kats-Ramayana).

Fig. 4. Sita and Hanuman (Panels XXXV, XXXVI) (Kats-Ramayana).

PLATE XXII

Mahadeva. Lara Jongrang (Krom, Pl. 39).

PLATE XXIII

Fig. 1. Images from Candi Banon.(Krom, Pl. 22).

Fig. 2. Images from Candi Banon.(Krom, Pl. 22).

PLATE XXIV

Fig. 1. Part of the Stone Gateway, Candi Merak.

Fig. 2. Decorated Fragments, Candi Merak.

Fig. 3. Fragment of Cornice, Candi Merak.

Fig. 4. Stoneblock for closing the Shrine (?) Candi Merak.

PLATE XXV

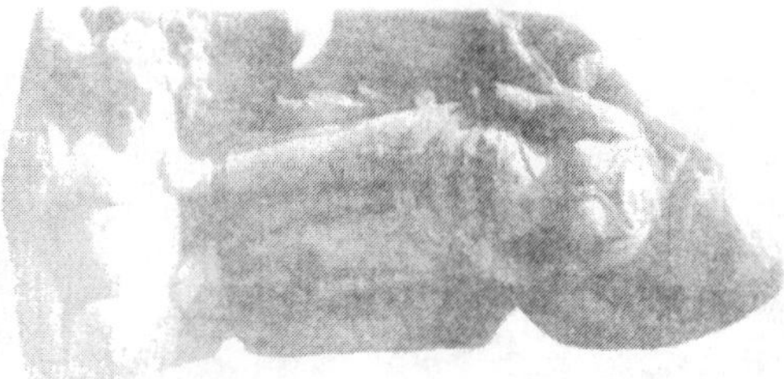

Fig. 1. Durga Image, Candi Merak.

Fig. 2. Fragments of Images, Candi Merak.

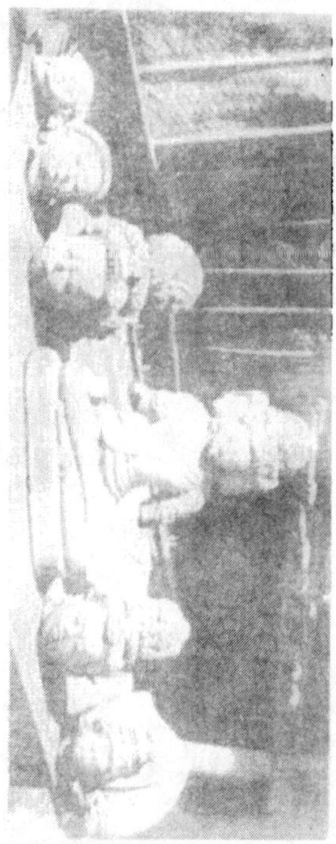

Fig. 3. Fragments of Gateway, Candi Merak.

PLATE XXVI

Image of Maitreya, Candi Plaosan (Krom, Pl. 44).

PLATE XXVII

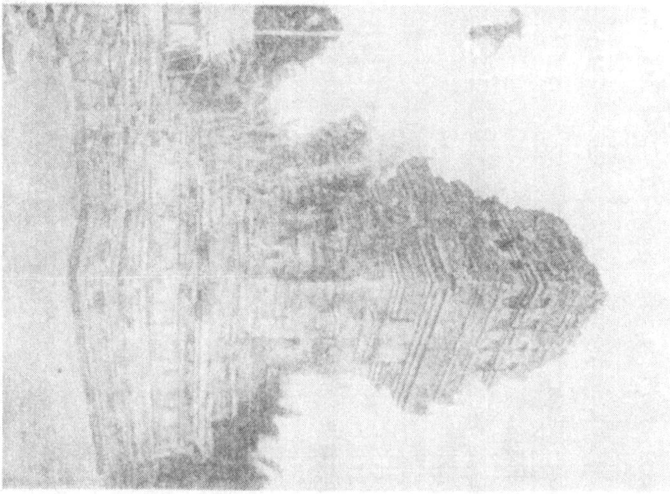

Fig. 1. Candi Kidal.(Krom, Pl. 49).

Fig. 2. Candi Jago.(Krom, Pl. 57).

PLATE XXVIII

Reconstruction of Candi Singhasari. (Krom, Pl. 51).

PLATE XXIX

Fig. 1. Gateway of Bajang-ratu. (Krom, Pl. 68).

Fig. 2. Candi Jabung. (Krom, Pl. 70).

PLATE XXX

Candi Pari (Krom, Pl. 74).

PLATE XXXI

Main Temple, Panataran (Restored). (Krom. Pl. 80).

PLATE XXXII

Fig. 1. Pyramidal Platform, Sukuh (Krom, Pl. 99).

Fig. 2. Hanuman Recites the Story of Sita Rama. Panataran (Panel 58). (Kats-Ramayana).

Fig. 3. Sita and Hanuman. Panataran (Panel 100). (Kats-Ramayana).

PLATE XXXIII

Sudhanakumara, Candi Jago (Krom, Pl. 63).

PLATE XXXIV

Prajnaparamita of Singhasari. (Krom, Pl. 54).

PLATE XXXV

Vienu Image of Belahan. (Krom, Pl. 47).

PLATE XXXVI

Harihara of Simping (Krom, Pl. 65).

PLATE XXXVII

Fig. 1. Image from Sikuning, E. Java (Krom, Pl. 94).

Fig. 2. Maharsi Trnavindu, Candi Singhasari (Pl. 79).

Fig. 3. Head of the Woman, Majapahit (I.A.L., III, Pl. V).

Fig. 4. Male Head, Sukuh (Krom, Pl. 99).

PLATE XXXVIII

Fig. 1. Water Spouts, Majakerta.(Krom, Pl. 103).

Fig. 2. Water Spouts, Majakerta.(Krom, Pl. 103).

PLATE XXXIX

Fig. 1. Kala-head, Candi Jago.(Krom, Pl. 52).

Fig. 2. Kala-head, Candi Singhasari.(Krom, Pl. 52).

PLATE XL

Fig. 1. Temple Guard (back), Panataran. (Krom, Pl. 84).

Fig. 2. Pedestal, E. Java. (Krom, Pl. 95).

PLATE XLI

Fig. 1. Entrance to Main Shrine, Candi Jago. (Krom, Pl. 61).

Fig. 2. Staircase Wing–Candi Jago. (Krom, Pl. 60).

PLATE XLII

Bronze Images, Nganjuk. (Krom, Pl. 109).

PLATE XLIII

Branze images (Swabe Colllection).

PLATE XLIV

Fig. 1. Bronze Image of Vairocana and Vajradhatvisvara Leiden Museum. (Juynboll–Catalogue, Pl. XI-2).

Fig. 2. Bronze Image of Sri. (Resink Collection) (Krom, Pl. 108).

PLATE XLV

Fig. 1. Bronze Image of Trailokya-Vijaya, Jogyakerta.

Fig. 2. (Cohn–Ind., Figs. 166-167)

PLATE XLVI

Fig. 1. Decorative Relief, Candi Jago. (Candi Jago, Pl. 189).

Fig. 2. Bronze Group of Siva and Parvati from Temanggung.
(I.A.L., III, Pl. IV).

PLATE XLVII

Fig. 1. Bell Cast in Bronze, from Kalasan (I.A.L., Vol. II, Pl. III, p. 74).

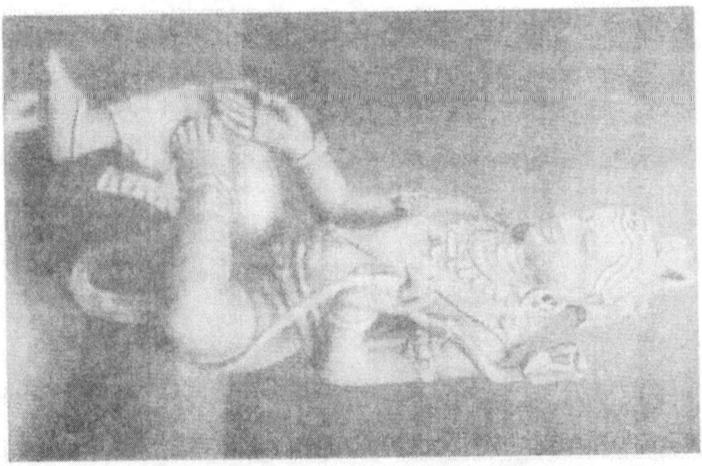

Fig. 2. Manjusri Statuette in Solid Silver Java A.D. 800 (?)
(I.A.L., II, Pl. II).

PLATE XLVIII

Fig. 1. Rock-hewn Temples of Gunang Kavi near Tampaksiring. (Krom, Pl. 48).

Fig. 2. General Plan of Temples in Bali (Moojen, Fig. 21).

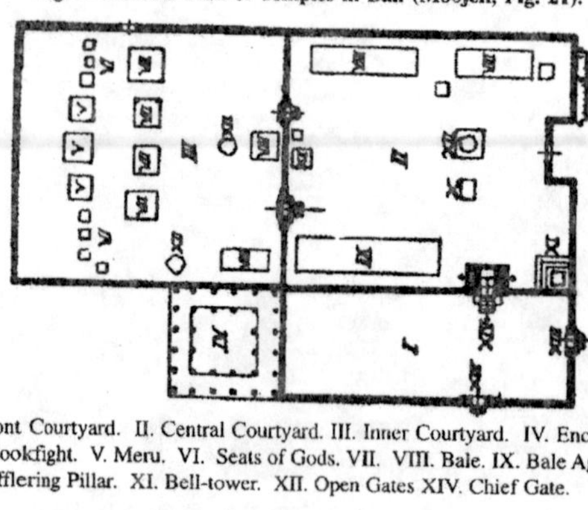

I. Front Courtyard. II. Central Courtyard. III. Inner Courtyard. IV. Enclosure for Cookfight. V. Meru. VI. Seats of Gods. VII. VIII. Bale. IX. Bale Agung. X. Offlering Pillar. XI. Bell-tower. XII. Open Gates XIV. Chief Gate.

PLATE XLIX

Meru and Gedong Kehen in the Besakih Temple. (Moojen, Pl. CCII).

PLATE L

Meru, Kesiman (Bali). (Moojen, Pl. LXXIV).

PLATE LI

Gateways, Singaraja Temple (Bali). (Moojen Pl. CI).

PLATE LII

Fig. 1. Maospait Temple at Tonjo (Bali). (Moojen, Pl. XCIII).

Fig. 2. Singaraja Temple, Offering Pillar, with Niche. (Moojen, Pl. CIII).

PLATE LIII

Stone Bell-tower, Blayu (Bali). (Moojen, Pl. LXVI).

PLATE LIV

Siva Image from Bedulu. (Stutterheim–Bali, Fig. 11).

PLATE LV

Fig. 1. Sacred Altars for Keeping Offerings, Padmasana, Bungkulan (Bali) (Moojen, Pl. CXXIV).

Fig. 2. King and Queen (1011 A.D.), Pura Sukavana, (Stutterheim–Bali Fig. 20).

Fig. 3. Female figure as Water-Spout, Goa Gaja. (Stutterheim–Bali, Fig. 21).

PLATE LVI

Fig. 1. Buddhist Image from Pura Subak, Kedangan.
(Stutterheim–Bali, Fig. 4).

Fig. 2. A Queen from Panataran
Sasih , Pejeng; 1342 A.D.
(Stutterheim– Bali, Fig. 44).

Fig. 3. Caturkaya, with Emblems of
Brahma,Visnu, and Siva at Pura
Panataran Sasih, Pejeng.
(Stutterheim–Bali, Fig. 49).

PLATE LVII

Fig. 1. Caturkaya, with Mask, Pejeng (Stutterheim–Bali, Fig. 50).

Fig. 2. Sacred Water-Pot, Pejeng (Stutterheim–Bali, Fig. 57).

PLATE LVIII

Fig. 1. Sculptured reliefs, Jeh Pulu.

Fig. 2. Sculptured reliefs, Jeh Pulu.

PLATE LIX

Fig. 1. Sculptured reliefs, Jeh Pulu.

Fig. 2. Sculptured reliefs, Jeh Pulu.

PLATE LX

Fig. 1. Gateway, Pura Beji Sangsit (Bali). (Moojen, Pl. CXLV).

PLATE LXI

Fig. 1. Nrisimha-figure as Water-spout, Pejeng. (Stutterheim–Bali, Fig. 58).

Fig. 2. Stone Buddha Image, Seguntang Hill, Palembang.

PLATE LXII

Fig. 1. Stone Buddha Image, Seguntang Hill, Palembang (front).
(A.B.I.A., 1931, Pl. XI).

Fig. 2. Stone Buddha Image, Seguntang Hill, Palembang (back).
(A.B.I.A., 1931, Pl. XI).

PLATE LXIII

Antiquities of Palembang (A.B.I.A., 1993, Pl. X).

(a) Bonze Head of Buddha Image

(b) Bonze Head of Buddha Image

(c) Bronze Image of Maitreya

(d) Bronze Image of Avalokitesvara

(e) Bronze Image of Buddha

PLATE LXIV

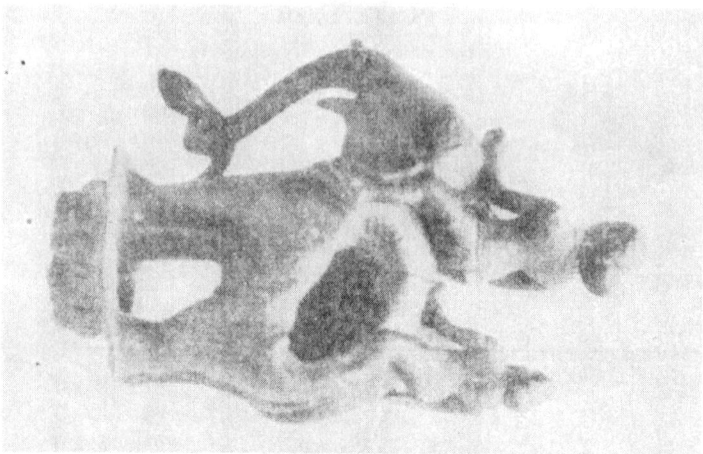

Fig. 1. Bronze Elephant with a female driver (Sumatra).

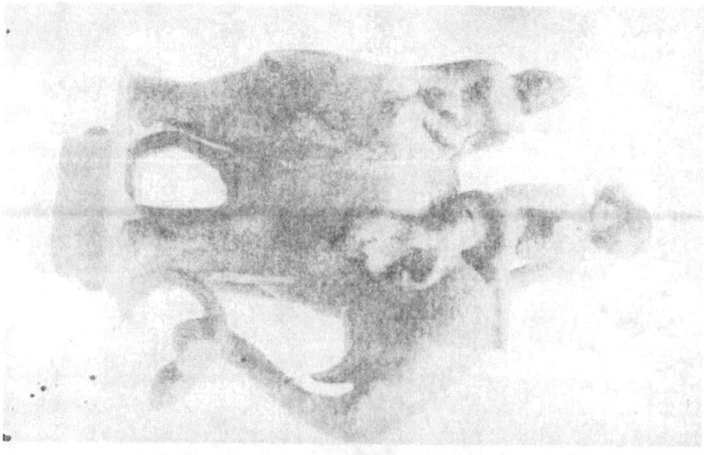

Fig. 2. Bronze Elephant with a female driver (Sumatra).

PLATE LXV

Fig. 1. Makara-head from Jambi T.B.G. (Vol. 45, p. 120).

Fig. 2. Biaro Bahal I (Sumatra), Main Temple. (North-West).

PLATE LXVI

Fig. 1. Biaro Bahal I (Sumatra), Main Temple. (North-East).

Fig. 2. Rakshasa figures, North Stircase, Biaro Bahal, Main Temple.

PLATE LXVII

Fig. 1. Biaro Bahal II, Main Temple. (North-East) (Sumatra).

Fig. 2. Biaro Bahal II, Main Temple. (North-West) (Sumatra).

PLATE LXVIII

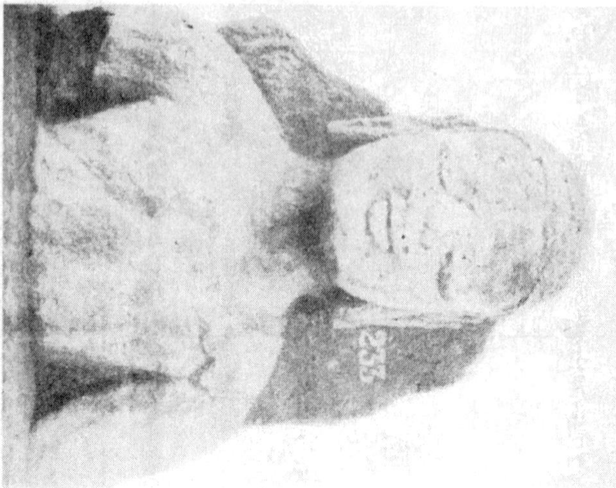

Fig. 1. Bust of a Buddha Image (Probably belonging to Biaro Bahal II).

Fig. 2. Image of Heruka, Biaro Bahal II.

PLATE LXIX

Fig. 1. Stupa to the North of the Main Temple, Bairo Bahal I.

Fig. 2. Stone Image Bajrasatva, Biaro Bahal I.

Fig. 3. Broze Image, Bairo Bahal I (Sumatra).

PLATE LXX

Fig. 1. Stone Image of Manjusri, Martanura (Borneo).

Fig. 2. Image of Mahadeva. Genung Kombeng (Borneo).

Fig. 3. Buddhist Image, Genung Kombeng (Borneo).

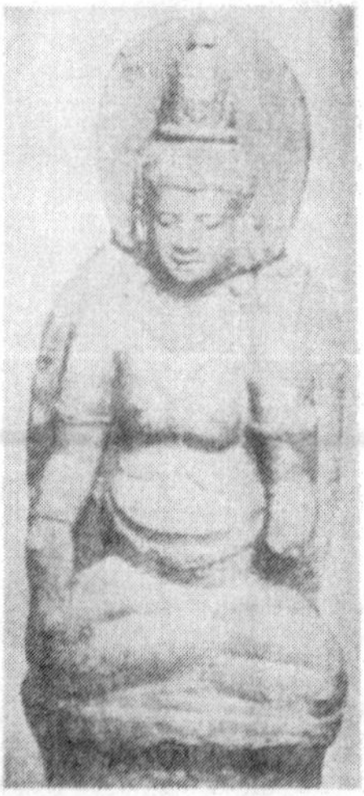

Fig. 4. Unidentified Image Genung Kombeng (Borneo).

PLATE LXXI

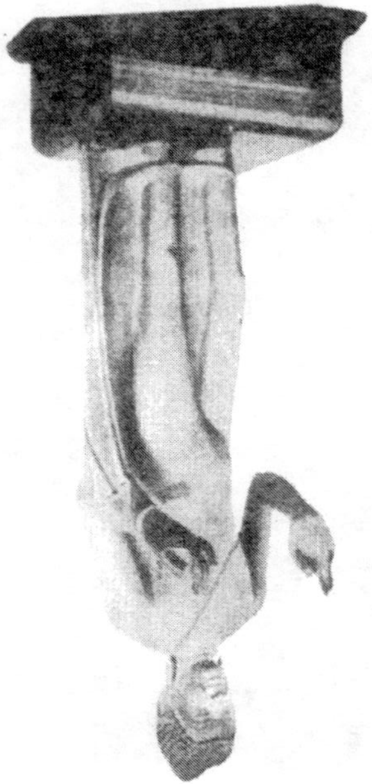

Fig. 1. Stone Image of Avalokitesvara, Palembang (A.B.I.A, 1931, Pl. XII).

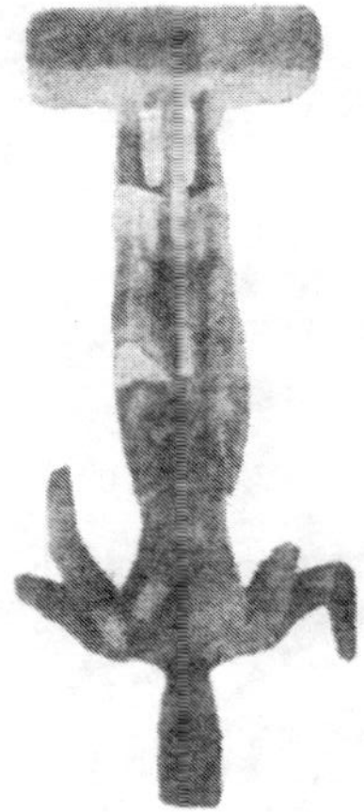

Fig. 2. Visnu from Phru No Hill Takua Pa (I.A.L., IX, Pl. II).

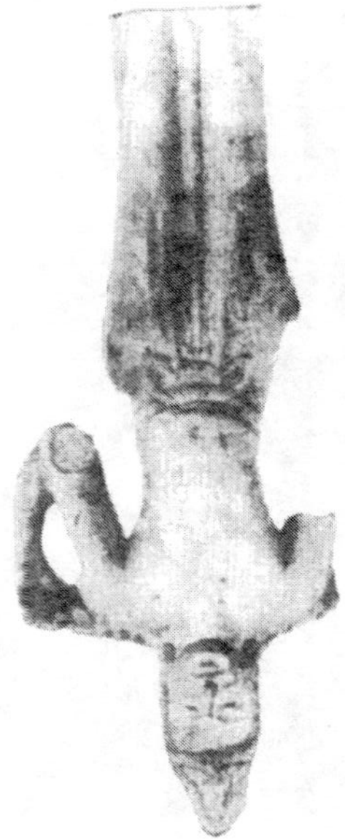

Fig. 3. Bronze Image of Buddha, Kota Bangun (Borneo).

PLATE LXXII

Fig. 1. Female figure, Takua Pa (I.A.L., IX, Pl. IV).

Fig. 2. Male Image Takua Pa (I.A.L., IX. Pl. IV).

Fig. 3. Three Stone Figures, Takua Pa (I.A.L., IX. Pl. IV).

PLATE LXXIII

Fig. 1. Visnu from Vieng Sra (I.A.L., I, Pl. XIV, p. 72).

Fig. 2. Visnu at Srivijay Hill (Pl. XV).

Fig. 3. Visnu from Vieng Sra. (I.A.L, I, Pl. V VII).

Fig. 4. Siva Bhairava from Vieng Sra.

PLATE LXXIV

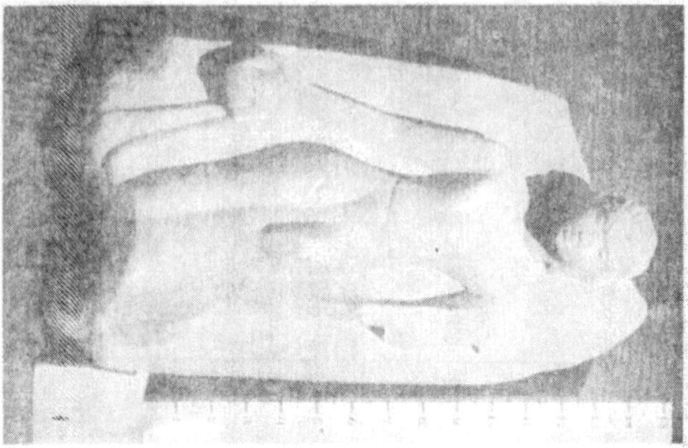

Fig. 1. Sandstone Buddha (I.A.L. IX, Pl. VI).

Fig. 2. Central Shrine of Phra That, Caiya (I.A.L., IX, Pl. VI).

Fig. 3 . Reliquary in the countryard of Vat Phra That, Nakan Sri Thammarat (I.A.L., IX, Pl. VI).

PLATE LXXV

Fig. 1. Golden Female figure (front), Philippines.

Fig. 2. Golden Female figure (back), Philippines.

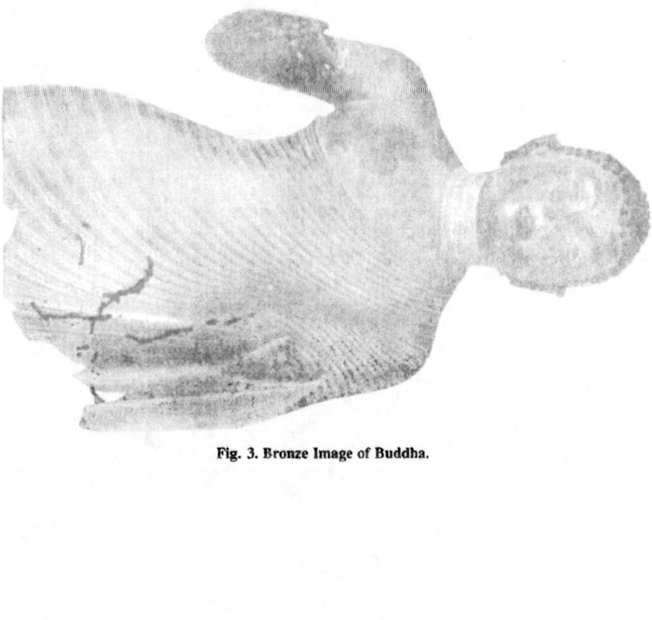

Fig. 3. Bronze Image of Buddha.

Law permitted a husband to sell his wife to another (171). But even here it is noticeable that a man was liable to punishment if he purchased a woman without the permission of her husband and kept her as a slave. But if he purchased her from the husband and married her himself he was free from any guilt.

The higher regard for women and the dominance of a husband over the wife are both reflected in the laws of adultery which indicate some peculiarity in Javanese conception. As stated before, many of these laws are taken from Manu, and, on the whole, the Javanese law resembles the Indian in regarding the offence of adultery as a serious one, and penalises not only the perpetrators and abettors of the crime, but also actions which might ultimately lead to adultery, *e.g.* speaking to a woman in loneliness, offering her presents, tempting her with money, *etc.* It recognises that human passions are difficult to control, and therefore forbids all actions and movements which inevitably tend towards an illicit connection (139). But the penalties prescribed are less severe. The extreme penalty of death, or mutilation of hands, accompanied by branding and banishment, is reserved only for the male offender. Manu's direction that the king shall cause the female offender to be devoured by dogs in a public place (VIII-371) has no parallel in Javanese law. The Javanese law mostly imposes fines, the amount of which varies with the gravity of the offence. But this fine is to be paid to the husband of the violated woman and not to the king (134-138). In other words, the offence is regarded more as a private wrong done to the husband, than a crime against the state. A further illustration of this principle is furnished by the fact that the husband had also the right to put the criminal to death if he were caught red-handed (134).

Before leaving the topic of women, it is necessary to point out, that although the laws regarding re-marriage of women, and payment of *sulka* or marriage-price are based on Indian

Law-books, the latter also contain regulations of exactly opposite character, forbidding both. These are, however, entirely absent from the Javanese Law-book, showing thereby the strong hold of the customs which formerly prevailed but later fell into disfavour or disuse in India. Again, the right of a wife to divorce her husband is unknown to Manu and foreign to the spirit of Indian law and practice, though Nārada (XII. 16, 96) permits it only in the cases of certain physical disabilities of the husband. Lastly, to the general rule that pledged property vests in the holder of the pledge after the lapse of a fixed period of time, there are some notable exceptions, *viz.*, those belonging to a married or unmarried girl, to the king, and to a Paṇḍita (206). These exceptions not only give a preferential treatment to women over men, but also supply another evidence that women could own real property (206). In all these cases the divergence from Hindu law may be explained by higher conception of the status of women among the indigenous people in Java.

This view is fully supported by the very interesting *Jayapattra* or Judgment, dated 927 (or 907) A.D. published by Brandes[1]. Here the case arose out of a sum of money lent to a woman who died without repaying it. Her husband was sued, but it was held by the tribunal, that the husband was not responsible for the payment when the wife borrowed without his knowledge and left no children. In other words, the wife had an independent status. It is also interesting to note that the tribunal consisted of Samget Pinapan and his wife who tried the case with the help of four assessors. The fact that a woman acted as a judge is also not without significance about the high status of women in general.

The Berbek Inscription[2] of Wawa, dated 927 A.D., refers to the hereditary ownership of property by Bingah's,

---

1. T.B.G., Vol. XXXII (1898), pp. 98-149; also O.V. 1928 (64), 1925 (59).

2. O.J.O., XXXII.

mother, a woman bearing the title *rake*. The property would descend to Bingah, but there could be no claim to it by Bingah's step-brothers or step-sisters, showing the independent possession of a wife apart from her husband.

Next to women, the Javanese law-book contains elaborate regulations about the slaves. The following causes are enumerated as grounds for reducing a man to the status of a slave (169, 270).

1. Imprisonment in war (called *dhvaja-hṛta*).
2. Born of parents who are themselves slaves (called *gṛhaja*).
3. Non-payment of debt or fine (called *daṇḍa-dāsa*).
4. Willingly accepting the status of a slave for food and shelter (called *bhakta-dāsa*).

A slave might change his master, by purchase or sale, gift, and inheritance.

Now the above closely follows Manu (VIII. 415), but differs from Nārada who enumerates fifteen kinds of slaves, including the above (26-28). According to the Javanese law all these slaves might obtain their freedom by payment of a requisite fee to their master (270, 166, 167). Manu is silent on this point, but Nārada states definitely 'that slaves by birth or those obtained by purchase, gift, and inheritance cannot be released from bondage, except by the favour of their owners.' In this respect, therefore, the Javanese law seems to be more liberal; but except in the cases of slaves belonging to classes 1 (166) and 4 (167), it does not lay down detailed regulations about their mode of obtaining freedom. These two classes of slaves could free themselves by paying a sum of 8000. Heavy penalties were prescribed for forcing a freed slave to work for his old master (160, 162, 172).

The slaves were regarded as the absolute property of the master. Not only were they to live and work according to his bidding, but he was also entitled to the property (128) and even the issues of his male and female slaves. If a male slave of one married the female slave of another, then their

3

children, if any, were divided among the two owners, the male children going to the owner of the male slave, and the female children to the other owner (10, 152, 153). Runaway slaves and those who helped them were severely punished (3). The murderer of a slave had to recompense the owner for his loss (7). The slave could be given as a pledge (101, 120), and such a slave was liable to capital punishment if he stole goods worth more than 100 from the owner of the pledge (118). A slave was, however, protected by law in many respects. He could be chastised, and even bound, by the master, but the latter was not permitted to strike him on the head (31 ; cf. Manu, VIII. 299-300). If a master made an attempt to outrage the modesty of a female slave, she could run away and would become automatically free (165). So were the slaves of a thief automatically set free (24). Any one who abducted a slave was liable to capital punishment (157). A master could marry a slave, and in such a case their children inherited the property of the father if the latter had no children by wives of equal birth (155). If one married the slave of another, the children would inherit one-fourth of his property, if he had other children, and the whole of it, if he had none by any wife of free birth (158).

In addition to regulations' about women and slaves, the Kuṭāra-mānava-śāstra deals with many other important topics of civil law such as debt, pledge, property, inheritance, *etc.*

The rules of debt are very comprehensive and follow closely those of Nārada and Yājñavalkya. Six kinds of interest are mentioned as in Bṛhaspati (XI-5). Detailed directions are given for preparing the necessary document (72), and three kinds of evidence are laid down as sufficient to prove the transaction,—*viz.*, documents, witness, and enjoyment of interest (74). Failing satisfactory evidences, trial by ordeal is prescribed though no details are given. The debts are classified according as they are re-payable or not by the debtor's children (79, 80), and judicial procedure for the recovery of debt is also laid down (81-84).

According to Nārada, "the guarantee to be offered to a creditor may be twofold: a surety and a pledge." Both of these are referred to in the Indo-Javanese law-book. It is interesting to note in this connection that only two kinds of surety are recognised, *viz.*, that for appearance of debtor (88), and that for payment (89). In this and other respects it agrees with Manu-smṛti, but not with Nārada and other law-books which recognise a third surety, *viz.*, that for honesty.

The rules about pledge are also laid down in great detail, and are based generally on the Hindu law. The use of a pledge without the permission of the owner is regarded as a grave offence as in Manu (VIII. 144, 150) and Nārada (I, 127-128), but the punishment is more severe. The offender has not only to give to the pledge-giver twice the value of the pledge but is also fined 20,000 as a thief (102). In connection with the laws about pledge we come across one important principle which has been the subject of serious discussion in this country. After saying that certain pledges, *e.g.*, clothes *etc.*, are forfeited after five years (99), it proceeds: "If some one pledges landed property, it is never forfeited, for the land is the property of the king, it only remains in possession of the creditor" (100). Thus it is clearly laid down that the ownership of the soil is vested in the king and no one else. Whether this rule is derived from an Indian Law-book, or whether it is an Indonesian modification, it is difficult to say. It may be added that a later section of the book lays down that a man loses his right over landed property, if another is in possession of it for twenty years with his knowledge (268). This is in accordance with Indian law as laid down by Yājñavalkya, Kauṭilya and Vyāsa.

Some idea of the king's right over land may be gathered from an inscription of king Tuloḍong, dated 919 A.D. [1] The king makes an endowment and grants some lands. About the waste-land it is simply recorded that it was fenced round

---

1. K.O., I.; Dacca University Studies, Vol. I, pp. 102 ff.

by the king. But as to the cultivated grounds we are told that he first purchased them from the headman of the village. There thus appears to be a distinction in the right of the king over lands according as they are cultivated or waste-lands.

The rules of property (including prescription), and those of sale and purchase follow the principles of Indian Law-books, but the illustrations given are mostly new. The rules of inheritance offer some striking novelty. If a man dies, leaving more than one child from the same wife, then the eldest son gets an additional share (*uddhāra*), which varies according to the value of the property left. In the most extreme case, the eldest takes four-fifths of the property, while the remaining fifth part is divided among his younger brothers (197). Now, some of the Indian Law-books recognise the claim of the eldest son to an additional share deducted from the state, also known technically as *uddhāra*, but both Manu and Viṣṇu-smṛti reckon it as one-twentieth, and Baudhāyana as one tenth. There is no Indian authority, known to us, for such a heavy share as four-fifths. It may be due to indigenous custom or misunderstanding of the original text.

The rules of inheritance vary if a man leaves children from wives of different castes. The children in that case obtain preferential treatment according to the caste of their mothers. A specific rule lays down that the property of a Brāhmaṇa with wives of four different castes should be divided into eleven shares (258). The idea, probably, is that the children should share in the proportion of 4, 3, 2, and 1, according as their mothers belong to the Brāhmaṇa, Kṣatriya, Vaiśya, and Śūdra castes, as is laid down in Manu (IX.153). But, then, the property is to be divided into ten and not eleven shares. The extra share perhaps belongs to the eldest. A man may, however, formally discard a son (78), and then the latter cannot inherit the property of his father.

In these rules of inheritance it is not quite clear whether both sons and daughters, or only the former, are to be regarded as heir, for, with a single exception, quoted above, the word used denotes children of both the sexes. Another remarkable point is that the children inherit the property of both the father and the mother, which is different from the Hindu laws. Another deviation from the latter is the total absence of all references to collateral descendants as heirs. Further, the word used for 'property' in these rules denotes always, at least if we take it in a literal sense, only movable property. As regards landed property, no rules of inheritance are clearly laid down, but there are two sections which run as follow :—

1. If any one puts forward a claim over a land and this claim proves unfounded, then he is fined by the king 160,000. It is called "falsely pretending to be a blood-relation" (132).

2. If any one does not permit his blood-relations to use the land, he is fined by the king 160,000, and is named "repelling his blood-relations". (133)

These two rules seem to indicate that land was regarded as the joint property of the family, and did not admit of divided ownership. But there are no clear statements on this point.

There are no definite rules about the inheritance of wife. But there is one rule, unfortunately fragmentary, which may be quoted in this connection. It runs as follows : 'If a married couple have no children, and one of them dies, then by the death of the wife the whole household property.........' (195). Jonker thinks that the missing portion referred to the right of the husband, but it might also include the corresponding right of the wife in case of the death of the husband. This view is strengthened by the regulation that immediately follows. It states that five years after marriage, but not before that, the household property of the husband and wife together with what each of them had obtained at the time of the marriage, shall be mixed up and regarded as common property, inheritable by each in the case of the death of the other (196). The same rule is laid down in another section where the period of interval is set down as 12 years, but it is distinctly laid down that the marriage-gift of the pair after that period shall be the property of the survivor, in case of the death of either the husband or the wife (123). It may be noted here that this merging of the property of the husband and wife is altogether foreign to Hindu law and must be regarded as an indigenous custom.

The right of the king to inherit the property of one who has no legitimate heir, with the exception of a Paṇḍita, whose property belongs to God (202-3), also closely follows the Indian legal principle, but the expression *'deva-dravyātmaka'* used in the Javanese book, cannot be traced to any existing Indian law-book.

In connection with inheritance we get a list of twelve classes of sons (*lit.* children). The list is expressly referred to Manu, and indeed closley, though not fully, agrees with that given in Manu-saṁhitā (IX. 158-160).

The twelve classes (259) are :

(1) The child of a woman, who was engaged with a man from her infancy and was afterwards given in marriage to him by the parents.

(2) The child of a re-married woman, if her character were pure and if the marriage had taken place with the permission of the parents.

(3) A child given by kinsmen.

(4) A child obtained from another.

(5) A child begotten on one's wife by another with his permission.

(6) A child cast off by his father.

(7) The child of an unmarried girl and whose father is unknown.

(8) The child of a woman pregnant at the time of her marriage.

(9) The child of a woman who divorced her husband, remarried another husband who died shortly, and then returned to her first husband.

(10) The child who is bought.

(11) The child who offered himself as such.

(12) The child of a slave-woman of low birth, accepted as such.

Of these the first six alone are entitled to inherit the property of their father, but the last six are not regarded as heirs (cf. Manu. IX. 158).

Chapter II

ECONOMIC CONDITION

From a very early period Malayasia formed one of the most important centres of trade in the world. We have already given an account of the early maritime intercourse between India and Suvarṇabhūmi, so far as it has been preserved in Indian literature in the shape of vague traditions, legends, and folk-stories. We now propose to refer briefly to the trade activities of this region so far as we can determine them by means of positive and reliable evidence.

Apart from the trade-relations of the various islands grouped under Malayasia, either among themselves or with Indo-China, India, China, and Arabia formed the three main centres of trade with this region.

As regards India, the earliest definite account is furnished by Fa-hien's travels. From Tāmralipti (modern Tamluk) Fa-hien "embarked in a large merchant vessel, and went floating over the sea to the south-west. After sailing day and night for fourteen days he reached Ceylon[1]". After two years Fa-hien again took passage in a large merchantman with a view to return to China. The detailed account of this voyage is so interesting and instructive regarding the early trade and maritime intercourse between Malayasia on the one hand and India and China on the other, that I make no apology for quoting the lengthy passage[2].

"Fa-hien took passage in a large merchantman, on board of which there were more than 200 men, and to which was attached by a rope a smaller vessel, as a provision against damage or injury to the large one from the perils of the navigation. With a favourable wind, they proceeded eastwards

---

1. Fa-hien, p. 100.   2. Ibid, pp. 111-114.

for three days, and then they encountered a great wind. The vessel sprang a leak and the water came in. The merchants wished to go to the smaller vessel; but the men on board it, fearing that too many would come, cut the connecting rope. The merchants were greatly alarmed, feeling their risk of instant death. Afraid that the vessel would fill, they took their bulky goods and threw them into the water. Fa-hien also took his pitcher and washing-basin, with some other articles, and cast them into the sea; but fearing that the merchants would cast overboard his books and images, he could only think with all his heart of Kwan-She-yin, and commit his life to (the protection of) the church of the land of Han, (saying in effect), 'I have travelled far in search of our Law. Let me, by your dread and supernatural (power), return from my wanderings, and reach my resting place!'

"In this way the tempest continued day and night, till on the thirteenth day the ship was carried to the side of an island, where on the ebbing of the tide, the place of the leak was discovered, and it was stopped, on which the voyage was resumed. On the sea (hereabouts) there are many pirates, to meet with whom is speedy death. The great ocean spreads out, a boundless expanse. There is no knowing east or west; only by observing the sun, moon, and stars was it possible to go forward. If the weather were dark and rainy, (the ship) went as she was carried by the wind, without any definite course. In the darkness of the night, only the great waves were to be seen, breaking on one another, and emitting a brightness like that of fire, with huge turtles and other monsters of the deep (all about). The merchants were full of terror, not knowing where they were going. The sea was deep and bottomless, and there was no place where they could drop anchor and stop. But when the sky became clear, they could tell east and west, and (the ship) again went forward in the right direction. If she had come on any hidden rock, there would have been no way of escape.

"After proceeding in this way for rather more than ninety days they arrived at a country called Java-dvīpa, where various forms of error and Brāhmanism are flourishing, while Buddhism in it is not worth speaking of. After staying there for five months, (Fa-hien) again embarked in another large merchantman which also had on board more than 200 men. They carried provisions for fifty days, and commenced the voyage on the sixteenth day of the fourth month.

"Fa-hien kept his retreat on board the ship. They took a course to the north-east, intending to fetch Kwang-chow. After more than a month, when the night-drum had sounded the second watch, they encountered a black wind and tempestuous rain, which threw the merchants and passengers into consternation. Fa-hien again with all his heart directed his thoughts to Kwan-she-yin and the monkish communities of the land of Han ; and, through their dread and mysterious protection, was preserved to day-break. After day-break, the Brahmans deliberated together and said, 'It is having this Śramaṇa on board which has occasioned our misfortune and brought us this great and bitter suffering. Let us land the *bhikshu* and place him on some island-shore. We must not for the sake of one man allow ourselves to be exposed to such imminent peril'. A patron of Fa-hien, however, said to them, 'If you land the *bhikshu*, you must at the same time land me ; and if you do not, then you must kill me. If you land this Śramaṇa, when I get to the land of Han, I will go to the king, and inform against you. The king also reveres and believes the Law of Buddha, and honours the *bhikshus*'. The merchants hereupon were perplexed, and did not dare immediately to land (Fa-hien).

"At this time the sky continued very dark and gloomy, and the sailing-masters looked at one another and made mistakes. More than seventy days passed (from their leaving Java), and the provisions and water were nearly exhausted. They used the salt water of the sea for cooking, and carefully divided the (fresh) water, each man getting two pints. Soon the whole was nearly gone, and the merchants took counsel and said, 'At the ordinary rate of sailing we ought to have reached Kwang-Chow, and now the time is passed by many days; —must we not have held a wrong course?' Immediately they directed the ship to the north-west, looking out for land; and after sailing day and night for twelve days, they reached the shore", to the south of the Shantung promontory in Chang-Kwang[1].

The next detailed account of this trade intercourse through Malayasia is preserved in the accounts, left by I-tsing, both about his own travels and those of 37 other Chinese pilgrims who travelled to India by sea-route.

I-tsing sailed from Kwang-tung in 671 A.D. in a Persian ship. After sailing twenty days he reached Śrī-Vijaya, and stayed there for six months. From Śrī-Vijaya I-tsing got on board the king's ship, and after halting for some time in Malayu (Jambi) and Ka-cha (Keddah) he sailed for Eastern India. Sailing northwards from Ka-cha he reached the island of the naked people after more than ten days. Then sailing towards the north-west the ship reached Tāmralipti in about half a month[2].

The accounts preserved by I-tsing about the voyage of the other pilgrims give us an idea of the extent of this maritime course.[3] Among the sixty Chinese pilgrims, whose account is given by I-tsing, about 37 availed themselves of the sea-route which was evidently used pretty frequently by the merchant vessels. Ho-Ling, Śrī-Vijaya and Kie-cha (Keddah) were the chief ports in Java, Sumatra, and Malay Peninsula, and there were also important harbours in Champā (Annam), Cambodge, and Siam. Śrī-Vijaya evidently was one of the most important centres of trade, and its king owned merchant vessels which also carried passengers. Lang-kia-su is also occasionally referred to as a port.

---

1. Ibid, p. 114, fn. 1. 2. I-tsing-Record, pp. XXVIII ff.

3. I-tsing-Memoire, cf. specially pp. 53, 57, 60, 64, 69, 100, 144, 158, 159, 176, 179, 183, 189-90.

The account of Vajrabodhi, preserved in Tokio Tripiṭaka, shows that, sailing from Ceylon in A.D. 717 with 35 Persian vessels, he passed through Śrī-Vijaya and many other countries.[1]

It is evident from these accounts that ships from India, Persia, Indo-China, and Malayasia were engaged in a brisk trade. The Chinese themselves seem to have taken but little share in it at the beginning. It was only in the seventh century that Chinese maritime enterprise began to manifest itself, and it was regarded as an unusually daring voyage of considerable length, when, in 607 A.D., the emperor sent a mission by sea to Siam (Chi-tu) to open commercial relations with it.[2] But there are reasons to believe that the sea-trade of the Hindus and Arabs with Malayasia and China had by this time assumed considerable importance.[3] It is difficult to determine exactly what parts were taken by the Malayasian states in this trade. But that Sumatra, Java, and Malay Peninsula had a fair share in it is beyond dispute, and appears clearly from the routes followed by merchant vessels.

The accounts supplied by I-tsing give us a fair idea of the general trade-route followed in the seventh century A.D. After having left China the vessel touched at a port in Annam. It then proceeded to Śrī-Vijaya, either by a direct voyage or by sailing along the coasts of Cambodia, Siam, and Malaya Peninsula. A third route was to proceed first to Java and then to Śrī-Vijaya, though sometimes Java was reached from Śrī-Vijaya. From Śrī-Vijaya it proceeded to Malayu (Jambi) and then to either Kie-cha or Lang-kia-su in Malay Peninsula. From one of these ports it sailed either north-west for Tāmralipti in Bengal, or westwards for Negapatam in Madras, and then to Ceylon. Sometimes a direct voyage was made to Ceylon.

A very detailed account of this sea-route from Canton to the Persian Gulf has been preserved in the itineraries compiled

1. J.A., Ser; II, Vol. XX, p. 7.

2. Chau Ju-kua, pp. 7-8.

3. Ibid, p. 9.

by Kia Tan between A.D. 785 and 805,[1] and everything indicates that the volume of foreign trade in China had grown enormously. In particular, the Muslim Arabs had far surpassed other nations in their maritime enterprise by the ninth century A.D. We have a series of interesting Arab narratives of this period concerning trade with China. "The ships engaged in China trade sailed from Siraf on the coast of Fars, where the goods were brought from Basra, Oman, and other places. They then went to Mascat, whence they sailed for Kulam-Male (Quilon), which port was reached in a month. Passing the Nicobar islands they made directly for Kalah (Keddah) on the Malay Peninsula, which was reached in a month from Kulam."[2]

Kalah or Kalahbar was the most important harbour in Malay Peninsula about this period. From this place a part of the goods was probably transported by land to the opposite coast of the Peninsula. The vessels proceeding to China touched at or passed by Jāba, Salāhit, Harlaj and Mayt, all situated quite close to one another, and in ten days reached Tiyuma, probably the island of Tiuman to the south-east of Malay Peninsula. They next made for Kundrang, near the mouth of the Mekong, reaching it in ten days. A further voyage of ten days brought them either to Champā, or Cundur-fulat (Pulo Condore). From either of these places they made directly for the Chinese ports.[3]

---

1. Ibid, pp. 10-14, Pelliot-Deux Itineraries, B.E.F.E.O., Vol. IV, pp. 131-413.

2. Chau Ju-kua, p. 15.

3 The sea-route described in the text is derived from the accounts of Sulaymān (851 A.D.), Ibn Khordādzbeh (844-848 A.D.), and Ibn Al-Fakīh (902 A.D.). These accounts have been translated by Ferrand (Ferrand-Textes). As Cundur-fulāt is identified with Pulo Condore, it is not easy to understand the route described by the Arab writers, *viz.*, from Kudrang to Champā (10 days), from Champā to Cundur-fulāt (10 days), and then from Cundur-fulāt to China, I have therefore taken these to be alternative routes.

The direct voyage of the Arabs to China was interrupted in the last quarter of the ninth century A.D. on account of serious political troubles in China. The foreign merchants had to leave China, and seek refuge in large numbers at Kalah.[1] At the beginning of the tenth century A.D. this port on the west coast of Malay Peninsula became the centre of the world trade where ships from the west met those coming from China. A graphic description of this port is given by Abū Zayd Ḥasan (c. 916 A.D.):

"The maritime country called Kalah, situated midway between Arabia and China, belongs to the empire of the Mahārāja (of Zābag). The area of the land is said to be 80 square farsang. The town of Kalah is the market where is centralised the trade in aloes, camphor, sandal-wood, ivory, tin, ebony, brazil-wood, all kinds of spices and articles of incense, and various other commodities, which it will take long time to mention in detail. The vessels from Oman come to this port, and from this port also depart vessels bound for Arabia".[2] Mas'ūdī, while describing this state of things, marks the contrast with the old days when there was a direct voyage between China and Arabia.[3]

It is evident from Mas'ūdī (943 A.D.) that Arab ships also made direct voyage to Zābag, the capital city of the vast empire. Henceforth the vast maritime empire of Zābag looms large in the Arab annals, and it is definitely stated by Edrīsi (1154) that on account of troubles and insecurity in China the trade of that country was diverted to Zābag and its dependent islands.[4] The frequent and prominent mention of Sribuza, (Śrī-Vijaya) shows that it also formed an important trade-centre.

The Chinese writings also support the conclusion that the foreign trade of China had passed into the hands of Arabs and Malayasians. This is evident from the following passages in Ling-Wai-tai-ta by Chou-Ku-fei (1178 A.D.)[5] :

---

1. Chau Ju-kua, p. 18.
2. Ferrand-Textes, p. 83.
3. Ibid, p. 96.
4. Ibid, p. 175.
5. Chau Ju-kua, pp. 23-25.

"Of all the wealthy foreign lands which have great store of precious and varied goods, none surpasses the realm of the Arabs (Ta-shi). Next to them comes Sho-po (Java); the third is San-fo-tsi; many others come in the next rank."

"San-fo-tsi is an important thoroughfare on the sea-routes of the foreigners on their way to and from (China). Ships (on leaving it, on their way to China) sail due north, and having passed the Shang-hia-chu islands [1] and through the sea of Kiau-Chi come within the confines of China.

"Ships coming from Java (Sho-po) go a little north-west (at first), but when they have passed the Shï-ïr-tzï rocks [2] they take the same route as the San-fo-tsi ships from below (*i.e.* south) of the Shang-hia-chu islands.

"The (Barbarian) kingdoms due south have San-fo-tsi as their commercial centre. Sho-po is the centre of those to the south-east. The Arab merchant vessels also made at first for San-fo-tsi and then proceeded to China by the same route as the San-fo-tsi ships."

We have already discussed above, in Book II, the location of San-fo-tsi and its great political importance from the ninth century onwards. That it rapidly developed into an important commercial centre is apparent from the above detailed account given by Chou ku fei.

Chau Ju-kua is even still more explicit in this matter. Referring to San-fo-tsi he says :[3]

"This country, lying in the ocean and controlling the straits (lit. gullet) through which the foreigners' sea and land (lit. ship and cart) traffic in either direction must pass, in old times used an iron chain as a barrier to keep the

1. They are usually identified with Pulo Aor, S.E. of Tyoman, although some wirters place them near Singapore (Chau Ju-kua, p., 23. fn. 3.)

2. These rocks are marked on Chinese maps of the sixteenth century as being north of Carimata island off the S.W. coast of Borneo (Chau Ju-kua, p. 24, f.n. 3).

3. Chau Ju-kua, p. 62

pirates of other countries in check. It could be kept up or lowered by a cunning device. If a merchant ship arrived it was lowered. After a number of years of peace, during which there has been no use for it, it has been moved and (now) lies coiled up on the shore.........

"If a merchant ship passes by without entering, their boats go forth to make a combined attack, and all are ready to die (in the attempt). This is the reason why this country is a great shipping centre."

Chau Ju-kua also refers to the articles of merchandise [1]. Exclusive of the native products which include tortoise-shell, camphor, varieties of gharu wood, laka-wood, cloves, sandal-wood, and cardamoms, there are also pearls, frankincense, rosewater, gardenia flowers, myrrh, aloes, asoefoetida, putchuk, liquid storax, elephant's tusk, coral trees, cat's eyes, amber, foreign cotton-stuffs, and sword-blades. The foreign traders who gather together in this country give in exchange gold, silver, porcelain-ware, silk-brocades, skeins of silk, silk-gauzes, sugar, iron, samshu rice, dried galangal, rhuburb, and camphor. About the coins, Chau Ju-kua says that "they have no stringed copper cash, but use chopped off lumps of silver in their business transactions." [2]

In the Tao-i Chih-lio there is a brief reference to trade activities in San-fo-tsi. "The native products are plum-blossom (and) flake camphor of middling quality, laka wood, betelnut, cotton stuffs and fine carved wood. The goods used by the Chinese in trading are coloured taffetas, red beads, shawls, coloured cotton stuffs, copper and iron pots, and such like [3]." It is evident that the trading importance of the place had diminished considerably along with decline in political power.

The same authority refers to another locality called Chiu-Chiang which is usually identified with Palembang. Both Ma Huan and Fei Hsin take this kingdom to be the same

---

1. Ibid, p. 61. 2. Ibid.

3. Rockhill—T'oung Pao, Vol. XVI (1915), p. 134.

as old San-fo-tsi, though this does not seem to be correct [1]. All these authorities refer to its agricultural wealth and trade activities. According to Tao-i Chih-lio "the profit they derive from their fields is double that of other countries. It is a common saying that if grain were planted one year the third year gold grew, meaning that the grain was changed into gold."[2]

The natural products of the land were gharu wood, laka wood, cotton superior to that of any other country, beeswax and very big crane's crest (a kind of bird). The goods used by the Chinese in trading are coloured beads, blue and white porcelain, copper caldrons, coloured cotton stuffs, big and little porcelain jars, and copper cash[3].

Samudra or Sumudra was another important centre of trade. A short history of this kingdom has been given before (Part I, pp. 370 ff). During the Sung dynasty it had the reputation of possessing much gold, silver, and silk, whilst the skill of its artisans was highly praised. It retained its importance down to the seventeenth century.[4] Ma Huan refers to it as an important emporium of the western seas. "This place is visited by many native ships and the trade in native articles is very important."[5] It was agriculturally poor, producing only rice, but neither barley nor wheat. But it produced pepper and sulphur while the people raised silk-worms. Gold and tin coins were used for trade. The gold coin was called ti-na-erh (dīnāra ?).[6] The place was filled with merchandise brought by passing foreign ships.[7] "Merchants from all sides collect at this place, and as the country is distant and the prices high, the Chinese who go there make more profit than anywhere else."[8]

---

1. Rockhill, op. cit., pp. 136-140.
2. Ibid, p. 135.
3. Ibid, pp. 136, 138, 140
4. Groeneveldt-Notes, p. 93.
5. Ibid, p. 87.
6. Rockhill, op. cit., pp. 154-55.
7. Ibid. p. 154.
8. Groeneveldt-Notes, p. 92.

5

The Chinese sources refer to various other localities in Sumatra,[1] but it is not necessary to refer to them in detail. Among their natural products may be mentioned camphor, tin, and fragrant resin, while coloured satins, silks, beads, and porcelain were included in the import from China.

Chau Ju-kua also gives some account of the trade activities in Java (Sho-po) which agrees with that in the History of the Sung dynasty.[2] Java was a rich agricultural country and produced rice, hemp, millet, sugarcane, beans, but no wheat. It had also gold, silver, elephant's tusks, rhinoceros-horns, pearls, camphor, tortoise-shell, aloes, sandalwood, aniseed, cloves, cardamoms, cubebs, laka wood, mats, foreign sword-blades, pepper, betel-nuts, sulphur, saffron, sapanwood and parrots. The people make salt by boiling sea-water. They also paid attention to the raising of silkworms and the weaving of silk ; they had various coloured brocaded silks, cotton, and damasked cotton gauzes (or damasks and cotton cloth). The foreign merchants gave, in exchange for these goods, gold and silver of various degrees of fineness, vessels made of gold and silver, silk stuffs, black damasks, orrisroot, cinnabar, copperas, alum, borax, arsenic, lacquer ware, iron tripods, and green and white porcelain ware.

Chau Ju-kua makes a special reference to pepper-trade. "There is a vast store of pepper in this country and the merchant ships, in view of the profit they derive from that trade, are in the habit of smuggling (out of China) copper cash for bartering purposes. Our court has repeatedly forbidden all trade (with this country), but the foreign traders, for the purpose of deceiving (the government) changed its name and referred to it as Su-ki-tan"

By this last name perhaps Central Java was meant. Chau Ju-kua devotes a separate chapter to it, but does not add

---

1. Rockhill, op. cit., pp. 141-159 ; Groeneveldt-Notes, pp. 77-78., 93-100.

2. Chau Ju-kua, pp. 75-85 ; Groeneveldt-Notes, pp. 15-19.

anything new. He refers to the abundance of pepper and remarks : "Traders are treated generously ; they are not charged expenses for either harbourage or board."

The account of Chau Ju-kua is supplemented by other Chinese writers. According to Tao-i Chih-lio (A.D. 1349) Java produced rice in such abundance that there was a surplus for export to other countries.[1] The same authority makes a special reference to sun-dried pepper of which every year ten thousand *catties* of the first quality and strength were prepared, and also to coloured cotton prints and parrots of the pan-ying-wu variety.[2] The coloured cotton prints or the Batiks have been one of the most famous industries of Java from the remotest period to the present day. The parrots of Java were evidently highly prized. Ma Huan not only refers to green, red, and five-coloured parrots, but also to parroquets that speak.[3] Fei Hsin (1436 A.D.) not only refers to parrots and 'parrot-peacocks', which can be taught to understand speech and to sing songs, but also to "hanging-down bird" with variegated plumage, which can absorb sweet perfume burnt during day and let it out at night by spreading out its tail and wings. The same writer observes : "This country is wealthy. There are pearls, silver, ya-ku stones, cat's-eyes, sapphires, rubies, che-ku, agate, nutmegs, long-peppers, put-chuck, indigo, everything that can be used, and traders are very numerous."[4]

There were several important ports in Java. In the fifteenth century A.D. Surabaya occupied the foremost place. Fei Hsin refers to it as the "principal mercantile centre for all goods, ships, and grain.[5] Next in point of importance was Geresik. To Ma Huan we owe the following account of its rise and importance : "Anciently it was a mud flat. The Chinese visited it and settled down there in numbers, when it was called Hsin-tsún or the "New Village". It counts over

1. Rockhill, op. cit., p. 237.
2. Ibid, p. 238.
3. Ibid, p. 245.
4. Ibid, p. 247.
5. Ibid, p. 248.

a thousand families and its chief is (*or* its chiefs are) from Kuang-tung. Foreign ships come here to trade, gold and precious and foreign things are in great abundance, and most of the inhabitants are rich[1]

There were several other ports among which Tu-pan (Tuban)[2] and Chang-ku (perhaps Changkir)[3] are prominently mentioned by the Chinese.

The Chinese authorities give us valuable information regarding the coinage of Java. According to Ling-wai-tai-ta (1178 A.D.), "they cast coins in an alloy of copper, silver, white copper, and tin; sixty of these coins are equal to one tael of gold; thirty-two are equal to half a tael of gold."[4] Chau Ju-kua, who quotes the above passage in his account of Sho-po, says, in connection with Su-ki-tan, that the people use as medium of trade, pieces of alloyed silver, cut into bits like dice, and bearing the seal of the Fan-Kuan stamped upon it. The expression Fan-Kaun means "foreign official", probably the resident headman of the foreign settlement, and the silver-dice referred to above were probably made by the Arab traders[5]. This kind of coin is apparently referred to by both Ma-Tuan-lin and Sung-Shi when they say: "They cut up leaves of silver to make coins for business purposes."[6] The name 'silver coin' is, however, given in Tai-i Chih-lio to the coins of the first variety made of an alloy of silver, tin, lead and copper. From the same authority we learn that these coins were used in business transactions in exchange for Chinese copper cash.[7] Ma Huan also refers to the use of Chinese copper cash.[8] The passage quoted above from Chau Ju-kua in connection with pepper-trade also shows the great demand of Chinese copper cash in Java.

1. Ibid, p. 241.
2. Ibid, pp. 240, 249.
3. Ibid, p. 242.
4. Chau Ju-kua, p. 78, p. 81 note 14.
5. Ibid, p. 82, p. 85 note 3.
6. Ibid, p. 81, note 14.
7. Rockhill, op. cit., p. 237.
8. Ibid, p. 240.

The Chinese account is corroborated by actual finds in Java; for while a great variety of brass and tin coins, and occasionally silver coins have been found in Java, no gold coin has ever been discovered there.[1]

The account of the prosperity and trade-activity in Java, given above, while generally true, should not be supposed to be applicable to all the parts of the island. Suṇḍa, for example, was an exception. It grew pepper of superior quality, but as the people were given to brigandage, foreign traders rarely went there.[2] The Chinese writers also refer to the piracy in some other localities which cannot be exactly identified.[3]

The Chinese authorities refer to various other islands of the Malay Archipelago with which the Chinese were engaged in trade. Principal among these are Banda, Timor, Madura, Borneo, Ceram, Kariṃata, Billiton, Molucca islands, and Sulu archipelago.[4] Among the native products which formed important articles of trade may be mentioned big elephants' tusks, tortoise shell, pearls, nutmegs, mace, cloves, pepper, cotton, betelnuts, skins, beeswax, laka wood, camphor, gharu wood and fine cotton cloths of the muslin type.

The things imported as exchange included silk, satins, cotton prints, calico printed with flowers, musical instruments, porcelain ware, coloured beads, copper caldrons, silver, ironware, gold, tin, alum, ivory, brimstone, and coral. The Moluccas islands were specially famous for cloves and attracted large number of Chinese merchants.[5]

It appears that black slaves were also exported from these islands. Tao-i Chih-lo includes them among the native products of Wen-tan (Banda),[6] and we learn from the History

1. Chau Ju-kua, p. 81 note 14.
2. Ibid, p. 70.
3. Rockhill, op. cit., p. 254
4. Ibid, pp. 257-271.
5. Groeneveldt-Notes, p. 117.
6. Rockhill, op. cit., p. 257.

of the Ming Dynasty that pirates from Borneo were engaged in slave-trade,[1] and that both in 1381 and 1382 the Javanese tributes to China included 400 black slaves of both sexes.[2] It may be mentioned that coins of lead were used in Borneo.[3]

As regards the Malay Peninsula, the earliest account of its trade activities is furnished by the Arab writers.[4] Reference has already been made to the importance of Kalah-bar as a port, and also to the glowing description of the wealth and grandeur of Zābag, which must have included a great part of the peninsula. The chief articles of trade seem to be clove, cardamom and other spices, aloe, amber, sandalwood, tin, and camphor.

The Chinese authorities[5] also refer to the trade activities of various other localities in the Malay Peninsula. The kingdoms referred to by Chau Ju-kua have been mentioned above, and some of them are also referred to by later Chinese authorities. Trade seems to have been carried on on principles of barter. With reference to Lengkasuka, Chau Ju-kua says: "Foreign traders barter there in samshu, rice, Ho-chi silks, and porcelain ware. They calculate first the value of their articles according to their equivalent in gold or silver, and then engage in barter of these articles at fixed rates."[6]

The native products of Malay Peninsula, so far as we can judge from the Chinese accounts of these kingdoms, included aloes, gharu wood, sandalwood, cardamom, wax, laka wood, ebony, camphor, elephants' tusks, rhinoceros-horns, tin, beeswax, tortoise-shell, betelnuts, resin, sago, and myrrh.

---

1. Groeneveldt-Notes, p. 138.
2. Ibid, p. 36.
3. Ibid, p. 108.
4. Ferrand-Textes.
5. Groeneveldt-Notes, pp. 119-140; Rockhill, op. cit, pp. 114-129; Chau Ju-kua, pp. 57-69.
6. Chau Ju-kua, p. 68.

Tin was one of the most important articles of trade and tin pieces were used as money. Among the foreign goods imported into the Peninsula may be mentioned silk, cotton stuffs, porcelain ware, gold, silver, copper, iron, lacquer ware, coloured beads, coloured taffetas, rice, sugar, wheat, and musical instruments.

From the fifteenth century A.D. Malacca rose to be the chief centre of trade in the Far East as Kalah-bar and San-fo-tsi were in earlier days. Its history and commercial importance have been already discussed above (Part I, pp. 383ff).

Chapter III

SOCIETY

The social organisation evolved by the Indian colonists in their new homes can only be dimly perceived. But enough remains to show that definite and deliberate attempts were made to introduce the Hindu social fabric, though they did not meet with as complete a success as in the case of religion.

The fundamental basis of the Hindu society, and one which distinguishes it from all other known societies, is the system of caste. That this was introduced in Java, Madura, and Sumatra is clear from the occurrence of the word "*Caturvarṇa*" in early records, and frequent reference to the Brāhmaṇas, Kṣatriyas, Vaiśyas, and Śūdras in literature and inscriptions.[1] It will be, however, too much to assume that this caste-system was the same as is prevalent in Hindu society to-day, and we are not sure if the caste-system there meant anything more than a theoretical recognition of the division of the people into four grades. But, then, it is necessary to remember that the same was also the case in at least many parts of India in earlier times, and that the influence of Buddhism and Tantrik religion obliterated the distinctions of caste to a considerable degree in later periods. It is, therefore, difficult to draw a sharp line of distinction between the system of caste in Java and that in India.

This view is strengthened by the fact that the Indian caste-system, such, for example, as is described in Manu-saṁhitā,

---

1. The four castes are named in the copper-plate grant of Keboan-Pasar in Eastern Java, dated A.D. 873 (O.J.O., Vol. IX), the Sidokata grant, dated A.D. 1323 (I.G.I.S., Vol. II, p. 131), and the Padang Roco (Sumatra) Inscription of king Kṛtanagara, dated A.D. 1286 (Part I, p. 299).

For Madura, cf. Congres I, pp. 262-3.

prevails in its essential features even to-day among the Balinese, the only people who have retained the old Hindu religion and customs. In order to convey an idea of the caste-system after its transplantation in the distant colonies, we can do no better than draw a picture of the system as it prevails to-day among the Balinese of Bali and Lombok.[1]

The people are divided into four castes, Brāhmaṇa, Kṣatriya, Vesya (Vaiśya), and Śūdra. The first three castes are 'twice-born' (*dvijāti*), while the Śūdras are '*ekajāti*' (once-born).

Marriage among different castes is prevalent, but while a man can marry a girl of his own or lower caste, a woman can only marry one of equal or higher caste. The union between a woman with a man of lower caste is punishable by death. The children of mixed marriages belong to the caste of the father, though they differ in rank and status according to the caste of their mother.

The Brāhmaṇas are divided into two broad classes according as they are worshippers of Śiva or Buddha. The first is again subdivided into five groups, originating mainly from the marriage with lower castes. For example, the Kamnuh, the highest class, is said to have sprung from a Brāhmaṇa father and Brāhmaṇa mother, while the Petapan, the lowest, was originally the offspring of a Brāhmaṇa father and a slave mother. But the classes were stabilised in Bali, the children belonging to the caste of their father irrespective of the caste of their mother.[2] To the Brāhmaṇa caste belong the Padaṇḍas or priests to whom reference will made in the chapter on Religion. Padaṇḍas of the highest rank observe strict *Brahmacarya* (celibacy), and usually the Padaṇḍas are expected to have only

1. For an account of the caste-system in Bali, cf. (i) Friederich—Bali, pp. 151-189. (ii) Crawfurd—Dictionary, pp. 29-30. (iii) Liefrinck-'Bijdrage tot de kennis van het eiland Bali', T.B.G., Vol. XXXIII (1890), pp. 233-472. (iv) Encycl. Ned. Ind., Vol. I, pp. 117-8. I have mainly followed the last

2. Liefrinck, op. cit., p. 237.

one wife. But in practice the Padaṇḍas marry wives, even from a lower caste. The Brāhmaṇas are usually styled 'Ida' (male) and Idayu (female).

The Kṣatriyas are also subdivided into five classes. Some, but not all the royal families in Bali belong to this caste. Their usual title is 'Deva' for the man and 'Desak' (*Skt.* Dāsī ?) for the woman.

Among the third caste, the Vaiśyas, the Aria (Arya ?) forms the chief group to which belong the royal families in Bali who are not Kṣatriyas. Their title is Gusti, for the male, and Gusti-ayu for the female. The 'Vargi' and 'Salit' form the other two Vaiśya-groups.

The Śūdras, known generally as Kaulas, are not despised as impure or untouchable. Impurity, according to the Balinese conception, is the consequence of certain acts such as, for example, (1) using water in which a dead body has been washed, (2) being reduced to slavery by legal process, (3) attempt to commit suicide, (4) refusing to become a *Satī* (*i.e.*, burning herself with her dead husband) after making a declaration to that effect, *etc.* The duration of impurity varies according to circumstances. Sometimes men of higher castes are degraded to the rank of a Śūdra.

The different castes are not tied down to specific occupations; for example, men of all castes take to agriculture. The Śūdras, in addition to agriculture, also follow other arts and crafts.

In Bali we meet with another characteristic feature of ancient Indian caste-system, *viz.*, the privileges enjoyed in law courts by the higher caste. Here, again, for the same offence, the law lays down punishment in inverse ratio to the superiority of the caste of the offender, and in direct ratio to that of the offended.

As to the superiority, although the four castes hold a relative position similar to that in India, the ruling princes, be they of Kṣatriya or Vaiśya caste, are regarded as superior to their Brāhmaṇa subjects. This is due to the theory that kings are representatives of God. It must be noted, however, that although superior, even a king cannot marry a Brāhmaṇa girl. In practice, however, even this is done by legal subterfuge. "Mr. Zollinger, in his interesting account of Lombok, gives an example. The young Raja of Mataram in that island, a Balinese, fell in love with the daughter of the chief Deva. In order to possess her, friendly legal ceremony became necessary. The Brāhmaṇa went through the form of expelling his daughter from his house, denouncing her as a "wicked daughter." She was then received into the Raja's house as a Vaiśya and became a princess."[1]

The days of impurity, to be observed in case of a death in a family, vary, as in India, according to caste. A Padaṇḍa, an ordinary Brāhmaṇa, a Kṣatriya, a Vaiśya, and a Śūdra, become pure respectively after five, ten, fifteen, twenty, and twenty-five days.

Two other social institutions in Bali may be referred to in connection with the caste-system. First, the *Satī* or the burning of a widow along with the body of her dead husband. This is forbidden in the case of the Śūdras, and in late periods came to be confined only to royal families. There were two kinds of self-immolation. In one case the wife first killed herself by the *Kris* (sword) and then her body was placed on the funeral pyre ; in the other case the wife jumped into the funeral pyre. Sometimes even the slaves and concubines of the dead also perished with him.[2]

Secondly, we may refer to the slaves as forming a distinct class in society. Slavery may be due to one of the following circumstances : (1) birth, (2) non-payment of debt or fines, (3) imprisonment in war, or (4) poverty. Although severely punished for crimes or attempts to escape, the lot of a slave is on the whole tolerable.[3]

---

1. Quoted in Crawfurd—Dictionary, p. 30.

2. For a detailed account of the 'Sati' system, Cf. Friederich-Bali pp. 145 ff.

3. Encyl. Ned. Ind., Vol. I., p. 118.

Whether all these customs which we find to-day in Bali also prevailed in Java and other parts of Hinduised Malayasia is difficult to determine. But the few references that we get are not incompatible with such a view. For in Javanese literature and Chinese accounts we get references to Brāhmaṇas and Kṣatriyas, and also to slavery and *Satī*. The Javanese literature and history throw some interesting light on certain phases of society, although they do not furnish materials for anything like a connected and complete picture. The system of marriage, for example, seems to show some divergence from Hindu customs. Polygamy was prevalent on almost as large a scale as in India, but the remarriage of widows, even of grown-up ladies with children, seems to have been a usual feature in Java, whereas it was all but unknown in India. For although sanctioned by the scriptures under special circumstances, an odium attached to it, and it hardly came into use, at least in the upper classes of society. In Java we have the famous instance of Ken Angrok or King Rājasa marrying the widow of Tunggul Ametung, the governor of Tumapel.[1] About common people we learn that in an annual gladiatorial combat (to be described later) in Java, the wife of the slain became the prize of the victor.

In general, the position of a woman in Java seems to have been much better than in India, so far at least as the political rights were concerned. Guṇapriyā Dharmapatnī ruled in her own rights, and in the official records her name was placed before that of her husband.[2] The records of Airlangga show that a lady named Śrī Sangrāmavijaya Dharmaprasādottungadevi occupied the post of 'rakryan mahāmantri i hino' next only to that of the king.[3] Rājapatnī succeeded Jayanagara, and her eldest daughter acted as regent for her although this daughter had a son.[4] Again, we know that after the death

1. Cf. Part I, Bk. III, ch. V.
2. Cf. Part I, Bk. III, ch. II.
3. Ibid.
4. Cf. Part I, Bk. III, ch. VI.

of Vikramavardhana, his daughter Suhitā ascended the throne although she had two brothers.[1] It is also interesting to note that on ceremonial occasions, such as the establishment of a freehold, the wives of officials are stated in the inscriptions to have received presents from the king along with their husbands.

The Berbek stone inscription of 927 A.D. refers to a lady as 'the mother of Bingah'. She carried the title rake, and founded a freehold which was to pass after her death to her own children and not to their step-brothers or step-sisters. This short record thus proves that even women, not belonging to the royal family, could hold office under the state and possess property in her own name with rights to dispose of it according to her own will[2].

There does not appear to be any *purdah* system in vogue, and the women freely mixed with men. This is evident from literature as well as present-day customs in Bali. Women could choose their own husbands, and we find actual reference to *Svayamvara* in the case of princess Bhreng Kahuripan[3]. There seems to be no restriction as to the degree of relationship within which marriage relation was prohibited. The case of Aji Jayanagara shows that even marriage with a step-sister was not forbidden[4].

An Old-Javanese prose work, Tatva-Ning-Vyavahāra, like Raghunandan's Aṣṭāviṁśati Tattva, seems to lay down rules for society. A sanskrit Śloka describing the origin of the four castes from the forehead, arms, thigh, and feet of Brahmā is quoted with an Old-Javanese translation. It then mentions the classes of food prohibited to the different classes. A list is given of the unclean animals such as dog, mouse, ape, snake, *etc.* It also deals with the marriage ceremony. How far books of this kind represent the actual state of society, it is difficult to say.

---

1. Cf. Part I, Bk. III, ch. VII.
2. Krom-Geschiedenis[2], p. 201.
3. Pararaton, p. 129.
4. Cf. Part I, Bk. III, ch. VI.

The duties of the four castes are given in some books of this kind. Others lay down the dates on which it is improper to institute a law-suit or when a husband should approach his wife, *etc.* (*cf.* Manu III. 45).

It was not the custom in Java to use match-makers in contracting a marriage. Some gold was paid to the relations of the girl and then the marriage took place[1]. In Borneo they sent, as marriage-presents, first the wine made of coconut-tree, then areca-nuts, and next a finger ring. At last they sent some cotton cloth or weighed out some gold or silver[2]. In Kora and Kalah (Malay Peninsula) they gave no other presents than areca-nuts, sometimes as many as two hundred trays[3].

The details of marriage ceremony in Java may be gathered from the following description.

"When a man marries, he goes first to the house of the bride to conclude the marriage, and three days afterwards he brings his wife home, on which occasion the relations of the bridegroom beat copper drums and gongs, blow on coconnut shells, beat drums made of bamboo, and burn fireworks, whilst a number of men armed with small swords surround them. The bride has hair hanging loose, the upper part of her body and feet naked ; round her waist a piece of green flowered cloth is fastened ; on her head she wears strings of golden beads, and on the wrists bracelets of gold and silver nicely ornamented.

"The relations, friends and neighbours bring *penang* and betel, whilst with garlands of flowers and leaves they adorn a little ship which they carry along with the newly married as a form of congratulation. Arriving at the house they beat drums and gongs and rejoice for several days after which they go away."[4]

Some of the Chinese accounts testify to a very high degree of conjugal love and fidelity. In Hsing-Cha Sheng-lan occurs the following passage about Ma-yi-tung which has been

1. Groeneveldt-Notes, p. 17.
2. Ibid, p. 108.
3. Ibid, p. 122.
4. Ibid, pp. 51-52.

identified with Banka. "They highly value chastity, and when a husband dies, his wife cuts her hair, lacerates her face and does not eat for seven days, sleeping all the time together with the dead body of her husband. Many die during this time, but if one survives after seven days, her relations exhort her to eat; she may then live but never marries again. On the day that the husband is burned, many wives throw themselves into the fire and die also."[1]

This last custom is also referred to in other Chinese accounts, and, as we have already seen above, has survived in Bali.

Adultery was punished with death both in San-fo-tsi[2] and Borneo.[3]

The Chinese writers have recorded various observations about the manner and customs of the people in different parts of Malayasia. These observations, made at different dates, and in respect of countries widely removed from one another, do not enable us to formulate a general picture of society. But they throw interesting light on various phases of the life of the people which is of great value. The following sketch gives the more salient features of the social institutions, in addition to those referred to above.

The king, the nobles, and the high officials formed an aristocracy which was sharply distinguished from the mass of people. The aristocracy lived in ease and luxury, evidently at the expense of the people.

The king occupied an exalted position and was sometimes regarded as divine. We learn from Chau Ju-kua that in San-fo-tsi, "when the king dies, the common people go into mourning by shaving their heads and his personal followers choose a voluntary death by leaping into the blazing fire."[4]

From a very early period the king imitated the grandeur and luxury of the Indian Court. According to an account of

1. Ibid, p. 79.
2. Chau Ju-kua, p. 61.
3. Groeneveldt-Notes, p. 107.
4. Chau Ju-kua, p. 61.

the sixth century A.D., the king of Lang-ya-su, "when he goes out, rides on an elephant, surrounded with flags of feathers, banners and drums, and covered by a white canopy."[1] The history of the Sung dynasty (960-1279 A.D.) says of the king of Java : "The king has his hair in a knot upon the top of his head, he wears golden bells, a silk robe, and shoes of leather. He sits on a square couch and his functionaries who see him daily salute him three times on going away. When he goes out, he rides on an elephant or sits in a carriage, and from five to seven hundred soldiers follow him. When the people see the king, they squat down until he has passed."[2] According to Chau Ju-kua, the ruler of San-fo-tsi was sheltered by a silk umbrella and guarded by men bearing golden lances.[3] The royal procession in Po-li was marked by even greater splendour as is evident from the passage quoted above, in Bk. 1, ch. IX. An idea of the primitive and simple court-life may be formed from the account of Pu-ni where "the king sits on a couch made of cords, and when he goes out he sits on a large piece of cloth (a hammock) and is carried by a number of men."[4]

The residence of the king and the nobles was built of brick and wood, sometimes covered by Chinese tiles, while the dwellings of the people were mostly bamboo cottages covered with straw, the walls being filled in with leaves, and the poles fastened with rattan.[5]

The Chinese description of the ordinary people is sometimes applicable only to wild primitive tribes who still inhabited parts of the country.

Take, for example, the following description of the Javanese in Ying-yai Sheng-lan which is also reproduced in the History of the Ming Dynasty. "The natives are very ugly and uncouth ; they go about with uncombed heads and naked feet

1. Groeneveldt-Notes, p. 10.
2. Ibid, p. 16.
3. Chau Ju-Kua, p. 70.
4. Groeneveldt-Notes, p. 108.
5. Ibid, p. 46. Chau Ju-kua, pp. 67, 70.

and believe devoutly in devils. The food of these people is dirty and bad, as for instance snakes, ants, and all other kinds of insects and worms which are kept a moment before the fire and then eaten ; the dogs they have in their houses eat and sleep together with them, without their being disgusted at all."[1]

This is evidently the class of people who were civilised by the Hindus. The Chinese account, which belongs to the last period of Hindu culture, shows that a large section of the people was still beyond the pale of Hindu culture and civilization.

Perhaps even the civilized element retained a degree of primitive ferocity such as is described in the same texts. "The temper (of the people of Java) is cruel and hasty ; young and old, high and low, all carry a sword at their side and on the slightest provocation they injure each other.'[2] We read in another text : "The men and women of this country take great care of their heads ; if another touches them, or if they get into a quarrel in trading, or if they are drunk and insult each other, they draw their dagger and begin stabbing, thus deciding the question by violence. If one is killed, the other runs away and conceals himself for three days after which time he has no more to account for his opponent's life. When, on the contrary, a murderer is caught on the spot, he is also stabbed to death immediately."[3]

Quite in keeping with this temper was an annual 'Gladiatorial combat' which is called by the Chinese "Meeting of Bamboo Spears." It was an annual gathering attended by the king and the queen. The combatants, armed with bamboo spears and accompanied by their wives or concubines, formed two ranks. At the sound of drum two men advanced with their lances and commenced fighting. After they were engaged three times, they were separated by their wives. If one was killed in the fight, the king ordered the victor to pay one gold coin to the relations of the deceased whose wife henceforth followed the

1. Groeneveldt-Notes, pp. 50, 40.
2. Ibid, p. 40.
3. Ibid, p. 47.

victor. The Chinese author justly remarks : "Thus they make a game of a deadly fight."[1]

The same primitive character may also be noted in their dress and food. The chief characteristic of the dress of the people was that both men and women usually kept the upper part of their body naked, and only put something like a modern *sarong* around the lower limbs below the waist. This is definitely recorded about the people of Lang-ya-su, Java, and Borneo.[2] The fact that the custom prevails even to-day in the island of Bali gives an authentic character to the Chinese statement. A woman without any covering for the upper part of the body would be regarded in modern India as a relic of barbarism. But it is only fair to bear in mind that even now the custom prevails among some South Indian tribes, and that ancient Indian sculpture as a rule represents female figures without any covering for the upper part of the body.

Rice formed the ordinary article of food, at least in Java. Another Indian characteristic was the chewing of betel. They drank wine made from flowers, cocoanuts (probably palm-tree), *penang* or honey, which were all intoxicating.[3]

The people had various amusements to enjoy their lives. Gambling seems to have been widely prevalent. The people of San-fo-tsi played *pa-kui*, chess or arranged cock-fight, in all cases staking money.[4] Cock-fighting was also a favourite pastime in Java. More innocent amusements were trips to mountains or rivers. We are told about Java : "In the fifth month they go in boats for their amusement and in the tenth month they repair to the mountain to enjoy themselves there. They have mountain ponies which carry them very well, and some go in mountain chairs."[5]

---

1. Ibid, pp. 50-1.

2. Ibid, pp. 10, 46, 51, 106. In the History of the Sung Dynasty, however, the dress of the Javanese is said to be wrapped round the breast and then going down below the knees (Ibid, p. 17).

3. Ibid, pp. 13, 49, 63. Chau Ju-kua, p. 60.

4. Groeneveldt-Notes, p. 75.

5. Ibid, p. 17.

The women of Java had their own modes of enjoyment. "On every fifteenth and sixteenth day of the month, when the moon is full and the night is clear, the native women form themselves into troops of 20 or 30, one woman being the head of them all, and so they go arm in arm to walk in the moonshine; the head woman sings one line of native song and the others afterwards fall in together; they go to the houses of their relations and of rich and high people when they are rewarded with copper cash and such things. This is called "making music in the moonshine."[1]

Music seems to be fairly cultivated all over Malayasia. The History of the Sung Dynasty (960-1279 A.D.) describes the Javanese musical instruments as transversal flute, drums, and wooden boards, and add that the Javanese can also dance.[2] Indeed the modern Javanese music (*gamelan*) and dancing, which justly enjoy a high reputation, give us a fair idea of their past achievements in these directions.

The modern Javanese orchestra, known as Gamelan, consists of a variety of musical instruments such as stringed instruments, wind instruments, instruments of percussion, instruments for the melody or accompaniment, and bass instruments. A detailed account of the various instruments under each of these heads cannot be attempted here, and the inquisitive reader is referred to the standing authorities in the subject[3]. "The various kinds of Gamelan are distinguished by the key in which the instruments are tuned...... A complete Gamelan requires a band of 24 players.... The Gamelan music has reached a great development at the court of Djokjakerta and the instruments there, which are of considerable antiquity, are held in great veneration[4]."

---

1. Ibid, p. 53. 2. Ibid, p. 17.

3. Kunst and Dr. Goris—Hindoe-Javaansche Muziekinstrumenten (1927); supplemented by T. B. G., Vol. 68 (1928), pp. 347 ff.

Kunst and Kunst-Van Wely—De Toonkunst Van Bali (1925).

4. J. Str. Br. R.A.S., No. 65, pp. 24-26.

The inscriptions refer to various kinds of music, *e. g.* those of *Gamelan*, *tuwung*, *regang*, *gandi*, *rāvaṇahasta*, drum, cymbal, and *brekuk*.

Dancing has always been a very popular entertainment in Java. It is referred to in various inscriptions, and sometimes even princesses are described as proficient in the art of dancing. Of the various kinds of modern Javanese dance both by men and women of different classes of society, a detailed and interesting description has been given by Raffles[1]. It consists in "graceful attitudes of the body and in the slow movement of the arms and legs, particulalry of the former, even to the distinct motion of the hand and fingers." In addition to the common dancing girls of the country, concubines of the sovereign, the hereditary princes, and of the nobles practise the art in public. As regards the concubines of princes Raffles remarks: "Their body and limbs are by slow movements thrown into every graceful attitude that the most flexible form is capable of exhibiting." The same author adds: "The nobles of the highest rank are accustomed, on particular occasions of festivity, to join in the dance with a common dancing girl. To dance gracefully is an accomplishment in every Javan of rank."

Music was also cultivated in other parts of Malayasia. As regards San-fo-tsi we are told: "For their music they have a small guitar and small drums. Slaves from Pulu Condore make music for them by trampling on the ground and singing".[2] The musical instruments used in Kora or Kalah, in Malay Peninsula, were "a kind of guitar, a transversal flute, copper cymbals and iron drums".[3]

The most important amusement known in Malayasia was of course the Wayang or shadow-play which originated in Java. As it still forms one of the most interesting and unique forms of amusement in Java, Bali, Lambok, Malay

1. Cf. Raffles—Java, pp 379-385.

2. Ibid, p. 63.

3. Ibid, p. 122.

Peninsula, and other places[1], naturally much has been written on its origin and character, and there is a vast literature on the subject. Reserving the discussion of this point for an appendix to this chapter we shall here confine ourselves merely to an account of the institution as it exists at present, for there are good grounds to believe that it has not materially altered its old character[2].

The Javanese have seven kinds of theatrical performances which may be broadly divided into three classes. First, the ordinary kind, in which the dramatic characters are represented by men. The only feature that deserves special notice herein is that the actors wear masks except when they perform before their sovereign. The former is called Topeng and the latter Wayang Wong.

Secondly, the Wayang proper. Although the term *wayang* is now used for theatre in general, it technically means a shadow-play. The essential features of a *wayang* proper are that the actors are represented by shadows which the puppets throw from behind on a white screen, in front of the audience. The puppets are made of leather, generally of buffalo's hide,

---

1. For an account of Malay and Siamese theatres Cf. I.A.L., Vol. VIII, pp. 43 ff.

2. There is a vast literature on this subject. Particular reference may be made to the following :—

(a) Rassers—Over den Oorsprong van het Javaansche Tooneel, B.K.I. (1931), pp. 317-450. This is the latest and most detailed discussion of the subject. Also cf. B.K.I., Vol. 81, pp. 311-381.

(b) G.A.J. Hazeu—Bijdrage Tot de Kennis Van het Javaansche Tooneel (Leiden, 1897).

(c) Krom—Geschiedenis[2], pp. 49 ff.

(d) Brandes, T.B.G. (1889), pp. 122 ff.

(e) Encyl. Van. Ned. Ind. (*s.v.* Tooneel). (An excellent summary of this is given in J. Str. Br. R.A.S., No. 65, pp. 19 ff).

(f) Kats—Het Javaansche Tooneel (1923).

(g) Jacob—Geschichte des Schatten-theaters (1925).

The account given is based principally on the authority No. (e) and also Raffles-Java, pp. 375-379.

and painted and gilt with great care. The performer (*dalang*) sits behind the screen under a lamp, and manipulates the puppets so as to suit their actions to the speech which he himself recites from behind on behalf of all the actors. The movements of the puppets are rendered quite easy as they are cut in profile and have loose arms which can be moved by wooden sticks. The *dalang* is, of course, the soul of the whole performance. He not only recites the speeches of all the actors but also repeats verses from the drama illustrating the spirit of the story, and adds descriptions necessary to render the action intelligible to the spectators. The music or *gamelan* forms an essential accompaniment of *wayang*, and like a band-master the *dalang* gives directions to the musicians seated behind him by means of a small hammer in his left hand. To render the war scenes sufficiently exciting he beats with his right foot two or three metallic plates kept ready for the purpose. Before the performance begins he puts in a cup an offering for the spirits and burns incense.

The most striking thing in a *wayang* is the grotesque form of the puppets or figures which cast shadows on the screen. They are strange distortions of human figures, with an unnaturally prominent nose, grotesque expression of face, and a curious disproportion between different limbs.

The *wayang* proper is of two kinds, *wayang purva* and *wayang gedog*. *Wayang purva* is the ancient and the most important one. Its themes are usually derived from the two Indian epics, the Rāmāyaṇa and the Mahābhārata, though they are sometimes mixed up with the Old-Javanese or real Malay-Polynesian myths. Even to-day it is the most popular form of theatre in Java.

The *wayang gedog* was first introduced during the Majapahit period and differs from *wayang purva* mainly in respect of the subjects of play. Raden Pañji, the prince of Janggala, is the hero of this later class of *wayang*, the themes of which are based on the stories of his love adventures and consequent fights with other princes. The dress and equipments of the puppets naturally vary to a certain extent in consequence of the difference of the subject-matter, but these are minor matters of detail.

The third class of theatre comprises Wayang Keliṭik or Karuchil, Wayang Golek and Wayang Beber. These are not, however, shadow-plays, the actors being represented respectively by flat wooden puppets, round dressed-up puppets, and pictures. No screen is used in any of these.

Thus on the whole we find that poetry, drama, music, and dance formed the highest classes of amusement, at least in Java, and the spirit of these was undoubtedly derived from India.

Lastly, we may turn to the final rites of a man, which form such a characteristic feature of every society. As regards the disposal of the dead, burning, throwing into water, and exposure to wilderness for being devoured by birds or dogs seem to have been the chief practices. It is said about Dva-pa-tan, usually identified with Bali, that "when one of them dies, they fill his mouth with gold, put golden bracelet on his legs and arms, and after having added camphor oil, camphor baros and other kinds of perfumery, they pile up firewood and burn the corpse." In Kora or Kalah (Malay Peninsula), after the bodies were burnt the ashes were put in a golden jar and sunk into the sea[1].

In this connection we may refer to the present practice of cremation at Bali[2]. It consists of a series of ceremonies and requires much time and much money. Immediately after death the body is embalmed, *i.e.*, covered successively with spices, coins, clothes, mats, and a covering of split bamboo. In this state the body remains for a length of time, until three days before the cremation, the corpse is stripped of its coverings and the relatives look upon the dead for the last time. The dead body is then placed on the funeral carriage which is a sort

---

1. Raffles—Java, pp. 52, 58, 108, 120, 122.

2. The account is based on the very detailed description given in Friederich–Bali, pp. 137-145.

of moving chariot, consisting of a base made of bamboo with a superstructure of bamboo or wood, in the form of a pyramid of three to eleven storeys. Of course the structure and its decoration vary with the wealth of the family and are very gorgeous in the case of princes.

The funeral carriage is then taken to the cremation ground in a long procession, accompanied by music, and also by armed men in the case of members of a royal family. The articles of daily use and holy water from the sacred places, both Hindu and Buddhist, are carried with the procession.

At the place of cremation the corpse is carried down from the carriage and placed into the coffin, which stands on a two-storeyed chamber and has the figure of a lion in the case of reigning princes, a cow in the case of other distinguished persons, and is usually a simple square wooden chest in the case of ordinary men, although even these sometimes use figures, *e.g.*, Gajamina, a monster half-elephant and half-fish. At last, after the Padaṇḍa has muttered the sacred texts and sprinkled the holy water on the body, a fire is kindled beneath the coffin. After the corpse is consumed the bones are collected and carried the next day with great state to the sea and thrown into it together with money and offerings.

It was believed that cremation exempted a man from any further change of shape, at least he remained for a certain time as a Pitā (father) in the heaven of the *devas* and as such demanded the worship and offerings of his surviving relations. But as every family was not able to bear the heavy expenses of cremation, they buried the body instead of burning it. Those who were buried could not enter heaven and assumed all sorts of shapes, and the Balinese specially believed that many of them were metamorphosed into wild dogs. It was, therefore, the bounden duty of every one, who was rich enough, to exhume the dead bodies of his poorer ancestors and burn them.

APPENDIX.

The origin of Wayang.

For the early history of Wayang we are dependent solely on stray references in Old-Javanese literature. It is mentioned, *e.g.*, in Arjunavivāha (st. 59), Vṛttasañcaya (st. 93), Bhārata-yuddha (st. 664), Tantu Panggelaran (pp. 103-4, 170-71, 258-60), Rāmāyaṇa (XXIV-112), Brahmāṇḍapurāṇa, Sumanasāntaka (XXVII, 1), and Rāma-Vijaya (VII-12). In Bali the earliest reference occurs in a record dated 1058 A.D. But there is a reference to Wayang in a recently published inscription which has been attributed to king Balitung (A.D. 898 to 910)[1].

Before the discovery of this inscription it was held "that as early as the first half of the eleventh century A.D. shadow-plays were shown at Kediri, in which shadows of figures cut of leather were projected on the screen, that they were so popular that they were referred to by the poets of the time, and that already in the twelfth century A.D. these shows were accompanied by an orchestra, consisting of flutes, small cymbals etc.[2]". But Dr. Hazeu held that the Wayang was known in Java about 800 Śaka or even probably earlier, and Brandes put this date as 700 Śaka. Dr. Hazeu's view now appears quite reasonable, but there is no satisfactory evidence as yet in support of Brandes.

While the older scholars generally attribute an Indian origin to Wayang, several scholars including Hazeu and Brandes are emphatically of opinion that the Wayang was invented in Java and not borrowed from the Hindus.[3] The

1. Ins. Nos. 10-11 of Balitung. Cf. Part I. p. 241.

2. J. Str. Br. R.A.S., No. 65, p. 20.

3. Hageman (Handeling tot de Geschiedenis Van Java, I, p. 47), Poensen (P.W. Jaarg, 17, p. 138), Veth (Java, I, p. 451), and Krom (op. cit.) are in favour of an Indian origin of Wayang, while Crawfurd (History, I, p. 240), Niemann (P.W. Jaarg, 17, p. 164 f. n. 2), Brandes (op. cit.), and Hazeu (op. cit.) are in favour of upholding its indigenous character.

arguments on which this view is based may be summed up as follows:—

(1) All the technical terms in connection with Wayang are purely Javanese.

(2) The Hindus never had a shadow-play.

(3) Originally Wayang was a typically Indonesian religious ceremony in honour of the gods or of forefathers as gods. Gradually it degenerated into a form of amusement, but even now it shows signs of having had a religious element.

The weakness of these arguments can be demonstrated very easily.

(1) It is always risky to infer the indigenous or foreign character of an article or a thing from the terms used to denote it. For example, in Bengal, the watch, clock and their accessories are known by indigenous terms (*ghaḍī*, *kāṭā* etc.), while the words for inkpot, pen and book are all foreign. Are we to conclude from this that while watch and clock are indigenous products of Bengal, the Bengalis owed their literary culture to Arabs and Parsis? Krom tells us that even to-day the Javanese are in the habit of giving indigenous names to articles imported from Europe and America. It stands to reason, therefore, that the indigenous names for Wayang and its accessories do not necessarily imply any indigenous origin of the institution.

(2) Nothing can be more erroneous than the assumption that the Hindus had never a shadow-play. Pischel[1] and Lüders[2] have shown that the famous Sanskrit drama Mahānāṭaka was originally intended for a shadow-play. As Winternitz[3] has already pointed out, Mahānāṭaka possesses great resemblance with the Wayang plays of Java. The date of Mahānāṭaka is not definitely known, but as it is quoted by Ānandavardhana, it must be earlier than 850 A.D. Further, a similar dramatic work, Dūtāṅgada by Subhaṭa (13th cent.

---

1. Sitzungsberichte der Berliner Akademie, 1906, pp. 498 ff.
2. Ibid, 1916, pp. 698 ff.
3. Geschichte der Indischen Litteratur, Vol. III, pp. 242-245.

A.D.), is expressly designated as Chāyā-nāṭaka (shadow-play). Among later works of this class may be mentioned Pāṇḍavābhyudaya, Rāmābhyudaya, and Subhadrā-Pariṇaya composed by Vyāsaśrī Rāmadeva (15th cent. A.D.), and a very modern work, the Sāvitrī-carita of Śaṅkaralāla (19th cent.). Pischel, however, thinks it probable that shadow-play is referred to in Mahābhārata and Bṛhatsaṁhitā. Sten Konow also is of opinion that the Indians knew shadow-plays in early period[1]. Dr. Coomaraswamy has shown that shadow-play with leather figures existed in South India and Ceylon in the twelfth century A.D.[2]

(3) As regards the religious character of the Wayang it is admitted that both in India and Greece the theatre originated in a similar way. Again, the worship of ancestors is common to both Indians and Indonesians. Further, no other Indonesian people, except the Javanese, have developed an institution like Wayang in connection with this worship. These facts, the truth of which cannot be doubted for a moment, considerably weaken the force of the arguments advanced by Brandes and Hazeu. For they discredit the view that the Wayang was necessarily connected with ancestor-worship, or *vice-versa*, and that even if it were so, it could not have been evolved in India, where also the worship of ancestor is a religious ceremony, and where, as in Greece, the theatre is known to have originated in religious ceremonies.

---

1. Das Indische Drama, pp. 4, 45, 90.

2. J.R A.S. 1930, p. 627 ; Coomaraswamy, p. 89

The following account of the popular shows called Pāvakkūttu, still current in Malabar, is of great interest in this connection.

"In these shows, dummy pieces of either leather or light pieces of wood, representing figures of heroes and heroines are displayed in public, to the accompaniment of vocal music, drums and cymbals. They are a favourite pastime with the masses of Malabar on the occasion of festivals in temples, and during certain seasons of the year. The Pāvakkūttu has for its plot only anecdotes from the Rāmāyaṇa." I.H.Q., Vol X, p. 144.

If we now turn to the broad facts of the case, the following may be regarded as undisputed.

(1) There is no evidence that the shadow-play was known in Java till the Hindu religion and culture were thoroughly established in that island.

(2) Shadow-plays have been undoubtedly known in India from an early period. The earliest work of the kind so far known is Mahānāṭaka which must have been composed before 850 A.D., *i.e.* before it is first referred to in Javanese literature.

(3) As in Wayang-Purva, the earliest type of Wayang in Java, so in the shadow-plays of India, the theme of the play is exclusively taken from the two epics the Rāmāyaṇa and the Mahābhārata.

(4) Wayang is not known to any other Indonesian people (except the Javanese and the Balinese).

If we add to these the predominant influence of Hindu culture in Java, particularly in the period when we get the first reference to Wayang in Java, there can be hardly any reasonable doubt that like so many other institutions the Wayang in Java had also an Indian origin.

It is needless to consider seriously the view, already refuted by Hazeu, that Wayang had a Chinese origin.

Chapter IV

LITERATURE

§ 1. JAVANESE LITERATURE

From an early date Indian literature was carried to Java, though the nature and extent of this importation are not exactly known.[1] The study of this literature led to the growth of an Indo-Javanese literature, which forms one of the most characteristic features of Indian colonisation in that island. Nowhere else, outside India, has Indian literature been studied with so much advantage and with such important consequences. The range and intrinsic value of this Indo-Javanese literature are, indeed, very great. As in other departments of civilisation, so here, too, a fine superstructure was built in Java upon foundations so well and truly laid by the Indians. It will be beyond my scope to enter into a detailed discussion of the contents and merits of this literature, and I shall therefore confine myself only to a general outline of the subject.

As we have seen above, the history of the Indian colony in Java may be divided into three broad chronological periods, according as the chief seat of political authority was in the west, centre, and the east of the island. For the first of these periods, we have no trace of any literature proper, although the inscriptions of Pūrṇavarman clearly testifiy to the knowledge of Sanskrit language and literature. This knowledge becomes more intensive and extensive during the second period. This is proved not only by inscriptions, but also by the

---

1. For an account of the Sanskrit texts now found in the island of Bali cf.

(i) Mededeelingen van de Kirtya Liefrinck van der Tuuk, aflef. I, Singharadja, 1929.

(ii) S. Lévi—Sanskrit Texts from Bali (Baroda, 1933).

extensive monuments of the period, both Brāhmancial and Buddhist, as the sculptures carved therein are mostly, if not exclusively, illustrations of Indian books. This period also probably saw the beginnings of Indo-Javanese literature ; I say probably, because only three books may be tentatively ascribed to this period, and the date of each of them is a subject-matter of great controversy. It is only when we come to the third period that we find the Indo-Javanese literature taking a definite shape. For nearly five hundred years (1000-1500 A.D.) this literature had an unbroken and flourishing career in the east under the patronage of the kings of Kaḍiri or Daha, Singhasāri and Majapahit.

The Muslim conquest of Majapahit brought to an end what is usually called the Old-Javanese literature. The subsequent development of Javanese literature took place in different localities. The Javanese who took refuge in Bali continued the literary efforts, and their literary products are referred to as Middle-Javanese. On the other hand, there was a revival of literary culture in Central Java, in the new Muslim kingdom of Matarām, and the result was the growth of what is called the New-Javanese literature.

While the Middle-Javanese literature may be regarded as a normal development from the Old-Javanese, the same cannot be said of the New-Javanese ; for although the literary traditions of the Old-Javanese still form its main basis, it shows a wide divergence from the latter in language, form, and substance. In other words, the process of Javanisation is more noticeable in New-Javanese than in the Middle-Javanese.

Two different views have been entertained regarding the origin of the New-Javanese literature. According to the older view[1] it is the result of a conscious but futile effort to imitate the Old-Javanese literature of the east, and its futility and the consequent artificial and degraded character are due to the

1. Cf., *e.g.*, G. A. J. Hazeu—Oud en Nieuw uit de Javaansche Letter-Kunde (1921), pp. 6-7.

influence of Islam. For the Islamic conquest of Java not only ushered in a period of political unrest, chaos, and confusion which proved fatal to all fine arts including literature, but also thrust in a wedge between the old and the new, obliterating, or at least considerably blurring the past and giving a new orientation to the present and the future.

According to the other and more recent view,[1] the rise of the New-Javanese literature in the new kingdom of Matarām was a revival of the literary traditions of Central Java which lay dormant for a period of nearly six or seven hundred years. The long gap or break in the continuity of the traditions is regarded as sufficient to explain the wide divergences from the Old-Javanese. The greater progress of Javanisation is further explained by the fact that the absence of political centres in Central Java loosened the hold of Indian civilisation and inevitably led to a corresponding increase in the indigenous influence.

The artificial classic language of the New-Javanese literature is called Kavi[2]. Formerly this word was used to denote the old language of Java in general, but now the term Old-Javanese is used to indicate the language which was current up to the fall of Majapahit, and the Middle-Javanese to indicate that used by the Javanese in Bali. We thus get three broad divisions of Indo-Javanese literature, *viz.*—

1. Old-Javanese.
2. Middle-Javanese.
3. New-Javanese.

In the following pages we shall make an attempt to give a short account of the first two only, as the third really falls beyond the Hindu period in Java.[3]

---

1. Berg-Hoofdlijnen, pp. 16-17. 2. Ibid., p. 20, f.n. 1.

3. Since this chapter was written, Mr. H.B. Sarkar has published his book "Indian Influences on the Literature of Java and Bali" which gives a more detailed account of many of the books which are only briefly touched upon here.

The Old-Javanese literature is marked by several important characteristics. Its poetry follows rules of Sanskrit metre, its subject-matter is derived mainly from Indian literature, and it has a strong predilection for using Sanskrit words and quoting Sanskrit verses. But even in subject-matter the deviation from the Sanskrit original is often considerable. We know that in India itself there were many local versions of Indian epic tales, and so it is difficult to say how far the difference in the Old-Javanese literature may be ascribed to this fact. Another factor may be looked for in the indigenous influence, but our complete lack of knowledge of the pre-Hindu literature in Java or other neighbouring islands[1] prevents us from estimating it at its proper worth.

As already said above, the beginnings of this literature may be traced to the period when Central Java was the political centre of the island. The earliest book that we may definitely refer to this period is an Old-Javanese version of a Sanskrit work, Amaramālā,[2] which like Sanskrit Amarakośa, and other Indian lexicons, contains synonyms of different gods, goddesses, and other animate and inanimate objects. This work was written under the patronage of king Jitendra of the Śailendra dynasty. Unfortunately this king is not known from other sources, and so we cannot trace his relationship to other kings of this well-known dynasty of Central Java.

Another work which may perhaps be ascribed to the same period is Sang hyang Kamahāyanikan, a Mahāyāna text, to which detailed reference will be made in connection with Mahāyāna Buddhism in the next chapter.

According to Poerbatjaraka the composition of the Old-Javanese Rāmāyaṇa has also to be referred to the same period.[3] This is one of the best and most famous works of

1. Berg-Hoofdlijnen, pp. 18-20.

2. Krom-Geschiedenis (Second Edition), pp. 150-151.

3. Gedenkschrift Kon. Inst. 1926, p. 265. T.B.G. Vol. 72 (1932), pp. 151 ff. The view is, however, opposed by Stutterheim (B.K.I., Vol. 85, pp. 483-7).

Indo-Javanese literature. Its subject-matter agrees quite well with that of Sanskrit Rāmāyaṇa, but it concludes with the reunion of Rāma and Sītā after the fire ordeal of the latter, and does not contain the story of her banishment and death. Some portions of this work, particularly in the last two *Sargas* or Cantos, have no corresponding passages in Vālmiki's Rāmāyaṇa, and are probably local additions. These portions may, however, be interpolations of a later date. The style is rich but simple, though occasionally the author makes an attempt to show off his learning.

The Old-Javanese Rāmāyaṇa is not a translation of the Sanskrit epic, but an independent work. Kern held the view that its author did not know Sanskrit and must have derived his materials from other sources.[1] It may be noted here that the story of Rāmāyaṇa had a wide currency, and we have both Malayan and Balinese versions of it, *viz.*, Seri Rāma and Rāma Kidung.

The name of the author of the Rāmāyaṇa and the date of its composition are not definitely known. Kern, who edited it, referred it to the beginning of the thirteenth century A.D. But according to Dr. Brandes and Dr. Stutterheim it belongs to a much earlier period. In a Wawatekan, Mpu Yogīśvara is cited as the author of the Rāmāyaṇa, and 1016 (=1094 A.D.) is given as the date of its composition. How far this tradition can be relied upon, it is, of course, difficult to say. As already noted, Poerbatjaraka refers the composition of Rāmāyaṇa to the period of Central Java. There is thus a wide divergence of opinion about the date of this famous work.[2]

---

1. Poerbatjaraka maintains that the author knew Sanskrit and was acquainted with Vālmiki's Rāmāyaṇa (T.B.G., 1932 pp. 168 ff.). Mr. M. Ghosh contends that the author was acquainted with Bhaṭṭikāvya and that his Rāmāyaṇa 'is partially a translation and partially an adaptation' of this Sanskrit work (J.G.I.S., Vol. III, pp. 113 ff.).

2. For Rāmāyaṇa cf. B.K.I., Vol. 71, p. 559 ; Krom-Geschiedenis[2], p. 174. For the spread of the Rāma-legend in Indonesia and its different versions, cf. (i). Stutterheim—Rāma-legenden und Rāma-reliefs in Indonesien (1924). (ii) J. Kats—The Rāmāyaṇa in Indonesia (Bulletin of the School of Oriental Studies, Vol. IV, pp. 579-585).

The next important landmark in connection with the development of Old-Javanese literature is the prose translation of the great epic Mahābhārata during the reign of Dharmavaṁśa. The Old-Javanese translation of Ādi-Parva, Virāṭa-Parva, and Bhiṣma-Parva may be definitely ascribed to the initiative and patronage of this king, while the Āśrama-Parva, Musala-Parva, Prasthānika-Parva, and Svargārohaṇa-Parva are of later date. There is also a version of Udyoga-Parva, written in very corrupt Sanskrit, and full of lacunae. The Virāṭa-Parva was composed in 996 A.D., just ten years before Java was overtaken by the great catastrophe which destroyed both Dharmavaṁśa and his kingdom.

The Old-Javanese translations closely follow the original epic, but are more condensed. Their style is very primitive and lacks literary merit. Their importance, however, cannot be over-estimated, as they made the Great Epic popular in Java and supplied themes for numerous literary works which exhibit merits of a very high order.[1]

The Old-Javanese Rāmāyaṇa was edited by Kern (1900). It is being translated by Juynboll in parts (Translation of Sarga XXIII appearing in B.K.I., Vol. 92 (1934).

1. There is an extensive literature on the Javanese Mahābhārata. Juynboll has edited the Ādi-(1906) and Virāṭa-Parvas (1912), and translated, in Dutch, three other Parvas, *viz.*, Āśramavāsika, Mausala and Mahā-Prasthānika Parvas (Drie Boeken van het oud-javaansche Mahābhārata, Leiden, 1893). The portion of the Bhiṣmaparva, corresponding to Bhagavadgītā, has been translated and commented upon by J Gonda (T.B.G., 1935, pp. 36 ff.) who will shortly publish an edition of the Bhismaparva-text. For Udyoga-Parva cf. B.K.I., Vol. 69, pp. 219-296. For a discussion of the relation of Old-Javanese Mahābhārata to the different Indian versions of the epic cf. T.B.G., Vol. 49 (1901). pp. 289-357. For further information cf.

(i) B.K.I., vol. 71, pp. 563-64. (ii) Sarkar-Literature, Chaps XI-XII. (iii) Lévi-Texts, pp. xxxii ff. (iv) Mahābhārata published by the Bhandarkar Oriental Research Institute, Ādi-Parva, pp. xxv-xxvi, App. II. Virāṭa-Parva, pp. xi-xv, App. II. (v) Verslag van het Zevende Congres van het Oostersch Genootschap in Nederland, 1933, p. 29.

The first work of this kind is Arjuna-Vivāha, written by Mpu Kaṇwa under the patronage of Airlangga (1019-1042 A.D.). It deals with an episode from the Mahābhārata in which Arjuna helps the gods in their fight against Nivāta-Kavaca. This is the first poetical work of which the date is known with certainty. It was a very popular work in Java. Its subject-matter formed the *motifs* of sculpture and the well-known lacon Mintarāga was based on it.[1]

Two other poetical works may be referred to the beginning of the Kaḍiri period. The first is Kṛṣṇāyaṇa by Triguṇa. It deals with the famous episode of the abduction of Rukmiṇī by Kṛṣṇa and his consequent fight with Jarāsandha. It contains a beautiful description of Dvārāvatī, the capital of Kṛṣṇa, and gives the name of 10 out of his 16000 wives. The poem supplied the themes of sculptured reliefs of the temple of Panataran.[2] The next work Sumanasāntaka[3] (death caused by a flower) is based on the story of the death of Indumatī, the queen of Aja and the mother of Daśaratha, so marvellously dealt with by Kālidāsa in his immortal work Raghuvaṁśa. While Aja was one day sitting with Indumatī, a garland of flowers fell from heaven upon the latter, and she died instantly. The poem was composed by Mpu Monaguṇa and refers to Śrī Varṣajaya. The Kṛṣṇāyaṇa also refers to a king of the same name. Krom thinks that this king is to be identified with Jayavarṣa (1104 A.D.). So these two works may be referred to the beginning of the twelfth century A.D.

---

1. B.K.I., Vol. 71, p. 561; edited by Friederich in V.B.G., Vol. 23; B.K.I., Vol. 82 (1926).

2. For contents cf. Cat. 1, Vol. I, p. 156; for the date cf. T.B.G., Vol. 57, p. 515 The work was formerly referred wrongly to the period of Airlangga.

3 B.K.I., Vol. 71, p. 561; Cat. I, Vol. I, pp. 144ff. For the date cf. T.B.G., Vol. 57, p. 516. For the relation of the poem to Kālidāsa's Raghuvaṁśa—cf. B.K.I., series 6, Vol. VI, pp. 391ff.

We next come to the most flourishing period of the Old-Javanese literature, *viz.*, the reign of Jayabhaya (1135-1157 A.D.). The greatest work of this period, which has all along enjoyed a very high degree of reputation is Bhārata-yuddha,[1] an independent work based on the Udyoga-parva, Bhīṣma-parva, Droṇa-parva, Karṇa-parva, and Śalya-parva of the Sanskrit Mahābhārata, in other words, those parts of the great Epic of India which deal with the great war. It is written in simple but epic style, and its grandeur, according to Juynboll, is comparable to that of the Greek epics. It was written by Mpu Sedah in 1157 A.D. by order of the Kaḍirian king Jayabhaya. According to one tradition, the poet incurred royal displeasure and the work was completed by Mpu Panuluh. As in the Rāmāyaṇa, there are many interpolations—mostly love-episodes—in this work. The continued popularity of the work is testified to by a New-Javanese version named Bratajuda.

Mpu Panuluh, who completed the Bhārata-yuddha, evidently during the reign of Jayabhaya, also composed another poetical work, Harivaṁśa,[2] during the same reign. This book, like its Indian prototype, deals with the abduction of Rukmiṇī by Kṛṣṇa and the consequent war with Jarāsandha and the Pāṇḍavas who helped the latter. This last episode is not in the original Indian work. Mpu Panuluh is also the author of a third poetical work, Ghaṭotkacāśraya.[3] It describes the fight between Abhimanyu and Lakṣmaṇa-Kumāra over a lady named Kṣitisundarī, in which Ghaṭotkaca comes to the help

---

1. B.K.I., Vol. 71, p. 560. The text was edited by J.G.H., Gunning (1903). Recently Poerbatjaraka and Hooykaas (Djawa, Vol. 14, No. 1, pp. 1-87) have made a critical study of the work, and have given a summary of its contents.

2. Cat. 1, Vol. I, pp. 143-44. For the date cf. T.B.G., Vol. 57, pp. 516-17.

3. Cat. 1, Vol. I, pp. 149-50. For the date cf. T.B.G., Vol. 57, p. 517. The poem refers in the first stanza to King Jayakṛta, who is probably the same as King Kṛtajaya of Kaḍiri.

of the former. This book has supplied the theme to many Wayang stories in Java and Malay Peninsula.[1]

Kāmeśvara II (1185 A.D.) maintained the brilliant literary traditions of the Kaḍirian court. The most famous work written under his patronage was Smaradahana.[2] This work is based on the famous episode of the burning of Smara or the god of Love by Śiva which has been so masterfully dealt with by Kālidāsa in his immortal work Kumāra-sambhavam. While Śiva was engaged in austerities, Smara (also known as Kāma, Madana, etc.) kindled in him the flames of passion. Enraged at this Śiva turned towards him, and a ray of fire proceeding from his body reduced the god of Love to ashes and he became Anaṅga or Bodyless. The subject-matter of the work, according to Pamañcangah, has been borrowed from Canda-Purāṇa which, according to Van der Tuuk, is the corrupt form of the well-known book Skandapurāṇa. The poem was composed by Dharmaya. It is dedicated to King Kāmeśvara, most probably Kāmeśvara II, though some scholars believe that it was Kāmeśvara I. In any case it belongs to the twelfth century A.D. The name of the king might have suggested his theme to the poet.

According to popular tradition, Dharmaya and Tanakung were two sons of Yogiśvara, the author of Rāmāyaṇa. The truth of this tradition may be doubted, but Tanakung was undoubtedly a contemporary of Dharmaya and wrote two poetical works Lubdhaka[3] and Vṛtta-sañcaya.[4] The latter work deals with rules of Sanskrit metre as applied to Old-Javanese, and was composed shortly before the fall of Kaḍiri

---

1. T.B.G., Vol. 25, p. 488.

2. B.K.I., Vol. 71; T.B.G., Vol. 58, pp. 461-489, 491ff. Krom-Geschiedenis,[2] p. 298, T.B.G., Vol. 57, p. 517. Berg-Inleiding (pp. 50ff.) and Mid. Jav. Trad. (p. 173). The text has been edited in Bib. Jav. series.

3. For contents cf. Cat. 1, Vol. I, p. 157.

4. Translated by Kern, V.G., Vol. IX, pp. 67ff.

in 1222 A.D. Lubdhaka, composed after this date,[1] relates the well-known story of the fight between the hosts of Yama (the god of death) and of Śiva over the body of a hunter. The latter spent the night of the Śivarātri festival on a Vilva-tree and threw a leaf of it over a Śivaliṅga lying beneath. He thus secured great merits, and so when after his death the servants of Yama took him away, the hosts of Śiva prevented them and a fight ensued. The work is also known as Śivarātri. Lubdhaka is here used as a proper name of a *niṣāda*, but it is a common word in Sanskrit meaning 'hunter.'

The famous Bhomakāvya[2] is also attributed to the period of Kāmeśvara II. It describes the defeat of Indra and other gods by Bhoma, or Naraka, son of Pṛthivī, and finally his death in the hands of Kṛṣṇa. A recently discovered work, Naraka-Vijaya, which describes the conquests of Naraka, also belongs to the reign of Kāmeśvara ;[3] but it is difficult to say whether he is the first or the second king of that name. For the Singhasāri period (13th cent.) we possess two works, the Lubdhaka of Tanakung and Rājapati-Guṇḍala,[4] a religious treatise. To the same period probably belongs also the Kakawin Kṛṣṇāntaka, which draws its materials from the Āśramavāsika-, Musala-, and the Prasthānika-parvas of the great epic. As the name shows, the death of Kṛṣṇa and the destruction of his family form the central theme of the work. It refers at the beginning to Śiva-Buddhamūrti, who may be identified with king Kṛtanagara.[5]

---

1. For the date of these two works cf. T.B.G., Vol. 57, pp. 518-19 ; Krom-Geschiedenis[2], pp. 298-9.

2. B.K.I., Vol. 71, p. 561, where it is referred to the period of Jayabhaya. Kern placed it in the 14th century A.D. For the date adopted cf. T.B.G, Vol. 57, pp. 517-518, and Krom-Geschiedenis[2], p. 298.

The text was edited with a Summary of contents in V.G.B., Vols. 22, 24.

3. Krom-Geschiedenis[2], p. 299. O. V., 1921, p. 70.

4. See next chapter.

5. Cat. 1, Vol. 1, p. 155. B.K.I., Series VI, Vol. VI, pp. 213-230. For the date cf. T.B.G., Vol. 57, p. 519.

In the fourteenth century, during the flourishing period of Majapahit we get a unique poem, the Nāgara-Kṛtāgama[1] written by Prapañca in A.D. 1365. Unlike the usual poems based on the Indian epics, it takes as its theme the life and times of Hayam Wuruk, the famous king of Majapahit, and supplies us most interesting information about the king, his capital city, his court, and his vast empire.

Prapañca names as his contemporaries, Kṛtayaśa, Brahmayaśa and several other authors. We possess two poetical works of another contemporary of Prapañca, *viz*. the Buddhist Mpu Tantular. Arjuna Vijaya[2], composed by him about 1378 A.D., describes an episode from the Uttarakāṇḍa of Rāmāyaṇa, *viz.*: the defeat of Rāvaṇa by Arjuna (*i.e.* Sahasravāhu or Kārtavīrya). It forms the basis of the New-Javanese poem Arjuna Sasrabāhu published by Winter (1853). Another work of the same author, Sutasoma or Purusādaśanta,[3] describes the fight between Sutasoma and the *rākṣasa* King Purusāda. It incidentally shows the very close relationship existing between Śaivism and Buddhism, so much so that the two might almost be regarded as identical.

The class of poetical works we have hitherto described is called Kakawin from Kavi meaning Kāvya. They are all written in Old-Javanese language and their subject-matter is derived mostly from Indian Epics and Purāṇas. In addition to the works mentioned above, there are many other Kakawins, which, however, cannot be dated even approximately. We give below a very brief account of some of them :—

1. Indravijaya[4]—story of Vṛtra's conquest and death, followed by that of Nahuṣa who secured the position of Indra for a short period.

---

1. Edited, with translation and notes, by Kern, V.G., Vols. VII-VIII. Republished with notes by Krom in 1919. For critical notes on the work by Poerbatjaraka, cf. B.K.I. Vol. 80, pp. 219-286.

2. B.K.I., Vol. 71, p. 561.

3. B.K.I., Vol. 71, pp. 561-562. Cf. Kern 'Over de vermenging van Sivaisme en Buddhisme op Java'. (V.G. Vol. IV., p. 149).

4. Cat. 1, Vol. I, p. 137.

2. Pārthayajña[1]—It describes Arjuna's asceticism by means of which he obtained weapons from Śiva.

3. Vighnotsava,[2] written by a Buddhist, describes the exploits of a Yakṣa king named Vighnotsava and particularly his fight with the *rākṣasa* king Suprasena.

4. Bratasraya[3] is a later development of the same theme.

5. Hariśraya.[4] It describes how the gods, threatened by Malyavān, king of Laṅkā, seek, at first the help of Śiva, and then of Viṣṇu, who kills Malyavān and restores to life, by *amṛta* or nectar, the gods who perished in the fight.

6. Harivijaya.[5]—It describes the churning of the ocean by gods by means of Mandara mountain.

7. Kālayavanāntaka.[6]—It describes, after the story given in Viṣṇupurāṇa, how Kālayavana invaded Dvārakā to avenge the death of Kaṁsa, and was ultimately reduced to ashes by Mucukunda, with whom the fugitive Kṛṣṇa had taken shelter. It also describes how Arjuna carried away Subhadrā when the Andhakas and Vṛṣṇis were celebrating a feast on Raivataka.

8. Rāmavijaya.[7]—Its theme is the defeat of Sahasravāhu Arjuna by Paraśurāma, son of Jamadagani and Reṇukā.

9. Ratnavijaya.[8]—It describes the fight between Sunda and Upasunda over Tilottamā.

10. Pārthavijaya.[9]—It is based on an episode from Bhāratayuddha, *viz.*, the death of Iravan, son of Arjuna and Ulupuy, and of Nīla.

11. An unnamed and incomplete Kakawin[10] gives the story of Udayana and Vāsavadattā in a modified form. Śatasenya of the lineage of the Pāṇḍavas had two sons, Udayana and Yugandarāyana. The abduction of Angaravatī, princess of Avanti, by Udayana forms the plot of the Kakawin.

1. Ibid., p. 140.
2. Ibid., p. 147.
3. Ibid., p. 148.
4. Ibid., p. 151.
5. Ibid., p. 152.
6. Ibid., p. 154.
7. Ibid., p. 159.
8. Ibid., p. 160.
9. Cat. 1, Vol. II, p. 493.
10. Ibid., pp. 496-497.

In addition to the Kakawins, based on epic themes, there are some, like Dharmaśūnya[1] and Dharmasavita,[2] of didactic or philosophical nature, and others like Lambang Salukat,[3] of an erotic character. We have, besides, a lexicon, Caṇḍakiraṇa[4] and two Kakawins Vṛttasañcaya[5] and Vṛttāyaṇa,[6] dealing with metre.

Special reference may be made to the Kakawin work, called in Java 'Nitiśāstra-kawin, but now known in Bali as Nītisāra.[7] The work may be referred to the closing years of the Majapahit period. It consists of a number of detached ślokas containing wise sayings, maxims, moral precepts, religious doctrines, *etc.*, such as we find in Sanskrit works called Nitisāra, Pañcatantra, Cāṇakya-śataka, *etc.* in India. In many cases the Javanese verses may be easily traced to the Indian original. For example we have close translations of the following well-known couplets

1. Duradhītā viṣaṁ vidyā ajīrṇe bhojanaṁ viṣam ।
   Viṣaṁ goṣṭhī daridrasya vṛddhasya taruṇī viṣaṁ ॥
2. Artha gṛhe nivarttante śmaśāne caiva bāndhavāḥ ।
   Sukṛtam duṣkṛtam cāpi gacchantamanugacchati ॥
3. Asaṁtuṣṭā dvijā naṣṭāḥ saṁtuṣṭāścaiva pārthivāḥ ।
   Salajjā gaṇikā naṣṭā nirlajjāśca kulastriyaḥ ॥

The work was very popular and has been rendered in many modern versions. It formed an important subject of study in Javanese schools until the introduction of western learning.

The Kakawins form the first of the three grand divisions of the Old-Javanese literature. The second division comprises doctrinal texts, like Sūrya Sevana, Gāruḍeya mantra, *etc.* which will be discussed in connection with religion.[8] We now turn to the third, the prose works, which may be

---

1. Cat. 1, Vol. I, p. 163.
2. Ibid., p. 162.
3. Ibid, p. 176.
4. Ibid., p. 170.
5. See pp. 69-70 above.
6. Cat. 1, Vol. II, p. 491.
7. The work has been recently edited by Dr. Poerbatjaraka (Bibliotheca Javanica, No. 4).
8. See next chapter.

subdivided, according to its contents, into four classes. Two of these, dealing with law and religion, have been discussed separately in connection with these topics, and the third comprises prose works based on Indian Epics and Purāṇas.

The Mahābhārata series begins with the Old-Javanese translations of the different Parvas of the Mahābhārata to which reference has already been made above. Another work of the same series is Koravāśrama,[1] a late work, in which a great deal of modification of the epic is noticeable. After the defeat and death of the Kauravas they are again brought to life by Vyāsa, and on Bhīṣma's advice, they practise asceticism in order to take their revenge on the Pāṇḍavas. Within this frame-work a large number of Purāṇic legends and Tāntrik doctrines have been included.

To this class also belongs Sāra-Samuccaya[2] (different from the law-book of the same name) an Old-Javanese translation of a large number of moral precepts chiefly drawn from Anuśāsanaparvan of the Mahābhārata. It is interspersed with quotations of Sanskrit verses from the epics and other Indian books such as Pañcatantra. The translations are fairly accurate and the author shows an intimate acquaintance with Sanskrit literature. The work is probably ascribed to Vararuci who is said in the beginning to have brought together the essence (Sāra) of the eighteen Parvas of the epics.

Navaruci,[3] a very popular work in Bali, describes the exploits of Bhīma. He kills two Nāgas and Indrabāhu, saves Droṇa from the wrath of Bhagavān Avaruci, practises asceticism in spite of the temptation offered by the Vidyādharis, and joins in time his brothers to save Indraprastha which the

---

1. Tantu, pp. 329-338. J.G.I.S., Vol. III, pp. 67ff.

2. B.K.I., Vol. 71, p. 505, B.K.I., Series VI, Vol. VIII, pp. 393-398. Tantu, pp. 303-4.

3. Cat. 1, Vol. II, p. 292. The text has been edited with a Dutch translation by M. Prijohoetomo (Batavia, 1934) who refers it to a date between 1500 and 1619 A.D.

Dānavas had planned to burn with Śivāgni. The work is also called Tattvajñāna and ascribed to Mpu Śivamūrtti. There are New- and Middle-Javanese redactions of this work (Navaruci-Kidung, Bimasuci). There is also a Kakawin Devaruci[1] dealing with the same theme.

Of the other epic, we have the prose translation of Uttarakāṇḍa[2] in Old-Javanese. It is interspersed with Sanskrit verses and its last two chapters are named Rāmaprasthānikam and Svarggārohanaṁ, agreeing in all these respects with the Javanese version of Mahābhārata. Like the Old-Javanese Rāmāyaṇa, it shows divergences from the original Sanskrit text. As already mentioned before, the Kakawins Hariśraya and Arjunavijaya derive their plots from this work. The banishment of Sitā is described as in Rāmāyaṇa. Among other episodes may be mentioned the killing of Vṛtra by Indra.

Of the Purāṇa class of works Brahmāṇḍa-Purāṇa[3] is undoubtedly the most important. It closely follows the model of Indian Purāṇa, though Javanese touches occur here and there. Even the preamble of the Purāṇa is reproduced ;—while Adhisīmakṛṣna was the ruler of the earth, Romaharṣaṇa, a pupil of Vyāsa, came to Naimiṣa forest, and recited the Purāṇa. The composition of the Purāṇa is, of course, ascribed to Vyāsa.

As regards the contents, we have first the story of the creation. Brahmā created the *aṇḍabhuvana*. He also created the four Ṛṣis, nine Devarṣis, and Parameśvara who is known under different forms. He also created *devas*, *asuras*, *pitṛs* and *mānuṣas*, *i.e.* gods, demons, manes and men, and the four castes originated from his mouth, arms, thigh and feet. Then he created Śatarūpā and Svāyambhuva Manu.

---

1. Cat. 1, Vol. I, p. 165. 2. Cat. 1, Vol. II. pp. 178-179.

3. V.B.G., Vol. 22, pp. 11-12, 43-50; B.K.I., Vol. 71, p. 563; Tantu, pp. 310-319; Cat. 1, Vol. II, pp. 166-167; B.K.I., Series VI, Vol. VII, pp. 272ff. Recently edited in the Bibliotheca Javanica Series; Acta Orientalia, XI, pp. 219ff.

After describing their descendants, in right Purāṇic style, the text describes the division of Jambudvipa among the nine sons of Agnīndra and the creation of the Veda in different Yugas. In Kaliyuga, Vyasa taught the four Vedas to his disciples, Jemini, Polaha, Vaiśampāyana and Sumantu, and Itihāsapurāṇa to his fifth disciple Romaharṣaṇa. Then follows an account of the disciples of these and further divisions of the Vedic literature, and incidentally the story of a dispute between Yājñavalkya and Śakalya in the court of Janaka, king of Mithilā. The text then gives a list of Vedic scholars, including women, Brahmarṣis, devarṣis, and rājarṣis, and the number of ṛks and yajus. It then describes the duration of the fourteen Manus, extent of a day and night of Brahmā, and the Mahāpralaya (great destruction).

The death of Vena and the origin of Pṛthu, the description of the seven seas and the seven dvīpas, varṣas, mountain-ranges, *etc.*, the divisions of Bhāratavarṣa, its rivers and mountains, *etc.*, are all given in detail in the style of the Purāṇas.

The contents of the work as well as the number of Sanskrit verses and passages occurring therein leave no doubt that it was based upon the Sanskrit original.

The existence of numerous manuscripts of Brahmāṇḍa-purāṇa and the veneration with which it is regarded in Bali even to-day, prove the extreme popularity of the work. Why of all the Indian Purāṇas, this one obtained a special celebrity in Java, it is difficult to say.

It may be mentioned here that there is also a poetical version of the Old-Javanese Brahmāṇḍapurāṇa. This Kakawin begins with the story of Vena and contains other legends such as those of Pṛthu[1]. The recently discovered Pṛtuvijaya Kakawin, composed by Aṣṭaguṇa, is very similar to Brahmāṇḍa-purāṇa Kakawin[2].

1. Cat. 1, Vol. I, p. 139. 2. Krom-Geschiedenis[2], p. 299.

Another work of the same class is Agastyaparva,[1] where Agastya describes to his son Dṛḍdasyu the creation of the world in right Purāṇic style. In the Mahāpralaya everything was destroyed, except Sadāśiva, who created anew the four elements, sky, air, earth and fire, and an egg from which arose Brahmā and Viṣṇu. Brahmā then created Prajāpatis, the ten Brahmarṣis (Dakṣa, Marīci, Ruci, Nilalohita, Bhṛgu, Atri, Anggira, Pulaha, Kratu, and Vaśiṣṭha), Manus, and the Pitṛs, of whom a detailed account is given. It mentions in this connection that the 27 *nakṣatras* are all daughters of Dakṣa and Asiktiki.

It then discusses the sins for which men go to hell and the meritorious acts which lead them to heaven. After dwelling in heaven or hell for an appropriate period, men are reborn in this world, in higher or lower rank, and even as plants and animals, according to their work. Only by *tapas* can a man avoid this re-birth. In this connection is given an interesting list of *karmas* or works in life and their consequences in the next birth

The thirteen daughters of Dakṣa, married to Kaśyapa, twelve children of Kaśyapa and Aditi, two sons of Kaśyapa and Diti (Hiraṇyakaśipu and Hiraṇyakṣa), their descendants, as well as those of Bhṛgu and other Brahmarṣis are described in detail on the model of the Purāṇas. In this connection we are told that Ilā, the wife of Pulastya, was the daughter of Tṛṇavindu, a disciple of Agastya, who is now practising *tapas* in 'Yavadvīpa-maṇḍala'.

The very detailed knowledge of Indian mythology and the occurrence of Sanskrit verses leave no doubt that the work was based upon an Indian text.

The Ādipurāṇa[2] begins with an account of King Biṣma-nagara of Praṣṭanagara, who was very learned and knew the

1. Tantu, pp. 319-326; Cat. I, Vol II, pp. 170 172. Poerbatjaraka-Agastya pp. 39ff. The text has recently been edited by Dr. J. Gonda in B.K.I., Vol. 85, pp. 329-415 and critically discussed in Vol. 92, pp. 331-458. The work is usually referred to as Anggastyaparva.

2. Tantu, pp. 304-310; Cat. I, Vol. II, p. 172.

Aṣṭādaśadharma, *i.e.* the eighteen duties, *viz.*, regulations about food and marriage, duties towards parents, friends, servants and the diseased, rules of games, trade, service, worship of gods, *etc.*

The king and the queen, directed by a divine command, go in a boat to meet Bhagavan Mūrtthitthasana on the island of Gavangan, and the latter instructs the royal pair. Within this framework is described the cosmogony, mythology, *etc.* after the model of an Indian Purāṇa but widely differing from it in details. The creation, for example, is described as follows :

Avarunting had eyes in different parts of his body and from them originated Mayanispṛha or Pañcamūrtti, earth, air, sky the gods, and the tribhuvanāṇḍa. Then he lost his eyes and created Lord Sardḍa. From the latter sprang Vindup(a)vana who married Trinayanā. These had the book Kalimahosadḍa and created the world, the gods, elements, sciences, *etc.*

Lord Tūryyanta sūkṣma, the son of Vindupavana, had three heads, which, when cut off, gave rise to three other beings who became the originator of Brāhmaṇa, Vaiśya, and Śūdra, and the lord himself, after the loss of his heads, originated the Kṣatriyas. His son Rāma married Mṛtyujīva and had 3 children, and then follows a long list of their descendants, persons not known from other sources.

Even well-known episodes, like the acquisition of Amṛta by the gods, are described in a different way.

The book is evidently of a very late date and has no connection with any known Sanskrit original, far less with Sanskrit Ādipurāṇa.

The Bhuvanapurāṇa[1] :—It begins by describing how Vaśiṣṭha was instructed by Parameśvara on the Kailāsa mountain about the four *āśramas* and *varṇas* (*i.e.* orders and castes). It contains many Purāṇic myths and legends. The Sanskrit verses quoted in it are very corrupt.

Tattva Savang-suvung[2].—It is a work on cosmogony. The creator named Sang hyang Taya practised Yoga, and Brahmā

1. Cat. 1, Vol. II, p. 174. 2. Ibid., p. 281.

and Visnu were born respectively out of his right and left eyes. Then, on his command, Brahmā created the first man Kaki Manuh and Viṣṇu, the first woman, Nini Manuh. Then the sun, moon, stars, earth, fire, *etc.* were created.

The fourth category of Old-Javanese prose literature comprises texts of secular character, dealing with a variety of subjects. A few specimens are described below :—

A. historical.—The Calon Arang[1] may be cited as a good specimen. The text, known in several versions, describes how the widow Calon Arang of Girah was angry that nobody asked her daughter in marriage. Being favoured by Durgā, she used her witchcraft to spread diseases among the subjects of Airlangga, king of Daha, and even burnt his troops. Thereupon King Airlangga took counsels with wise men such as Tanakung Kaṇva and Monaguṇa. Then he went to the learned Bharādah who lived with his daughter Medhavatī in the monastery named Viśyamuka. Bharādah succeeded in killing Calon Arang and then the king went with his two sons Jayabhaya and Jayasabha to Girah.

Airlangga wanted to appoint Jayasabha as king of Bali, but was dissuaded by Paṇḍita Kuturan. It was then decided to make Jayabhaya, king of Jaṅggala or Koripan, and Jayasabha king of Kaḍiri or Daha. The latter, however, marched against his elder brother. A messenger sent by the latter told Jayasabha, by way of warning, a story of the Mahābhārata (Ādiparva), how two brothers, Supratika and Vibhāvasu, were, on account of mutual enmity, transformed into an elephant and tortoise, and devoured by Garuḍa at the command of Kaśyapa. Bharādah, however, reconciled the two brothers and revived the dead soldiers. The book enumerates the subject states of Daha as follows :—

Malayu, Palembang, Jambi, Singhapura, Patani, Pahang, Siyam, Cempa, Cina, Koci, Kling, Tatar, Pego, Kuṭavaringin,

---

1. Ibid., pp. 299-300 ; The text is edited with a translation by Poerbatjaraka in B.K.I., Vol. 82 (1926).

Bangka, Suṇḍa, Madhura, Makasar, Seran, Goran, Vaṇḍan, Moloko, Dompo, Bhima, Timur, Sasak, Sambawa, Kangean.

There are two or three Middle-Javanese poetic versions of this work.[1]

Two other works dealing with what may be called the history of the Kakawin literature deserve special mention.

Prastuti Ning Kakawin[2] gives a list of Kakawins together with their authors. Another, a Wawatekan,[3] adds also the date of composition of the works. The data supplied by these books may be shown in the following tabular form :—

	Name of the Kakawin.		Author.		Date in Śaka era.
1.	Rāmāyaṇa	...	Yogīśvara	...	1016
2.	Sumanasāntaka	...	Mpu Monaguṇa	...	1020
3.	Arjuna-Vivāha	...	Mpu Kano (pupil of Yogīśvara).		1022
4.	Pārthayājña	...	Mpu Vijātmaka (or Vidyātmaka).		1075
5.	Sumavaraṇa	...	Mpu Salukat (son of Yogīśvara).		......
6.	Pāṇḍavavīra	...	Mpu Sḍah (pupil of Mpu Salukat)		......
7.	Bomāntaka (or Bhomakāvya.)		Mpu Ṛsirangan or Mpu Bradah	...	1019
8.	Banolakṣaṇa	...	Mpu Ragarunting	...	......
9.	Smaradahana	...	Mpu Dharmaya	...	1021
10.	Arjuna Vijaya	...	Mpu Tantular	...	1031
11.	Kṛṣṇāyaṇa	...	Mpu Triguṇa	...	1041
12.	Lubdhaka	...	Mpu Tanakung	...	1050
13.	Ghaṭotkacāśraya	...	Mpu Panulung	...	1061
14.	Bhārata-yuddha	...	......	...	1079
15.	Usana Bali Kakawin		Nirartha	...	1141

The books Nos. 1-8 are given in the first text while those with dates are given in the second. It may be added that

1. Cat. 1, Vol. I, pp. 248-9.
2. Cat. 1, Vol. II, p. 286.
3. Ibid., p. 287.

these data, particularly the dates, cannot be accepted as true without further evidence.[1]

B. Linguistic.—The chief lexicons are Adiśvara,[2] Ekalabya[3] Kṛtabasa[4] and Caṇṭakaparva.[5] They are written in Indian style giving the synonyms of gods, animals, trees, and other well-known objects and words. The Kṛtabasa, *e.g.*, gives 29 names of Indra, 31, 27, 29, 48, 9 and 8 synonyms, respectively, of Fire-God, Wind-God, Kāma or God of Love, Moon-God, Yama, and Bṛhaspati, and 29, 59, 4, 28 and 48 words signifying respectively king, paṇḍita, food, birds and snakes.

The Sanskrit metre is dealt with in Caṇṭakaparva which differs in many respects from Vṛtta-sañcaya, the famous Kakawin on the subject referred to above. These, together with grammatical works[6] dealing with Sanskrit conjugation, formation of compounds, *etc.*, show the active pursuit of that language in Java until the very end.

C. Medical texts, such as Anda[7] and Usada.[8]

D. Texts on Erotic like Smaratantra,[9] Angulipraveśa[10] and Smararacaṇa.[11]

E. Miscellaneous texts on calendar,[12] music,[13] birds,[14] animals,[15] etc.

After having made a brief survey of the Old-Javanese literature we may next turn to the Middle-Javanese.

The extent and compass of the Middle-Javanese literature is fairly large. The most important works are those of historical character written both in prose and in poetry.

---

1. Cat. I, Vol. II, p. 287. According to Krom the data are absolutely untrustworthy (T.B.G., Vol. 57, p. 511).

2. Cat. I. Vol. II, pp. 205-206.
3. Ibid., pp. 206-207.
4. Ibid., pp. 207-214.
5. Ibid,, pp. 219-222.
6. Ibid., pp. 215-218.
7. Ibid., pp. 246-247.
8. Ibid., pp. 248-253.
9. Ibid., pp. 253-255, 257-258.
10. Ibid., pp. 255-256.
11. Ibid., p. 258.
12. Ibid., p. 225.
13. Ibid , p. 264.
14. Ibid., p. 308.
15. Ibid., p. 309.

The poetical works of the Middle-Javanese literature use new kinds of metre and are known as Kidung.

Of the prose works the most important is Pararaton[1] which has been so often referred to in the historical portion of this work. It begins with the story of Ken Angrok (or Arok) and gives the outline of the political history of Java for nearly three centuries during the Singhasāri and Majapahit periods. The proper title of the book is Pararaton (Book of Kings) though it is sometimes referred to as Ken Arok or Ken Angrok. According to the colophon, the work was composed in 1613 A.D.[2] In spite of legendary character of the first part, the work may be regarded as one of the most important historical works, although some of the dates and events recorded therein have not proved true in the light of modern researches.

The Usana Java[3] contains traditions about the history of Bali. It begins by describing how the king of Vilvatikta (Majapahit) sent his brother Arya Damar and Gajah Mada to conquer Bali and how Arya Damar killed the Balinese general Pasunggiri. It then describes the establishment of Deva Agung in Gelgel and the division of the island among the chief nobles. The work gives undue prominence to Arya Damar and his family, but almost ignores Gajah Mada, the founder of the royal family of Karang Asem. The Usana Java means really the old history of Java. It is thus a wrong name for this work.[4]

The Usana Bali,[5] also called Mayāntaka, is another historical work of this kind, but it also gives some account of the popular religion. It was written by Nirartha in the sixteenth century A.D.[6]

---

1. This was originally edited by Brandes, and the edition was revised by Krom (V.B.G., Vol. 62), 1920. 2. Ibid., p. 201.
3. B.K.I., Vol. 71, p. 571 ; Cat. 1, Vol. II, p. 388.
4. Mid. Jav. Trad., p. 13.
5. B.K.I., Vol. 71, p. 571 ; Cat. 1, Vol. II, pp. 385-7.
6. Mid. Jav. Trad., p. 41.

This book is 'exclusively intended for the people and not esteemed by the priest. The Usana Java is held in honour by all castes'.[1]

Besides the two historical works referred to above, there is another, Batur Lelavasan, dealing with the old history of Bali.[2]

Next we have to deal with a class of historical chronicles known as Pamañcangah.[3] We have not only general works of this name but also local chronicles such as Pamañcangah Gelgel, Pamañcangah Badung, *etc.* Of the work known simply as Pamañcangah we have both a prose and a Kidung version. It describes the establishment of a Javanese colony from Majapahit in Bali and continues its history up to the fall of Gelgel and the rise of Klungkung. The text is followed by three appendices. The first deals with the history of Badung, the second with the history of Ñalyan which lies to the east of Gianjar, and the third relates to the destruction of Gelgel and the foundation of the Kraton of Klungkung. The first appendix is also known separately as Pamañcangah Badung, while the second and third together form a separate work called Pamañcangah Ñalyan.[4] The Kidung version of the Pamañcangah contains the second and third, but not the first. In addition to these four there are also other Pamañcangahs dealing with local history.

The book called Tattva Sunda[5] deals with the story of Hayam Wuruk's marriage with a Suṇḍa princess which ended in such a terrible tragedy (cf. Bk. III., Ch. VI.).

The same tragic tale forms the plot of the poetical-historical work called Kidung Suṇḍa.[6] Among other works of this kind

1. Friederich-Bali, p. 92. 2. Mid. Jav. Trad., p. 12.

3. To Berg belongs the credit of giving a correct account of these works (Mid. Jav. Trad., p. 15, which supersedes that given in B.K.I., Vol. 71, p. 571, and Cat. 1, Vol. II, pp. 392-4).

4. Juynboll includes it among Balinese works (Cat. 11, p. 153).

5. Cat. 1, Vol. II, pp. 388-9.

6. Cat. 1, Vol. I, pp. 234-5, 257-8. The text is edited by Berg in B.K.I., Vol. 83 (1927), pp. 1 ff. There are different versions of the Kidung.

may be mentioned Kidung Rangga Lawe[1] composed in 1543 A.D. The poem is called Pañji Vijayakrama in the manuscripts. The Kidung may be really divided into two parts. The first part gives the history of Vijaya and the foundation of Majapahit, and the second part deals with the revolution of his trusted officer Rangga Lawe. According to Berg the first part may be called Pañji Vijayakrama, and the second part, Rangga Lawe.

A still more detailed and romantic version of the history of Vijaya is found in Kidung Harṣa-Vijaya.[2] It partakes of the character of the Pañji romances in a far greater degree, and not only contains elaborate descriptions of feasts, merriments, and love-scenes, but often introduces the hero as Pañji raden Ino. The Pararaton, Kidung Pañji-Vijayakrama, and Kidung Harṣa-Vijaya show the three successive stages in the evolution of a simple historical tale into a romance.[3] The revolution and downfall of Sora, which followed that of Rangga Lawe, froms the subject-matter of Kidung Sorandaka.[4] It differs from Pararaton and adds many more details. It however agrees in the main with Kidung Rangga Lawe and strengthens Berg's view that the latter is not based on Pararaton, as Brandes held, but rests on an altogether different source.[5]

Of the remaining poetical works, called Kidung, the most important is the Pañji series, *i.e.* those dealing with the romantic adventures of the famous hero Pañji.[6] The most

---

1. Cat. 1, Vol. I, pp. 255-257; Mid. Jav. Trad., p. 10.
2. Edited by Berg in B.K.I. Vol. 88 (1931) pp. 1-238.
3. Ibid. pp. 2-3.
4. An account of it is given by Berg in Feestbundel, Vol. 1, pp. 22 ff.
5. Mid. Jav. Trad. pp. 61-63. B.K.I. Vol. 88 (1931), pp. 1-2.
6. For a general discussion of the origin and nature of the Pañji works cf. De Pandji-Roman by W. H. Rassers (1922), particularly the learned introduction of the work, and Poerbatjaraka's article in T.B.G., Vol. 58, pp. 461-489. For an account of the individual works cf. Cat. 1, Vol. I, pp. 182-217.

well-known work of this class is Malat. It is as voluminous as the Rāmāyaṇa, and forms the source of all later Javanese and Malayan works of the Pañji-cycle. Among other Javanese Pañji-works may be mentioned: Mantri Wadak, Menur Wilis, Misa Gagang, Smaravedana, Uṇḍakan Pangrus, Wangbang Wideha, Waseng, Puruṣādaśanta, Ajar Pikatan, Smaravijaya, Ḍangḍang Peṭak and Ḍangḍang Hireng.

The crown prince of Kahuripan, the hero of this cycle of legends, is known by various names. He is represented as a wonderful stranger and a young lover wandering about on horseback in search of his lost beloved, Candra Kiraṇa of Daha. He is an enigmatic and shadowy figure, and his character is full of contradictions. On the one hand he is a sentimental lover, almost on the verge of madness for his long lost beloved, but, on the other, he is fully alive to the charms of other women and only too eager and unscrupulous in gaining them. He changes his name and form, gets involved in endless complications, and plays his rôle sometimes among men in the earth and sometimes among gods in heaven.

There are good many versions of this story in Javanese and Malayan literature, and quite a large number of texts on this subject. The story is also widely spread all over Indonesia, *viz.*, Java, Sumatra, Bali, Lombok, Borneo, Celebes, and also Malay Peninsula and Indo-China. The Pañji legends also serve as the subject-matter for Wajang Gedog and Topeng Dalang. All these invest the Pañji literature with a special interest, and there has been much speculation about the nature and origin of this cycle of legends.

At the first glance, one would not be inclined to invest the stories with any historical character, inasmuch as the scene is laid in the kingdom of Medang, Janggala, and Majapahit, three kingdoms which came into existence at long intervals and never flourished side by side. But the scholars like Van der Tuuk, Kern, and Rouffaer were of opinion that in spite of this seeming contradiction a historical character forms the nucleus of this voluminous mass of legends. Recently Poerbatjaraka has gone a step further and tried to demonstrate that the origin of the two chief figures in the story, the crown prince of Janggala and his beloved (or wife) Candra Kiraṇa, princess of Daha, is to be looked for in the historical king Kāmeśvara I of Daha (c. 1115-1130 A.D.) and his Queen Śrī-Kiraṇa-Ratu of Janggala. Of course, we are then to presume that the story-tellers have just reversed the titles, by representing the hero as prince of Janggala and the heroine as princess of Daha.[1]

Whatever we may think of this theory, there can be hardly any doubt that the Pañji-legends represent the purely Javanese literature as opposed to that which is based on or influenced by Indian element. This view has been ably put forward by Rassers in his masterly work on the subject. He is further of opinion that the story originated in Java and then spread from that centre all over Indonesia and Indo-China. Lastly, he has tried to demonstrate that many mythical beliefs formed the groundwork of this cycle of legends.

Next to the Pañji-cycle may be mentioned the class of folktales and fables known as Tantri. Some of these works are written in poetry, *e.g.*, Tantri Keḍiri[2] and Tantri Ḍemung,[3] but the oldest work, Tantri Kāmandaka,[4] is written in prose. These works are based on Hitopadeśa and Pañcatantra, but contain many new stories. This class of literary works is found not only in Javanese but also in Balinese, Siamese, and Laotian, showing the great popularity of the work. The preamble is, however, different. Instead of the usual introductory episode of Viṣṇuśarman instructing his royal disciples, the stories are put in the mouth of a queen, the last of a long

---

1. Van Stein Callenfels stresses the importance of the rôle played by Airlangga and concludes that "persons and events in the Javanese history between 1007 and 1128 A.D. have formed the basis of the Pañji-stories" (Congres I, pp. 301 ff.)

2. Cat. I, Vol. I, pp. 239-244. 3. Cat. I, Vol. I, pp. 244-248.

4. Edited with a Dutch Translation by Dr. C. Hooykaas in the Bibliotheca Javanica Series (1931). For a summary cf. Cat. I, Vol. II, p. 395; cf. also my article in I.H.Q., Vol. IX, pp. 930-1.

series who were daily married and put off by the king for a new one, thus reminding us of the introduction of the Arabian Thousand and One Nights.

Many Kidung works are merely new versions of well-known works. Thus we have Ādiparva Kidung, Rāmāyaṇa Kidung, Sumanasāntaka Kidung, Koravāśrama Kidung, Panañcangah Kidung, Pararaton Kidung. Indraloka Kidung, Navaruci Kidung, Calon Arang, *etc.*

Epic and mythological stories form the basis of many poetical works of the Kidung class. The Bhīmasvarga[1] describes the journey of Bhīma to hell in order to release the soul of his father Pāṇḍu. The exploit of Bhīma also forms the plot of Navaruci Kidung.[2] One of the most popular Kidungs is Śrī Tañjung.[3] It relates how Sidapakṣa, son of Nakula, married his cousin Śritañjuṅ, the daughter of Sahadeva, how the king sent him to heaven in order to seduce his wife, and how, on his return, Sidapakṣa killed her on the suspicion that she had committed adultery, but was convinced of her innocence by the delicious scent emitted by her blood. Śritañjun was then restored to life by Durgā. Another work by the same author, Sudamala,[4] forms a sort of introduction to Śrī Tañjung and describes the exploit of Sahadeva. Śiva cursed Umā for adultery and transformed her into a monster, when she was called Durgā. Sahadeva delivered her from this fate, and on her advice cured Tambapetra of his blindness and married his daughter. The two Vidyādharas, Citrasena and Citrāngada were cursed as they looked upon Śiva and Umā during their bath, and became two *Rākṣasas.* Being defeated by the Pāṇḍavas they regained their old forms.

The Kidung Kuntī yajña[5] describes the exploits of the Pāṇḍavas and specially Arjuna who was twice married and

---

1. Cat. 1, Vol. I, p. 267. Its relation with Old-Javanese Mahābhārata is discussed by Juynboll in Kern-Album, pp. 73-74.

2. Cat. 1, Vol. 1, pp. 236-237.

3. Ibid., pp. 259-261.

4. Ibid., pp, 262-263.

5. Ibid., p. 226.

twice killed. The second time he fought with his own son by Suprabhā and both were killed. But Suprabhā restored them to life and told them their relationship.

There are many other Kidungs based on epic and mythological stories such as Darmajati,[1] Arjuna Pralabda,[2] Candra Berava,[3] Wangbang Astuti,[4] *etc.*

The Sang Satyavan[5] is of more than passing interest as it gives a Javanese version of the famous episode of Sāvitrī. The god Satyavan was incarnated in the earth and married Suvistri, the daughter of Yayāti and Devayānī. As he pretended to die, his wife killed herself, but was restored to life. Then he went to a monastery and his wife also followed him there. On the way he terrified his wife by assuming the forms of a dragon and of a tiger, and lastly by causing storms. But Suvistri reached the monastery and at last met her husband.

There are some Kidungs with independent plots of romantic character and not based upon epic or mythology, *e.g.* Aji Dharma,[6] Jaya Prameya,[7] Kṛtasamaya,[8] Pañji Margasmara,[9] Vargasari,[10] Durma,[11] *etc.* There are also Kidungs whose contents are of philosophic, didactic, and erotic character.

§ 2. BALINESE LITERATURE.

A historical treatment of Balinese literature is beset with a preliminary difficulty which is perhaps unique in the history of the world. The fact is that almost all the works of Old- and Middle-Javanese literature, which we have discussed in the last section are now to be found in the island of Bali alone, whereas they are either totally absent in Java or are

1. Cat. 1, Vol. I, p. 269.
2. Ibid., pp. 221-224.
3. Ibid., pp. 249-50.
4. Ibid., pp. 265-67.
5. Ibid., p. 270.
6. Ibid., pp. 272, 219.
7. Ibid., pp. 224-25.
8. Ibid., p. 225.
9. Ibid., pp. 227-8.
10. Ibid., pp. 250-252,
11. Ibid., p. 273.

merely represented there by very modern versions. During the flourishing period of the Majapahit empire, there was a powerful Javanese colony in the dependent island of Bali, and it grew to be a centre of Javanese literature (cf. Bk. IV, Ch. V). When the fall of Majapahit forced the Javanese to take refuge in Bali, they not only carried with them the literature they had, but also continued to enrich it in the land of their adoption.[1] It is, therefore, not always easy to distinguish between what was written in Java and what was written by the Javanese in Bali, save in respect of works whose dates are known, or whose language clearly marks them out as Old-Javanese. In our discussion of Indo-Javanese literature we have included all works written in Old- and Middle-Javanese languages, irrespective of the question whether they were written in Java or Bali. Under Balinese literature we shall only treat of those which are written in Balinese.

The existing works in Balinese language may be divided into eight classes according to their subject-matter.

I. Balinese translation or version of Javanese works :—

In this class may be mentioned seven Balinese poems *viz.*, Ādiparva Kidung, Rāma Kidung, Bhāratayuddha Kidung, Bimasvarga, Arjunavivāha, Vṛttasañcaya, Calong Arang, Variga Kidung, and one prose text, Uttarakāṇḍa.

We may mention here another work called Viratantra[2] which describes an episode from the Rāmāyaṇa, *viz.*, the fight between Kumbhakarṇa and Hanumān.

1. That both these facts contributed to the growth of Javanese literature in Bali has been shown by Berg (Mid. Jav. Trad. pp. 41-46). While modern historians lay stress mainly upon the second factor, *viz.*, the migration of the Javanese to Bali after the fall of Majapahit, Balinese tradition and a few literary facts, definitely known to us, point to the cultivation of Javanese literature in Bali during the palmy days of Majapahit.

2. Cat. II, p. 146.

II. Religious, philosophical, didactic, and mythical works.

(a) Ḍe Gunati[1]—The diseases and bodily defects are attributed to actions of previous birth. The poem also deals in detail with the duties of the king, the punishment in hell, and the reward in heaven.

(b) Yama Purvanasattva[2]—This prose text describes the fate of the soul of a dead man in the hell.

(c) Limbur[3]—This poem is named after the heroine. Although ugly she had sufficient influence over her husband to procure the death of a step-son. The son goes to heaven but she suffers all kinds of punishment in hell.

(d) Bagus Diyarsa[4]—This poem describes how Bhaṭāra Guru, disguised as a beggar, was treated with hospitality by Bagus Diyarsa. Thereupon his son was taken to heaven by, Bhaṭāra Guru and saw the various heavens. It refers to the heaven of Aśvin as the residence of Wajang players.

(e) Pamañcangah Maospahit[5]—This mythological prose text describes how Yang Meleng and Yang Ratih introduce the cultivation of rice on earth. They had three children, Śiva, Sadāśiva and Paramaśiva from whom were born respectively the Brāhmaṇas, Buddhists, the Bhujangas, and the different castes. It concludes with a dissertation on the respective duties of these castes.

(f) Pamañcangah Manik Angkeran.[6] This is one of the oldest prose works in Bali, being composed in Śaka 1221 (1299 A.D.). Manik Angkeran is reduced to ashes by Basuki, who, however, restores him to life again by mantra Gāruḍeya at the request of his guru. Manik Angkeran then settles in Balatung and his descendants are known as Gusti Ngurah Sidemen.

Among other works of this kind may be mentioned the poems Darma Sembada,[7] Covak,[8] Kidung

1. Cat. II. pp. 80-81.
2. Ibid. p. 204.
3. Ibid, pp. 114-15.
4. Ibid, pp. 99-100.
5. Ibid, p. 153.
6. Ibid, pp 152-3.
7. Ibid, p. 80.
8. Ibid, pp. 83-4

Anacaraka,[1] Tatas ing Varah,[2] and the prose work Teges ing Buvana,[3] all of didactic and philosophical character, the prose texts Kandampat[4] and Smarabuvana[5] on cosmogony, and the poem Kidung Dina[6] which lays down the days that are favourable or unfavourable for various actions.

III. Kāvyas or fictions in poetry.

(a) The poem called Cupak[7] belongs to a class which is very popular in all Austronesian languages. In the Suṇḍanese this class of literature is known as Kabayan. The principal characteristic of this class of poems is that it depicts the hero in all kinds of undignified situations so that he is represented as a coward, and braggart, gluttonous, liar, faithless, *etc.*

The story of the Cupak is as follows :—Cupak and Grantang wander about in order to escape the father of the latter. Cupak betrays his selfishness in all respects, *e.g.*, taking for himself all the food, though it is carried by his friend. They arrive at Daha whose princess is abducted by Limandaru. Cupak boasts that he will bring her back, but when the two friends meet Limandaru, Cupak climbs up a tamarind tree. Grantang, however, frees the princess by killing Limandara. While Grantang was asleep, a Rākṣasa carries away the princess, but Cupak offers no resistance. The two friends trace the Rākṣasa and the princess to a well. Grantang goes down with the help of a rope held fast by Cupak and brings back the princess. But when he goes down the second time to kill the Rākṣasa, Cupak leaves the rope and returns to Daha with the princess. There he takes all the credit to himself and boasts how he killed Limandaru after the latter had killed Grantang. As a reward for this he is declared the successor to the throne.

---

1. Ibid, pp. 81-82.
2. Ibid, p. 83.
3. Ibid, p. 151.
4. Ibid, pp. 150-51.
5. Ibid, pp. 151-2.
6. Ibid, pp. 111-12.
7. B. K. I., Vol. 71, p. 574, Cat. 11, pp. 84-86, 128-129.

In the meanwhile Grantang kills the Rākṣasa, and comes out of the well. As soon as he reaches Daha, he is thrown into the sea by Cupak, but is somehow saved. He manages to send to the princess the ring she had given him. The lovers then meet and are married, while Cupak is banished for his treachery.

To this class of poems belong also Pan Bongkling[1], the popular version of which was composed in the middle of the nineteenth century A.D., Eṇder[2] and Pan Brayut.[3] The first describes in detail a battle between a Balinese and a Muhammadan king.

(b) Rara Vangi[4]—Rara Vangi, a beautiful maiden of Badung, was in love with Raṇapati, but as the king was after her she fled to Bañjar. The king of this latter place also fell a victim to her charms. He contrived to have Raṇapati put to death and Rara Vangi was forcibly taken to the palace. But as soon as the king approached her she stabbed herself to death. The king, mad with despair, killed all his wives and went to the forest where he died. But Raṇapati and Rara Vangi were united in heaven, while the dogs of hell awaited the soul of the king of Bañjar. Raṇapati and Rara Vangi were reborn in earth, punished the king of Badung, and returned to heaven.

(c) Buvang Sakti[5]—The hero, orginally called Jayamṛta, was named Buvang Sakti by the king of Manangkabo whom he served. He then killed a tiger and a rangsasa (rākṣasa) and lastly the king of Pañcanagara, whose widow Devi Sitarum he married. Later, he was taken prisoner and killed.

(d) Japatvan[6]—Japatvan, the hero, went through the grace of gods to heaven to bring back his elder brother's wife who had died shortly after her marriage. After drinking Amṛta there he came back and became a king. The author gives a detailed description of hell and shows acquaintance with Vāyupurāṇa and Ādiparva.

---

1. Cat. II, pp. 122-26.
2. Ibid, pp. 78-80.
3. Ibid, pp. 126-8.
4. Ibid, p. 77.
5. Ibid, p. 104.
6. Ibid, p. 105.

(e) Mantri Java.[1] Mantri Java goes from Java to Bali and falls in love with princess Pacar Cinamburat. As he returns without her, she follows him and they get secretly married. The mother of Mantri Java becomes angry and orders him to marry the princess Limbur. The latter by means of spells, makes her husband forget Cinamburat whereupon the latter kills herself. But soon the hero freed himself from the charms of Limbur and Cinamburat is restored to life. Now they get married with the permission of the parents while Limbur falls into disfavour and dies.

(f) Purvajati[2]—The hero leaves his two wives, but their two sons, when grown up, go out in search of their father. In course of their wandering they fight with a rākṣasa, a Garuḍa, a tiger, a lion, and an elephant. At last they meet Adi Guru who ask them to fight with Sindhurāja as he abducted their mothers. These two come to hell on account of their faithlessness to their husband, but, on the intercession of their children, go to heaven.

(g) There are also poems belonging to Pañji cycle, among which two deserve special mention, *viz.*, Megantaka[3] or Mantri Malaka and Begus Umbara[4] or Mantri Koripan. Among other less known works may be mentioned Pakang Raras,[5] where Śiva and Nārada play some part.

The story of Megantaka is briefly as follows :

Hambara Pati, crown prince of Hambara Madija, meets princess Hambara Sari of Nusa Hambara. They fly and were shipwrecked. The princess reaches the Malacca coast. Prince Megantaka meets the princess during hunting and carries her to his palace. Hambara Pati, too, comes to Malacca court, meets his beloved, and escapes with her to Hambara Madija. He comes alone to the palace of his father, is forced to marry the hideous Limbur, and the latter secretly puts Hambara Sari to

---

1. Ibid, p. 117-8. 2. Ibid, p. 130.
3. Edited and translated by R. Van Eck (V. B. G., Vol. 38).
4. Cat. 11, pp. 101-2. 5. Ibid, pp. 120-21.

death. Hambara Pati, however, flies from his wife and discovers the dead body.

Megantaka invades Hambara Pati's land, defeats him, enters the capital, and finds the dead body. We next find the soul of Hambara Sari in heaven. The nymphs Suprabhā and Tilottamā bring her back to earth. Megantaka and Hambara Pati meet the princess and all come back to the court of Hambara Madija.

(h) Dreman.[1] This poem is well-known from the edition and translation of the text by J de Vroom and a rendering in verse by Kern.

A man named Jatiraga had two wives. The first Tan-porat was an ideal virtuous wife, while the second Dreman was a capricious, bad-tempered, haughty, and prodigal woman. Nevertheless the good-natured but weak Jatiraga favoured the younger Dreman and poor Tan-porat had a hard lot. She however bore her misery without demur and with ideal patience. Dreman died and was carried to hell. Jatiraga died in grief for her and also went to hell for the ill-treatment of his wife. Tan-porat died after a long time and went to heaven for her virtuous conduct. There, to her great regret, she did not find her husband and learnt that he was suffering in hell. Without a moment's hesitation she decided to give up the bliss of heaven for the pleasure of living with her beloved husband in hell. Then the gods intervened and brought the husband to the heaven.

The poem thus depicts the ideal virtue and chastity of a woman, and Kern has compared it to the story of Griseldis which was famous in Mediaeval Europe.

(i) Raden Saputra[2] or Ratna Manik, so called after the hero and the heroine. The hero goes to the cemetery and fights with tigers and spirits. There he sees in dream the beautiful heroine, and the latter also sees him in dream at

1. Edited, with translation, by De Vroom in T. B. G., Vol. 21, pp. 323 ff. Kern also translated it in verse (V. G., Vol. XIV, 131).

2. Cat. II, pp. 130-31.

the same time. He meets her while bathing and the two get married. On hearing this Detya Putih, king of Giri Kañcana attacks him. (The Ms. abruptly ends here.)

There is a New-Javanese version of this story. The Madurese poem of the same name gives an altogether different story.

(j) Lingga Peta[1] :—The poem describes the virtues of the poor but beautiful courtier of this name. The king loved him on account of his beauty, loyal devotion, and charming manners. His beauty made him a great favourite of the young girls, but Lingga Peta never yielded to their temptations. A cunning plot was laid by the courtiers who were jealous of his reputation and royal favours, and Lingga Peta was put to death. When an inquiry was made as to the cause of his death, the father of a girl named Hi K'toet Lajang said that as the hero wanted to outrage the modesty of his daughter he had killed him. But the gods intervened and restored Lingga Peta to life. He was born in a noble family and ultimately became the king.

IV. Historical poems.

There are numerous works dealing mostly with recent history.

(a) Jambenagara[2] or Siyat Sasak describes in the guise of a romantic story the conquest of Matarām by the Dutch.

(b) Ung Bañjar[3]—The conquest of Bañjar by the Dutch in 1858 forms the subject-matter of the poem.

(c) Ung Buleleng[4]—The Dutch expedition against Buleleng in 1846 is described in this poem.

(d) Ung Giañjar[5] gives the local history of the kingdom under Deva Manggis.

---

1. Edited by De Vroom (T. B. G. Vol. 21, pp. 402-446, 534—597), Cat. 11, pp. 115-16.

2. Cat. 11, pp. 104-5.

3. Ibid, pp. 139-40.

4. Ibid, pp. 140-41.

5. Ibid, pp. 141-42

(e) Ung Kaḍiri[1] describes the destruction of Kaḍiri in Lombok.

(f) Ung Mangvi[2] gives the local history of this kingdom.

V. Poems dealing with stories and fables.

(a) The 'Tantri Bali'[3] agrees generally with the Javanese Tantri books.

(b) Guṇakaya[4] is a different redaction of Tantri Bali.

(c) The numerous Satva[5] texts belong to this class and contain folktales both of men and animals.

VII. Dharma-lakṣana, a book on Śilpaśāstra, exists only in one corrupt manuscript. It is attributed to Viśvakarmā and must have been based on an Indian original or a Javanese translation of the same.[6]

VI. There are, besides, poetical works on medicine (*e.g.* the poem Ñeling)[7], birds (Kidung Paksi)[8] and erotics (Tuñjung Biru[9], Ñalig etc.)[10]

VII. S. Lévi refers to a grammatical work Kāraka-saṁgraha with a Balinese commentary which cites Pāṇini.[11]

VIII. The works called Wariga[12] enjoy a high reputation in Bali. These are the calendars for calculating time, and correspond to Indian Pañjikā. The most well-known work is Wariga Garga, based upon a Javanese text, and containing both Indian and Malayo-Polynesian elements.

The Balinese have lunar months, but by intercalary months they transform them into a solar system. There are twelve months, all having the usual Sanskrit names, but ten of them (*i.e.*, all except Jyaiṣṭha and Āṣāḍha) have also corresponding Balinese names.

---

1. Cat. II. pp. 142. 2. Ibid, p. 143.
3. Ibid, pp. 135-6. 4. Ibid, p. 136.
5. B. K. I. Vol. 71, p. 577. Cat. 11, pp. 179-183.
6. The text is referred to by Bosch (Congres I, p. 116).
7. Cat. II. p. 120. 8. Ibid, p. 112.
9. Ibid, pp. 86-87. 10. Ibid, pp. 90-91.
11. Versl. 6de. Congr. oost. Gen. (1929) pp. 8 ff.
12. Friederich—Bali, pp. 191-200.

There is also an alternative method of calculating time. This is formed by a combination of the Polynesian week of five days with the Indian week of seven days; this combination gives us 35 days which form the basis of the Balinese calendar. We find these combinations of 35 days six times in each Balinese year of 210 days, but they are not called months. On the other hand each of the 30 weeks has its own name.

The astrological calendar of the Balinese deals in detail with the stars and planets and their influence over human destiny. It is entirely of Indian origin.

The era used is the well-known Śaka era.

§3. The Malayan Literature.

No trace now remains of the pre-Muhammadan Malay literature. But that such a literature existed and originally grew up under the influence of Indian or Indo-Javanese culture there can be hardly any doubt. The best evidence thereof is furnished by the clear traces of such influence in the Malay literature that has developed since the Muhammadan conquest.

The Malayan texts which show this influence at its best are those based on Indian epics. The story of the Rāmāyaṇa forms the basis of Hikayat Seri Rāma[1]. While giving the essential part of the story, *viz.*, the abduction of Sītā by Rāvaṇa, the death of the latter with his family in the hands of Rāma, and the part played by Hanumān, the present text differs widely on some vital points. For example, Kaikeyī is made a sister of Rāma and married to Bibhīṣaṇa. Rāma was jealous to find in possession of Sītā a portrait of Rāvaṇa (which she had really made for Kaikeyī) and sent her to her father Maharṣi Kāla, *etc. etc.*

1. Cat. III, pp. 40 ff. An analysis of this work, and comparison with Sanskrit Rāmāyaṇa is given in J. Str. Br. R. A. S., Nos. 70-71.

On the other hand it contains even details like the twin sons of Sītā, purification of the latter by fire, the death of Indrajit and Kumbhakarṇa, the episode of Jaṭāyu[1] *etc.* There are indications that the Malayan version was based on the Tamil recension of the Rāmāyaṇa.

The Mahābhārata formed the basis of several versions of Hikayat Pāṇḍava, such as Pāṇḍava Lima, Pāṇḍava Jaya, Angkavijaya, *etc.* There are, besides, many Wajang stories derived from Javanese Bhārata-yuddha and many others in which Arjuna appears as the hero[2].

The Indian influence is equally clear in the numerous stories and fables with which Malayan literature abounds. Even the heroes and heroines of Malay romances bear Indian names. It may also be added that the Malay language abounds in Sanskrit words[3].

The Indo-Javanese influence is clearly proved by the Malayan versions of Bhomakāvya, Hikayat Maharaja Boma, and Bhīmasvarga, and also the numerous Pañji-texts, such as Hikayat Chekel Waneng Pati, Hikayat Pañji Kuda Sumirang, Hikayat Jaran Kinanti Asmarandana, Hikayat Pañji Susupan Mesa Kelana, and Hikayat Naya Kusuma[4].

---

1. For the discussion of the different forms of the Rāma-saga cf. p. 65, fn. 2.

2. Cf. Encycl. Ned. Ind., s. v. Litteratur (Maleisch); Cat. III, pp. 50 ff.

3. Cf. J. Str. Br. R. A. S., Nos. 57 (p. 183), 76, 85 (p. 41).

4. Encycl. Ned. Ind., op. cit.

Chapter V.

RELIGION

In the last chapter of Book I we have described in a broad outline how the religious systems of India—both Brāhmanical and Buddhist—were spread in Malayasia and took deep root in its soil even during the early period of Hindu colonisation. As centuries rolled by, the Indian religions made a more thorough conquest of the land, and it would hardly be an exaggeration to say that so far as faiths, beliefs and religious practices are concerned, the colonies in the Far East were almost a replica of the motherland. Of course, we should not expect that the indigenous faiths and practices vanished altogether. As in India itself, these were partly eliminated by, and partly absorbed into the higher and more developed system, but in some respects the latter also was affected and moulded by the former.

All these observations are specially applicable to Java, the only colony which furnishes us detailed evidence of the various stages of religious development.

§1. The Brahmanical religion in Java.

About the beginning of the eighth century A. D. we find the Paurāṇik form of Brāhmanical religion firmly established in Java. In essence it consisted of the worship of three principal divinities, *viz.*, Brahmā the creator, Viṣṇu, the protector, and Śiva the destroyer, together with their Śaktis or divine spouses and a host of minor gods and goddesses related to them. The beginning of this form of religion can be traced as early as the fourth or fifth century A. D.[1] But

1. See above, Bk. I. Chap, X.

the period under review contains more detailed evidence regarding its nature and characteristics. These evidences are derived principally from four sources, *viz.*, (1) Inscriptions, (2) Temples, (3) Images, and (4) Literary sources. These enable us to draw a picture of the religious systems of Java such as existed from the eighth century A. D. down to the last days of Hindu civilisation.

We may begin with the Cangal inscription[1] which records that in the year A.D. 732 king Śrī Sañjaya set up a *liṅga* on a hill, for the sake of the peace of his kingdom. The first verse gives the astronomical details of the auspicious hour when the ceremony took place. The author then eulogises Śiva in the most extravagant terms in the next three verses, while the fifth verse is dedicated to Brahmā and the sixth to Viṣṇu. These hymns refer to the familiar attributes of each of these gods. With regard to Śiva mention is made of his three eyes, the matted hair with the sacred Gaṅgā and the moon on his head, the body besmeared with ashes, and the necklace made of serpents. He is possessed of supreme *aiśvarya*, and adored not only by the hermits but also by Indra and other gods. He is the lord of the *bhūtas* (living creatures) and in his infinite mercy maintains the world by means of his eight forms. Brahmā is described as of golden colour, the preceptor (*guru*) of the world, worshipped by hermits and gods, the source of the threefold ends of life *viz.*, *dharma*, *artha*, and *kāma*, and one who has organised society by the rules of the Vedas. Viṣṇu is described as lying with his consort on the body of the serpent king, floating on the vast sea, deeply absorbed in his meditation, and adored by the gods for the sake of deliverance.

The five verses of the Cangal inscription thus give an admirable summary of the essential conceptions of the Paurāṇik

1. V.G., Vol. VII, p. 115.

2. Goris, pp. 101-105. Brāhmāṇa may denote the votaries of Brahmā, though sometimes it seems to take the place of Śaiva.

Trinity. It also clearly indicates that the position of supremacy among them was undoubtedly accorded to Śiva. That it was not a mere personal or local factor, but generally true of both Central and Eastern Java clearly follows from a study of the literature, inscriptions and monuments of Java. Thus the records of Airlangga refer to the three principal sects as Śaiva (or Māheśvara), Saugata (*i.e.* Buddhist), and Ṛṣi or Mahābrāhmaṇa. Goris has analysed the list of religious sects enumerated in ten different texts. All of them mention one or more Śaiva sects, but only four refer to the Vaiṣṇava sect and three to 'Brāhmaṇa' or 'Brāhmāṇa' (devoted to Brahmā ?).

Again, by far the great majority of temples in Java are dedicated to Śiva, and the largest number of the detached images so far discovered are those of Śiva and the members of his family.

The same conclusion is borne out by Amaramālā, the earliest literary text bearing upon religion that we have so far come across in Java. In giving the synonyms of differnt gods it begins with those of Śiva and calls him Guru and Īśvara *i.e.* God *par excellence.* If we consider the famous Lara-Jongrang group of temples, the last great monument of Central Java, we find only a further illustration of the same truth. In this famous group, which will be described in detail in a subsequent chapter, we find the central and the biggest temple dedicated to Śiva with two smaller ones on its two sides for Brahmā and Viṣṇu, and with a temple of Nandī in its front. All these are unmistakable evidences of the supreme position accorded to Śiva in the Javanese form of Hindu trinity.

This great god Śiva was regarded not only as the agent of the destruction of the world, but also of its renovation. He had thus both a benevolent and a terrible nature. These two aspects are represented in Javanese iconography by the two human forms of the god known as Mahādeva and Mahākāla or Bhairava.

The image of Mahādeva[1] has usually one head, though in one instance it has five. He has a third eye on his forehead, his head-dress is adorned with a moon and a skull, and a snake takes the place of the *upavīta* or the sacred thread. He has usually four arms, rarely two, holding fly-whisk (*cāmara*), rosary (*akṣamālā*) a book, lotus, water-pot, and trident (triśūla).

The image of Bhairava or Mahākāla has a terrible expression of face, protruding eyes and teeth, and wild hair, while the sacred thread is replaced by either snakes or a garland of skulls. He has two or four arms holding mace (*gadā*), sword (*khaḍga*), noose, snake, and a dagger (or knife), along with the usual attributes of Śiva, such as trident, rosary, and fly-whisk. A variety of the image of this god, which is perhaps called *Cakracakra* in the attached inscription, deserves particular mention. Here the god sits on the body of a jackal or of a dog, and not only is his seat surrounded by skulls, but the same form the ornaments of his head, ear, neck and arms. A string of human heads forms his sacred thread, and a number of bells forms a belt round his belly. In his four arms are found a trident, a drum (*ḍamaru*), a dagger, and a bowl made of an iverted human skull.

To these forms of Śiva correspond two different forms of his Śakti. The Śakti of Mahādeva is Devī, Mahādevī, Pārvatī, or Umā, the daughter of Himālaya. In her four arms she holds lotus, fly-whisk, rosary, flower, snake, trident or palm-leaf manuscript. A particular form of this goddess is Durgā or Mahiṣāsuramarddinī. She has six, eight, ten or twelve arms, holding various weapons, and is represented as killing the demon who assumed the form of a buffalo.

The Śakti of Mahākāla or Bhairava is Mahākālī or Bhairavī. She is represented as sitting on a dead body, and human skulls

1. The description of the images that follows is mainly based on Krom-Kunst, Vol. I, Ch. III, and Juynboll's Catalogue Vol. V, and is intended to give the reader only a general idea. In enumerating the attributes I have given a list of those that are usually found, though not necessarily in one and the same image.

form her sacred thread and ornaments of head and neck. In her two arms she holds a trident and a small dish for keeping the blood of the victims. Sometimes she is depicted as a terrible figure with protruding eyes and teeth and a dreadful face, holding fast in her arms the body of the human victim.

The well-known figure of Ardhanārī, combining in one body those of Śiva and Durgā, is also found in Java. The right half of the body is that of Śiva, while the left half is that of Durgā, both being indicated by proper attributes.

The image of Gaṇeśa, the son of Śiva and Pārvatī, is very common in Java, and follows in general the Indian prototype. He has the head of an elephant, and ornaments made of human skulls. He has usually four arms and his sacred thread is formed by a snake. As in India, Gaṇeśa was regarded as the god of wisdom, and one who removes all obstacles and difficulties. It is evidently this last aspect which accounts for the presence of Gaṇeśa-figures in large numbers, and even in solitary places on hills or rivers where men were apprehensive of great dangers.[1]

The war-god Kārtikeya, another son of Śiva, is also well-known in Java. He is generally represented in an ordinary human form riding on a peacock. But sometimes he has six heads and twelve arms, holding various weapons.

Lastly, it may be mentioned, that Śiva was also worshipped in the form of Liṅga (phallus), although, as Stutterheim has tried to demonstrate, the Liṅga form was connected with ancestor worship in Java, and might have been prevalent in Java before the Hindu immigration.[2]

Viṣṇu, the second member of the trinity, never attained in Java a position or importance equal to that of his rival Śiva, though under some dynasties he enjoyed very high honour

1. Cf. B.K.I. Vol. 86 (1930) pp. 308-310.

2. Ibid, pp. 311-12. For Liṅga worship in general, cf. T.B.G. Vol. 64 (1920), pp. 227 ff.

and rank. He is usually represented with four arms having the well-known attributes, conch-shell (*śaṁkha*), wheel (*cakra*), mace (*gadā*), and lotus (*padma*), though occasionally the number of arms is only two. His Śakti, Śrī or Lakṣmī, is usually represented with four arms holding lotus, corn of ear, fly-whisk and rosary. Viṣṇu's rider (*Vāhana*) Garuḍa is also represented in Java, generally with human form, though occasionally the beak, claws and wings of a bird are added. Viṣṇu is often depicted in *ananta-śayana* posture, such as has been described in the Cangal inscription noted above, and most of his *avatāras* or incarnations, specially Kṛṣṇa, Rāma, Matsya, Varāha, and Narasiṃha, are represented by images. Sometimes there are two female figures on the two sides of the image of Viṣṇu, which are usually known as Lakṣmī and Satiavana in Bali. The last is probably to be restored as Satyabhāmā. In that case the image may be regarded as that of Kṛṣṇa with Satyabhāmā and Rukmiṇī on two sides.[1]

The devotees of Viṣṇu were undoubtedly less in number than those of Śiva and Buddha, and Vaiṣṇavism ranked in importance next only to Śaivism and Buddhism. This appears quite clearly from the comparatively smaller number of the images of that god found in Java. The religious literature of Java also supports this view, as it contains less traces of that religion than of the other two. Even the Mahābhārata, where Kṛṣṇa, the avatāra of Viṣṇu, plays such a leading part, is strongly Śaivite in character.[2]

The images of Brahmā, the remaining member of the trinity, are comparatively few in number. He is easily recognised by his four heads facing the four directions. He has four arms holding rosary, fly-whisk, lotus and water-pot. His rider (*vāhana*) *haṁsa* (swan) is sometimes depicted in its normal form, but sometimes also as a human being with the head of a swan above, indicating his true nature. Sarasvatī, the Śakti of Brahmā, is represented with two or four arms, riding on a

1. B.K.I. 1908, pp. 412-420.

2. Ibid.

peacock. The Tengger hill to the east of Singhasāri is referred to as the sacred hill of Brahmā in an inscription dated 1405 A.D.[1]

The image of Trimūrti *i.e.* of Brahmā, Viṣṇu and Śiva combined together, is also found in Java. It has three heads, all of the same appearance, though in rare cases the central head is indicated to be that of Śiva by the skull and the moon. The image has four arms holding rosary, fly-whisk, lotus, book and the water-pot.

Another image, which is very popular in Java, is usually styled Bhaṭāra-Guru. It is a two-armed standing figure of an aged pot-bellied man with moustache and peaked beard, and holding in his hands, trident, water-pot, rosary and fly-whisk. This image is usually regarded as a representation of Śiva Mahāyogin (the great ascetic), and his universal popularity is explained by supposing that an originally Indonesian divinity was merged in him. Mr. Poerbatjaraka has, however, shown by a comparison with Indian figures that the image represents the sage Agastya. The extreme veneration for, and the popularity of the worship of Agastya in Java are reflected in the inscriptions, and Poerbatjaraka's, view seems eminently reasonable.[2]

In addition to the principal gods and goddesses described above, we come across the images of various minor gods in Java to which a brief reference may be made. Of the eight dikpālas *i.e.* minor gods guarding different directions,[3] we meet with the familiar images of Yama (the god of death), Varuṇa (Water-god), Indra (the king of gods), Agni (the fire god), Nairṛta, and Kuvera (the god of wealth). The first three have distinctive attributes, *viz.*, mace, noose and thunderbolt, while Agni is known by his rider, the ram. The representation of

1. Brandes—Not. Bat Gen, 1899, pp. 64-69.

2. Poerbatjaraka—Agastya, specially Chapter VI.

3. Probably all of them were represented in the Śiva temple at Lara-Jongrang cf, Bk. VI. Ch. I, section 7.

Kuvera also follows exactly the lines adopted in Hindu and Buddhist pantheons of India,—a pot-bellied man, seated on a low cushion, with small bags of money scattered around, and holding a lemon in the right hand and an ichneumon in the left. Kuvera's wife Hārītī is also known in Java. There are also images of Sūrya (sun-god) holding a lotus and seated in a chariot drawn by seven horses, and Candra (moon-god) holding a flag and carried in a chariot drawn by four or ten horses. Kāma (god of love) is represented as seated on Makara with a bow and arrow in his hand.

It is unnecessary to go further into iconographic details. In short, almost all the gods of Hindu pantheon are represented in Java, and the following observation of Crawfurd,[1] made more than a century ago, can hardly be regarded as an exaggeration. "Genuine Hindu images, in brass and stone, exist throughout Java in such variety, that I imagine there is hardly a personage of the Hindu mythology, of whom it is usual to make representations, that there is not a statue of".

No account of Javanese Hinduism can be regarded as complete without a reference to some of the rituals and ceremonies and philosophical concepts which formed an essential part of the religious life of the people. Our knowledge in this respect is derived not only from the old Javanese texts but also from modern practices in the island of Bali where Hinduism is still a living religion.

Dr. Goris has given a detailed account of the rites, ceremonies and *mantras* used in connection with Sūrya-sevana or the worship of Sun[2]. It may be noted at the outset that the Sun was identified with Śiva (perhaps also with Viṣṇu) and the Sūrya-sevana really means the worship of Śiva in the form of the Sun. The order of the different ceremonies is not absolutely certain, but the arrangement suggested by Goris may be followed.

---

1. History of the Indian Archipelago Vol. II. p. 207.

2. Goris, pp. 12-53. cf. also Lévi—Texts.

1. The first ceremony is the *Talabhedana* and *Karaśodhana*, *i.e.*, the purification of the hand and the individual fingers with appropriate *mantras*. One of these mantras, which is frequently repeated, and is based on Hindu scriptures, runs as follows.

ओं हं हृदयाय नमः, ओं अर्काय शिरसे नमः, ओं भूर्भुवः स्वरे ज्वालिनि शिखाये नमः, ओं हुं कवचाय नमः, ओं रः फट् अस्त्राय नमः।

2. Then follows *prāṇāyāma* or control of breath with appropriate *mantras*, including the Gāyatrī.

3. The first consecration of water beginning with the mantras :

ओं परमशिवगङ्गाय नमः
ओं ह्रौं ह्रीं वौषट् परमशिवामृताय नमः।

There are also a hymn to the goddess Ganges, and what is called Sapta-tīrtha-*mantra*, or an invocation to the rivers Gaṅgā, Sarasvatī, Sindhu, Vipāśā, Kauśikī, Yamunā and Saraju.

4. Then follow a variety of *mantras*, to be uttered with appropriate *mudrās* and *āsanas*. The *Caturaiśvarya mantra* is an invocation to Dharma, Jñāna, Vairāgya, and Aiśvarya, each of which is represented as *Siṅgharūpa* (form of a lion), and white, red, yellow or black in colour. The *Navaśakti mantra* is a salutation to Dīptā, Sūkṣmā, Jayā, Bhadrā, Vimalā, Vibhūti, Amoghā, Vidyutā, and Sarvatomukhinī. The *tritattva mantra* is similarly a salutation to Śiva-tattva, Vidyā-tattva, and ātma-tattva. The *Kūṭa* mantra runs as follows.

ओं ह्रां ह्रीं सः परमशिवादित्याय नमः। or according to a variant reading ओम् ह्रां ह्रीं सः शिवसूर्य्यपरन्तेजस्स्वरूपाय नमः।

This is interesting as showing the identity of Śiva and Sūrya and thereby explaining the inner significance of the Sūrya-worship. The concluding *mantra* is a salutation to sarva-deva, sapta-ṛṣi, sapta-pitṛ, and the Bhūtas. There are other *mantras* consisting of salutations to vowels and consonants (*Oṁ aṁ āṁ namaḥ,......oṁ kaṁ, khaṁ, gaṁ namaḥ etc.*)

5. Then follows the consecration of *ganṭhā* (*i.e. ghanṭā* or bell) with appropriate *mantras* beginning as follows :—

ओंकारम् सदाशिवम् जगद्नाथहितंकरम् ।
अभिवाद्यवदनीयं गण्ठाशब्दं प्रकाशने ॥ etc.

Then follows the invocation to Śiva to forgive the sins of the worshipper. It contains some beautiful stanzas which are recited even to-day all over India :

पापोऽहं पापकर्माहं पापात्मा पापसम्भव: ।
त्राहि मां सर्व्वपापेभ्य: केनचिद मम रक्षतु ॥
ओं मन्त्रहीनं क्रियाहीनं भक्तिहीनं महेश्वर: ।
यत् पूजितं मया देव परिपूर्णम् तदस्तु मे ॥

6. A second consecration of water with a variety of *mantras* follows. In addition to recitation of mystic syllables it includes invocation to the Trinity and the sacred rivers. A specimen of each is quoted below :

1. ओं ओं परमशिवशून्यात्मने नम: ।
ओं ओं सदाशिव निष्कलात्मने नम: ।
ओं ओं सदारुद्र अन्तरात्मने नम: ।
ओं ओं महादेव निरात्मने नम: ।
ओं मं ईश्वर परमात्मने नम: ।
ओं उं विष्णु अन्तरात्मनि नम: ।
ओं ओं ब्रह्म आत्मने नम: ।

2. ओं गङ्गा सिन्धु सरस्वती सु-यमुना ।
गोदावरी नर्म्मदा कावेरी सरयू ।
महेन्द्रतनयचर्म्मण्वती वेणुकाम् ।
भद्रनेत्रवती महासुरनदी ।
ख्यातश्च य गन्धकी (गण्डकी ?) ।
पुण्य पूर्णं जलै समुद्र संहित कुर्व्वन्ति मे मङ्गलम् ।

7. Then comes invocation to (1) *Gandha* (perfume) (2) *Akṣata* (corn) (3) *Puṣpa* (flower) (4) *Dhūpa* (incense) (5) *Dīpa* (lamp) and (6) *Patanganan* (sandalwood) ?

To this are sometimes added *mantras* about Udakāñjali and Pādyārghya.

8. The Mṛtyuñjaya (also called Dīrghāyu or Sapta-Vṛddhi)

The following *mantra* selected from a large number will indicate the objects which the worshipper had in view.

ओं आयुर्वृद्धि यशोवृद्धि वृद्धि प्रज्ञा सुखश्रिया ।
धर्मसन्तानवृद्धिश्च सन्तु ते सप्तवृद्धयः ॥
यावत् मेरौ स्थित देव यावद् गङ्गा महीतले ।
चन्द्ररेखा गगणे यावत् तावत् भुवि जयी भवेः ॥

In connection with this we have a Trimūrti *mantra* or invocation to trinity from which it appears that all the three gods have three eyes, but Brahmā has four faces, Viṣṇu three faces and four arms, while Īśvara has five faces and ten arms.

9. The next process is called *ma-bhasma*, where the priest besmears his body with sandal-paste and utters various *mantras* such as :

(a) ओं इदं भस्मं परं गुह्यं सर्व्वपापविनाशनम् ।
सर्व्वरोगप्रशमनं सर्व्वकलुषनाशनं नमः स्वाहा ॥
(b) ओं भूर्भुवः स्वः ।

After this the priest consecrates his headgear (*śiroviṣṭa*) and sacerdotal thread (*yajñopavīta*) with appropriate *mantras*. One of these *mantras* "*Bhargo Devasya Dhīmahi*" is a part of the famous Gāyatrī. Another *mantra* is a fragment of a Vedic hymn which can be easily restored as follows :—

ओं (त्रिव सूत्रं) यज्ञोपवीतं परमं पवित्रं ।
प्रजाप (तेर्यत् सहजं पुरोस्तात्) ।
आयुष्यं (अग्र्यं प्रतिमुञ्च शुभ्रं) ।
(यज्ञोपवीतं) बलमस्तु तेजः ॥

This *mantra* is found in Kāṭhaka Āraṇyaka, Brahmopaniṣad and the Gṛhya Sūtras (Baudhāyana, Vaikhānasa and Pāraskara).

Thus while the *mantras* used in Java and Bali are mostly taken from Paurāṇik and Tāntrik texts, the presence of the two last mentioned *mantras* perhaps indicates acquaintance with later Vedic literature.

10. The priest then silently performs *japa* and *dhyāna* with the help of his rosary containing 108 beads. By this process the soul is carried from abdominal cavity to the end of the top-knot (dvādaśāṅgula) of the hair, and Śiva takes its place in the body. Then several *mantras* are uttered including invocations to Śiva, Viṣṇu and Sūrya.

11. After a short while new *mantras* are uttered, whereupon Śiva leaves the body and the soul comes back to its proper place. Then follows an invocation to Sūrya under ten different names. Immediately after this, the priest takes off his head-gear, indicating that as he has again become an ordinary human being, he should no longer retain the symbol of Śiva. He then wipes off his face with his moist hand, puts a flower in his Śikhā (top-knot), places the remaining flowers in the water-pot and puts off the rosary. This finishes the ceremony.

Some unpublished Javanese texts give an account of the ceremonials connected with the worship of Viṣṇu. We may quote as specimens, a few *mantras* addressed to (A) Viṣṇu, (B) his avatāra (incarnation) Narasimha, and (C) his vāhana (rider) Garuḍa.[1] These *mantras*, written in Sanskrit, are always accompanied by Old-Javanese version which explains and comments on them and sometimes adds new elements.

(A) (1) The Viṣṇu-stava describes the features and attributes of the great god.

ओं ओं नमो विष्णु त्रिमुखं त्रिनयनचतुर्भुजं कृष्णवर्णं स्फटिकाक्ष: सर्व्वभूषणनीलनं चक्रहस्त महातीक्ष्ण आत्मरक्ष हृन्पृस्थान: अमृतसञ्जीवनी देव सर्व्वग्रह विनाशनम् फट् स्वाहा।
[हृन्म् – liver.]

1. Cf. Juynboll's article in B.K.I. 1908, pp. 412-20.

The idea that the god lives in different parts of the body is very common in these mantras.

(2) The Viṣṇu-pañjara *mantra* refers to different Avatāras and surnames of Viṣṇu as protecting (*a*) different parts of the body, and (*b*) different directions.

(a) पादौ रक्षन्तु गोविन्दो जंघाभ्यश्च त्रिविक्रमः ।
ऊर्व्वन्तं केशवो रक्षेत् पृष्ठे रक्षन्तु वामनः ॥
बाहवौ वासुदेवश्च नरसिंहः हृदिस्थितः ।
कण्ठे रक्षन्तु वराहः कृष्णश्च मुखमण्डलम् ॥
नेत्रे नारायणो रक्षेत् ललाटे गरुड़ध्वजः ।
कपाले वैनतेयश्च केशवो शिरः संस्थितः ॥

(b) पूर्व्वेंष्यां पुण्डरीकाक्ष अग्नेये श्रीधरस्तथा ।
पुरुषोत्तमो वरुणां वायव्यां पीतवाससः ॥
गदाधरश्च कौवीर्थां ऐशान्यां ब्रह्मर्मधिष्ठेत् ।
पातालं कूर्म्म रक्षन्तु आकाशश्च सुदर्शनः ॥
विष्णुपञ्जरं विष्णोहम् विचरामि महीतले ।
राजद्वारे पते घोरे संग्रामे रिपुसंकटे ॥
डाकिनीभूतप्रेतेषु भयो नास्ति कदाचन ।
अपुत्रो लभते पुत्रः धनहीनो धनं लभेत् ।
मुच्यते सर्व्वरोगेषु विष्णुलोकं स गच्छति ॥

(B) Narasiṁha-dhyāna. It begins with ओं नरसिंहाय सर्व्वशत्रुविनाशाय फट् । Then follows a long list of epithets of the god, as holders of different weapons, each ending with the adjective Sarva-śatru-vināśāya. These weapons are *Khaḍga* (sword), *Śaṁkha* (conch-shell), *Sudarśana Cakra* (discus), *Gadā* (Mace), *Cāpa* (bow), *Śara* (arrow), *Tangka* (chisel) and *Ardha-Candra* (half-moon).

The Narasiṁhāyudha-*mantra*, whose aim and effect is to kill the enemy contains a description of the god.

तप्तहाटककेशाग्र ज्वलत्पावकलोचनः ।
वज्राधिकनखस्पर्श दिव्यसिंह नमोस्तु ते ॥

(C) Gāruḍeya mantra.

महाभैरवरूपश्च सुदंष्ट्रनखलोचनः ।
महानासो महाग्रीवो वायुवेगसमन्वितः ।
ज्ञानः कामगमश्चैव नाभिर्वैनायकाकृतिः ॥
सप्तश्चैवार्कसन्निभः ऊर्ध्वाभिन्नभ्रमाकृतिः ॥

(read मूर्द्धा)

महापीतं भवेद् वर्णं जान्वन्तं पादमूलकं ।
महाश्वेतं भवेद् वर्णं नाभ्यन्तं जानुमूलकं ।
महारक्तं भवेद् वर्णं हृदमूलान्तकण्ठान्तकं ।
महाकृष्णं भवेद् वर्णं वदनादिशिरान्तकं ॥

It is added in Old-Javanese, that this *mantra* is to be uttered before meals in order to get rid of the fear of poison, this evidently alluding to the enmity between Garuḍa and the snakes. It should be added here that the mythology of Garuḍa was very popular in Java and Bali and plays a prominent part in the art and literature of the Far East. The Garuḍa myth forms the subject-matter of many sculptures in Java and paintings in Bali. [1]

We have referred to these ceremonies and *mantras* in some detail, not only to indicate the important part they played in religious life, but also to demonstrate the extent and thorough-going nature of the influence which Hinduism had exercised in these far-off colonies. The fact that these *mantras* and ceremonies are prevalent in Bali even to-day would prove the complete mastery of ritualistic Hinduism which was once the conspicuous feature of the religious life of Malayasia.

But although the rituals formed the chief feature of Hindu religion in Java as in India, the knowledge of philosophical concepts was not altogether lacking[2].

---

1. Cf. "De Geschiedenis Van Garuḍa" by Juynboll—Gedenkschrift, 1926, pp. 156-170.

2. For details cf. Goris pp. 54-69.

Not to speak of the later Tāntrik philosophy and the ideas associated with it, we have clear reference in Javanese texts to such philosophical concepts as *praṇava*, *pradhāna-puruṣa-saṁyoga* (of Sāṁkhya), *prāṇāyāma* (of Yoga), *tri-śakti*, *tri-puruṣa*, *daśa-bāyu*, *pañca-mahābhūta*, *pañca-tanmātra*, *etc.* It is obviously impossible to go deep into these matters and we therefore refrain from discussing these any further.

Of far greater interest, at least for our present purpose, is to give some details about the religious myths, legends and stories which may be regarded as constituting an important part of the popular form of religion. These may be easily gathered from a study of the extensive religious literature of Java. Unfortunately this vast store is yet mostly unexplored and we can do no better than take as our basis a typical text like Tantu Panggelaran which is known to us in a critical and scholarly edition.[1]

It is an Old-Javanese work dealing with religion, and was probably composed towards the end of the Hindu-Javanese period. It gives us a picture of the religious condition of Java, which conforms in the main to what we have said above. As this work may be taken as a representative specimen of its class we may refer to its contents at some length, in order to elucidate the religious conceptions in Java, at least in its ultimate phase.

The Tantu is a work of the nature of Purāṇa and contains theology, cosmogony, mythological stories etc. The late Prof. Kern remarked that, to judge from the names of gods, goddesses and other divine beings, one would imagine himself to be in the world of Indian gods, but what is told of them differs in many respects from Indian versions. How this difference arose it is difficult to say. It may be due either to a misunderstanding of the Indian texts, or to the growth of local legends in Java, or perhaps partly to both. We should also not exclude

1. De Tantu Panggelaran uitgegeven, vertaald en toegelicht door Th. Pigeaud (Hague, 1924)

the possibility of there being originally other versions in Indian texts, now lost, from which the Javanese author drew his inspiration. Of course, as is quite natural, the author transfers the scene of the most important events to Java. Thus he begins by saying that originally Mount Mahāmeru and Mount Mandara were in Jambudvīpa, but then the Lord Jagatpramāṇa with his spouse Parameśvarī went to Java and began to practise *yoga* in a place called Ḍihyang (Dieng). Under his orders Brahmā and Viṣṇu created mankind—men being created by the former and women by the latter—in a spot marked by Mount Pavinihan. Then the great Guru Lord Jagannātha (also called Lord Mahākāraṇa) directed the various gods to minister to the different needs of men, both material and spiritual. These gods are Brahmā, Viśvakarmā, Īśvara, Viṣṇu, Mahādeva, and Ciptagupta who dwelt in different parts of Java and performed the specific duties assigned to them. After doing their part they went back to heaven, leaving their children to continue their work. Specific mention is made of Viṣṇu and his spouse Śrī. They had five sons who took to various crafts and became progenitors of different classes of men.

But there was one difficulty. Java was subject to frequent quaking, and in vain did the gods create mountains to stop it. Then the Lord Mahākāraṇa one day called together the gods, the ṛṣis (Nārada, Kapila, Ketu, Tumburu, Sapaka and Viśvakarmā), the Surāṅganās, the four Lokapālas (Indra, Yama, Varuṇa, and Kuvera), Vidyādharas and Gandharvas and asked them to go to Jambudvīpa and bring the Mandara mountain (also called Mahāmeru) to Java. They came to India and broke off the upper half of the mountain, the lower portion remaining *in situ*. Then Brahmā assumed the shape of a tortoise, on which the mountain was placed, and Viṣṇu became a snake, with which it was towed, admidst thunder and storm, by the gods, ṛṣis etc. The latter were tired by their efforts and felt thirsty. They drank water, which contained the poison Kālakūṭa, and were all killed. Then Lord Parameśvara drank off the poison, and thereby his throat became black and he was called *nīlakaṇṭha*. He converted the poisonous water into *amṛta* (tattvāmṛta), and as soon as it was sprinkled over the dead bodies of the gods, etc, they were restored to life. Then the Lord asked the daityas, dānavas, and rākṣasas to help the gods and the Mount Mandara was brought safely to Java. As it bore the traces of gods, this Mandara, the Mahāmeru (great mountain), also came to be called Kailāsa mountain.

At first the mountain was fixed in the western corner of Java. But as the western half of Java subsided and the eastern half rose higher up, the Mandara was removed to the east. But the lower portion of the mountain remained in the west and a few pieces fell on the ground in course of transplantation. These became the hills known as Katong, Wilis, Kampud, Kawi, Arjjuna, and Kumukus. As the Mandara was thus damaged in one end it remained unstable till it was fixed up on the Brahmā mountain. Henceforth the island of Java ceased to quake and became stable. Therefore the Mahāmeru was named Niṣadha.

This somewhat extensive quotation would give the reader a fair idea of the Javanese adaptation of the Hindu mythology. Nobody can fail to trace the source of the above story in the Paurāṇik tale of Samudra-manthana, and in the remaining part of the story we have the well-known episodes of (1) the amṛta being taken by the Rākṣasas, (2) the stealing of amṛta by Viṣṇu in the disguise of a beautiful woman, and (3) the enmity of Rāhu towards the sun and the moon, etc. But if the source is beyond doubt, the local adaptation is equally clear. The main object of the whole episode has been cleverly altered to suit the peculiar conditions of Java, and details of the story have been deliberately invented to associate the gods with the different localities of Java.

Apart from local colouring we may note some peculiarities in the Javanese story. In the first place, Śiva or Mahādeva is distinguished from Īśvara, so that with Brahmā and Viṣṇu there are four chief gods instead of three.[1] But in other places reference is made to three gods.[2] Thus we are told that as soon as the Mandara mountain was firmly fixed up in Java, the Lord Parameśvara granted three riders (Vāhanas) to the three gods, white Bull to Lord Īśvara, white swan to Lord Brahmā, and the Garuḍadhvaja to Lord Viṣṇu.[3] The splitting up of Īśvara and Mahādeva (or Śiva) into two gods, and the name Garuḍahvaja for Garuḍa may be regarded as due to misunderstanding on the part of the Javanese authors.

It is also worthy of note that in addition to the Hindu Trinity, there is throughout a conception of a supreme god[4] called variously Jagatpramāṇa, Jagannātha, Mahākāraṇa, Parameśvara etc., or simply Guru. But indications are not wanting that here, again, there is a confusion of thought; for this great god is also represented as the husband of Umā,[5] thereby betraying his identity with the Indian God Śiva. This great god is named Lord Guru (Bhaṭāra Guru) who had from Umā two children, Kāmadeva, the most beautiful of gods, and a girl called Smarī, and later on two more sons called Gaṇa and Kumāra. Kāmadeva being enamoured of Smarī, Rati, born out of her body, became his wife, another instance of the confusion of ideas.

On the whole the perusal of a text like Tantu Panggelaran enables us to realise how the theology, mythology, religious concepts, and the philosophy of Paurāṇik Hinduism made a thorough conquest of Java. The same view is strengthened by a study of the other religious texts, of which a short account is given in the appendix to this chapter.

§2. Buddhism

We now turn to the other great religious sect, *viz.* Buddhism. We have seen above that the Hīnayāna form of

1. Ibid, p. 131, 139.
2. Ibid, p. 157.
3. Ibid, p. 137.
4. Ibid, p. 157.
5. Ibid, p. 140.

Buddhism was prevalent all over Malayasia towards the close of the seventh century A.D.[1] But the next century saw a great change at least in Java and Sumatra. The Hīnayāna form was practically ousted by Mahāyāna which had a triumphal career in Sumatra and Java during the period of the Śailendra supremacy.

In Java it led to the erection of the famous Barabuḍur and several other magnificent temples which will be described in detail in a subsequent chapter. The predominance of Mahāyāna was not, however, limited, only to a particular period and locality. Its monuments are also found in Eastern Java. The religion has left a prominent trace in caṇḍi Jago and many small temples which are scattered all over the island. It may be presumed, therefore, that Buddhism, particularly its Mahāyāna form, became a very popular religion in Java among the masses. The same thing may also be said of Sumatra. On the whole it may be safely presumed that as in the old days, Suvarṇadvīpa continued to be a strong centre of Buddhism. The international character of Buddhism gave Suvarṇadvīpa a status and importance, and brought it into intimate contact with India and the other Buddhist countries. It has already been stated above that the Śailendra kings were in close touch with the political powers of India and that the Buddhist preachers from Bengal exerted influence on Javanese Buddhism. It is also on record that eminent Buddhist scholars like Atiśa Dīpaṅkara[2] of Bengal (eleventh century A.D.) and Dharmapāla[3] of Kāñcī, who was a Professor at Nālandā in the seventh century A.D., went to Suvarṇadvīpa as it formed an important seat of Buddhist learning. The study of Buddhist literature in Java is proved not only by the discovery of important Buddhist texts but also by the sculptures of Barabuḍur and other religious monuments which

---

1. Cf. Bk, I. Ch. X.
2. Sarat Chandra Das—Indian Pandits in the land of snow, p. 50.
3. Kern—Manual of Buddhism, p. 130.

presuppose a wide range of knowledge in its various branches.

The international character of Buddhism perhaps explains the absence of any material modification of its principal tenets and belief. This is best illustrated by a study of the Buddhist iconography in Java. Here the entire hierarchy of the Mahāyānist gods makes its appearance. The Ādi-Buddha and Prajñā-Pāramitā, the Dhyānī Buddhas and Mānuṣī Buddhas, the Bodhisattvas and the Tārās, all make their appearance almost in identical forms and names, and we also meet with the familiar postures called *Mudrā* in the delineation of these images. A more detailed reference to these will be found in the chapter dealing with Art. Here it will suffice to state that in addition to the image of Gautama Buddha, those of Bodhisattva Avalokiteśvara were most popular in Java and Sumatra, though Maitreya and Mañjuśrī were also great favourites. The images of Tārās were also very familiar. Slight discrepancies are sometimes noticeable in the Javanese representation of these divinities. Thus, in India, Śyāmā-Tārā is represented with the right hand in vara-mudrā, and a lotus (*utpala*) in the left, while Javanese image with these attributes is expressly named as Māmak(h)ī. Śyāmā-Tārā is, on the other hand, represented in Java in the dharma-cakra-mudrā, holding a lotus without stem. Again, Locanā, Śakti of Akṣhobhya, is in Java represented as the Śakti of Vairocana. But with these minor modifications the entire Mahāyānist Pantheon seems to be well-represented in Java.

The later phases of Mahāyāna Buddhism in India are also met with in Java. We may note in particular four of them, *viz.* (1) The adoption of Hindu gods in the Buddhist pantheon, (2) introduction of minor and miscellaneous divinities, some of a terrible appearance, (3) the development of Tāntrik mode of worship, and (4) the gradual rapprochement between Mahāyāna and Brāhmanical religion.

As in India, Hindu gods like Brahmā, Śiva, Gaṇeśa and Indra were adopted in the Buddhist pantheon, but they were relegated to an inferior and sometimes even to a degraded position. In the earlier period they were represented as attendants of Buddhas and Bodhisattvas, but in later times their images, even those of Śiva and Pārvatī, are represented as being trodden under foot by the Buddhist gods. The change seems to be due to the introduction of a class of minor gods in Mahāyānism. These are regarded as protectors of the devotees or defenders of the faith, though they occupied a rank distinctly inferior to the aristocratic family of Buddhas, Bodhisattvas and Tārās referred to above. As prominent examples of these may be mentioned Trailokyavijaya, Hevajra, Bhṛkuṭi, Heruka, Mārīcī, Hayagrīva and Kuvera. The last-mentioned one, although originally a Hindu god, was taken over into the minor Buddhist pantheon and thus escaped the fate which overtook his superior gods. Some of these minor gods are of either monstrous or terrible appearance, like their Indian prototype, but in one case at least, that of Mārīcī, the Javanese form presents a benign human figure in *vara-mudrā* attitude, in striking contrast to her Indian prototype, with a hideous pig-face, standing in a menacing attitude on a chariot drawn by seven pigs.

The image of Trailokyavijaya[1] found in Java aptly illustrates the point noted above. It stands on the prostrate bodies of Śiva and Gaurī and has four (or five) heads, eight hands and a necklace composed of the images of Amitābha. It is represented in *vajra-huṅkāra-mudrā*, and holds in his hands a variety of weapons, such as sword, thunderbolt (*vajra*), discus, elephant-goad, noose, bow, and arrow.

Among the minor gods of monstrous and terrible appearance mention may be made of Hayagrīva and Heruka. Hayagrīva, as the name indicates, has the head of a horse (sometimes

1. See Pl. XLVI.

placed above three ordinary human heads), wild hair adorned with human skulls, and *upavīta* made of a double line of snakes. He holds in his hands various attributes, such as mace, sword, bow, and arrow.

The image of Heruka is very rare, even in India, only three being known up to date. As such it is interesting to note a recent discovery of this image in the Bairo Bahal Temple (No. II) in Sumatra[1]. The image corresponds to the *sādhanā* and to its Indian proto-type. The god is represented in a dancing attitude with a devilish smile (or grin) in his face. His hairs rise up like flames and he wears a garland made of human skulls (and probably joined together by entrails as the *sādhanā* says). He holds the thunderbolt in his right hand and a human skull serving as a wine-bowl in his left. On his left shoulder lies a *khaṭvāṅga* (a club or mace) and to its upper end is fastened a flapping banner with small bells.

The evolution of these monstrous and terrible gods in the Buddhist pantheon unerringly indicates its later degraded form known generally as Tāntrism, which comes into prominence simultaneously both in Hinduism and Buddhism. The object of Tāntrism, to take the most favourable view, was to obtain, by supernatural or magical practices, the highest spiritual power or bliss even in this life without having to undergo a series of births as original Buddhism contemplated. But both the objects and the means were not unoften extremely degraded. Instead of the attainment of spiritual power not a few strove only for the acquisition of material advantages. As to the depraved and revolting nature of the means we may mention the Pañcatattva or Pañcamakāra which enjoins upon the devotees the free enjoyment of *madya* (wine), *māṁsa* (meat), *matsya* (fish), mudrā (various postures), and *maithuna* (sexual intercourse), and also of the *cakra*, *i.e.* secret sitting in a circle of men and women practising mysterious and obscene rites. It is unnecessary to go into details about the development of

1. See Pl. LXVIII, Fig. 2. O.V. 1930, p. 139 pl. 40-42.

this aspect of Tantrayāna or Tantra-cult for which adequate information is available in the many standard treatises. The following passage from Kern's *Manual of Buddhism*[1] admirably sums up the general view of the subject.

"The development of Tāntrism is a feature that Buddhism and Hinduism in their later phases have in common. The object of Hindu Tāntrism is the acquisition of wealth, mundane enjoyments, rewards for moral actions, deliverance, by worshipping Durgā, the Śakti of Śiva—Prajñā in the terminology of the Mahāyāna—through means of spells, muttered prayers, Samādhi, offerings &c. Similarly the Buddhist Tantras purpose to teach the adepts how by a supernatural way to acquire desired objects, either of a material nature, as the elixir of longevity, invulnerability, invisibility, alchymy; or of a more spiritual character, as the power of evoking a Buddha or a Bodhisattva to solve a doubt, or the power of achieving in this life the union with some divinity."

The Tantrayāna, even in its most debased form, Kālacakra-tantra, prevailed in Java and Sumatra, as we have already seen above[2] in connection with the history of king Kṛtanagara. About a certain text of this sect the late Dr. R. L. Mitra observed as follows:

"The professed object is devotion of the highest kind, but in working it out, theories are indulged in and practices enjoined which are at once the most revolting and horrible that human depravity could think of. The work is reckoned to be the sacred scripture of millions of intelligent beings[3]."

It is not perhaps difficult to explain the rise of Tāntrism in Java. The Tibetan historian Tāranātha informs us that the Pāla period witnessed a great development of the cult. As we have seen above, the Śailendra kings were in close touch with the Pāla kings of Bengal, and learned Buddhist priests from Bengal exerted great influence over the religion of

1. p. 133. 2. Cf. Part I, p. 304.

3. Nepalese Buddhist Literature, p. 261.

Sumatra and Java. It is, therefore, perhaps not unreasonable to assume that Tāntrism, like Mahāyānism, flowed from Bengal to Malayasia. This view is further strengthened by the date of the Buddhist Tāntrik text Sang hyang Kamahāyānikan. This work, which deals with the theory and practice of Tantra, and to which more detailed reference will be made later on, was probably composed in the Śailendra period and revised in the reign of Siṇḍok by Sambharasūryāvaraṇa.[1] To the same author is also ascribed the Javanese Subhūti-tantra[2] which formed the most favourite subject of study of king Kṛtanagara. Thus Tāntrism, which flourished later in Eastern Java, had already its beginning in the tenth century A. D. while the Pālas were yet ruling in Bengal.

Recently the Dutch scholar Moens has dealt in great detail with this last and decadent phase of Buddhism in Sumatra and Java, and we refer the inquisitive readers to his learned article[3] for the theological and philosophical aspects of the question. It will suffice here to state that we can trace the influence of Tāntrism in the eleventh and twelfth centuries A.D. by the prominent parts played by Tāntrik teachers during the reigns of Airlangga and Jayabhaya.[4] During the thirteenth century it had two great devotees in kings Kṛtanagara of Java and Ādityavarman of Sumatra. The accounts of these two kings, the images of Bhairava, Heruka and other Tāntrik gods and goddesses as well as the Tāntrik texts give us unmistakable proof of the nature and extent of this degraded form of Buddhism which ultimately proved its ruin.

Reference has already been made (Bk. III. Ch. IV) to the religious activities of Kṛtanagara. It is a sad comment on the religious condition of the time that this great king,

---

1. Goris, p. 156. Krom—Geschiedenis², p. 219.
2. Krom—op. cit., pp. 219-220.
3. T.B.G., Vol. LXIV (1924), pp. 521 ff.
4. Cf. the story of Bharāḍa (Bk III. Ch. III). A high official of Jayabhaya with jurisdiction over spiritual matter is called Bhairava-mārgānugamana and 'yogiśvarādhikāra.' (Krom—Geschiedenis² p. 295.)

believed to be an incarnation of Jina, and undoubtedly endowed with power and talents of a high order, could indulge, perhaps in sincere faith, even in such obnoxious practices as *pañca-makāra* and *sādhana-cakra*. According to Moens the king was represented after his death by a Bhairava image which is now at Leyden.[1] The image is a terrible and repulsive one, a naked corpulent figure decorated with human skulls all over his body, dancing on a seat made up of or supported by human skulls. It has protruding teeth and bulging eyes, and holds in his four hands a trident, dagger, *ḍamaru*, and an inverted human skull forming a bowl of wine. Whether this Bhairava image really represented the deified form of the king may be doubted, but it seems almost certain that the image verily personifies the crude and obnoxious religious faith of the time.

Moens has also proved that King Ādityavarman was a great follower of the Bhairava cult. According to his interpretation the Suroasa inscription of 1297 Śaka seems to refer to *Kāpālika* practices indulged in by King Ādityavarman. The king assumed the title Viśeṣadharaṇi after performing, according to the Bhairava cult, the highest consecration ceremony which included a human sacrifice in the cremation ground. Seated on a corpse, he was drinking the blood of the victim who was being consumed in a blazing fire. Here, again, although this interpretation is not absolutely certain, the inscriptions of Ādityavarman leave no doubt that the king was a follower of Tantrayāna, and indulged in its obnoxious practices. He looked upon himself as an incarnation of Bhairava and his queen as that of Mātaṅginī, one of the ten Mahāvidyās.

From a study of Tantrayāna we may now pass on to the last phase of Mahāyāna, *viz.* a syncretism of the different Hindu and Buddhist gods. It is a well-known fact that in its very origin Mahāyānism shows clear influence of both

1. T.B.G., Vol. LXIV, plate facing p. 546.

Vaiṣṇavism and Śaivism. That there was growing tendency of rapprochement between the last two sects is indicated by the image of Hari-Hara, *i.e.* the joint representation of Śiva and Viṣṇu, and a clear expression of the identity of the two gods in religious texts. Now, in a similar way, there was an attempt towards a synthesis between Vaiṣṇavism and Buddhism by regarding Buddha as an incarnation of Viṣṇu. With the development of Tantrayāna these identities assumed a more definite form.

The close association between Śiva and Buddha is a characteristic feature of Javanese religion. The two deities have been identified in such books as Kuñjarakarṇa and Sutasoma. This question has been dealt at length by Kern and Rassers.[1] In modern Balinese theology Buddha is regarded as a younger brother of Śiva, and there is a close rapprochement between the two doctrines. A similar Śiva-Buddha cult existed in Java. Further researches have shown that Śiva, Viṣṇu, and Buddha were all regarded as identical and so were their Śaktis. Here, again, the point is well illustrated by the case of king Kṛtanagara. He called himself Narasiṁha-mūrti, *i.e.* an image of Viṣṇu in the incarnation of Narasiṁha (Man-lion). But he was also known as Śiva-Buddha, and was represented after his death by an image of Śiva-Buddha. His father king Viṣṇuvardhana was represented after his death by the images of both Śiva and Buddha, while the cousin of the latter, who shared the royal honours with him, was called Narasiṁha-mūrti, but was represented by an image of Śiva. These are not instances of faith in different gods, but rather of a belief that these different gods are identical. The evidence thereof is furnished by the growing popularity of the image of Hari-Hara at this period. It may be remembered that Kṛtarājasa, the son-in-law and successor of Kṛtanagara, is represented by a fine image of the god Hari-Hara.

---

1. Kern—V.G. IV (149-177). Rassers—Gedenkschrift, B.K.I. 1926, pp. 222-253,

The Tāntrik texts definitely identify the three gods in the form of Bhairava. Thus Tārā-tantra says : "He, Janārdana, is the excellent Deva in the form of Buddha, the Kulabhairava". The images of Bhairava which we meet with in Java and Sumatra may, therefore, be regarded as the visible symbol of the Tāntrik syncretism of the gods of different sects. This gradual obliteration of sharp differences between the different sects and a growing conviction of their essential unity, in spite of outward observances, is also very clearly reflected in Javanese religious literature.

We have already surveyed a few texts regarding Hinduism in Java and may now pass on to those belonging to Buddhism. The earliest and best-known works in this field are Sang hyang Kamahāyānan Mantranaya and Sang hyang Kamahāyānikan, both Mahāyāna texts.[1]

The first work consists of Sanskrit verses with Javanese translation, while the second consists of a somewhat free Javanese version of a Sanskrit original, interspersed with a number of original Sanskrit verses. The latter text is known in several redactions. It was probably composed in the Śailendra period and modified at a subsequent date. During or shortly after Siṇḍok's reign, in the first half of tenth century A.D.,[2] it was further modified in a manner which has been regarded as a Hinduised or Śaiva version of a Buddhist original. This in itself is of great significance, as marking an important landmark in the religious evolution of Java.

As to the two texts, one may justly feel doubts as to how far the Sanskrit original really portrays the actual faith and belief in Java. But the selection of one or more particular Mahāyāna texts for commentary and translation, and their

---

1. Sang Hyang Kamahāyānikan—Oud-Javaansche Tekst met inleiding, vertaling, aanteekeningen door J. Kats (The Hague, 1910). For the dates and gradual additions to the text, cf. pp. 5-9, and also Goris, pp. 151-156.

2. Cf. Part I, p. 260.

currency in Java for a long period undoubtedly entitle us to regard them as giving a fair picture of the Mahāyāna doctrines as prevalent in Java.

The Sang hyang Kamahāyānikan is a much larger text than Kamahāyānan Mantranaya, and, as the preamble says, is an exposition of the sacred principles of Mahāyāna. It begins with an admonition against austerities and torture of the body, and sums up its views in this respect as follows : "Take care of your body, because on the welfare of the body depends happiness, happiness leads to a fixed mind, fixed mind is means to Samādhi and the Samādhi is the means to the attainment of Nirvāṇa".

The ultimate aim is to get rid of the passions, *rāga* (anger) *dveṣa* (jealousy, aversion or envy) and *moha* (infatuation). For this purpose one should not be attached to the various branches of learning such as Tarka (logic), Vyākaraṇa (grammar), and even the Purāṇas, Āgamas, the religious texts of Samayakoṣa, Tantra etc. One should equally avoid stories, recitations, music, dance and similar things.

But one should follow the six great virtues (Ṣaṭ-pāramitā). These are defined as (1) dāna (2) śīla (3) kṣānti (4) vīrya (5) dhyāna (6) prajñā. Dāna or gift is of various degrees beginning from the offer of food and drink to that of son, wives and even of the flesh and blood of one's own body. Śīla is explained as abstention from doing evils in body, speech and mind, evils done by body being further defined as slaughter of a living being, taking of what belongs to another, sexual pleasure, and telling lies. Kṣānti is explained as that attitude of mind which makes no difference between friends and foes, or high or low, and which is calm and friendly even to the angry. Vīrya is constant effort to do good deeds both day and night. These good deeds are enumerated as the writing of sacred texts, the worship of the gods, reading of sacred texts, the installation of stūpa and images of Buddha, practice of Yoga, reciting mantras before the images of Buddhas and the devīs, contemplation of welfare of all created beings *etc*.

Dhyāna is explained as a realisation of unity between oneself and all other created beings, attachment to truth, and mercy for all both high and low. Prajñā is defined as the realisation that Śūnya (void, emptiness) is the essence of all existing things. To these six pāramitās are added four others, maitrī (friendliness), karuṇā (mercy), muditā (joy) and upekṣā (evenmindedness), making a total of Ten Pāramitās.

Five Goddesses represent the essence (tattva) of these Ten Pāramitās. The goddess Vajradhātvīśvarī, wise, beautiful and devoted to her husband, is said to be the six pāramitās. Of the remaining four Locanā, Māmakī, Pāṇḍaravāsinī and Tārā represent respectively maitrī, karuṇā, muditā and upekṣā.

The author then proceeds to explain the four Yogas, taught by Dignāga, the four Bhāvanās leading to them, and the four Ārya-satyas. The four Yogas are belief in the existence of the great god (Bharāla) (1) in the ākāśa (firmament), (2) in our body, (3) in the world, and (4) in the śūnyamaṇḍala (circle of emptiness). The four Bhāvanās are possibilities of getting rid of *rāga* (anger), *dveṣa* (aversion), *moha* (infatutation) and the *kleṣas* (sufferings). The four Ārya-satyas (sacred truths) are duḥkha-satya (truth of the sorrow), nirodha-satya (truth of its suppression), samudaya-satya (the truth of its origin), and mārga-satya (the truth of the ways). The ten Pāramitās, the four Ārya-satyas, together with Yoga and Bhāvana constitute the Mahā-guhya or the great mystery.

Then comes the Parama-guhya or the excellent mystery, which concerns itself with the body of the great god (Bharāla). Here we get an interesting account of the theology of Mahāyāna according to the Yogācāra system. The starting point is Advaya, whose union with Advaya-Jñāna created Divarūpa. From Divarūpa sprang Bhatāra Buddha and from the latter originated Śākyamuni. From the right and left side of Śākyamuni originated Lokeśvara and Vajrapāṇi. These three had respectively white, red and blue colours and dhvaja-, dhyāna-, and bhuḥsparśa—mudrās. They were called Ratnatraya, 'the Buddha, Dharma and Saṅgha'.

From one face of Śākyamuni originated Śrī Vairocana. knowledge divided himself and created Akṣobhya and Ratnasambhava. Similarly from Vajrapāṇi originated Amitābha and Amoghasiddhi. These five Tathāgatas were named Bhaṭāra Sarvvajñāna.

From the all-embracing knowledge (śaśvata-jñāna) of Vairocana originated the almighty gods Īśvara, Brahmā and Viṣṇu. At the command of Vairocana they created the three worlds, Svarga, Martya and Pātāla.

The text then proceeds to give an account of some of the Buddhist philosophical conceptions, such as the five Skandhas (*rūpa, vedanā, saṁjñā, saṁskāra, and vijñāna*), the five vījākṣaras (*auṁ, huṁ, traṁ, hrīḥ, aḥ*), trikhala (*rāga, dveṣa, mohā*), trimala (*artha, kāma, śabda*), trikāya (*kāya, vāk, citta*), triparārtha (*asiḥ* or love, *puṇya, bhakti*), pañcadhātu (*pṛthvī, āpaḥ, tejas, vāyu, ākāśa*), pañcarūpaskandha (*kalala, arbuda, ghana, peśi* and *praśākha*), pañca-jñāna (*niṣprapañca* or *śāś vata, prabhāsvara* or *adarśana, grāhya-grāhakarahita* or *ākāśamata, sarvvadharma-nairātmya* or *pratyavekṣaṇa*, and *kṛtyānuṣṭhānajñāna*).

The text concludes with an account of the Tathāgatadevīs or female counterparts of the Buddhas. These are Dhātvīśvarī, Locanā, Māmakī, Pāṇḍaravāsinī and Tārā, wives respectively of Vairocana, Akṣobhya, Ratnasambhava, Amitābha and Amoghasiddhi. The last four goddesses have as their essence (*tattva*) *maitrī, karuṇā, muditā* and *upekṣā*. The first two, Dhātvīśvarī and Locana, are really one in essence (tatva). They are co-workers of Vairocana, possess Śāśvata-jñāna, and have the forms of the omnipotent *viz*., Satvabajrī, Ratnabajrī, Dharmabajrī, and Karmmabajrī.

The short account of the text given above would give us a fair insight into the leading conceptions of Mahāyānism in Java. Its close resemblance and minor differences from the form of the religion current in India are interesting subjects of study, but cannot be attempted here. Specially noteworthy is the attempt to bring the Hindu Trinity, Īśvara, Brahmā and

Viṣṇu, in organic relation with the Buddhist pantheon. It is also remarkable that these Hindu gods are admitted to be the creator of the three worlds. We thus get a valuable evidence of the syncretism of the gods of different sects which formed a conspicuous feature of the religious spirit of the age.

A more popular but degraded form of the Mahāyāna doctrine in Java is preserved in the Kamahāyānan Matranaya. It contains a short preamble followed by forty-one Sanskrit verses with Javanese commentaries. The preamble refers to the mystic syllables *oṁ*, *aḥ*, *huṁ* and also to the (equivalent) words 'paramārtha, kāya, vāk, citta, vajra'[1] The first verse is a sort of introduction in which a preceptor addresses his disciple: "Come, my boy, I shall teach you the Mantrācāryanaya rules of Mahāyāna (mahāyānaṁ mantrācāryanayaṁ vidhim)." This Mantrācāryanaya is evidently a full form of Mantranaya, the title of the book. This Mantranaya has been rightly identified with the Mantrayāna. About its nature and origin Waddell observes: 'The excessive use of the mystic *mantras*, consisting mostly of unmeaning gibberish, resulted in a new vehicle named the Mantrayāna which is a Tāntrik development of the Yoga-phase of Buddhism. It teaches that one can attain the Buddhahood by the mysterious knowledge of *kāya*, *citta* and *vāk*.'[2]

---

1. It is interesting to note a corresponding formula in the following Tibetan prayer:

"We pray you to give us the gifts of the True Body, Speech and Mind, Oṁ! aḥ! huṁ" (Waddell—The Buddhism of Tibet p. 442). The same author further observes: "Before commencing any devotional exercise, the Lama gently touches his forehead either with the finger or with the bell, uttering the mystic oṁ, then he touches the top of his chest, uttering aḥ, then the epigastrium, uttering huṁ" (Ibid p. 423). This close resemblance can be easily explained if we remember that both ibet and Java got their religious inspiration mainly from Bengal.

2. Waddell—op. cit. pp. 143-145, p. 145 fn. 2.

17

As a matter of fact, the text is throughout devoted to an exposition of the Tantrayāna or Vajrayāna both in its theoretical and practical aspects. The ideal of the attainment of Buddhahood is clearly expressed in the following verse :

एष मार्गवरः श्रीमान् महायानमहोदयः ।
येन यूयं गमिष्यन्तो भविष्यथ तथागताः ॥

"This is the famous Mahāyāna system which yields both material and spiritual bliss (*bāhya-ādhyātmika sukha*, as explained in the Javanese commentary), and by following which you will become Tathāgata (Buddha). A clear reference to the five kinds of sensual enjoyments is contained in the following verses :—

नास्ति किंचिदकर्तव्यं प्रज्ञोपायेन चेतसा ।
निर्विशंकः सदा भूत्वा प्रभुङ्क्ष्व कामपञ्चकम् ।

The plain meaning of the above seems to be that a votary who has attained prajñā, can do everything and should always fearlessly enjoy the five senses. The Javanese commentary on this verse is a characteristic one. It says that since it is difficult to avoid *karma*, he should work for the possession of the highest spiritual knowledge and the sensual enjoyments are forbidden to him.

It is definitely said in other verses that one should not torment his body by austerities (तपोभिः नातिपीडयेन्), but should become a Buddha by following pleasurable ways (यथासुखं सुखं धार्यौ).

There are references to Maṇḍala, and several verses refer to the high honour which should be shown to Guru (preceptor). The Guru is equal to Buddha and should never be despised. A devotee should dedicate to his Guru not only his own life but also his son, and even his wife[1], not to speak of material wealth. For while Buddhahood is normally attainable only by immense troubles through millions of births, the Guru enables

---

1. This seems to foreshadow the revolting practices prevalent among certain sects in India.

the disciple to attain Buddhahood even in this life. Thus we read :

> यद्यावमन्येदाचार्यं सर्वबुद्धसमं गुरुं ।
> सर्वबुद्धावमानेन नित्यं दुःखमवाप्नुयात् ॥
> नित्यं सम्समयाचार्यं प्राणैरपि निजैर्भजेत् ।
> अदेयैः पुत्रदारैर्वा किम्पुनर्विभवैश्चलैः ॥
> यस्मात् सुदुर्लभं नित्यं कल्पासंख्येयकोटिभिः ।
> बुद्धत्वमुद्योगवते ददातीहैव जन्मनि ॥

The text concludes with the exulting description by the Guru of the Buddhahood to be attained by the devotee on that very day.

> अद्य वः सफलं जन्म यदस्मिन् सुप्रतिष्ठितः ।
> समाः समा हि देवानामद्य जाताः स्वयंभवः ॥
> अद्याभिषिक्ता युष्मन्तः सर्वबुद्धैः सवज्रिभिः ।
> त्रैधातुकमहाराज्ये राजाधिपतयः स्थिताः ॥
> अद्य मारं विनिर्जित्य प्रविष्टाः परमं पुरम् ।
> प्राप्स्यथैव बुद्धत्वं भवद्भिर्नात्र संशयः ॥

In addition to the above, the text of Kamahāyānan Mantranaya contains clear references to Mahāyānist conceptions of various Buddhas, and particularly to Bajrasattva the chief of all the Buddhas. The esoteric character of the teaching is clearly indicated by a verse which forbids the devotee to communicate the secrets of bajra, ghaṇṭā and mudrā to those who do not belong to the Maṇḍala. It is not necessary to go into further details, but on the whole the text gives a very interesting picture of the form of Mahāyāna, called Vajrayāna.

§ 3. Different sects.

After giving a brief description of the principal features of the two great religious systems, *viz.*, Buddhism and Paurāṇik form of Hinduism, we may conclude this account with a reference to the various religious sects that flourished in Java. These religious sects are enumerated in different texts, but the lists do not always agree. Goris has drawn up a classified list of these sects by an analysis of ten different texts.[1] These are :

(1) Śaiva or Siddhānta (*var.* sidanta, śridanta) sometimes also called Śaiva-siddhānta or Siddhānta-Śaiva.

(2) Pāśupata..

(3) Bhairava.

(4) Vaiṣṇava.

(5) Bauddha or Saugata.

(6) Brāhmaṇa (or Brāḥmāṇa)

(7) Ṛṣi.

In addition there is reference to Alepaka or Lepaka, a Śaiva sect, and Yogita which cannot be identified.

The epigraphic data in general confirm the above list. The Bendosari inscription mentions Bhairava, Sora and Bauddha sects. Sora has been identified with Siddhānta, but may also stand for Saura (Sun-worshipper) which would then give us a new sect.

The Tantu Panggelaran, to which reference has already been made above as a source of mythological stories, also tells us a great deal about the origin of the different Maṇḍalas or Orders of religious ascetics called Viku, no doubt derived from Indian 'Bhikṣu'. The first Order is said to have been founded by the Great God called Guru, and the lesser gods and demigods completed the task. While the stories of the foundation of the different Maṇḍalas by different Gurus no doubt belong to the domain of mythology, the Tantu clearly testifies to the existence of these different Orders, and gives us some idea not only of the localities which formed their head-quarters, but also of the nature of their organisation.

1. Goris, pp. 101-4.

In connection with the Maṇḍalas the Tantu refers to the various religious sects (*pakṣa*) to which they belonged. Among these specific mention is made of Śaiva, Saugata (Buddhist), and Bhairava sects, with the addition of two more, *viz.*, *pakṣa kasturi* and *pakṣa tyāga*, which were offshoots of the Bhairava sect. The Tantu gives a detailed account only of the Bhairava sect, a circumstance which agrees well with what has been said above regarding its wide prevalence in Java during the last days of Hindu civilisation. As the account also throws light on its relations with other sects, it would be well to give a short summary of the passage.[1]

"The Great God, Lord Guru, took the form of a Viku, a Bhujangga of the Śaiva sect. He was called Mahampu Palyat or empu Mahāpalyat. He dwelt in the cemetery of Kalyasem, south-east of Paguhan, and began to practise the religious performances (*tapas*) in accordance with the usages of the Bhairava sect. He ate human flesh at midnight. Twelve years later he attended an assembly of the king of Galuh with a human skull (for drinking) and five pots (*kaṇṭora*) for drying human flesh. The king said: "As he eats human bodies and destroys the creation of Brahmā, expel him from Java and throw him into the sea". Palyat merely uttered a wild laughter (*hahaha*) and returned to the cemetery. Next morning the king's agents threw him into the sea, but the day after he was again back at his cemetery. Then they tied him to a stone and again threw him into the sea, but he again came back. Then they burnt his body and threw the ashes into the sea, but Palyat could not be killed. Amazed at the exhibition of the magical power by the Paṇḍit, the king's emissaries fell at his feet when the latter said: "I belong to the island of Kambangan and have a Bhujangga-maṇḍala there. As the king is angry, I shall go back to my own land; a piece of stone will I take as my boat". The bewildered servants of the king became his disciples and accompanied him. They were

1. Tantu, pp. 171 ff.

consecrated with the names empu Janādhipa and empu Narajñāna. When they returned to Java the king of Galuh appointed them respectively as his Guru and Purohita (priest).

Some time later empu Mahāpalyat came back to the island of Java. He divided his body in two parts, and there arose one Saugata (Buddhist) empu Waluh-bang and one Śaiva, empu Barang.

Empu Barang settled in mount Hyang at the cemetery of Kalyasem and a large crowd of men belonging to the Bhairava sect soon gathered round him. They collected heaps of dead bodies, ate human flesh, and drank from human skulls. The king of Daha thereupon sent two brothers, both Buddhist, to kill empu Barang. Although the two brothers were really incarnations of Brahmā and Viṣṇu, and they threw empu Barang into sea, and burnt his body, they did not succeed in killing him. Then empu Barang went to Jambudvīpa, accompanied by the two brothers. There he converted, by his magic power, the Brāhmaṇas who were worshippers of Haricandana. He came back to Java, and being welcomed by the king of Daha, presented to him a golden image of Viṣṇu which he had modelled after the one which was worshipped in Jambudvīpa.

The Buddhist Waluh-bang now approached empu Barang and requested him to found the Kasturi sect. Empu Barang founded the first maṇḍala of the Kasturi sect. Similarly he became the founder (devaguru) of the Tyāga sect. Thus both Kasturi and Tyāga sects were offshoots of the Bhairava sect."

The above account leaves no doubt about the growing importance of the Bhairava sect. It also shows that any hard and fast distinction between the different sects was fast disappearing. Buddhism, Śaivism and Vaiṣṇavism are all brought into association with the Bhairava cult which evidently arose out of them and was now exercising supreme influence in its turn.

The same impression is produced by a general study of the religious literature of the period. Although different sects are named and there are treatises dealing specifically with different religions, the theoretical or practical distinction between them is not quite clear. Pigeaud observes from a study of the Tantu, Koravāśrama, and Pararaton 'that the religious faiths in Java were marked by a strong influence of Tāntrism, but of different sectarian dogmas or church-organisations there is little trace.'[1] There were no doubt different religious groups or orders, but the characteristic differences between them are nowhere made explicit. The *Tutur*, *mantras* etc. in religious books are neither Śaiva nor Buddhist, but applicable to both, and the sectarian predilection of the author can only be gathered by the names of gods which he invokes. Most likely the different Orders were distinguished only by different rites and ceremonials. This conclusion is strengthened by a passage in Koravāśrama[2] in which the three sects are named Śri-danta, Brāhmaṇa and Buddha, and distinct rituals are laid down for each. The names of sects are peculiar and the distribution of the gods among the different sects is equally so, Buddha, for example, being identified with Mahādeva. But the climax is reached when Brāhmaṇa is substituted as the name of a sect, in place evidently of Śaiva, and it is expressly laid down that the Brāhmaṇas born in Java are much superior to those born in Jambudvīpa, who indeed deserve to be called Śūdra.

The passage, however, lays great stress on observances and rituals and these seem to be the hall-marks of the different religious orders. We may well imagine, therefore, that the decadent phases of Hinduism in Java were not unlike those in Bengal where Buddhism, Śaivism and Vaiṣṇavism were gradually merged together and a body of rituals and ceremonies came to be the chief characteristics of religious faiths, at least among the masses.

---

1. Op. cit, p. 39.
2. Quoted by Pigeaud, Ibid, p. 36.

It is refreshing to note, however, that better minds in Java, as in India, could soar above these trivial externals and catch a glimpse of the highest spiritual truth. As an example of this we may refer, at some length, to Caturpakṣopadeśa,[1] a treatise dealing with sects.

It divides the orders of ascetics into five classes (pakṣas) named after five elements (earth, water, fire, air and sky) and describes the vows, religious practices, manners of living, and various usages and customs of each. The object of their *vrata* (vow) is either to become rich, powerful, beautiful, accomplished, successful, *etc.* or to attain *svarga* (heaven) or *mokṣa* (liberation).

The means for attaining all these ends are enumerated as tapa, vrata, yoga, samādhi (samaḍi), puṇya and dharmma (ḍarmma). There are five classes of ascetics *viz.*, those who live on fruits (*phala-vāsī*), roots (*mūla*), water (*salila*), air (*pāvaka or pavana ?*) or nothing (*nira*). The text then proceeds to say that *rāga* (passion) and *dveṣa* (hatred) are the two chief enemies of the ascetics, against which they should always be on guard. If the five classes of ascetics fall victims to these two, then they should, respectively, be like monkey, swine, the *Vāḍavānala* (mythical submarine fire), serpent and stone. If men are only free from passion and hatred, then it is immaterial where they live, whether in hill, wood, cave, sea-beach or island. One who is not free from passion and hatred does not deserve the name of Paṇḍita.

This high moral tone is in keeping with the spiritual insight of the author who realised the unity of the all-pervading soul in spite of the seeming varieties of religious faiths, beliefs and practices. He illustrates this by two homely examples. As a man puts on clothes of different colours, but still remains one and the same, so is He, the Creator, one and the same, although He appears in different garbs to different men or different sects. Again, if there are thousand pitchers full of water, men would

1. Ibid, pp. 42 ff.

see thousand suns reflected in them ; but if they would only look up, they would see only one sun whose images they are. So only one God pervades all creatures though we mistake Him for many.

Speaking of the different sects with different practices, the author says that they are like men who obtained different kinds of jewels or precious stones, and then each claimed that his was the best of all. Each put his precious jewel in a case and left it as a legacy to his successors. Gradually, owing to neglect or want of proper care, the jewls were lost and there remained only the empty cases. So are the present religious sects or orders. They have lost the costly jewels, *i.e.* the noble spirituality of their founders, and their outward observances and ceremonials are merely like those empty cases. How did they lose the costly jewels, *i.e.* the noble spiritual truths ? By passion and hatred. Let them, therefore, be on guard against these two, and without laying too much stress on their peculiar dresses and habits, let them make an effort to get back the costly jewels and preserve them by keeping a vigilant watch.

Passages like these furnish striking examples of the higher tone of morality and spiritual insight that continued down to the latest days of Hinduism in Java. The treatise, on the whole, confirms the picture we have drawn above of the religious sects.

§ 4. Religion in the Island of Bali

In the foregoing account we have mainly confined our attention to Java. Of the other regions, our knowledge is very limited except in the case of the island of Bali and the western part of Lombok (colonised by the Balinese) where Hinduism is still the prevailing religion. An historical study of this religion is, however, beset with two difficulties. In the first place, we are unable to trace the successive stages of its development, and secondly, it is difficult to determine how much of it was imported from Java and how much or how little really belongs to the Balinese. The older writers definitely affirm that every vestige of Hindu religion and literature that we find to-day in Bali is derived from Java. Recent researches[1] have proved that this sweeping assertion is untenable, and that Bali possessed a distinct Hindu culture before the influx of Javanese elements began in the eleventh century. Still the fact remains that since the eleventh century Javanese culture profoundly affected that of Bali, and after the fall of the Majapahit empire, large groups of Javanese fled to that island and Javanese religion and literature found there a last resting place. All these so profoundly modified the civilisation of Bali that it is impossible now to distinguish what is Javanese from what is Balinese proper. It has been pointed out above that our knowledge of ancient Javanese literature is derived mostly from what has been found in Bali. And one who goes through any account of Balinese religion, such, for example, as is given by Dr. R. Friederich, will be struck with the similarity, at almost every step, with what has been said above regarding the Brāhmanical religion in Java. As a matter of fact the present religious views and practices in Bali may justly be regarded as a fitting supplement and an apt illustration of the picture we have drawn above of the Brāhmanical religion in Java.

Nevertheless as Hinduism is still a living religion in Bali we get naturally more details about its actual working than is possible in the case of Java. The following account[2] of Balinese religion should, therefore, be regarded more as a supplement to the sketch we have drawn above than as an independent picture.

As we have seen above Buddhism was introduced in Bali as early as the sixth century A.D. But gradually the Paurānik

---

1. Cf. above, Bk. IV, Ch. V.

2. The account is based on the following works :

1. Encycl. Ned. Ind. (*Sv.* Baliers) 2. Friederich-Bali. 3. Liefrinck—Bijdrage tot de kennis van het eiland Bali (T.B.G. Vol. 33, pp. 233-252.)

form of Brāhmanical religion, with predominance of Śaivism, exerted its sway. To-day the two sects not only exist peacefully side by side but there is even a theological and doctrinal rapprochement between the two. The Buddha is regarded as the younger brother of Śiva, and on the occasion of the important ceremonial feasts, there are always four Śaiva and one Buddhist priests. The latter faces the south while three of the former face the other directions, and the fourth sits in the middle. Even at the cremation of princes, the consecrated water brought by a Śaiva priest is mingled with that of a Buddhist. To the mass of people, there is hardly any consciousness of the difference between the two sects, and their view is represented by the popular saying "ya Śiva, ya Buddha" (He who is Śiva is Buddha). In their eyes Śiva and Buddha are one and the same.

The predominance of Śiva in the Brāhmanical pantheon is unquestioned, perhaps even in a far greater degree than in Java. Most of the peculiar characteristics and attributes of Viṣṇu are given to Śiva, while Brahmā and Viṣṇu are both regarded, rather as different forms of Śiva than as separate gods. Indeed Śiva is more or less regarded as the supreme deity, though his aspect as a member of the Trinity is not lost sight of altogether. In other words, the three gods were regarded as mere different aspects of the one indivisible supreme God, though the latter was expressed in terms of one of them *viz.* Śiva. As in Java, the three gods were known under various names, and their Śaktis were, Umā or Pārvati (of Śiva in his benificent aspect), Kālī and Durgā (of Kāla *i.e.* Śiva as destroyer), Śrī or Lakṣmī, the goddess of fertility and protector of agriculture (of Viṣṇu), and Sarasvatī, the goddess of knowledge and fine arts (of Brahmā). Among the host of inferior divinities mention may be made of Indra, Yama, Varuṇa, Kuvera, Kāma, Vāsuki (Serpent king, a member of Śiva's family), Sūrya, Candra, Rāhu *etc.* The incarnations of Viṣṇu and the members of Śiva's family, particularly Gaṇeśa, are also well-known.

The numerous evil spirits or Butas (*Skt.* Bhūtas) form a characteristic feature of Balinese theology. They are supposed to live in water, trees, or hills, and must be propitiated by appropriate offerings and worship. It has been said that the worship of these spirits occupies the people almost more than that of the benificent gods.

The Balinese mind is strongly dominated by a religious feeling inasmuch as they have a strong belief in the unbounded influence of gods and Butas, *i.e.* good and evil spirits over the entire destiny of man. Their whole life may almost be described as an unceasing struggle to befriend the former and to appease the latter. The religious performances thus occupy a prominent place in Balinese life, and their ultimate object may be described as honouring the gods and ancestors and propitiating the evil spirits. The Balinese worship may be divided into two classes, domestic and public. The most important in the first category is Sūrya-Sevana or worship of Śiva as Sūrya (Sun), to which a detailed reference has already been made above. The following account of an actual performance,[1] given by an eye-witness may serve as an apt illustration.

"The Padaṇḍa is clothed in white, with the upper part of the body naked, after the Balinese-Indian manner. He sits with his face to the east, and has before him a board upon which stand several small vessels containing water and flowers, some grains of rice, a pan with fire (Dhūpapātra) and a bell. He then mumbles, almost inaudibly, some words or prayers from Vedas (*sic*), dipping the flowers into the water and waving them and a few grains of rice before him (towards the east) with the forefinger and thumb of his right hand, whilst at the same time he holds up the pan containing fire. After having proceeded with his prayers for some time, during which he makes all kinds of motions with his fingers and turns his rosary, he appears to be inspired by the deity ; Śiva has, as it were,

1. Friederich—Bali, p. 99.

entered into him; this manifests itself in convulsions of the body, which grow more and more severe, and then gradually cease. The deity having thus entered into him, he no longer sprinkles the water and flowers towards the east alone, but also towards his own body, in order to pay homage to the deity which has passed into it. The bells are not used in the ordinary daily worship, but only at the full and new moons and cremations."

In addition to Sūrya-Sevana, there are other domestic religious ceremonies of the type described in the Gṛhya-Sūtras, performed on important occasions of a man's life, such as the birth of a child, the cutting of the navel-string when the child is 12 days, 42 days, 3 months or 1 year old; the name-giving ceremony; the piercing of the ears; first menstruation; marriage; conception; death; cremation; funeral; birthdays of family members; and also on occasions of illness, beginning of harvest *etc.*

Each house has got a domestic chapel where daily worship is offered to the tutelary deity or deities with flowers and delicacies. These are prepared by the ladies of the family who bring them to the chapels and reverently deposit them before the god with a *Sembah.* (bow). The chapel is usually enclosed by a wall, along the side of which are wooden or stone niches dedicated to particular gods who receive occasional worship.

For public worship, each *deśa* (district) has three or four general temples or Puras *viz.*:

1. Pura Desa or the principal temple dedicated to the general and local gods.

2. Pura Dalem, the temple for the dead, in or near the cremation ground, dedicated to the goddess Durgā.

3. Pura Segara (*Skt.* sāgara or sea) on the sea-coast dedicated to the Sea-God Baruṇa.

4. Pura Bukit, on the foot or on the top of a hill, dedicated to the gods of the hills.

To these may be added the Pura Subak, dedicated to Śrī, the goddess of fertility and cultivated fields. These are small, and, as a rule, located in a prominent part in the field overlooking the entire area irrigated by the same canal or irrigation system. All these temples are built more or less on the same plan, which will be described in detail later on. Lastly we may mention Pura Panataran, founded and maintained by the king.

Among the numerous temples in Bali six (ṣaḍ-kahjangan) are said to enjoy special distinction. Of these six, again, the one in Basuki, at the foot of the Gunung-agung hill, is the most distinguished. It was founded by the first Deva-Agung, and the Balinese princes make a pilgrimage there once a year, each having his own special place for prayer and worship. As to the other five, there is no certainty, as each district claims that distinction for one or more of its temples. Usually the following are reckoned to have a legitimate claim to be counted under this head : Pura Batur (Bangli), P. Lempujang (Karangasem), P. Batu-Kao (Tabanan), P. Jehjerok (Gianjar), P. Jugal Vatu (Badong), P. Gua-Lalavah (Klungkung), P. Sakenan (Badong), and P. Pejeng (Gianjar).

The Brāhmaṇa priest of the Balinese temples is called Padaṇḍa and is held in high honour. Another functionary, called 'Pamangku' or simply 'Mangku' also enjoys high distinction. He is not only the guard of the temple, but performs some of the religious ceremonies when the Padaṇḍa is absent. He is usually recruited from common people and may belong to any caste, but has to undergo a special training.

In addition to the Padaṇḍa and Mangku the Balinese require the service of an invisible spirit called 'Jro-taksu' or simply 'Taksu' for the purpose of communication with the god. A small temple is dedicated to him, but as he cannot speak, he is invited to pass into and speak from the body of one of the persons present. If he does so, the person 'possessed' by him loses his consciousness and then answers the questions of the people and communicates to them the desires of the god or what the people want to know from him. Sometimes, however, the god himself enters into the body of a person and then there is direct communication between the god and his votaries. On all important occasions, and before any important undertaking, the pious Balinese seek to know the divine will in this way.

In addition to the regular worship in the temples there are annual religious ceremonies or feasts on fixed dates. *e.g.* (1) Menjepi, on a new-moonday, for driving away the evil spirits : (2) Usaba (utsaba ?) in honour of Śrī the goddess of agriculture ; (3) Sara-Sevati (Sarasvatī) for consecration of books or manuscripts ; (4) Tumpek-landep, for consecration of weapons ; and others on the birth days of principal gods, and chiefs, on the anniversary of the foundation of each temple, on the coronation of kings, on the conquest of a state, on the outbreak of epidemics for the welfare of domestic animals, etc.,

The worship of the *pitaras* or ancestors forms an important part of the Balinese religion. Each dwelling house has got one or more small temples for this purpose, and there are occasional gatherings on sacred spots, believed to be the original dwelling places of these ancestors. At stated periods of the year, the *pitaras* return to the bosom of their families and are entertained with games and amusements. There are, besides, three religious ceremonies known as Pegursi, Galungan, and Kuningan for honouring the soule of the dead and holding close communion with them. In these offerings are placed near the graves, for the souls of those whose bodies are yet unburnt, and also in the Pura Dalem, for the souls freed from the body, after burning.

The worship consists mainly of presenting offerings and chanting (or secretly uttering) *mantras* from scriptures. These vary for different deities and different occasions. The offerings are usually made up of ordinary articles of food (grains, fruits and meat) and drink, clothes, and money. Animal sacrifices are chiefly reserved for Kāla, Durgā, Butas, Rakshasas and other evil spirits. Hen, duck, young pig, buffalo, goat, deer and dog are usually sacrificed. But sometimes we hear even of human sacrifices.

The well-known accessory articles of Indian worship such as *Ghṛta* (clarified butter) *Kuśa*-grass, *tila* (sesamum) and *madhu* (honey) are also used in Bali. One of the most important items is the holy water. Although rivers in Bali are named after the sacred rivers in India, *viz.*, Gaṅgā, Sindhu, Yamunā, Kāverī, Sarayu and Narmadā, the Balinese recognise that those rivers are really in Kling (India), and the water of these Balinese rivers is not regarded as holy. The water is therefore rendered sacred by the priests by uttering *mantras*, such as we have seen in the detailed ceremony of Sūrya-Sevana, and is then called *amṛta*.

The Padaṇḍa or priest who conducts the worship is usually a Brāhmaṇa. He attains to this position by learning the sacred texts, both Sanskrit and Kavi, and following a course of religious training, under a *Guru*, who then formally consecrates him. He has a peculiar dress, and identifies himself, both spiritually and materially, with the supreme deity. But the religious rites may also be performed by the three other castes, after they have followed a similar course of training. In that case the Kṣatriyas and Vaiśyas are called *ṛṣis* and the Śūdras become *dukuh*. But these are very rare. Even women, if properly qualified, may serve as priests, and are called Padaṇḍa-istri (Padaṇḍa-Strī). The Padaṇḍa is expected to lead an ideal life. He must never tell lies or give way to evil passions. He must abstain from pig's flesh, and observe the proper rituals in his bath and dress. The Padaṇḍa belonging to the highest class also observes celibacy throughout his life. It must be mentioned, however, that this high ideal does not apply to Buddhist Padaṇḍas.

The Padaṇḍa is rewarded for his services by a portion of the offerings. Remnants of his food and drink (which he takes after finishing the religious ceremony) are regarded as holy and are consumed by the people present. The *Toyatirta* or holy water used in the ceremony is eagerly solicited and even bought by the people. Besides domestic and public religious ceremonies his services are also required on the occasion of cremations. In addition to these he works as teacher, astronomer, and astrologer for the public. One of his most important functions is to consecrate every newly made weapon, as otherwise it would not be effective.

§5. Traces of Hinduism and Buddhism in other parts of Malayasia

A. **Sumatra :—**

Next to Java, the island of Sumatra has preserved the most interesting remains of both Hinduism and Buddhism. We have already referred to some of the characteristic traits of religion in this area and note below the more important archaeological finds related to them.[1]

I. The ruins of brick temples, called biaro, are found in large number in the Highlands of Padang and Tapanuli. Some of them are fairly large, *e.g.* Biara si Pamutung at the mouth of the Panai river, and many contain Brāhmanical and Buddhist images. Ruins of stone temples exist in the Residency of Palembang.

II. Buddhist Stūpas ore also fairly large in number, more noteworthy being those of Tanjung Medan and Muara Takus in which golden plates with mystic syllables in Nāgarī script were discovered. There are also numerous Dāgabas.

III. Images from the Highlands of Padang, Tapanuli Palembang and Jambi :—

(a) Stone images of Buddha, Bodhisattva, and minor deities *e.g.* Heruka.

(b) Silver image of Vajrasattva (form Buo).

(c) Bronze images of Buddha and Lokanātha.

(d) Stone images of Śiva, Gaṇesa, Nandi, Brahmā or Trimūrti.

(e) Bronze images of Gaṇeśa and Kuvera.

IV. Remains of Hinduism, though far more meagre, are found in Padang, Ketapang (Lampong), Kota Pinang (Siak), Benuvang (Rokan), Acheh and Indragiri.

1. Encycl. Ned. Ind. (*Sv.* oudheden).

V. Large number of Buddhist inscriptions, specially those of Ādityavarman, have been found in the district of Fort Van der Capellen, the very centre of Menankabau. Reference has already been made to them in connection with Java[1].

B. **Malay Peninsula** :—

The archaeological remains clearly indicate that both Buddhist and Brāhmanical religions continued to flourish in the Peninsula after the seventh century A. D[2]. The Ligor inscription of 775 A. D., already noted above, demonstrates the predominance of Buddhism in that region during the eighth century A.D[3]. To the same period belongs a Buddhist Sanskrit inscription originally found at Vat Maheyong near Ligor and now preserved at Vat Boromanivet, Bangkok[4]. Next, in order of time, is a Bronze Buddha image, discovered in Takua Thung district and now preserved in the royal palace at Bangkok. The usual Pāli Buddhist formula 'Ye dhammā' etc. is engraved on it in characters of about the ninth century A.D[5]. An inscription of the same or the following century, found at Pasir Panjang in the Great Karimun islands, clearly refers to the Mahāyāna form of Buddhism[6]. The influence of Mahāyānism in Malay Peninsula is further proved by two miniature paintings of an image of Avalokiteśvara in a Buddhist Manuscript. According to

1. Cf. above, Bk. IV, Ch. I.
2. Cf. above Bk. I, Ch. V.
3. Cf. above, Bk. II, Ch. I.
4. B.C.A.I., 1910, p. 152. Fournerau-Le Siam Ancien, Vol. I. p. 125.
5. B.C.A.I, 1910, p. 151, f.n. 3.
6. The inscription written in North Indian character reads as follows :—"Mahāyānika Golayantritaśrī Gautama Śrīpada". Brandes translated it : "Illustrious feet of the illustrious Gautama, the Mahāyānist, who did possess an armillary sphere" (J. Mal. Br. R.A.S. 1932, p. 21). Kern translates it : "Illustrious foot of the Buddha who is identified with the Golayantra (the eternity) by the Mahāyānikas" (V.G. VII, pp. 139-142). Brandes referred the inscription to the period between 700 and 900 Śaka.

the short inscriptions below the figures they represent 'Avalokiteśvara of the Valavatī hill in Kaṭāha-dvīpa.' Evidently this particular image enjoyed some degree of celebrity in the Buddhist world[1].

More interesting and detailed evidence of the prevalence of the Mahāyāna form of Buddhism in the Peninsula is furnished by a large number of clay tablets. A number of them was discovered in Keddah in a cave nine feet below the floor. Kern read therein the Buddhist formula 'Ye dharmā' etc. in North-Indian Nāgarī characters of the tenth century A.D. . Another group of such tablets was found in two caves, Vat Han and Phu Khao Chai in the state of Trang[3]. Five of these have been described in detail by Mr. R. D. Banerji[4].

They usually bear impressions on one side only which consist of one or more figures, either of a Buddha or some other deity or deities of the Mahāyānist Buddhist Pantheon or a Caitya, accompanied by the Buddhist formula 'Ye dhammā hetu' etc. or some other suitable quotation from the Buddhist scriptures.

The characters of the inscriptions are, in the opinion of Mr. Banerji, North Indian Nāgarī (Western variety) of the eleventh century A.D. Mr. Banerji has very rightly pointed out that the figures on the tablets are decidedly Indian, offering a striking contrast in this respect with those obtained from Burma and other places in the Far East. Among them Mr. Banerji has identified, in addition to the Buddha figure, which usually occupies the centre, Lokeśvara, of the Hari-hari-hari-Vāhanodbhava type[5], Bodhisatva Avalokiteśvara,

1. Foucher—Etude, I, pp. 102, 194, pl. IV, fig. 4. There is also reference to another image at Kalaśavarapura (Ibid, pp. 89, 191, 209, pl. III, fig. 3. See Part I, pp. 75 ff.).

2. J. Str. Br. R.A.S. No. 39 (1903) pp. 205-6.

3. Man, 1902, No. 125 ; B.C.A.I. 1912, p. 172.

4. J.A.S.B ,N.S. Vol. III, 1908, pp. 459-470.

5. Foucher—Etude, II, p. 35.

surnamed Padmapāṇi (Amoghapāśa type), and Mahattarī[1] Tārā.

A third group of tablets has been discovered in Patani states and elsewhere on the east side of the main range which forms the backbone of the Malay Peninsula[2]. Mr. Banerji has described a single specimen of this group. It contains six figures, the central one being identified as Dhyānī Buddha Amogha-Siddhi. Mr. Banerji has pointed out that these short thickset figures form a good contrast to the tall graceful lithe figures of the Trang tablets. Mr. Lajonquière[3] has described thirteen of them found in Phu Khao Khrom (near Bandon) and three different types in Khao Khuha. All of them bear Buddhist figures. M. Coedès has devoted an interesting article to these Votive Tablets which are known as Brah Bimb, and referred them to the tenth century A.D. [4].

An account of the ancient religious edifices in Malay Peninsula, which we owe mainly to Lajonquière,[5] throws fresh light on the religious condition of that land. At Caiya or Jaya, on the northern side of the Bay of Bandon there is an old brick sanctuary, recently restored, which contains an image of Buddha. The decorative figures in different parts of the building are both Brāhmanical and Buddhist, and Lajonquière is of opinion that originally the principal image was either a Śiva or Viṣṇu, and Buddha was merely regarded as a secondary god in the Brāhmanical pantheon. In the same locality have been found two Buddha statues of

1. Ibid, p. 64. The figure on the tablet is strikingly similar to the figure No. 23 in Foucher—Etude, I.

2. J.A.S.B., N.S. Vol. III pp. 461, 469.

3. B.C.A.I., 1912 pp. 137 ff, 163-4.

4. Etudes Asiatiques Vol. I, pp. 145 ff. Specially cf. pp. 157-8 pll. VIII-IX.

5. B.C.A.I., 1909, pp. 227 ff. 1912, pp. 127 ff. Corrections in B.E.F.E.O., Vol. XXVII, pp. 501-2. Also cf. B.E.F.E.O., Vol. XXXI, pp. 373 ff., and I.L.A., Vol. IX, No I, pp. 18 ff.

twelfth and thirteenth centuries[1]. About fifty miles to the south are the ruins of the temple of Vieng Sra (or Sras) containing an image of Viṣṇu. Not very far are the ruins of a Vihāra with an image of Buddha. But by far the most magnificent remains of Buddhism are those of Nakhon Śrī Thammarāt (Ligor), where, according to a local tradition preserved by Chau Ju-kua, Buddha manifested himself after his *nirvāṇa.* Ruins of *stūpas* and temples, no less than fifty in number, the Vihāras, of some of which the colonnade alone exists, and the fine images of Buddha testify to the great hold of Buddhism in that region before the Thai conquest. Of these the *stūpa* called Vat Phra. That was the most magnificent and served as the model of similar constructions in the valley of the Menam. The main *stūpa*, about 80 yds. high, was surrounded by 171 statues of Buddha. The other sculptures represented various Buddhist legends such as his journey to heaven, cutting his hair etc.

There are also a few Brāhmanical temples in Nakhon Śrī Thammarat where 'Hindu ceremonial was performed until about thirty years ago, and which are still in the care of a small colony of Brāhmaṇas of Indian descent.' One of them, Ho Phra Isuon (wrongly called by Lajonquière Phra Narai) contains very fine bronze images of Brāhmanical gods[2]. Of them, a Gaṇeśa bears an inscription in South Indian character. The finest is perhaps that of Naṭarāja Śiva, of the South-Indian pattern.

Turning now to the Western Coast we find in Malacca itself an image of a Makara, which is no doubt the sole remnant of a Hindu temple in the neighbourhood. Further north, Takua Pa and its neighbourhood also furnish interesting relics of the old times to which reference has already been made above. In conclusion we may refer to an inscribed image of Buddha, of perhaps eleventh century A.D., found at Mergui,

---

1. The two Buddha images of Jaya are referred to by Coedes who has edited the inscriptions engraved on them (B.E.F.E.O. Vol. XVIII, No. 6. pp. 32-36.)

2. B.E.F.E.O. Vol. 31, p. 374. I.A.L. Vol. IX No. 1, p. 22.

in the extreme north of the Peninsula, if we take that geographical name in its more extended sense.

Lastly we must refer to a series of caves, converted into Buddhist sanctuaries, in the hill ranges *e.g.* at Phu Khao Lab Lo (Chumphon); Phu Khao Krom (Bandon), Mahacpoi, Deng, Pathavok and Mak in Nakhon Śrī Thammarāt; Ronphibun; Vat Han and Phu Khao Cai in Trang; Phukhao Othaln and Kuha in Pathalung, and at Yala near Patani. These contain numerous Buddha images, and some of them also votive tablets of clay to which reference has been made before.

The evidence furnished by the archaeological finds described above leaves no doubt that down to the time of the Thai conquest both Buddhism and Brāhmanical religion flourished in the northern and central part of the Malay Peninsula. There was no antagonism between the two religions which flourished side by side. The Buddhism was mostly Mahāyānist in character, but of Tāntrik development we have as yet no clear trace.

The prevalence of the Indian culture and religion is also indicated by the literature of the Malay Peninsula, to which reference will be made later. Many Hindu customs may still be traced among the Malays[1].

C. **Borneo** :—

The existence of both Buddhism and the Paurāṇik form of Hinduism in Borneo is indicated by the ruins of temples and detached images. Unfortunately, it is very difficult to assign even any approximate date to them. In addition to those referred to above, in Bk. I, Chap. VIII, we may enumerate the following[2] :—

I. **Western Borneo** :—

1. A stone Nandi form Pontianak, the chief town and administrative headquarter of Western Borneo.

---

1. Journal of the Federated Malay States Museums Vol IX, part I (Hindu survivals in Malay customs).

2. Unless otherwise stated, the list is based upon Encycl. Ned. Ind., Vol. III, p. 198.

2. Remains of temples at Sanggau and Monggo Batah on the two banks of the river Sekayam in which stone images of Gaṇesa, Nandi and Liṅga were found.

3. A golden Liṅga was found in the bed of the Kapuas river.

4. Ruins of temples at Ngeris on the Sekadan.

5. A stone Liṅga and Yoni at Nanga Seravi on the Melavi.

II. **Southern and Eastern Borneo :—**

1. A stone image of Durgā at Rantavan in Barabai.

2. A bronze Buddha figure at Serapat in Buntuk.

3 Remains of a brick temple at Margasari with stone images of Nandi and Liṅga.

4. A stone Nandi at Sebulu.

5. A Buddha image at Kota Bangun.

6. Ruins of temples in Bahu-Dajaks.

7. A stone Nandi and Liṅga at Rata on the upper Mahakam river.

In addition to the above there are ruins of temples in various localities, and the natives report finds of bronze images.

III. **Northern Borneo :—**

An image of Gaṇeśa has been discovered at Lembang, Sarawak. Krom refers it to sixth or seventh century A.D., but Sir John Marshall is of opinion that it belongs to about the thirteenth century A.D.[1].

In addition to these images the prevalence of Hindu religion among the natives of Borneo is proved by the fact that "the religious beliefs and superstitions of the Dyaks are clearly based upon Hindu mythology"[2].

D. **Other islands :—**

While detailed and definite evidences are available regarding the spread of political and cultural influences of the Hindus in respect of Malay Peninsula, Sumatra, Java (including

1. J. Str. Br. R.A.S. No. 85 (1922), p. 210.
2. Rum-Serams, p. 38.

Madura), Bali (including a portion of Lombok settled by the Balinese), and Borneo, it may be easily presumed that the influence, at any rate, of Hindu culture must have pervaded the whole of Malayasia. The political influence of the Indo-Javanese empire of Majapahit over numerous islands in the east must have facilitated such a transmission. But positive evidences are not altogether lacking in support of this presumption. These evidences may be classified as (1) archaeological, (2) philological, and (3) anthropological, and a brief reference to them will suffice to show that Hindu religion and culture had spread over the whole area, reaching Philipine Islands in the north and New Guinea in the east.

1. A golden image of Śiva was found at Amahai in Seram while stone images of Trimūrti and Kāla have been found at Tato in the Timor islands. Hindu remains have also been found in Bima (Timor group) itself as well as at the entrance of the Bay of Bima.[1]

2. The Language of Celebes indicates a strong influence of Hindu culture in that island. Not only theological terms, but also other words in Sanskrit, indicating progress in civilisation, are found in the language of the Bugis.[2] Besides, the Bugi alphabet as well as that of Makassar are both of Indian origin.[3] A Buddha image has been found in Celebes.

3. The influence of Hindu culture in Celebes is also supported by anthropological evidence. Even to-day traces of Hinduism are found in Bolaang Mogando in Northern Celebes. Traces of Śiva-worship have been found in South Celebes where the name Bhaṭāra-Guru is well-known in local legends and myths.[4]

Philological and anthropological evidences again indicate the prevalence of Hindu religion in Sumba islands where the

---

1. Encycl. Ned. Ind. Vol. III, p. 199.
2. Crawfurd—Dictionary, p. 91.
3. Encycl. Ned. Ind. Vol. I, p. 323.
4. Rum-Serams, pp. 40, 44, 51, 55.

people worship stones called 'Deva' (Sanskrit word for god).[1] The Sasaks of Lombok, too, professed Hinduism before their conversion to Islam.[2]

As regards the more distant regions, we have distinct testimony of European writers who had unique opportunities of making local investigations. Thus Crawfurd observes as follows in respect of the Philippine islands: "The religion of the Philippine islands was a very rude and very superficial Hinduism, engrafted on many local superstitions, and was evidently derived directly from the Malayan nations." Crawfurd also refers to a number of Sanskrit words in the most cultivated languages of the Philippinos.[3]

About Halmaheira or Jailolo in the Ternate group of islands, Horst remarks after referring to their three principal gods: "The Hindu origin of this somewhat debased form of Trimurti is too evident to require any detailed discussion."[4] The same author has also attempted to prove in a long dissertation that the religious ceremonies in the temples of New Guinea are reminiscences of the worship of Śiva.[5]

We may thus legitimately conclude that Hindu religion and culture spread to the furthest limits of Malayasia and perhaps even beyond.

In conclusion, we may refer to some of the religious practices and beliefs in Malayasia as recorded by the Chinese writers.

Chau Ju-kua relates that each succeeding king of San-fotsi, before ascending the throne, casts a golden image of Buddha to represent his person, and makes offerings of golden vessels to him. The same writer adds that when any one in that kingdom is dangerously ill he distributes his weight in silver among the poor of the land, as this is held to be a means of delaying death.[6] The History of the Sung Dynasty also

1. Crawfurd-Dictionary, p. 421.
2. Ibid, p. 221.
3. Ibid, p. 348.
4. Rum-Serams, p. 68.
5. Rum-Serams, Chs. III-IV.
6. p. 61.

says, in respect of Java, that when the men are ill, they take no medicine, but only pray to the gods and to Buddha.[1]

As might have been expected, some localities were associated with Gautama Buddha. Thus Chau Ju-kua says that there is a mountain in Ligor where Śākyamuni Buddha manifested himself after his *nirvāṇa*, the event being commemorated by a bronze elephant at this place.[2] The same writer adds that in Fo-lo-an there was a procession on Buddha's birthday with music and beating of cymbals.[3]

Religious sacrifices are also referred to. According to History of the Sui dynasty (581-671 A.D.) the people of Poli performed their sacrifices during the dark fortnight (lit. the time that there is no moon). They filled a bowl with wine and eatables and let it float away on the water. In the eleventh month they had a great sacrifice.[4] According to Tung Hsi Yang Kau (1618) the people of Brunei always sacrificed living animals in their temples[5]. We read in Hsing Cha Sheng-lan (1436) that the people of Pahang make human images of fragrant wood and kill people in order to make a sacrifice of the blood, when they pray for luck or try to ward off evil. Groeneveldt remarks on this passage that the worship of Śiva or Kālī, in its worst form, existed in Pahang[6]. But the rites may also refer to Tāntrik practices, such as we have described in the case of Ādityavarman.

1. Groeneveldt—Notes, p. 17.
2. p. 57.
3. p. 69.
4. Groeneveldt—Notes, p. 83.
5. Ibid, pp. VIII, 102.
6. Ibid, p. 136, and f.n. (3).

APPENDIX

Religious Literature in Java

In order to properly understand the religion of a country it is necessary to have an idea of the texts on which it was based, and by which it was inspired, guided, and controlled. The religious texts in Java, from the very nature of the case, must have consisted primarily of (i) Sanskrit texts, imported from India or composed in the island, (ii) the Old-Javanese translations or adaptations of such texts, and (iii) independent Old-Javanese works.

We have a few texts belonging to each class and have already referred to some of them in course of the above discussion. We give below a short account of the more important ones among the rest. It is to be understood, however, that some books of class iii may really belong to class ii, for they may be really translations of some Sanskrit texts, yet untraced, and not independent works as they are now supposed to be.

I. Sanskrit Texts

It is quite clear from references in literature and inscriptions that Sanskrit literature was highly cultivated in Java and Bali, and that a very large number of Sanskrit texts, mostly imported from India, existed in these islands. With the loss of contact with India and the gradual passing away of knowledge of Sanskrit, these texts have almost entirely disappeared, and only a very small number of short doctrinal texts have survived on account of religious exigencies. It is curious to note that although even the priests of Bali do not understand a word of Sanskrit, and have not even heard the name of India, they still recite the Sanskrit *mantras* in their daily rituals and ceremonies. The few Sanskrit texts that we find to-day in Bali no doubt owe their existence to this fact alone, and cannot give us any adequate idea of the vast Sanskrit literature that must once have formed favourite subject of study among the people. We give below a short account of these texts on the authority of S. Lévi who has recently published them[1].

I. Vedas. Frequent reference is made in the Javanese records to the four Vedas, and proficiency therein was greatly prized. High hopes were therefore raised when Friederich announced the existence of fragments of all the four Vedas in Bali. A controversy has been going on since then regarding the genuineness of these Vedas. The matter may now be said to be set at rest by the researches of S. Lévi. He has shown that the text known as 'Caturveda' in Bali is no other than the Nārāyaṇātharvaśirṣopaniṣad. "What the pedaṇḍas mean when speaking of the four Vedas is only the four sections of the Upaniṣad respectively known as the 'heads' (Śiras) of the Ṛg, Yajus, Sāma, and Atharva Veda[2]." The text of this Upaniṣad, as current in Bali, has been published by S. Lévi along with the Indian original[3].

II. The second text noted by S. Lévi is known as Veda-parikrama-sāra-saṁhitā-kiraṇa[4]. It gives an account of the daily worship, which we have described above. It contains the Sanskrit *mantras*, with directions for the occasion of, and the appropriate rituals and ceremonies accompanying their use. Specimens of these *mantras* have been quoted on pp. 107 ff. above.

III. The Stotras (or Stavas) form the next important texts[5]. These are 'regular parts of the ritual' and are addressed not only to principal deities, Śiva, Viṣṇu, Buddha, Sūrya, Vāyu, Varuṇa, and Yama, but also to various minor Brāhmanical and Buddhist gods such as Umā, Gaṅgā, Gaṇapati, Soma, Pṛthvī (Earth), Rabi, Vāsuki, Śrī and Sarasvatī. There are also Stotras for the Pitṛs (manes), the syllable oṁ etc.

---

1. Lévi—Texts.
2. Ibid, p. XV.
3. Ibid, pp. 3-6.
4. Ibid, pp. XVIII-XXI, 7-32.
5. Ibid, pp. XXI-XXIX, 35-70.

The original Sanskrit texts of some of these have been traced, and others may be found in course of time. The possibility of some being composed in Java or Bali cannot be altogether excluded. Some of these stotras are very beautiful, and, as Lévi remarks, 'deserve to be classic, even in India.'

IV. Buddhaveda.[1] This is the Buddhist counterpart of the Brāhmanical Veda and contains a full account of the daily worship of the Buddhist priest. It includes many pieces well-known in Nepal and elsewhere. According to Lévi "the verses and *mantras* are clearly derived from some Tantra, probably Śaiva Tantra."

V. In addition to the above, there are scattered verses of moral or semi-religious purport as well as *mantras* for the consecration of sword, ships, houses, *etc.* There is, for example, the verse "Oṁ Ahalyā Draupadī Sītā Dārā [for Tārā] Mandodharī tata pañcakanyā smare nityam," a slightly corrupted form of the well-known Sanskrit verse which is known in every Hindu household in India.[2] The following poem, known as Daśaśīla[3], which admirably sums up the Hindu ideal of life, may form an apt conclusion of this section.

आनृशंस्यं क्षमा सत्यमहिंसा दम आर्जवम् ।
प्रीतिः प्रसादो माधुर्यं मार्दवं च यमा दश ॥

II. Old-Javanese with Sanskrit original

1. Bhuvana-Kośa.[4] It appears to be an Old-Javanese translation of a Sanskrit work, the Sanskrit verses being followed by translation in Old-Javanese prose. It is called Jñāna-Siddhānta-Śāstram and is described as Parama-rahasya or an esoteric text.

1. Ibid, pp. XXIX-XXXI, 73-84.
2. Cat. I, Vol. II, pp. 321-384.
3. Lévi-Texts, p. 109.
4. Goris, pp. 75, 94-98 ; Cat. 1. Vol. II. p. 261.

The framework of the text is formed by the dialogue between Śiva and Muni Bhārgava about 'Nirvāṇa' or final emancipation. It deals with cosmogony and metaphysics, betraying clear influences of the Purāṇas, specially Agni-purāṇa, in the case of the former, and Vedānta philosophy in the case of the latter. It also deals with the twelve *tattvas*, after the Sāṁkhya and the Yoga philosophy of India, and a great part of it is devoted to Tāntrik mysticism.

The ultimate reality is called Parama Brahma, Mahāsūkṣma, and Śānta-parama-nirmala. The Mahāyogī, or great ascetic, burns his sins by his asceticism as fire burns a tree, and then attains *nirvāṇa* by the realisation that his soul is identical with Śiva. This is undoubtedly a Vedāntic doctrine.

2. Bhuvana-Saṁkṣepa[1]—It is an Old-Javanese translation of a Sanskrit work with a number of the original Sanskrit ślokas interspersed in the text.

It lays down the Paramatattva or the great mystery of Śūnyavāda *i.e.* the great void. Mokṣa or final emancipation consists in a negation of all things and ideas. Thus we read :—

न भूमिर्न जलम् व्यापि: न तेजो न च मारुत: ।
न सूर्यचन्द्र सर्वेपि नाकाशं नान्तरं भवेत् ॥
न बुद्धि: न मनंकार: न विष्णु न ब्रह्म ईश्वरं ।
न निष्टे न मध्योत्तम: न शिव देवता पुन: ॥

Then follows the Bhuvana-Saṁkṣepa proper, in the form of instructions given by Śiva to Umā and Kumāra. The ultimate reality is described as Niṣkala from which originated *mātra*, *nādānta*, *nāda*, *vindu*, *candra*, *viśva*, *tryakṣara*, *Brahma* etc. Then follows an account of the Sapta-dvīpa (seven continents), *Sapta-parvata* (seven mountain ranges), *Sapta Samudra* (seven seas), and *Saptatīrtha* (seven sacred rivers).

---

1. Goris, pp. 94-98 ; Cat. I. Vol. II, p. 261-3.

We are next told that the fundamental elements of the body correspond to the pañca-mahā-bhūta (flesh=earth, blood=water etc.). Then the five prāṇas (prāṇa, apāna, samāna, udāna, vyāna) are located in different parts of the body. Then the three *tattvas* (ahaṁkāra, mana and buddhi) are identified with Brahmā, Viṣṇu and Śiva, and the three *guṇas* (sattva, rajas and tama) with three aspects of Śiva *viz*: Mahādeva, Rudra and Śaṁkara.

3. Tattva Sang Hyang Mahājñāna[1]—It is a philosophical dissertation between Bhaṭāra Guru (Śiva) and Kumāra, written in Sanskrit verses followed by Old-Javanese translation and commentary. One of its verses runs as follows :—

आप्सु दैवो द्विजातीनां ऋषीनां दिवि दैवत: ।
शिलाकाष्ठेषु लोकानां मुनीनां आत्म दैवत: ॥

The Old-Javanese commentary says that it describes the *adhikāra* (proper sphere of the religious activity) of the different groups. The Brāhmanas perform rituals and ceremony in the holy water, the ṛṣis look to the gods of heaven, and the munis or ascetics look to the *ātmā* or realisation of the soul. The common people, on the other hand, believes in stone and streams and in images and temples.

4. Bṛhaspati-tattva[2]—It is an Old-Javanese work interspersed with Sanskrit ślokas. It enumerates the different religious sects and then discusses Karma-Vaśana (actions in this life and their consequences hereafter), and refers to the famous parable of the blind men and the elephant to indicate the incomplete nature of the different conceptions about God. It then refers to a number of philosophical doctrines *viz*: the *tattvas* (*pradhāna, triguṇa, buddhi, ahaṁkāra, indriya, pañca-mahābhūta*); *aṣṭeśrarya* (*aṇimā* etc. or *dharma, jñāna*, etc.); the *tripramāṇa* (*pratyakṣa, anumāna*, and *āgama*);

---

1. Goris, pp. 98-101 ; Cat. 1. Vol. II, pp. 272-3.
2. Goris, pp. 101-107.

the *aṣṭasiddhi* (*dāna*, *adhyayana*, *śabda*, *tarka*, *sohṛdam* with the three *adhyātmika siddhi viz.*, *adhyātmika*, *adiderika*, and *adibhotika duḥka*); the *pañca-tanmātra*, the *pañca-mahā-bhūta*, the *ṣaḍrasa* etc., etc.

III. Independent Old-Javanese works

5. Sapta-bhuvana[1]—This book gives a mystic interpretation of a number of categories containing seven elements, *e.g.*, the *sapta-giri* (seven mountains) in the east, the *saptāgni* (seven fires) in the south, the *saptauṁkāra* (*a*, *u*, *m*, *oṁ*, *nāda*, *vindu* and *ardhacandra*) in the west, the Sapta Veda (seven Vedas—details not given) in the north, the *saptaloka* (seven heavens) above, and *sapta-pātāla* (seven hells) below. It identifies the *navagraha* (nine planets), the *sapta-dvīpa*, and *sapta-samudra*, with the different parts or elements of human body, the eight mountain-ranges with the tattvas, etc.

6. Ṛṣiśāsana[2]. It begins with a verse about Manu, the first king, who gave Śivaśāsana to the Śaivas. It then refers to the four kinds of Śāsana, *viz*: (1) Dharmaśāsana; (2) Rājaśāsana for kings *e.g.* Sara-samuccaya, Manuhagamanava; (3) Devaśāsana for religious sects; and (4) Ṛṣiśāsana for Yogīśvaras. It then deals in detail with the Yogīśvaras specially dwelling upon their rights over the freehold property enjoyed by them.

7. Devaśāsana[3]. It also deals with the position of the Yogīśvara or Devaguru, the head of a Dharma or maṇḍala. He enjoyed large power and privileges and was under the patronage of the king, and often related to him. The Devagurus were the same as Bhujanggas or the spiritual leaders referred to in Nag. Kr.

---

1. Goris, pp. 108-115; Cat. 1, Vol. II, p. 275.
2. Tantu, pp. 299-300.
3. Tantu, pp. 289-291.

8. Rājpatiguṇḍala[1], attributed to king Kṛtanagara, resembles Devaśāsana in its contents and deals with Yogīśvaras and Bikus (both male and female) and the different sects.

9. Śivaśāsana[2]. It deals in detail with the privileges of spiritual leaders, specially those in respect of the sovereign.

10. Vratiśāsana[3]. It deals in detail with the rules and regulations to be observed by a religious disciple. His food, dress, rules of purity, moral conduct, religious rituals, *etc.* all come within the purview of this work, and follow on the whole the Indian ideal.

11. Śilakrama[4]. It deals in detail with the duties of a Śiṣya (disciple) towards his *guru* (preceptor).

12. Wit ing Tapabrata[5], describes the different kinds of asceticism.

13-14. Nitibrata and Pabratan[6] deal with different kinds of Bratas or religious vows and ceremonies.

15. Pratasti Bhuvana[7]. It begins with a description of the four Yugas—Kṛta, Tretā, Dvāpara, and Kali—giving names of the prominent kings, sacred books, and a general description of the people in each. Among the kings of Kaliyuga it mentions several names which may be easily identified with well-known kings of Java. The Linggapurāṇa is placed in Dvāpara, while Kuṭamanava and Samūrccaya, together with Manūḥ-śāśana and Ṛṣi-śāśana are mentioned in respect of Kaliyuga. Origin and privileges of maṇḍalas, the high position of Śiva-maṇḍala and the duties and privileges of Biku are described in detail.

1. Tantu, pp. 291-294.
2. Tantu, pp. 300-302.
3. Tantu, pp. 295-299.
4. Tantu, pp. 302-3.
5. Cat. 1, Vol. II, pp. 284-5.
6. Cat. 1, Vol. II, pp. 266-269.
7. Tantu, pp. 294-295.

16. Kuñjarakarṇa[1] is a Mahāyānist work in which the philosophy and principles of that sect are expounded in the shape of a story. Yakṣa Kuñjarakarṇa receives religious instructions from Dhyānī-Buddha Vairocana, and, at his command, goes to the hell or abode of Yama, not only to witness the miseries entailed by sin, but also to take lessons from Yama. On his return Vairocana again taught him religious doctrines and philosophy.

The book also contains the story of Pūrṇavijaya, a Vidyādhara and a friend of Kuñjarakarṇa. The latter learned, while in hell, that Pūrṇavijaya was destined to suffer great miseries in hell on account of his many sins. On his advice Pūrṇavijaya, too, became a disciple of Vairocana, and got religious instructions from him. Accordingly when he went to hell and was going to be thrown into a red-hot pan on fire, the firepit disappeared and a Kalpataru appeared in its place. He was then set free and came back to the world. Then the two friends Kuñjarakarṇa and Pūrṇavijaya went to Mahāmeru and practised hard austerities for twelve years. As a result of this they became Siddhas and went to heaven.

The text lays stress on the immortality of the soul, the transmigration, the effect of *karma* or action upon the next birth, and the penance and austerities as a mode of self-purification. The Mahāyāna doctrine pervades the entire work.

Kern, who translated the text, refers it to the twelfth century A.D., but Juynboll places it two centuries later.[2]

17. The superiority of Buddhism is the subject-matter of another Old-Javanese work, Singha Langghyāla[3] which belongs to the same period as Kuñjarakarṇa. It describes how

---

1. Edited and translated by Kern (V.G. Vol. X). On the origin and spread of the Buddhist story all over the world, cf. T.B.G. Vol. 71 (1931), pp. 107-132.

2. B.K.I. Vol. 72, pp. 401. ff.

3. Cat. 1, Vol. II. pp. 169-70.

Cāya-puruṣa, the Śaiva king of Śvetanadipura, undertook an expedition against Kāmarūpiṇī the Buddhist queen of Singha Langghyāla, but failed. His brother Lakṣmīkiraṇa, a Vaiṣṇava, then made a similar attempt, but fared no better. Rati and the Vidyādharīs came to the help of the Buddhist queen against the joint forces of the two brothers. At last Śiva intervened. The text seems to be an allegorical representation of the rivalry between the three religious sects and the innate supremacy of the Buddhists.

18. Putrupasaji.[1] It deals with worship of different gods and describes the benefit accruing from the eating of all kinds of animals,—fish, birds, fourfooted animals, insects etc. It also gives a list of animals that men should not eat and also a list of mountains which should be visited by men desirous of going to heaven.

19. Raṇayajña.[2] It describes the different hells to which men go after death according as they are killed by different weapons. The battlefield is compared to a sacrifice (hence the name of the book), the body and the blood *etc.* correspon-ding to the fire-wood, oil, *etc.*

---

1. Cat. I, Vol. II. pp. 270-271.
2. Cat. I. Vol. II, pp. 271-272.

Book VI

ART IN SUVARNADVIPA

BOOK VI

Chapter I

THE ARCHITECTURE OF CENTRAL JAVA.

§1. General Classification.

Apart from the pre-historic artifacts described above in Bk. I Ch. III, the earliest monuments in Java belong to its central region and may be referred to the period during which that region played the supreme political rôle in the island. It would be wrong to infer from this fact that art did not develop in the earlier Hindu colony of Western Java over which Pūrṇavarman ruled nearly three centuries before. As regards Eastern Java, we have positive evidence that it possessed temples which were older than those of Central Java.[1] But the monuments of Western Java, even if there were any, have vanished altogether, without leaving any trace behind, while nearly all the existing temples of Eastern Java belong to a much later period. The disappearance of these old monuments may be partly accounted for by supposing that they were built of wood or other perishable materials. As regards Eastern Java, which was in continued occupation for nearly five hundred years after the fall of Central Java, the older structures were possibly replaced in many cases by later buildings. In any case, the fact remains that so far as the actual remains go, the earliest monuments in Java belong to the Central region and do not carry us further back than perhaps eighth century A.D.

1. For example, the construction of a temple of Agastya is referred to in the Dinaya inscription, dated A.D. 760. Cf. Part I, p. 248, fn. 3.

This fact is extremely unfortunate, as it hides from our view the early and formative stage of that Indo-Javanese art of which we find the fullest development in the classical monuments of Central Java. At the time when these were erected, more than four centuries had elapsed since the first Indian colonists had settled in Java. During this long period, the principles of Indian art which these colonists had introduced in their new home must have taken deep root in the soil, and undergone process of evolution. How far these modifications are inevitable consequences of normal growth amid strange surroundings, and how far they are to be attributed to a deliberate working of local factors, it is at present impossible to say. But certain it is that when this developed form of art first comes into our view, it can hardly be regarded as purely Indian. Although its essential characteristics are unmistakably Indian, it has already developed into a type which neither actually exists nor probably ever existed in India. In other words, we come across a full-fledged Indo-Javanese art, and that at its very best.

The history of this Indo-Javanese art is thus written in decay,—to quote a familiar phrase of Fergusson. It may be conveniently divided into two broad periods. First the Central-Javanese period ranging from 700 to 900 A.D., and secondly, the East-Javanese period from 1200 to 1500 A.D. The art of each of these periods may again be sub-divided, on sectarian, chronological or regional basis, though none of these principles is entirely satisfactory. For the sake of convenience of treatment we shall study it under the following scheme, which is more or less a combination of all the three.

I. Central Java.

(a) Hindu monuments in Dieng Plateau and its neighbourhood.

(b) Buddhist monuments in the Prambanan Valley and Kedu plain.

(c) Hindu monuments in the Prambanan valley.

(d) Monuments in other localities.

II. Eastern Java.

(a) Early Monuments.
(b) Monuments of the Singhasāri period.
(c) Monuments of the Majapahit period.
(d) Post-Majapahit period.

III. Sculpture of Central Java.

IV. Sculpture of Eastern Java.

§2. General Plan

The Indo-Javanese art, like its parent art in India, may be described as the hand-maid of religion. All the monuments of this art, so far discovered, are religious structures, and religion has provided its sole aim and inspiration from beginning to end.

The religious structures in Java are known by the general appellation Caṇḍi. The word originally denoted any monument over the ashes of the dead, ranging from a single stone column to a complete structure. Krom suggests that the word is derived from Caṇḍikā, a name of the goddess Durgā, who is specially associated with the dead and whose temple is invariably present in a Balinese cremation ground even to-day. Howsoever that may be, it is evident that the word Caṇḍi gradually came to denote a temple in cremation ground, and ultimately any temple.[1]

Before describing the individual temples in Central Java, it will be convenient to begin with a general description of the essential features of its temple-architecture. Any deviations from this general plan will be noted in the description of the particular temple where they occur.

---

1. Krom—Kunst, Vol. I, pp. 142-3. Stutterheim (Djawa, 1927, p. 188) thinks that 'Caṇḍi' in the sense of a general temple is a wrong use of the term by modern archaeologists.

The Javanese temple of the standard type may be divided into three parts as follows

(1) Basement ;

(2) Main Body (referred to sometimes as Body)

(3) Roof.

The basement, as well as the main body of the temple, consists, like the classic entablature, of three distinct parts which we may designate as the base, wall (the central vertical part), and cornice (corresponding to Greek architrave, frieze and cornice). The base and the cornice have also the same essential features in the basement and in the main body of the temple.

I. Basement. The base consists of a flat plinth supporting a bell-shaped ogee- and a roll-moulding, though occasionally one or more string-courses (fillets or mouldings) are added to give the whole thing a complex character.

The cornice, consisting of one or more projecting string-courses or mouldings, is enriched with ante-fix ornaments which serve to distinguish the different parts and emphasise the corners. Just below the cornice is a frieze-band usually enriched with ornaments.

The walls of the basement are usually divided into panels (sometimes sunken) by pilasters, and often richly ornamented with figure-sculpture, scroll-work etc.

II. Main Body. The main body of the temple is usually square (sometimes rectangular) on plan with a porch or vestibule in front and projections on all other sides. The vestibule leads to the only entrance of the temple which has no other opening.

The walls on three other sides are divided into panels as in the case of the basement, though sometimes there is a projecting niche in the centre of each. As already stated, the walls stand on a base and support a cornice both of which have the same features as those of the basement. The walls of the main body of the temple are, of course, naturally of greater height in proportion to the base and cornice than is the case with the basement.

III. The Roof. The roof consists of a series of gradually diminishing storeys, each repeating on a minor scale the general plan of the temple itself, *viz.*, a cubic structure with four niches on four sides. To the four corners are four diminutive turrets which again are miniature reproductions of the temple.

In the cases of some great structures, the upper stages of the roof are made octagonal, instead of rectangular, in order to relieve the monotony. The roof was crowned by an ornament, the exact nature of which is uncertain, as no single specimen has been discovered *in situ*. Judging from the fragments and also from the corner turrets, it appears to have been of the shape of a cushion with a high and pointed finial. Sometimes the cushion supported a bell-shaped *stūpa* ending in a pinnacle.

The interior of the temple is a plain square chamber. Its walls, rising vertically up to a certain height, support a series of horizontal courses of stone which, projecting one in front of the other, form an inverted pyramid of steps, and is terminated by a high and pointed hollow cone,—the whole corresponding to the storied pyramidal roof outside. Stucco or plaster work is found in some temples. In some cases it was part of the original plan, but in others it is a later addition. Sometimes even colour or paint was used. The decorative ornaments which consisted of well-known Indian motives such as rosette, garland, floral scroll, arabesque, various naturalistic designs and floral or geometrical patterns will be described in connection with individual temples. It may be noted here that all these patterns are derived from India and there is no trace of local flora or fauna. One very frequently occurring motive, however, deserves particular notice. The Dutch archaeologists describe it as Kāla-Makara. It really consists of two separate motives Kāla and Makara though sometimes they are found united to form a single combined motive. The Kāla-head (also called Banaspati) is shaped like the head of a monster, and is taken to be an effigy of the terrible god Kāla. But it is really derived from the Indian motive of lion's head and Coomaraswamy rightly describes it as a grotesque Kirttimukha[1]. It is a conventional lion's head with protruding eyes, broad nose, thick upper lip with two big projecting teeth on two sides. The Makara is a favourite motive of ancient Indian art. There are differences of opinion regarding its original significance. According to Vogel, it was originally a representation of crocodile. On account of a strange combination of elephantine and fish-like properties Grunwedel describes it as a 'sea-elephant'[2]. In Java the Makara has the body of a fish and the head of an elephant, and is often developed into a floriated ornament.

The Kāla-head is usually placed right over a gateway, or above a niche, in the centre of the enclosing arch, ending in a Makara-head at its two ends. Makara-heads are also placed at the foot of door-jambs. These motives are also found at the top of the staircase and various other parts of the building. In short, the Kālā-Makara motive, combined, or separated into two elements, occurs almost everywhere, and is one of the most favourite decorative devices of Indo-Javanese art. Though its elements are originally derived from India, it is, according to vogel, "the outcome of an indigenous combination and development[3]," and should be regarded as Indo-Javanese rather than Indian. This may be doubted, as the complete design also occurs in India[4].

The decorative reliefs and sculptures in Central-Javanese temples were always restrained and in perfect correlation with the general architectural plan. They were designed to

1. Krom—Kunst, Vol. I, p. 162; Indian Art, pp. 60-61; Coomaraswamy, pp. 202-3.

2. Indian Art, pp. 60-61; Grunwedel—Buddhist Art, p. 57. Stutterheim regards Makara as a zodiac sign (I. A. L. Vol. III, pp. 27 ff.)

3. Indian Art, p. 62.

4. J. G. I. S., Vol. II, pp. 38 ff.

accentuate and emphasise the outline, rather than overshadow it by exuberance, or distort it by wrongly conceived ornamental patterns.

Two peculiarities of Javanese temples may be noted here. In the first place, columns and pillars are wholly lacking. Secondly, the arches are all constructed on horizontal principle, as in ancient India, and the true or radiating arches are conspicuous by their absence.

These two peculiarities made it impossible for the Indo-Javanese architects to cover large spaces by means of big arches and domes. Hence they could not plan any temple on a very big scale. They sought to make up for this deficiency, either by developing the projecting bays on the three sides into separate side-chapels, with separate roofs, or by surrounding one main temple by a large number of subsidiary temples, so as to give a monumental or colossal character to the whole structure.

Individual temples or groups of temples were surrounded by an enclosing wall. It is also likely that the gate of this enclosure was covered by a structure like south-Indian Gopuram. No trace of such a structure has, however, been found in Central Java. Its existence in Eastern Java, in the later period, is proved by actual remains and literary descriptions, and it may be presumed that this element of architecture was also taken from Central Java.

The stone used for the temples is usually trachyte, but a softer kind of sandstone or marlstone has been used in Lara-Jonggrang, Plaosan, and Sajivan temples. Mortar was used in the upper part of the temples, though not in the base, where the shaped and dressed stones were simply set side by side and kept in their position by various devices of connecting-stones.

§3. Dieng Temples

It is generally assumed by the Dutch archæologists that the groups of temples on the Dieng plateau are the oldest temples now extant in Central Java.[1] The arguments which may be brought forward in support of this view are based, in the first place, on a number of inscribed stones which formed part of the temples, and an inscribed gold plate which belonged to the treasury of a temple; and secondly, on the architectural motives of decoration. The alphabets of the incriptions are similar to what we find on one bearing a date 731 (=809 A.D.). The decorative motives also belong to the earliest phase of Indo-Javanese art. On these grounds the temple-groups of Dieng are regarded as contemporaneous with, if not earlier than the Caṇḍi Kalasan which was built in 778 A.D. It must be admitted, however, that these arguments cannot be regarded as conclusive.

The plateau of Dieng, called in old time Dihyang, has a height of about 6500 ft. and is surrounded by hills on almost all sides. About the centre of this plateau, standing in a line north to south, are four temples called Caṇḍi Arjuna, Caṇḍi Srikaṇḍi, Caṇḍi Puntadeva, and Caṇḍi Sembadra, all facing west, while there is a fifth, Caṇḍi Semar, which lies opposite to Caṇḍi Arjuna, and faces east. That these five temples belonged to the same group is indicated by the fact that they were all surrounded by one enclosing wall.

There are three other isolated temples on the same plateau, called Caṇḍi Dvaravati, Caṇḍi Gaṭotkaca and Caṇḍi Bima. In addition to the remains of other temples, Caṇḍi Parikesit, Caṇḍi Nga-Kula Sadevo, there is a long underground tunnel, which served as a drain-pipe of the Arjuna group of temples.

The names of five of these temples are borrowed from the heroes and heroines of the Mahābhārata, Puntadeva, being a Javanese name for Yudhiṣṭhira. These names have, of course, been given in later times, and although they indicate the

---

1. But vogel holds a different view; cf. Indian Art, p. 68. For a description of the Dieng temples, cf. Krom—Kunst, I, pp. 165-204. Plates 1-4.

popularity of the great Epic, they do not throw any light on the original nature of these temples, any more than do the similar modern names of the temples of Māmallapuram.[1]

The Dieng temples, generally speaking, belong to the standard type described above. The ornament was very restricted and simple, being composed mostly of plain courses, pilasters, and ogee mouldings. The projections on three sides contained niches. The lotus-cushions in these niches with holes in the centre prove that they once supported images of gods which have now disappeared. These niches, the door of the vestibule leading to the temple, and niches on two sides of it (where they occur) on the front wall of the temple, were all crowned by Kāla-Makara ornament.

The Caṇḍi Puntadeva has finer decoration than the rest. The ante-fix ornaments are more profusely used both in the basement and the main body of the temple. The niche in the centre of each of the three walls covers its entire length and has an ornamental base and border-frame. At about two-thirds of its height, there is a sort of upper niche, whose decorated base with an ante-fix, ogee mouldings, and cushion cover the entire upper part. The walls are enriched with ornamented corner-posts and decorated pilasters. The first or the lowest stage of the roof, which alone is preserved, almost exactly repeats the main features of the temple and is adorned with corner towers. There are two flights of steps, each enclosed between stone curbs with volute ends. One of them leads to the top of the basement and the other continues the ascent up to the door of the vestibule. The vestibule repeats the features of the main temple on a smaller scale, but has a separate and lower roof composed of two slanting panels from a central rib, and having, of course, no stages above.

1. Failure to recognise this obvious point has led Mr. Havell to the view that the temples were dedicated to the Pāṇḍava heroes, and he has accordingly interpreted the human heads in Caṇḍi Bima as those of the great hero Bhima. This is, of course, quite wrong. cf. Vogel in J. R. A. S., 1917, pp. 371-376.

Among the Dieng temples Caṇḍi Bima (Pl. 1, Fig. 1) or Vṛkodara deserves more particular notice as it differs in many respects from the standard type. The ground plan is almost square, the front and back sides being 16 and the other two sides about 14 ft. in length. There are projections in the centre of the three side-walls while the vestibule is fairly large, with a projection of about 6½ ft. and width of about 11½ ft.

The niche, on one side, is provided with Kāla-Makara ornament, and the side-posts of all the niches are ornamented; but otherwise, the flat walls of the three sides are severely plain. The cornice rests on a double-ogee moulding, the upper of which is teethed or indented with small beam-ends, while below it, and just above the flat panels, there is a projecting course decorated with garland motive.

The special characteristic of the temple, however, lies in its roof. The first stage of the roof is a repetition of the base-mouldings, the upper ogee moulding being decorated with double lotus-petal motive. Above the cornice of this is a plain ogee moulding, a low flat band, and an upper ogee decorated with double lotus-petal. We have thus a repetition of the main features of the first stage though on a very small scale.

The second stage of the roof which springs up immediately above these, is characterised by a double row of three arched niches on each side, one such double row being on the projection, and one on each side of it. The niches on the side also occupy the corner, thus leaving very little of the plain part of the roof exposed. The four niches in each corner may thus be viewed as a whole as forming a corner turret, and it is surmounted by a very short round column ending in two round courses. From the lower of these hangs a garland, and the upper supports a lotus cushion.

The third stage of the roof is similar to the first stage, though the upper ogee moulding has got a single, not double lotus-petal, with a garland hanging beneath. But the most striking difference consists in a double row of niches on the projections which, together with the two niches of the second stage and those of the upper one, form a successive series of niches vertically placed one above another.

The fourth stage was a repetition of the second stage with slight modifications. The upper part of the roof has completely disappeared.

The arched niches are of horse-shoe pattern and resemble the caitya-windows of India. They have plain borders and contain human heads or rather busts in high relief (Pl. XII, Fig. 2) or some ornamental motives.

The general appearance of the roof is very different from the normal type, and may be regarded as unique.

Dr. Coomaraswamy takes the corner turrets to be three-quarter ribbed *āmalakas* and suggests that a complete *āmalaka* crowned the summit. In his opinion 'the roof structure corresponds exactly with that of a typical Indo-Aryan Śikhara, such as that of the Paraśurāmeśvara at Bhuvaneśvar.'[1] It is difficult to subscribe to this view, at least without a great deal of reserve. As he himself admits, the roof "consists of diminishing horizontal stages" and thus preserves the essential features of Dieng Temples and Dravidian style.

The vestibule repeats the features of the main building on a small scale. It had a separate roof with two stages corresponding generally to the first two stages of the roof of the main building. The top of this roof covered from view only the first stage of the main roof. The doorway in front of the vestibule cuts through the mouldings of its basement and reaches down to the plinth.

It is not necessary to give a detailed description of the other temples of Dieng. Although they are comparatively small in dimensions, their simple and clear outline, and restrained but well-conceived decorations endow them with a special importance. The sculptures are also characterised by a

1. Coomaraswamy, p. 202.

simplicity and vigour worthy of the temples which they adorned.[1] On the whole the art of Dieng is characterised by a sobriety and dignity which reminds us of the Indian temples of the Gupta period.

The images found in the plateau of Dieng belong exclusively to the Brāhmanical pantheon. We have images of Śiva, Durgā, Gaṇeśa, Brahmā and Viṣṇu. The temples were thus Brāhmanical, and to judge from the extant remains, mainly of Śaivite character. The representation of the three chief gods with their riders is very important from iconographical point of view. For the riders have all human bodies, and only the head of a bull or a swan, or the beak of a bird on the human body indicates the riders of Śiva, Brahmā and Viṣṇu.

A general view of the architectural remains of Dieng indicates that it was a holy place of pilgrimage rather than a town with a considerable number of settled population. Beyond the normal requirements for priests and servants of the temples and the occasional rush of pilgrims, there are no vestiges of a large number of dwelling houses, and there is hardly any space for the accommodation of a large population. The Dieng or Dihyang, to call it by its old name, thus resembled the Jaina City of Temples in India, such as Śatruñjaya or Palitānā. We learn from the Chinese accounts that the king of Java visited it once a year, and presumably the nobles and other classes of people made occasional pilgrimages to this holy place.

To the south and east of the Dieng Plateau we come across the ruins of a large number of ancient temples. To judge from a number of inscriptions scattered about in the neighbourhood, they belong probably to the middle of the ninth century A.D. The isolated remains also indicate that they were mainly Śaivite in character. These temples, built on the standard type, offer sometimes examples of exquisite decoration.

---

1. Detailed discussion of sculpture will be found in Chapter II.

Among these, Caṇḍi Pringapus[1] has been rendered famous by the enthusiastic description of Brandes. It is a small beautiful temple measuring about 16½ ft. by 15 ft. It is of the standard type save that the basement consists merely of a plinth and plain walls without any moulding, and that there are no projections on the three sides of the temple. The walls are, however, divided into three panels by pilasters, and the sculptures on these panels as well as those on the front constitute the excellence of the temple. Brandes has compared the decoration of this temple with that of Mendut and emphasised the fact that artistic principles of construction did not differ according to the sectarian character of the structures. In conclusion attention may be drawn to the repetition of cornices, an architectural peculiarity which played such a prominent part in later East-Javanese art.

Another interesting group of temples is that on Mount Ungaran known as Gedong-Sanga[2] which lies to the east of Dieng and south of Semarang. The name Gedong-Sanga means nine houses and no doubt refers to the nine groups of temples which are now found on two ranges of hills, separated by a deep ravine which to-day forms the boundary between Semarang and Kedu. It is a difficult question to decide whether all the temples belong to one series. The difficulty of communication between them, caused by the depth of the ravine, would, no doubt, incline us to regard them as two different groups. But the similarity of architecture is in favour of regarding them all as belonging to one and the same series. It is conceivable that in old times the communication was rendered easier by means of a sort of staircase which is now lost.

---

1. Krom—Kunst, Vol, I, pp. 210-215, Pl. V. Brandes—Oudheidkundig Rapport, 1903, p. 10.

2. Krom—Kunst, Vol I, pp. 224-239, Pll. 6-7. Detailed descriptions of the recent explorations are to be found in O. V. 1916, 1917 etc.

23

The temples of Gedong-Sanga are not arranged in a definite plan like those of Dieng, but lie scattered about on different plateaus without any symmetery of plan. They belong to the standard type and need not be described in detail. They were mostly Śaivite in character, but some were devoted to worship of Viṣṇu. Among the verious images found in these temples particular mention may be made of a new form of Durgā. Instead of standing she sits on the bull, and holds the Asura, not by the hair, but by the neck.

§4. Buddhist monuments in the Prambanan Valley

From the Dieng Plateau and its neighbourhood we come to the Prambanan valley[1] which forms the rich treasure-house of the products of the art of Central Java. It is dominated by a hill-range in the east and watered by the Opak river which runs across it from north to south, while a smaller river, Sarageḍug, runs south from the hill. The Prambanan valley proper lies to the north and west of the hill-range, along the Opak, while the Saragedug constitutes a separate valley named after it. These two valleys and the hill range itself contain a large number of Hindu and Buddhist temples belonging to different types and different periods.

The region stands on the border of the modern districts of Jogyakerta and Surakerta. It was a seat of one or more cities or capitals, and not merely a city of temples like Dieng.

Of the Buddhist temples in the Prambanan valley the famous Caṇḍi Kalasan[2] (Pl. II, Fig. 2) deserves to be mentioned first. An inscription dated 778 A.D.[3] informs us that the temple was built by a Śailendra king and dedicated to the Buddhist goddess Tārā. The image of Tārā which must have once occupied the shrine has now disappeared.

1. Krom-Kunst, Vol. I, pp. 240 ff, Pl. 9.
2. Krom—Kunst, I, pp. 257-264, Pll. 11-12.
3. See above, Bk. II, Chap. I.

The inscription also refers to the gift of the village Kalasa, a name preserved in modern Kalasan, a neighbouring village. Hence the temple is referred to as Caṇḍi Kalasan. As we can assign a fixed date to this structure, it forms one of the few definite landmarks in the history of Indo-Javanese architecture.

The basement of the temple, which is in a very damaged condition, offers the normal type *i.e.* square in shape with projections on four sides. The temple stands on this basement leaving a margin on all sides, about 15 ft. wide, which obviously served as a processional path. The little that is left of the base of the temple shows that it conformed to the normal type and its central vertical part was decorated.

The main body of the temple is also square on plan with projections on four sides. These are formed into four chapels accessible by a double flight of stairways, one from the ground to the top of the basement, and another from the basement-terrace to the door of the chapel itself. The chapel on the eastern side is really an ante-chamber leading to the main cella in the centre, but the other three chapels do not communicate with it, and are really subsidiary and independent shrines.

The door of the chapel forms the most striking feature of each of the side-walls. A fantastic Kāla-head of colossal proportions forms the crowning piece of the decoration above it, and extends over the entire upper part of the wall up to the point where the roof begins. The hair of the monster is conventionally arranged in various curls in the shape of a pyramid. From the terrible mouth of the monster hang down five lotus-flowers, and out of its two corners appear two lions from which issue two flowering branches ending in the usual Makara on the two sides of the doorway.

The actual door-opening is set in a sort of niche. The two pilasters of the niche are crowned by two Gaṇa figures who support with their hands a beautiful framework above the double-curved arch of the niche. This entire framework is nicely carved with leaf-scroll and birds. It has a central piece with pointed ends, both above and below. The lower end divides the arch of the niche into two segments and the upper one almost reaches the lotus-flowers hanging from the mouth of the monster. This central piece may also be regarded as a conventionalised pattern of Kāla-Makara ornament. Immediately above the doorway, set within this niche, is the figure of a goddess holding a lotus-flower in each hand.

The decorated door-frame, described above, covers only a narrow vertical portion in the centre of the wall. At the two ends of the wall, and extending over its entire length, are again two vertical decorations of recalcitrant spirals within two plain flat posts. The portion of the wall, on each side, between this decorated corner-piece and the central doorway, is plain above, with a richly ornamented human figure in a niche below, just above the Makara figures on the two sides of the doorway.

The two side-walls of the projection as well as the remaining parts of the main wall on either side of the projection are decorated in the same style. Two long but narrow recalcitrant spirals within two flat posts form the two vertical borders of the broad central part. This central part has an arched niche, whose opening covers its lower half, and the decorations above the opening, the upper half. The two pilasters on two sides of the niche support a beautiful framework. Its lower part is formed by the Kāla-head whose two ends, immediately resting on the pilasters, are formed by two pairs of Makaras, each pair looking in opposite directions and projecting a little beyond the top-piece of the pilaster. Above the Kāla-head is the representation of a richly decorated temple, emerging out of a mass of cloud below, in which are found floating two divine beings on each side with lotus-flowers in their hands.

The niches must have contained figures which have, however, all disappeared, only the footstools remaining *in situ*. The holes visible above and beneath the niches indicate the existence of some sort of screens which were necessary to protect the images from rain and sun.

The upper end of the decorated walls contains an architrave of three flat bands supporting a richly decorated frieze, and lastly the cornice, with ante-fix ornaments. The decoration of the frieze consists of a row of dwarfish *Gaṇas* below, and a row of garlands and rosettes above. The ante-fix ornaments of the cornice are Gargoyle heads in the angles, and figures of goddesses in the centre.

The roof begins immediately above the cornice and at first follows all the windings of the walls below. Its base, similar to that of the temple itself, supports a row of decorated niches, alternately larger and smaller, most of which contained Buddha images. These belong to the class of the four Dhyānī-Buddhas, Akṣobhya, Ratnasambhava, Amitābha and Amonghasiddha, facing the appropriate directions, as in Barabuḍur.

The second and third stages of the roof are octagonal and carry niches with images of Dhyānī-Buddhas.

From the middle of the third stage arises the crowning ornament of the roof, *viz.*, a large bell-shaped *stūpa* with a high pointed pinnacle.

We may now turn to the interior of the temple. The chapels on the three sides are about 11½ft. square. The walls rising straight up to a projecting cornice, approach one another by means of projecting steps, and then, rising up for some distance like a perpendicular boiler, ultimately end in a point. Each of the side-walls has a niche, about 3½ft. wide, decorated with Kāla head and scroll-work, and above it two divine figures on two sides. The back-wall contains a footstool which has place for three images.

The chapel on the east side is naturally somewhat different. It measures about 11 ft. by 8 ft. and has three small niches on each of the side walls. The back-wall has an opening which gives access by four steps to a door-opening above, from which descending again by three steps one comes to the main cella.

This chamber is about 24½ ft. square. The plain walls rise straight up to the cornice, where in each corner a big projecting angular stone gives the room an octagonal appearance. Then the walls approach one another by projecting steps, rise perpendicularly high for some distance, and then again inclining towards one another end in a top-piece just under the bell-shaped *stūpa* of the roof. In the north and south walls, at the height of about 13½ ft. from the floor are two small apertures, about 4 ft. wide, which opened into the side-chapels and were no doubt meant for purposes of ventilation.

The back-wall of the cella is entirely covered by the throne which once contained an image of Tārā,[1] as we learn from the Kalasan Inscription. On two sides of the throne are the usual *motifs*, a lion standing on a half-lying elephant, while the horizontal top-frame of the back of the throne has two Makaras on two sides.

Finally, it may be noted here that the building was covered by stucco paint. That this was original part of the plan, and not a later addition, clearly appears from the fact that the decorations and sculptures were not fully worked out as the finishing touch was to be given by the stucco-work.

About half a mile to the north of Caṇḍi Kalasan lies the Caṇḍi Sari or Caṇḍi Bendah[2] (Pl. II, Fig. 1). It is a rectangular building about 19 yds. by 11 yds. with the longer sides running north-south, and the main entrance at the middle of the eastern side. The high basement and the lower portion of the structure is very much damaged, and the vestibule which stood in front of the main entrance has entirely disappeared.

---

1. Mr. Schnitger says that the throne must have been meant for a person with hanging legs, and so it was for a male god, and not for the goddess Tārā; as such the Kalasan inscription cannot also belong to the temple. (Oudheidkundige Vondsten in Palembang, Bijlage B. 2nd Ed. p. 3 notes).

2. Krom—Kunst, I, pp. 264-269, Pl. 13.

It is a two-storeyed building, the upper storey being set back a little behind the lower. The division is marked by a projecting cornice. A similar cornice divides the second storey from an attic or parapet wall on the top, which, being adorned with niches and gateways, looks like a third storey from below. This is crowned by a number of Dāgobas with high pinnacles.

The centre of the eastern face of the first storey is covered by an ornamented doorway. Leaving some blank space on either side—where evidently the vestibule was attached to the main building—the rest of the wall on each side is decorated by an ornamented window-opening flanked by two decorated panels. The other three faces are similarly decorated, there being two window-openings on the northern and southern faces and three on the western.

The gateway has the usual Kāla-Makara ornament, the Makaras resting on kneeling elephants, and having birds in their open jaws. The window-opening is flanked by Kinnaras and supports a richly decorated framework ending in two Makaras. The panels contain human figures, a male on the one and a female on the other side of the window-opening.

The decoration of the second storey resembles that of the first, only a window-opening takes the place of the central door on the eastern face, and there are two small niches on two sides of it with a divine figure in each.

In the parapet walls above the second storey, there are three niches corresponding to the three window-openings below, and two additional smaller niches, corresponding to those of the floor beneath. These niches are empty, but perhaps the bigger ones with heavy decorations on the top contained the images of Dhyānī-Buddhas.

The richness and variety of the decorations of the niches and windows constitute the most striking feature of the temple.

The doorway leads to a rectangular chamber divided into three compartments, 11½ ft. by 19 ft. each, by walls over 3½ ft. thick. There were communicating doors between these rooms and in the left hand chamber was the staircase for going to the upper storey. All the rooms had niches, and the two side-rooms also window-openings. There was a broad altar-like bench against the back-wall of the three rooms on the ground-floor, and probably they contained images of Buddhas and Bodhisatvas.

The exact nature or purpose of the building is difficult to determine. The lower floor was evidently used as a temple. The upper floor is generally believed to have been used for residential purposes. The fact that there are arrangements for opening and shutting the windows lends support to this view, though it generally offends religious sentiments that human beings should live above the heads of the gods.

The Caṇḍi Sari may thus be regarded as a combined temple and monastery. Some scholars hold that it is the monastery referred to in the Kalasan Inscription. Krom, however, refuses to accept this view, partly on account of its distance from Caṇḍi Kalasan, and partly on the ground that Caṇḍi Sari can by no means be regarded as exclusively a monastery,

Next to Caṇḍi Sari the two groups of temples, Caṇḍi Lumbung and Caṇḍi Sevu deserve our attention. The Kelurak inscription,[1] dated 782 A.D., was found in the neighbourhood, and must have originally belonged to one of them, probably the former.

The group called Caṇḍi Lumbung[2] consists of the main temple and sixteen others around it, arranged in the form of a square with five on each side. The main temple belongs to the standard type, but the others have no projection except on the front. Neither the size nor the decoration of these temples mark them out as prominent ones.

Far different, however, is the case of Caṇḍi Sevu the biggest Buddhist sanctuary except Barabuḍur[3] (Pl. II, Fig. 2).

---

1. See above Bk. II, Chap. I.

2. Krom—Kunst, I, pp. 272-4, Pl. 14.

3. Krom—Kunst, I, pp. 274-294. Pll. 15-18. O. V. 1915 (141), 1917 (42-45, 76-78), 1919 (pp. 90 ff.)

A rectangular paved courtyard, measuring about 200 yds. by 180 yds., is surrounded on each side by two rows of temples, altogether 168 in number. The main temple which occupies the centre of the courtyard is similarly surrounded by two rows of temples in the form of squares, with 12 and 8 respectively on each side, thus making a total of 72. The main temple is thus surrounded by 240 temples, and there are traces of five more between the first two and the last two rows. The group thus formed had, again, one anterior temple on each side, at a distance of about 330 yds. There was thus a total of 250 temples including the main temple.

The main temple, situated on an elevated plane, formed the worthy centre of this vast complex of sanctuaries, each successive row of which was on a lower plane than the others. The sloping roofs of the vestibules of the first and last rows of temples accentuated the gradual slope and gave a pyramidal appearance to the whole.

Very little remains of the subsidiary temples, and there is no need to describe them in detail. A short inscription, engraved on one of them reads as follows: "*Mahāprattaya sang Ranggunting*" (*var.* Ragunting, Ragarunting, Rangg̃anting) *i.e.* "gift of Ranggunting". There are several other short dedicatory records of this kind. These make it evident that the subsidiary temples were the gifts of private persons. These short records may be referred on palaeographical grounds to the ninth century A.D.[1]

The main temple stands on a raised pavement, about 40 yds. square, enclosed by a balustrade with four gateways in the middle of the four sides. The general plan of the temple resembles that of Caṇḍi Kalasan. It is square on plan with projections on four sides, three of which form three separate chapels, while the fourth,—here, again, that on the east—forms

1. Krom refers them to the beginning of the ninth century A.D. (op. cit, p. 283) but Stutterheim refers them to the second half of the ninth century A. D. (B. K. I., Vol. 85, pp, 494 ff.)

an antechamber to the main shrine. There are, however, two important differences. In the first place the path of circumambulation on the basement does not go round the entire temple, but is interrupted by the wall of each side-chapel. Each of the side-chapels has, however, a rectangular vestibule at the back which communicates with the circumambulation path by a door, and thus one can walk round the central shrine through these vestibules. Secondly, in Caṇḍi Kalasan one and the same roof covers the main and the subsidiary chapels, while in Sevu, the four side-chapels have all independent roofs, with that of the central shrine towering above them all.

The vertical panels in the basement are decorated with vase and lotus motive, while the balustrade round the temple is adorned with figures engaged in dance and music. The walls of the temple are severely plain but the monotony is broken by two niches at the two ends. The walls of the side-chapels were, however, richly ornamented with complex variegated patterns including rosette-circles with flowers and animals, combination of trident and wheel etc. The frieze of the chapels just below the cornice was decorated with human figures under a band of birds and garlands.

A short staircase leads to the interior of the side-chapel which measures $11\frac{1}{2}$ by $7\frac{3}{4}$ ft. At the back a door leads to the vestibule referred to above. On the right and left hand walls are three niches with pointed arch, one larger between two smaller ones. The pilasters of these niches rise out of a vase with lotus and end in a lion's head. In the four corners of the room, as well as in the central niches of the side-walls, are footstools for images.

The back-vestibule also has three niches on its back-wall (which is also the outer side of the wall of the cella), with a footstool for images in the central niche. The images have, however, all disappeared.

The back-vestibule on the eastern side had of course a doorway through which by means of a staircase one could reach the cella measuring about 18 ft. square. The walls of the cella are plain and the construction of the arch above was of the usual type. Its back-wall was wholly covered by the throne which once contained a colossal seated image, probably of bronze.[1]

§ 5. Buddhist monuments on the Kedu Plain

About the time when the older temples were erected in the Prambanan valley, or perhaps a little later, the foundation of the famous Barabuḍur marked the Kedu plain as another important centre of religious sanctuaries in Java. Numerous temples, both Brāhmanical and Buddhist, must have at one time clustered round this central figure. Two of them deserve special mention, as they were more closely associated than others with the Barabuḍur. These are Caṇḍi Mendut and Caṇḍi Pavon.

The recent "restoration" of Caṇḍi Mendut (Pl. III.) gives a somewhat different idea of the structure as a whole from what it originally was. But it is not difficult to follow the essential features of this beautiful temple.[2]

The basement measuring about 30 yds. by 26 yds. has a height of 12 ft. The projections are shallow except on the front, the north-west, where room had to be made for the porch leading to the doorway of the temple. The basement is composed in the usual way, with a nice tooth-band, between the lower ogee and roll mouldings, and several square fillets both above and below the vertical part. The vertical part contains a number of decorated panels separated by pilasters, the whole being nicely arranged with a view to produce a very good effect by the play of light and shade.

---

1. Stutterheim describes a small bronze fragment which he believes to be part of the head of the image (B. K. I., Vol. 85, pp, 487-491 and plate).

2. Krom—Kunst, I, pp. 295-320, Pll. 19-21.

A flight of steps enclosed between stone curbs leads to the top of the basement. In addition to the Kāla and Makara ornaments at the top and the bottom, the curb walls of the steps were decorated with panels representing Jātaka scenes.

The temple occupies the centre of the basement leaving round it a passage, about 8 ft. broad. It is surrounded by a railing which has decorated panels and also twelve spouts with Makara-heads for draining out water.

The temple is about 15 yds. square with small projections on three sides and a large porch in front. The base of the temple has some additional courses in the lowest part, *viz.*, a vertical plinth, divided into rectangular panels, a frieze with garland motive etc. The panels are all decorated, sometimes with recalcitrant spiral of floral design combined with birds, and sometimes with illustrations of familiar fables about animals etc.[1]

The walls of the temple are divided into three parts by the projections, a broad vertical compartment in the centre with two smaller ones on two sides. Each of these has a broad plain flat post with a smaller one decorated with recalcitrant spiral at each end. The intervening space is decorated by a vigorous and beautiful sculpture. It represents a divine figure with attendant worshippers, flanked by two pilasters, rising out of a vase and supporting two Gaṇa figures. The addition of trees and flowers adds infinite grace to the well conceived scenes.

The central panel on the north-east has an eight-armed goddess richly ornamented and seated on a lotus-cushion. Above the halo behind her head is a conventional tree richly bedecked with foliage, garlands, and umbrellas. On each side of the goddess is a human figure, also richly ornamented and with a halo, holding a lotus stalk in one hand and a fly-whisk in the other. The goddess holds in her right hands, conch-shell, thunderbolt, discus and rosary, and in the left a round

---

1. Cf. Notes by Crucq ; O. V. 1930, p. 323.

object, axe, elephant-goad and probably a book. In the background are divine worshippers floating in clouds, *etc.*

The corresponding panel on the opposite side has a lotus-pond from which arise three lotus-cushions, one bigger in the centre with two smaller on two sides. On the central one supported by two Nāgas sits the chief figure, perhaps a female, richly ornamented and with a halo. Of the four hands two are placed on the lap, in dhyāna-mudrā, and the other two hold a rosary and a book. On the two side-cushions sit two worshippers, one with a flower and the other with a jewel on a lotus-cushion. On each side is a tree, with pots of money or treasure near the foot, while in the background is another big tree with umbrellas, divine figures, *etc.*

The central panel of the back-wall has the figures of Bodhisatva Avalokiteśvara in the centre, in a field as richly decorated as the other two.

The central panel is of course lacking on the front side, its place being taken by the vestibule.

The identification of the two goddesses in the central panel on the two sides is a matter of difficulty. Foucher has identified the one on the north-eastern side as that of Cundā, and the corresponding one on the opposite side has been taken to be the same goddess in her benevolent form. But the presence of Avalokiteśvara on the back-wall has induced others to regard the goddess as Tārā. The lotus-pond scene supports this view, as it agrees with the mythical legend about the birth of the goddess.

The eight side-panels have each the figure of a Bodhisatva in the centre. By small variations in the drapery and attributes the artist has left no doubt of his intention to represent the eight Bodhisatvas who were held in special honour in the Mahāyāna pantheon. Beginning from the panel to the proper right of the doorway these are, (1) Sarvanivaraṇa-viskambhī, (2) Maitreya, (3) Samantabhadra, (4) Kṣitigarbha, (5) Vajrapāṇi, (6) Mañjuśrī, (7) Khagarbha, and (8) Padmapāṇi.

The walls of the temple end in the usual frieze and cornice. The frieze is decorated by birds and garlands. The ante-fix ornaments above the cornice, as well as others in the building, show Kāla-Makara ornament in arabesque.

Of the roof two stages alone remain, and these repeat the main features of the building. Only in the centre of the projections false niches are placed to break the monotony of horizontal line, and bell-shaped *stūpas* on lotus-cushions are placed all round, 24 in the first and 16 in the second stage. The third stage was also perhaps similar to the first two, and the whole was crowned by a bell-shaped *stūpa* on a lotus-cushion, fragments of which have been found within the temple area.

The cella of the temple is reached through a covered doorway 21 ft. by 8 ft. This has decorated panels on two sides, illustrating the Kalpadruma, and giving the figures of Kuvera, Hārītī (or, as some would identify, Yakṣa Aṭavika and Hārītī)[1] and other figures.

Two steps from this doorway lead down to the cella. It has the figure of a trapezium, the front wall being 24 ft. while the back-wall and the two side-walls being about 22 ft. long. The usual inward slope of the walls begins at the height of about 13 ft.

In the back of the cella, on a raised floor, are three thrones, one bigger between two smaller ones, containing the seated images of Buddha, between two Bodhisatvas.

The thrones are all of the same type (Pl. XIV). The lower portion consists of a plinth, ogee moulding, toothed band, and several square fillets. The vertical part is decorated with crosses and rosettes and several projecting and receding bands. There is a projection in the centre supporting a double petalled lotus on which the god sits. The back-piece of the throne consists of two uprights joined by a horizontal top-bar. The top-bar ends in two Makara-heads looking sideways,

1. Congres I, pp. 325-348.

and just below them, leaning against the uprights and looking sideways is the figure of a lion standing on a kneeling elephant on each side. On the top-bar rests the nimbus of the Caitya-window pattern.

In the case of the Buddha both the legs hang down and rest on a lotus on a footstool in front. In the case of the Bodhisatvas one leg is folded on the lap while the other hangs down in a similar way.

The Buddha image, about 10 ft. high, is built of a single stone. In the footstool beneath him are figures of two deers with a wheel between them, showing the well-known symbol of *Dharma-cakra-pravartana mudrā*. Steps are provided on both sides for giving access to the image.

As usual the Buddha figure is clad in the simple robe of a monk, while the rich ornaments decorate the figures of the Bodhisatvas who represent probably Avalokiteśvara and Mañjuśrī.[1] All the three images belong to the finest type of Indo-Javanese sculpture and indicate a high degree of artistic excellence.

There are six niches in the walls of the shrine, and they were probably used for burning lamps.

The temple of Mendut was not an isolated monument. It was the principal one of a large group of temples which occupied a rectangular court-yard 120 yds. by 55 yds. Traces of a brick wall surrounding this court-yard, and of a bigger structure on the northern side of it can still be traced.[2]

As already noted above, the temple of Mendut faced north-west, and the only opening to its enclosure was on the south-west. These characteristics are very unusual, but are found again in the case of Caṇḍi Pavon. Now Caṇḍi Pavon

---

1. The identification of the three figures is a matter of dispute. Krom regards them as Avalokiteśvara—Buddha—Vajrapāṇi (Geschiedenis[2], p. 152), while Moens regards them as Avalokiteśvara—Buddha-Mañjuśri—Vajrapāṇi (T. B. G. Vol. 59, pp. 569 ff). Stutterheim accepts the latter view (B. K. I., Vol. 85, pp. 503 ff.)

2. Krom—Kunst, I, pp. 320 ff.

lies at a distance of 1257 yds. from Caṇḍi Mendut, and if an imaginary line connecting the two be continued straight in the same direction for 1913 yds. we arrive at Barabuḍur. This fact naturally points to some connection between these three buildings. There is also a popular tradition that there was once a paved road from Barabuḍur to Mendut *via* Pavon. But whether there was any such connection or not, the discovery of a few short records in Mendut and its style of decoration leave no doubt that it belongs to the age of Barabuḍur. Besides, in a sense, Mendut may be regarded as supplementary to Barabuḍur. For while the latter presents only images of Dhyānī-Buddhas and its sculpture represents the previous lives of the Buddha, the Master in his last earthly life is represented only in Mendut.

The small but charming temple of Pavon (also called Dapur and Brajaṅalan) is of the standard type[1] (Pl. IV). The panels of the basement were decorated with sculptures, but these are mostly gone. The basement supports a paved terrace on which the temple stands, leaving a broad passage around. Each of the three side-walls is divided into three panels, a broader one on the projection and two smaller ones on the two sides. Each of the smaller ones contains a human figure—either a male or a female—richly ornamented and with a halo. The central panels are divided into two parts. The upper part contains a vase and lotus with two rectangular window-openings on two sides. In the lower part is a *kalpa* tree in the centre flanked by a pair of Kinnaras below and a second pair of flying figures (Gandharvas) above.

The most striking features of the roof are the corner-towers supporting bell-shaped *stūpas*, and the big central tower, with a *stūpa* of the same shape, which crowns the top, there being also a similar but smaller tower, with *stūpa*, over the central projection on each side. The lower portion of the roof, which supports these, consists of a series of receding string courses.

1. Krom—Kunst. I, pp. 345-350, Pll. 23-4.

A decorated stairway in front of the basement led to the doorway of the cella. This is about 10 ft. square, and against its back-wall is an empty footstool. The niches—one on each side-wall—are likewise empty.

The sculptures of the temple of Pavon are of the same style as those of Barabuḍur, and this beautiful small temple is now regarded as only an anterior temple to the great monument.

We now come to the most famous and the world-renowned monument, the Barabuḍur.[1] The name Barabuḍur, spelt

---

1. There is a vast literature on this subject. For a short description, cf. Krom-Kunst, I. pp. 330-400 which also gives on p. 399-400 references to important publications up to 1922. For a detailed account one may consult the big volumes by Krom and Erp with two big volumes of Plates. The English Edition of the first part, *viz.* "Krom—Barabuḍur, Archaeological description" (Nijhoff, 1927) in two volumes deals exhaustively with sculpture but not with the architectural details which are contained in the second part, *viz.* 'T. Van Erp—Bouwkundige Beschrijving' (Nijhoff, 1931). Readers, unacquainted with Dutch, may consult Verneuil—Java (l'arts), Paris, 1927.

For different theories about the nature and significance of the monument, cf.

(1) H. Parmentier—Nouvelle hypothese sur la forme prevu pour le Borobudur (Feestbundel, Vol II, p. 264.)

(2) Poerbatjaraka—Het Borobudur Problem ; B. K. I. Vol. 81 (1925), pp. 523-537.

(3) Stutterheim Tjaṇḍi Barabudur—naam, vorm, beteekenis (Weltevreden, 1919) ; Djwa, Vol. 13, No. 4.

(4) The monumental dissertation by Paul Mus-"Barabuḍur, les origines du Stūpa et la transmigration, Essai d'Archéologie religieuse comparée." (B. E. F. E O. Volume XXXII, pp. 269-439, Vol. XXXIII, pp. 577-980, Vol. XXXIV, pp. 175-400, in progress.)

(5) Coedés—review of the last two in I. A. L., Vol. VIII, (1934), No. I, pp. 33-4.

For recent identifications of reliefs, cf.

(1) S. Lévi in (i) Oostersch Genootschap, 6th Congress (Leiden, 1929), pp. 7-9 and (ii) Ann. Bib. Ind. Arch., 1929, pp 1-7.

(2) "Sculptuur, Tekst en Traditie op Barabuḍur" by N. J. Krom (Gedenkschrift, K. I., 1926, pp. 110 ff.).

(3) "The identification of the first sixteen reliefs of the second main wall of Barabuḍur," B. K. I., Vol. 89 (1932), pp. 173 ff.

also as Borobuḍur, Burubudur, Borobado, etc., has proved an enigma to all. Various explanations of this name have been offered by different scholars, but none is convincing in the least. Raffles, and others after him, have split up the name into two parts 'Boro' and 'Buḍur'. According to some, the first is the name of the district, and the second means 'ancient.' Poerbatjaraka, however, takes Buḍur as the name of the locality and Vara as the equivalent to Vihāra. Others have taken the second part to be a corrupt form of 'Buddha' and the first, a qualifying adjective, meaning 'great' or 'many'. These and other explanations[1] are, however, beset with serious difficulties, and no great weight can be attached to them. It is probable, as Krom thinks, that Barabuḍur is the Javanese name of the locality, as both the parts of the word occur elesewhere in connection with place-names. It is possible, however, that the sanctuary had an additional sanskrit name.

The date of the construction of Barabuḍur is not definitely known. It is somewhat strange that there is not only no record of the foundation of this famous monument, but it is even never referred to in any inscription. Some curious accidents have, however, enabled us to get some idea of its antiquity. It will be noted below how the original base of the monument was, in course of the construction, covered by a heavy stone embankment. As the sculptures of this base were thus deliberately hidden, the artists did not care to scratch out the short inscriptions which were placed above the panels for the instruction of the engravers. These records remain for the present as the only basis for forming an approximate idea of the age of the building. The palaeographic examination of these records led Kern to refer them to about A. D. 850, and this view has generally been accepted. Recently

---

1. Krom—Kunst, 1, pp. 331-2. Congres I, pp. 287 ff.

Two other interpretations by Stutterheim and P. Mus will be noticed in connection with their theory about the real character of the monument.

Krom has re-examined the records with the help of fresh data, and has assigned them to the second half of the eighth century A. D. The construction of Barabuḍur may thus be referred to the century 750-850 A.D.[1]

The Barabuḍur is situated on the top of a hillock which commands a fine view all round across the green plains of Kedu to the distant hill-ranges that surround them. The site was admirably chosen for what was destined to be the greatest monument of Indo-Javanese art, and an immortal tribute to the genius and resources of a gifted people and the culture and refinement of the civilisation of which they were the product.

The site was, however, even more suitable than is apparent to a modern visitor. There was a rocky eminence on the top of the hillock which served admirably as the core of the huge structure. The big monument that stands before us to-day in its massive grandeur is really an outer covering of that primitive rock which lies hidden beneath it.

The noble building (Pll. V, VI) really consists of a series of nine successive terraces, each receding from the one beneath it, and the whole crowned by a bell-shaped *stūpa* at the centre of the topmost terrace. Of the nine terraces the six lower ones were square in plan, while the upper three were circular. Of the six square terraces the lowest four have double, and the upper two, only single projections on each side. The lowest terrace has an extreme length of 131 yds. (including projections) and the topmost one a diameter of 30 yds. The five lower terraces were each enclosed on the inner side by a wall supporting a balustrade, so that four successive galleries are formed between the back of the balustrade of one terrace and the wall of the next higher one (Pl. VII, Fig. 1.). The three uppermost terraces are encircled by a ring of *stūpas*, each containing an image of Buddha within a perforated framework (Pl. VIII, Fig. 1.). From the ninth terrace series of circular steps lead on to the crowning *stūpa*.

---

1. Krom—Kunst, I, pp. 332-335.

Just in the middle of each of the four sides there is a stairway on each terrace leading to the next higher one. In the case of the six lower terraces the stairway is covered by a doorway (Pl. VII, Fig. 2).

There has been much speculation as to the real nature of the monument. It is usually described as a *stūpa*, but its difference from a normal *stūpa* is so glaring that some explanation is necessary to justify the nomenclature. This explanation, however, varies with different scholars. Some look upon the crowning *stūpa* as the essential part of the structure and regard the rest of the monument merely as its base. But, then, the different elements of the *stūpa* become so obviously disproportionate, that the explanation can be hardly regarded as entirely satisfactory. Accordingly others justify the term *stūpa* by the semicircular outline of the shilouette of the whole structure which may be clearly seen in twilight against the background of a setting sun. It is probable that both the explanations are right and the artists wanted to emphasise the *stūpa* character of the building not only by the crowning *stūpa* but also by the general design of the building as a whole.

Poerbatjaraka, however, maintains that Barabuḍur corresponds to the description of a *stūpa* given in Mahāparinibbāna-sutta and Divyāvadāna. Parmentier offers a novel hypothesis. He thinks that the architect originally designed, after the model of the Burmese *stūpas*, a big *stūpa* on the square base of the sixth terrace. But earthquake or some other natural phenomena made him afraid that the base might prove too weak to support the huge superstructure. It was then that he built a stone embankment round the bottom to give additional strength to the building and gave up the original design.

Dr. Stutterheim also regards the monument as a *stūpa*, but he believes that the architect deliberately built the *stūpa* on a pyramid. He traces the explanation of this architectural expedient to a passage in the Old-Javanese text Sang hyang Kamahāyanikan which compares the human body to a *stūpa*-

prāsāda i.e. a *stūpa* combined with a terraced building. He argues that like the microcosm of human body, the Barabuḍur is also a symbolic microcosm of which the superposed stories symbolize the different stages of the ecstasies of *dhyāna*.

Paul Mus points out that in the Old-Javanese text, referred to above, the human body, which is identified with a *stūpa-prāsāda*, is expressly said to have outwardly the shape of a *stūpa* and inwardly that of a *prāsāda*. He, therefore, holds that the architect did not put the *stūpa* above the pyramid as Stutterheim believed, but really set the pyramid inside the *stūpa*. Mus holds that 'Barabuḍur is the realisation in space of a *maṇḍala* of stone, a sculptured *maṇḍala* to which the descriptions supplied by the 'Lotus of Good Law' apply very exactly. Stutterheim also agrees with this view to a certain extent, and holds that the base of Barabuḍur is of the form of a *maṇḍala*. Both Stutterheim and Mus take 'buḍur' as a Malay word meaning 'to appear', and interpret Barabuḍur, respectively as 'Vihāra on the height', and 'Vihāra of the secret appearing'.

There is thus a general consensus of opinion that the structure is a *stūpa*. It must be confessed, however, that in any case, the Barabuḍur is undoubtedly a monument of strikingly original character, and the artist, refusing to follow the beaten track, evolved a new conception of a *stūpa* structure. His daring genius has produced a structure of unique design and unparalleled grandeur.

But whatever be the real character of the building, the principles of construction followed are those of a temple. The wall of the lowest terrace really formed the basement. Originally it consisted of a plinth, a vertical part decorated with reliefs, ogee and roll-mouldings combined with various string courses, a decorated frieze, and a cornice, very nearly in the style of Mendut. Unfortunately the lower half of this basement is now hidden from view. For in course of the construction of the building the base appeared to be too weak to support the huge superstructure, and hence a broad stone embankment was built round it to give it additional strength. This massive stone embankment has a height of about 12 ft. above the original floor, a breadth of more than 21 ft., and a length of 120 yds. At the height of 4.2 ft. from the ground is a projection round it, 9.6 ft. broad. Although adopted as a measure of necessity, this solid mass of stone has not only covered half the proper base and thereby hidden from view the first series of sculptured reliefs, but it has also distorted the original plan and disturbed the harmony of the building to a certain extent. Two receding stone-courses and an ogee moulding connect the embankment to the original basement, the ogee merging into the upper-half of the roll moulding of the latter. The upper portion of the basement, which alone is now visible above the solid stone embankment, consists therefore of the broad decorated frieze together with the roll-moulding below and the cornice above. The broad frieze, now at a short height above the stone floor, was originally designed to be looked at from the much lower level of the first terrace, and its sculptures are of a purely decorative character. These are arranged in alternate succession of a group of three (rarely two) closely allied panels followed by an independent one. The last depicts a sitting or kneeling human figure between two pilasters joined by a Kāla-Makara lintel. Of the group on its sides, the central panel contains a man, rākṣasa, or a nāga between two female figures, all standing. The side panels (or panel) contain each a standing female figure.

Two projecting courses above this decorated frieze lead to the cornice. The latter supports the balustrade which is nearly of the same design in all the terraces. It consists of a row of arched niches separated by panels. In the lowest terrace the sides of the niches form a continuous arch, with a band of foliage running all round, and a leaf and foliage ornament forming the centre-piece. In the other balustrades the arch, which encloses only the upper half of the niche, is formed by the usual Kāla-Makara ornament. The lower half of the two sides of the niche consists of two carved pilasters supporting dwarfish Gaṇa figures which hold aloft the Makara-endings of the arch.

All the niches are flanked by a flat carved pilaster on each side, reaching up to nearly half their height. The arch of the niche as well as these pilasters support a superstructure which resembles the terraced roof of a temple, such as that of Pavon with bell-shaped *stūpas* (of slightly modified form in the lowest terrace) in the corner and the centre. The entire piece may thus be described as a niche-temple, and this aspect is emphasised by the image of a Dhyānī-Buddha in each of the niches. These niche-temples play a very prominent part in the scheme of decoration of Barabuḍur, and there are no less than 432 of them in the whole building.

The images of the different Dhyānī-Buddhas are arranged in these niche-temples according to a definite principle. Those of Akṣobhya, Ratnasambhava, Amitābha and Amoghasiddha occupy respectively the niches on the east, south, west and north sides of the four lower balustrades. The images in the niches of the fifth or uppermost balustrade, on all sides, represent Vairocana.

The niches are separated by sunken panels crowned by bell-shaped ornaments. The panels are decorated by relief-figures of men and women, sometimes with halo and attributes, and thus representing divine beings. But on the whole the reliefs are of decorative character.

The general arrangement of the galleries (Pl. VII, Fig. 1). is characterised by a uniform design though there are great variations in details. The walls of the terrace contain broad horizontal sculptured panels. Above these we find several projecting courses, a frieze decorated by garland and rosettes, and lastly the broad heavy cornice with a number of ante-fix ornaments. Beneath the sculptured panels, the arrangement differs in different galleries. In the first gallery this part is absolutely plain, while there are two or more courses in the others.

The method of dividing the sculptured reliefs from one another also differs in different galleries. In the first gallery there is a double row of reliefs separated by a horizontal floral band. In the upper row the series of reliefs are divided from one another by a flat post with recalcitrant spiral resting upon an animal figure, while a decorated pilaster serves the same purpose in the lower row. These posts and pilasters are richly ornamented with infinite variations of detail.

In all the other galleries there is only a single row of relief. In the second gallery the division between relief panels is marked by a pilaster, in the third gallery by a pilaster between two spirals, and in the fourth by a spiral between two pilasters.

On the inner side of the balustrade, the back sides of the niche-temples have sculptured reliefs between projecting courses above and below them, while the backs of the intervening panels are used for decorative reliefs depicting Kalpa-tree, Kinnaras etc., or, where they continue the main story, are occupied only by minor personages, attendants of the chief personages represented in the bigger panels *etc.*

The breadth of galleries is about 6½ ft., the first one being a little smaller. The height between the successive galleries varies from 12½ ft. to 8 ft.

As already said above, there is a gateway over the staircase in the middle of each side of the gallery (Pl. VII, Fig. 2). The arch of the gate is made by successive layers of overhanging stones, the projecting ends of which, instead of being removed, are beautifully decorated. The centre of the arch shows the Kāla-Makara ornament from which two floral spirals hang down and end in two Makaras on two sides of the entrance. The doorway is crowned by a miniature temple-roof like the niches of the balustrade. The beautiful decorations of the doorways and the masterly plan in which they are set—commanding from a single point a fine view of all the doorways and staircases from the lowest to the highest—introduce an unspeakable charm and invest them with a high degree of importance in relation to the whole construction.

Each of the terrace-walls is furnished with twenty gargoyles for discharging rain-water. In the lowest wall they have the shape of a Makara, while in the four upper ones they are monster-heads, both being delicately carved with endless details.

The three upper terraces (Pl. VIII, Fig. 1) form a striking contrast to the six lower ones, not only by their round shape, but also by the total absence of ornaments and decorations of which there is a plethora in the galleries below. The radii of the three terraces are respectively 28½ yds., 21 yds. and 15 yds., and there are 32, 24 and 16 *stūpas* round them. The construction of these *stūpas* is simple and almost uniform. A round band on a flat circular plinth supports a double-petalled lotus, and on this rests the bell-shaped body of the *stūpa*, crowned by a pinnacle on a flat cushion. There are regular small openings around the body of the *stūpa*, diamond shaped in the two lower terraces and square in the upper. The cushions supporting the pinnacles are square in the two lower terraces and octagonal in the upper. Each of these *stūpas* contains a Buddha image (Pl. XIII) which can be seen through the openings. This image represents most probably the sixth Dhyānī-Buddha, Vajrasattva.

The central *stūpa* similarly rests upon a double lotus, cushion. There are, however, no openings round the body of the *stūpa*. Instead we find an ornamental band, with hanging garlands, round it. The pinnacle is octagonal and rests on a double cushion, octagonal above and square below. The height of the *stūpa* upto the cushion of the pinnacle, is about 23 ft.

Of the pinnacle nothing remained *in situ* and only its lower portion has now been restored. Van Erp has demonstrated that this octagonal pinnacle, tapering as it rises, was encircled at the top by nine plain bands as we see in the pinnacles over the *stūpas* in Nepal and Tibet, and the whole was crowned by three umbrellas of gradually diminishing size with an octagonal jewel at the top.

The central *stūpa* was absolutely closed and its interior was not meant to be seen by anybody. There is, however, a circular chamber within, and above it a smaller cell. This chamber was ransacked long before any systematic investigation began, and so the relics, if any were deposited there, have been irretrievably lost.

A few words must be said about the series of sculptured panels (Pll. XV—XIX) in the galleries which form the most striking feature of Barabuḍur. On the whole there are eleven series of sculptured panels : one on the foot of the monument, covered by the stone embankment ; two rows on the wall and two on the back of the balustrade in the first gallery ; and one on the wall and one on the back of the balustrade in each of the other three galleries. The total number of these sculptured panels would be about fifteen hundred.

It is beyond the scope of the present work to deal with these in detail. Their technical aspect would be dealt with in connection with sculpture. As regards the interpretation of these sculptures the reader may consult with advantage the two big English volumes of Dr. Krom.

The difficulty and uncertain nature of the interpretation, as well as of the proper method of approaching the task may be illustrated by the first series of reliefs *i.e.* those on the covered base. Krom has given an exhaustive description of these sculptures and we may quote a few lines to give some idea of their nature.

"We find here many scenes from the daily life of the common people, scenes of murder and fighting, the capture and killing of all kinds of animals, *etc.*.....Finally we find a number of panels depicting the horrors of hell and the pleasures of heaven."

As regards the interpretation of individual scenes Krom tried to explain some of them with the help of the short inscriptions. But he understood the futility of his endeavour and remarked as follows :

"There is on the base of the Barabuḍur a text sculptured that brings before his (visitor's) eyes in regular sequence the working of the Karman, the law of cause and effect as it is manifested in re-incarnation, in heaven and hell. Which text it may be we do not know."[1]

Quite recently S. Lévi has succeeded in discovering this text, and has demonstrated in a convincing manner that the reliefs on the base of Barabuḍur are a continuous illustration of the Karmavibhaṅga. While this discovery has made the interpretation of many of the sculptures quite easy, it shows also the hopelessly erroneous character of many of the early interpretations suggested by Krom and others.

It may be safely presumed that the sculptures in the different galleries follow certain prescribed texts, and it is not possible to interpret them without the help of those texts. Fortunately, it has been possible to trace them in many cases, and thus the work of interpretation has been comparatively easier in these instances.

The upper row of reliefs on the wall of the first gallery represent unmistakably the scenes from the life of Gautama Buddha and the sculptors have followed a text which, if not identical with Sanskrit Lalitavistara, resembles it in all essential points.

The lower row on the wall of the first gallery, the two rows of reliefs on the balustrades of the first, and the single row on the balustrade of the second gallery,—all illustrate the *Jātakas, i.e.* previous births, and *Avadānas* or great deeds of the Buddha. A part of these (135 in number) is based upon the Jātakamālā. As to the rest, some individual scenes here and there have been traced to Avadānaśataka or Divyāvadāna, and a few of the reliefs can also be explained with the help of scattered stories in the Buddhist literature. But no texts, coinciding with the whole series of reliefs, have yet been found, and thus it is not possible to give a satisfactory interpretation of them.

---

1. Krom—Barabuḍur, Vol. I, p. 61.

The reliefs on the wall of the second gallery follow the text known as Gaṇḍavyūha which describes how Sudhanakumāra, who made sixty-four persons his *gurus*, passed through a hundred austerities and ultimately obtained perfect knowledge and wisdom from Mañjuśrī.[1]

The reliefs on the walls of the third and fourth galleries have not been satisfactorily interpreted. A particular Bodhisattva plays the chief part in each of them. The Boddhisattva of the third gallery is most likely Maitreya, and the one in the fourth has been identified by Krom with Samantabhadra. It is probable that the reliefs illustrate some anecdotes about these Bodhisattvas. But Dr. Bosch has suggested that they are continuations from the wall of the second gallery, illustrating in more details the visit of Sudhanakumāra to Maitreya and Samantabhadra according to a different and enlarged version of Gaṇḍavyūha, bearing the title Samantabhadracaryā-praṇidhānasūtra.

The reliefs on the balustrade of the third and the fourth gallery have not been identified. Maitreya plays an important part, but the general purport of the legends is very obscure.

In spite of the undeniable excellence and high aesthetic merit of the sculptures one must clearly comprehend the general design of Barabuḍur in order to appreciate its real value. As already noted above, the monument consists of a series of nine terraces, each leading to the next higher one by a staircase on each side. In order to have a full view of the monument a visitor should, therefore, first move round the base or the lowest terrace, then ascend to the next one by one of the stairways, and again walk round the terrace, and so on, until he reaches the top. As he moves round the second, third, fourth and fifth terraces he will find himself in a gallery enclosed on one (inner) side by the wall and on the other (outer) side by

1. The identification, originally made by Krom, has been further elucidated by Bahadur Chand Sastri who had the advantage of consulting the original text of Gaṇḍavyūha, whereas Krom had to depend only on summary (cf. B. K. I. 1932, pp. 173-181.)

the back of the balustrade crowning the wall of the next lower terrace. Both of these are covered with sculptures, and hence they occupy the chief attention of the visitor. If, however, he turns his eyes upwards towards the interior he will find the front of the balustrade (particularly the niche-temples) crowning the wall on the inner side. It is obvious also that to any one who looks at the monument from the outside these niche-temples with Buddha images rising in successive rows one behind the other will engage his chief attention.

As already noted above, the first four terraces have double projections on each side. The visitor will have, therefore, to pass round thirty-six angles in going over each of the first three galleries, while there are only twenty such angles in the next gallery, the terraces having only single projections on each side. These angles are emphasised by beautiful niche-temples with images of Dhyānī-Buddhas.

As the visitor completes his round over the fourth gallery and ascends to the sixth terrace, the view becomes altogether different. He leaves behind him the windings of the gallery with its series of sculptured reliefs on both sides. Instead he has to walk round a circle made up of small bell-shaped *stūpas*. After a further ascent of three such terraces he at last finds himself in front of the holy of the holies, the crowning *stūpa*.

This general view of Barabuḍur must be clearly grasped by any one who seeks to realise its essential nature. From an æsthetic and religious point of view the object of the artist seems to be quite clear. By the gradual ascent the mind is carried to higher and higher region till it reaches the sublime and the lofty. The decoration is deliberately suited to this end. The miseries of life and the lives of saviours *i.e.*, both present and future Buddhas, are depicted in endless details in the superbly decorated sculptures of the lower terraces which also contain the images of the five Dhyānī-Buddhas in the niches. But as the visitor rises still higher, his attention is drawn to the sixth and the most sublime Dhyānī-Buddha, whose figures are partially visible through the lattice-work of the series of *stūpas.* But he has to ascend higher still, both literally and figuratively, and when at last he reaches the summit, there is the crowning *stūpa* with solid walls, typifying the Mahāśūnya or the Great Void, the logical end of the Buddhist conception of life's journey.

The artistic conception of Barabuḍur is thus transparent and sublime, and gives a vivid expression to the most abstract and profound philosophy of the Buddhists. If the excellence of art consists in giving a beautiful visual expression to a noble and lofty ideal, Barabuḍur must be accorded the highest rank among the great monuments of the world. Alike by the grandeur of conception and infinite beauty of its details, it captivates the heart and carries the mind to a mystic height of joy inexpressible. It is the highest artistic expression of a most abstruse philosophy of life, and inspires awful reverence and a heartfelt homage and devotion to the eternal spirit which forms the essence of all religions.

Other temples in the Kedu plain.

In addition to Mendut, Pavon, and Barabuḍur, there were many other sanctuaries in the neighbourhood whose ruins now lie scattered in almost every direction. Mention may be made of Caṇḍi Ngrajeg, Caṇḍi Vurung, Caṇḍi Ngawen, Caṇḍi Banon etc.

The last named one was a Śaivite temple and judging from the fine life-size images of Śiva and Viṣṇu mnst have once been a famous sanctuary.

The Caṇḍi Ngawen group of temples[1] lies in the district of Muntilan, 3 miles to the south of the head quarter of that name, and to the east of the *Desa* Ngawen. It comprised five temples in a row from north to south, nos. II and I being somewhat bigger than the rest. No. II was restored in 1927 and offers sufficient details for forming an idea of its

1. O. V., 1927, pp. 50-83; Pll. 7-18, Plans I-vii,

general plan and characteristic features. It is a fine example of a classic temple of Central Java. The main body of the temple, as well as the high broad basement on which it stands, is square in shape with projections on four sides. The basement consists of the usual courses and mouldings with a standing lion at each corner. The most characteristic feature of the temple is, however, the detached portal on the east which consists of three parts, the main entrance in the centre, flanked by two side-walls with niches. The three parts of the portals had separate roofs of several stages.

Each side-wall of the temple had three niches, one in the centre flanked by two on the two sides. The roof consisted of a number of gradually receding stages with antefix ornaments and towers at the corner and in the middle of each.

The decorations of the temple are of high quality. The sculptures are vigourously designed and nicely executed. The squatting gaṇa-figures, the fine human figures on the two sides and below the door-way, and the foliage-ornament with elephant indicate the palmy days of Javanese art.

Later Buddhist sanctuaries

In addition to Barabuḍur, there are three or four monuments to which the name *stūpa* may be applied with some degree of certainty.

Two of these,[1] of almost identical design but now in considerably damaged condition, are in *Desa* Palgading, on the way from Jogyakerta to Bulus, and about five miles from the former place. The *stūpas* are bell-shaped and tower-like with a pinnacle, which, however, is lost, and whose exact form cannot therefore be determined. A decorated band encircles the *stūpas* a little above the centre. The base of the *stūpa* is polygonal and supports a circular band above which is a succession of five rings each receding a little from the lower one. The *stūpa* stands on a high square plinth consisting of a base, cornice, and

1. O. V., 1925, pp. 61 ff. Pll. 15-20.

the vertical central part. The cornice is decorated with antefix ornaments in the corner and the centre, and just below it is a sculptured frieze-band. The vertical central part is composed of sunken panels divided by pilasters. The panels are decorated with relief figures. The base consists of two receding terraces and an ogee-shaped lotus petal band connects it with the central part.

There was another similar but bigger monument between these two, but of this the ruined basement alone remains. On grounds of the style of the relief figures the monuments have been referred by Bosch to 750-850 A.D.

There is also a small high *stūpa* near Jogyakerta which somewhat resembles those in Sumatra.[1]

The fourth monument of this type, originally situated at Cupuvatu, but now removed to the house of the Resident at Jogyakerta, is one of the most graceful productions of the Central Javanese art. The decorative bands are finely conceived and well-executed[2] (Pl. VIII, Fig. 2).

§ 6. Later Buddhist monuments in the Prambanan valley.

The account of the Buddhist monuments in Central Java may be concluded with a short reference to Caṇḍi Plaosan and Caṇḍi Sajivan which may be regarded as the latest of this noble series.

The Caṇḍi Plaosan[3] lies about 1630 yds. to the north-east of Caṇḍi Sevu, and is the furthest monument in the Prambanan valley in that direction. Within a rectangular enclosure it consists of three separate groups of structure, each of which is again within a separate inner enclosure (Pl. IX). The southernmost group consists of a terrace in the centre, surrounded by circular pedestals on three sides and sixteen

---

1. I. A. L., Vol. I, p. 75.
2. Krom—Kunst, I, pp. 255-6, Pl. 10.
3. Krom—Kunst, II, pp. 4-17, Pll. 41-44.

small rectangular temples in two rows on the front or western side. It is separated from the central group by an open space. The northern group which immediately adjoins to the central group consists of a square terrace in the centre surrounded on all sides by circular pedestals.

The central group which constitutes the most important part has also circular pedestals and rectangular temples on all sides, but the central portion is covered by a rectangular enclosure containing two *vihāras* (monasteries) separated by a partition wall. All the three groups face west.

The two *vihāras* have the same design. Each of them has a rectangular ground plan with a projection in front (*i. e.* the west) for the vestibule. This led through a porch to a central compartment communicating with two others on two sides. It thus resembled in the main the Caṇḍi Sari, and like it had an upper floor, which, however, is completely lost. Each of the three chambers measured 19 ft. by 11½ ft. The profile of the basement had the usual mouldings.

The two niches of the porch contained each a Bodhisattva figure, and each of the three main chambers had three images on an altar along the back wall. Of these three images, two were Bodhisattvas on two sides, and the central figure, now lost, probably represented the Buddha. The Bodhisattva figures, some of which are in a good state of preservation, are of excellent workmanship, and the artist has succeeded in a remarkable degree in bringing out the divine expression of serene majesty which is the essence of the Buddhist conception of gods (Pl. XXVI). The decorative bas-relief sculptures on the outer walls of the vestibule, and the figure-reliefs on the sculptured panels in the inner walls of the main chambers are fine productions of artistic skill. The former contain the Triśūlacakra motive and the lion's heads conventionalised into floral patterns, which are characteristic features of the art of Eastern Java, and to the same category belong the images of the armed guardians of the temple. The relief figures have not been definitely interpreted but represent, according to Krom, the royal founder with his queen and officers.

The smaller temples surrounding the two *vihāras* were fifty-eight in number and contained each an image of a Dhyānī-Buddha. The circular pedestals were probably the bases of small *stūpas* which contained ashes of dead monks or other celebrities.

In the northern group, the central terrace had twenty-one images of Dhyānī-Buddhas and Bodhisattvas when Ijzerman saw it. The number of circular bases of *stūpas* was 65.

In the southern group there were eleven images on and around the terrace, sixteen temples and forty-five *stūpa*-bases.

There are indications that other structures were associated with this group, and the outermost enclosure which can be traced in the surrounding fields covered an area measuring about 380 yds. by 110 yds. These structures have, however, wholly perished.

The Caṇḍi Sajivan is situated about a mile to the south-east of Prambanan. The basement is square in shape, each side measuring about 21 yds. It is about 6 ft. high and has a deep projection in front. The profile of the basement has the usual mouldings which are continued round the projection. The central vertical part is decorated with sculptured panels, representing animal stories from the Pañcatantra, Jātakas[2] and the Tantri-texts. In front of the projection is a flight of steps enclosed between stone-curbs, which end in Kāla-Makara ornament and whose sides are sculptured with figures round a Kalpa-tree. These figures represent most probably some *yakṣas* though Van Erp identified them as Yama and his attendants. The stairway led not to the temple itself but to the top of the projection which probably served as a

---

1. Krom—Kunst, II, pp. 17-23, Pl. 45. J. R. Van Blom Tjaṇḍi Sadjiwan (Leiden, 1935).

2. Krom's interpretations of the Jātaka reliefs (pp. 18-19) were corrected by Crucq in O. V., 1930, p. 221.

vestibule. A second staircase led to the doorway of the shrine. The doorway was decorated with Kāla-Makara ornament, of which the Makaras alone exist, looking sideways with a dwarf behind supporting the pilaster which served as the door-post. The Makara and the dwarf rested on a rectangular block with two sculptured panels on its two sides. The front depicts an elephant with a rider in the centre and two lions on two prostrate human figures on two sides. The side-panel, at right angle to the former, depicts human figures. Behind this is visible a portion of another panel depicting the forepart of an elephant.

A long passage leads from the doorway to the cella which is nearly square, each side measuring about 20 ft. On each side-wall is a niche and a window $4\frac{1}{2}$ ft.$\times 1\frac{1}{2}$ ft. These windows, visible from outside, are a very unusual feature in a temple. Along the entire back wall was a projecting throne meant for the images of Buddhas and Bodhisattvas.

The body of the temple, looked from outside is a shapeless mass of stones. It rose immediately behind the cornice of the basement, scarcely leaving a passage round it. It was square in plan with broad but shallow projections on four sides, thus differing from the ground plan of the basement. The base was of the usual plan but nothing remains of its decorations.

Remains of the images of two temple-guards of the usual type were found amidst the scattered ruins. Mention may be made also of a carved stone with the image of goddess Śrī, with two elephants pouring water over her from two pots. Traces have also been found of an enclosing wall at a distance of about 44 yds. from the temple.

There are remains of temples to the south and south-east of Sajivan and they may be traced over the whole valley to a distance of about two miles east from Prambanan. But no useful purpose would be served by a detailed description of these ruins.

§7. Brahmanical temples in the Prambanan valley.

The earlier Hindu temples in the Prambanan valley are not of great importance and may be briefly described.

On the Gunung Ijo,[1] on the eastern side, there is a group of eleven temples, consisting of the principal shrine, 3 rows of 3 temples each, and an isolated temple. The main shrine, about 50 ft. square, is of the normal type. The other temples measure about 29½ by 23 ft. All these temples have their entrance on the west and are mostly in a dilapidated condition, walls and roofs having almost disappeared altogether. The main shrine contained a Śivaliṅga and the temples were thus Śaivite in character. A short inscription, found in one of the smaller temples, indicates the probable age of the group to be about the ninth century A.D.

Ruins of temples are also met with in Saragedug valley,[2] but these are shapeless mass of ruins. Mention may be made of Caṇḍi Abang in the south-western corner, being the only temple made of brick so far found in the Prambanan valley. Of course the large number of bricks lying scattered about in the valley indicate the use of this material for buildings, but very few brick-temples have actually been met with in Central Java.

The Buddhist monuments of Kalasan and Sevu described before were the early great monuments of the Prambanan valley. Later than these is the famous Lara-Jongrang group which constitutes the most important Hindu temples in Java.

The Lara-Jongrang group,[3] usually referred to as Prambanan temples *par excellence* or properly so called, derives

---

1. Krom—Kunst, I, pp. 247-250,

2. Krom—Kunst, I, pp. 250-254,

3. Krom—Kunst, I, pp. 440-489, Pll. 35-40. On pp. 489-90 will be found references to literature on this subject, published up to 1919. A good description with plates is given in Verneuil—Java (l'arts) Paris, 1927. Rapporten, 1909, gives illustrations of the temples (Pll. 117-133).

its name from a stone image of Durgā of that name in one of the minor temples. She is looked upon by the natives as the petrified princess at whose desire the temples were built in one night by an unsuccessful suitor for her hands. The story goes that the unwilling princess consented to marry him only on condition that he would raise six temples over six pits in one night, and as he was prevented from completing his task only by the artifice of the princess, he cursed her to be converted into stone. The image is still the object of veneration and worshipped by the native people and the Chinese.

The Lara-Jongrang group consists of eight main temples, enclosed by a wall, with three rows of minor temples round the wall on each side (Pl. XI. Fig. 1). A second enclosing wall surrounded them, and there is trace of even a third. The number of minor temples in each row is sixteen, counting twice the last three temples on each side of each row, and thus making a total of 156. In addition to these, isolated temples are found which probably belonged to a fourth row. The wall surrounding them is almost a square, measuring nearly 285 yds. on each side, while the third wall was about 437 yds. square. Little, however, remains of these two walls, or of the minor temples which were all of the same pattern. These all faced away from the main temples and had an inner chamber of about 8 ft. square reached by a small stair-case. There is a well-hole in the middle of the chamber which usually goes down right up to the foundation. These pits have been ransacked by treasure-seekers, and occasionally ash-urns have been found, but there are no images in any of these temples. It may be noted that each row of these temples stood on a successive higher level so that the innermost stood about 3 yds. higher than the ground level. About 2 yds. behind the innermost row of these minor temples rises the first enclosing wall, about 15 ft. high and 6½ ft. wide. It surrounds a raised terrace on which the main temples stand. The terrace is about 110 yds. square and was accessible by staircases from the four gates, one in the centre of the enclosing wall on each side. These gates have now vanished, and the corresponding openings in the second enclosing wall indicate the existence of similar gates which all faced the four cardinal directions.

As already noted above, there are eight temples on the terrace. Of these six are arranged in two rows of three each, running north to south, and between them are the remaining two, placed close to the surrounding wall and a little to the east of its northern and southern gateways. The western row contains the three biggest temples, all facing east, and the three smaller temples of the eastern row are just opposite to them facing west.

Of the three temples in the western row, the central one is the biggest and the most renowned, and contains an image of Śiva (Pl. X). The one to the north has an image of Viṣṇu, and that to the south, an image of Brahmā. Of the three temples on the opposite row, the middle one contains the image of Nandi, and the other two probably contained images of the riders of the other two gods, though we have no definite evidence on this point. It has been suggested that these two were also Śaivite containing a Liṅga and a Mahāyogi.[1] There are, however, no actual remains in the other two temples to indicate their sectarian character.

We may now proceed to describe in some detail the Śiva-temple in the centre. Its basement has a length of more than 30 yds. The length of the projection in front of it is about 22 yds. of which 6 yds. is covered by the stairways and the small temples in the angles formed by them. Thus the portion of the basement free from the projection is a little more than 4 yds. on each side, which is also the depth of the projection. The height of the basement is about 10 ft.

The basement supports a platform on which the temple stands, leaving a margin about 7 ft. wide on each side, which served as a path of circumambulation. The platform is enclosed by a balustrade decorated with reliefs on both

1. O. V., 1927, pp. 14-17.

sides. On the outer side it consists of a regular series of a projecting niche followed by a sunken panel. Each of these niches contains three figures—three females, three males, or a male between two females—holding one another in a very intimate way, and is flanked by a chiselled pilaster on each side. The two pilasters support a superstructure consisting of a splendid Kāla-Makara between two lions. The Kāla-head is richly carved, its two curls ending in two Makaras facing each other. Between the two are lotus plants, coming out of the mouth of the Kāla, and supporting three hanging bells. The figures in the niche undoubtedly represent divine beings while those in the panels, represented as dancing or singing, are perhaps heavenly nymphs or Gandharvas. The figures and decorations on the balustrade are executed with a masterly skill and may be regarded as the very best that the Javanese artist has ever been able to achieve.

The inner side of the balustrade consists of a continuous series of relief-sculptures depicting the story of Rāmāyaṇa from the beginning up to the expedition to Laṅkā. The story was presumably continued on the balustrade of the temple dedicated to Brahmā. These reliefs (Pll. XX-XXI) which will be noticed at some length in connection with sculpture, constitute the chief importance and grandeur of the Lara-Jongrang temples. They may justly be regarded as the Hindu counterpart of the Buddhist reliefs on Barabuḍur and are hardly, if at all, inferior to them.

The main body of the temple stands in the centre of the platform. The base of the temple looks like a second or upper basement, and may be regarded as such, particularly as there is above it the temple-base proper, on which the walls of the temples rest. The two bases, or a second basement and the proper base of the temple, are separated by a cornice decorated with antefix ornaments, and thus they were intended to be looked upon as two distinct parts of the building.

The upper basement, or the lower base of the temple—it is difficult to say which would be the more proper designation—

rests on a plinth about 1 yd. high. This consists of a plain flat band supporting a series of decorated panels. The decoration consists of a lotus-vase, the spiral leaves of which, flowing on either side, cover the entire field. Sometimes winged shell is substituted for the vase. This vase-motive, so common in Java, is executed here with a great deal of freedom and masterly skill.

A cornice with projecting antefix-ornaments separates the plinth from the upper part of the second basement, about 3 yds. high. It consists of the usual ogee and roll mouldings, the central vertical part and the cornice, with a number of small courses, all vigorously executed. The band below the cornice is decorated with garland and Kinnara *motif*, and ante-fix ornaments, with the same *motif*, are placed above the cornice. At each corner of the cornice is a magnificent gargoyle. The central vertical part consists of a series of twenty-four sculptured panels. The indentation of the upper basement and the general arrangement of these panels follow those of the lower basement. Similar flat posts, flanked by carved pilasters, separate one panel from another and each of these panels consists of a projecting central part with two sunken panels on two sides.

There is thus no doubt that the Lara-Jongrang temples were Brāhmanical in origin and dedicated to the well known Hindu Trinity. But Śiva is undoubtedly held up as the great god, Brahmā and Viṣṇu obviously playing a minor, if not a subordinate, rôle.

In the opinion of some scholars the Lara-Jongrang temples were originally meant as burial-chambers, the great Śiva temple being destined for the king, and the others for his relations and nobles according to their rank. This view rests mainly upon the popular tradition of the origin of the temples from pits, and is strengthened by the actual finds of well-holes in all of them and ash-urns in some. It is, however, also equally possible that the buildings were originally planned as temples and used as burial places only in subsequent times, or as an after-thought, by way of a subsidiary use. This view finds support in the actual practices in Bali, from which it would further appear that the main Śiva temple was the royal temple and the subsidiary temples represented the different suburbs and quarters of the capital city, each of which was expected to take care of and provide for the regular worship in the particular temple assigned to it.

According to Rouffaer king Dakṣa (915 A.D.) was the founder of Lara-Jongrang. The arguments by which he supports this view cannot be regarded as convincing, but the scholars agree that the foundation of the temple belongs approximately to this period.

The temples of Lara-Jongrang possess a uniformity of design and decoration which relegates them all to the same period and excludes the possibility of successive additions at different times. All the three great temples are square in plan with prominent projections on all sides. In the biggest one, the central temple of Śiva, the projections have been converted into side-chapels. Consequently it has stairways on all the four sides, leading to the main shrine and the three side-chapels. But the temples of Brahmā and Viṣṇu have only stairways in front leading to the main shrine. Further, in the Śiva temple there are small temples in the angles formed by the stairways with the basement.

The peculiarity and the special excellence of these temples lie in the dimensions and decorations of the different parts of the temples and each of these requires a separate and detailed description.

The basement consists of the usual roll and ogee mouldings below, and the cornice at the top, but the central vertical portion forms the special characteristics of these temples and its decoration has been called the 'Prambanan motif'. It consists of a projecting niche, containing a standing lion, with a sunken panel on each side containing a conventional tree between two Kinnaras or animals. All this is enclosed by a border of beautiful rosette pattern and is flanked by a plain flat vertical post on each side. This entire thing, which forms, so to say, a unit, is separated from its next repetition by a broad flat post with two chiselled pilasters on two sides. The lion in the projecting niche is a free-standing conventional figure looking to the front, and the sides and top of the niche are decorated with Kāla-Makara ornaments. The Kāla-head is, however, represented by merely gracefully curved outline, without protruding eyes or teeth, and is combined with rich, variegated floral and spiral patterns with a small bell hanging from its centre. The tree in the side-panel stands on a vase and is crowned by an umbrella, sometimes with birds sitting on its branches. It is splendidly decorated, specially by lotus in various stages of development, and might have been easily mistaken for a bouquet of flowers, but for the birds. The figures on two sides of the tree are generally Kinnaras—usually a male and a female—but sometimes replaced by animals or birds.

As stated above the panels repeating this general motive are separated by a flat post and the separation is further emphasised by the antefix and other ornaments placed above and beneath this post.

It is necessary to add that while the basement of the six main temples follows this general plan, there are endless minor variations in the execution of details, not only in the different temples but even in the different panels of the same temple. It will be hardly an exaggeration to say that probably no two panels exactly agree in the representation and decoration either of the niche with the lion or of the panels with trees. This endless diversity takes away the monotony and displays an artistic skill of a very high order, which can be truly appreciated only by a minute examination of the different panels.

We may now proceed to describe in some detail, the Śiva-temple in the centre. Its basement has a length of more than 30 yds. The length of the projection in front of it is about 22 yds. of which 6 yds. is covered by the stairways and the small temples in the angles formed by them. Thus the portion of the basement free from the projection is a little more than 4 yds. on each side, which is also the depth of the projection. The height of the basement is about 10 ft.

The basement supports a platform on which the temple stands, leaving a margin about 7 ft. wide on each side, which served as a path of circumambulation. The platform is enclosed by a balustrade decorated with reliefs on both sides. On the outer side it consists of a regular series of a projecting niche followed by a sunken panel. Each of these niches contains three figures—three females, three males, or a male between two females—holding one another in a very intimate way, and is flanked by a chiselled pilaster on each side. The two pilasters support a superstructure consisting of a splendid Kāla-Makara between two lions. The Kāla-head is richly carved, its two curls ending in two Makaras facing each other. Between the two are lotus plants, coming out of the mouth of the Kāla, and supporting three hanging bells. The figures in the niche undoubtedly represent divine beings while those in the panels, represented as dancing or singing, are perhaps heavenly nymphs or Gandharvas. The figures and decorations on the balustrade are executed with a masterly skill and may be regarded as the very best that the Javanese artist has ever been able to achieve.

The inner side of the balustrade consists of a continuous series of relief-sculptures depicting the story of Rāmāyaṇa from the beginning up to the expedition to Laṅkā. The story was presumably continued on the balustrade of the temple dedicated to Brahmā. These reliefs (Pll. XX-XXI) which will be noticed at some length in connection with sculpture, constitute the chief importance and grandeur of the Lara-Jongrang temples. They may justly be regarded as the Hindu counterpart of the Buddhist reliefs on Barabuḍur and are hardly, if at all, inferior to them.

The main body of the temple stands in the centre of the platform. The base of the temple looks like a second or upper basement, and may be regarded as such, particularly as there is above it the temple-base proper, on which the walls of the temples rest. The two bases, or a second basement and the proper base of the temple, are separated by a cornice decorated with antefix ornaments, and thus they were intended to be looked upon as two distinct parts of the building.

The upper basement, or the lower base of the temple—it is difficult to say which would be the more proper designation—rests on a plinth about 1 yd. high. This consists of a plain flat band supporting a series of decorated panels. The decoration consists of a lotus-vase, the spiral leaves of which, flowing on either side, cover the entire field. Sometimes winged shell is substituted for the vase. This vase-motive, so common in Java, is executed here with a great deal of freedom and masterly skill.

A cornice with projecting antefix-ornaments separates the plinth from the upper part of the second basement, about 3 yds. high. It consists of the usual ogee and roll mouldings, the central vertical part and the cornice, with a number of small courses, all vigorously executed. The band below the cornice is decorated with garland and Kinnara *motif*, and ante-fix ornaments, with the same *motif*, are placed above the cornice. At each corner of the cornice is a magnificent gargoyle. The central vertical part consists of a series of twenty-four sculptured panels. The indentation of the upper basement and the general arrangement of these panels follow those of the lower basement. Similar flat posts, flanked by carved pilasters, separate one panel from another, and each of these panels consists of a projecting central part with two sunken panels on two sides.

The sculptures on the panels are, however, altogether different from those of the lower basement. Here, the central projecting panel contains a human figure in high relief, seated, between two lotus-stalks, on a cushion in Indian style, and decorated with rich ornaments. The twenty-four figures in the twenty-four panels are all seated in various *mudrās*, and distinguished from one another by some easily recognisable attributes. The halo round the head indicates that they represent divine beings. The sunken panels on either side contain two or three persons each, evidently followers of the chief figure.

The identification of the chief figures was for long a perplexing problem. At one time they were supposed to represent the Bodhisattvas, although the temple was manifestly a Śaivite. Miss Martine Tonnet, however, succeeded in demonstrating that these figures represent the Dikpālas, protectors of the different directions, such as Indra, Yama, Varuṇa and Kuvera[1]. Although the detailed identifications of all the figures, as suggested by Miss Tonnet, may not be accepted, her general view seems to be beyond question.

Of the main body of the temple the base alone remains, the roof and the upper portion of the walls having almost entirely disappeared. The base shows peculiarity in two respects. In the first place, the ogee and roll mouldings are repeated twice, and secondly, instead of being plain as they usually are, the upper ogee and roll mouldings are decorated respectively with lotus-leaf, and ovolo (bead and reel ?) ornaments. It may be noted that both these peculiarities, so unusual in Central Java, were further developed in East-Javanese art. Above these upper ogee and roll mouldings rise the walls of the temple, which are too ruined to admit of even a general view of their nature and appearance. They were decorated with projecting niches, of which one fortunately still exists.

The niche resembles that of Caṇḍi Kalasan and probably contained an image standing on a decorated pedestal. It was bordered by the usual Kāla-Makara ornament and crowned by a projecting superstructure showing a high pointed roof—probably a representation in miniature of the roof of the temple—with two figures on two sides in an attitude of devotion.

The niche was flanked by a tripartite post ; a broader one in the centre, decorated with recalcitrant spiral, between two plain smaller ones with only conventional lotus flower at the foot

1. B. K. I., 1908, pp. 128-149.

and the top. Beneath the central post was a small niche which contained a detached image of a lion standing on an elephant's head. The space between the niche and the smaller post was decorated with lotus and rosette *motif.*

The mouldings above the wall are wholly lost and can only be guessed from the scattered fragments. It appears that just above the post with recalcitrant spiral was a moulding of palmettes. The many dwarfish Gaṇa-figures which lie on the ground show that there was a band decorated with these figures as is the case at Caṇḍi Kalasan.

We may now turn to the inside of the temple. As already said above, one of the stairways leads directly from the ground to the main shrine, while the three others lead to the side-chapels.

The main stairway begins at a distance of about 8 feet from the projection of the basement. The lowest step is about 7½ ft. broad and so are the remaining seventeen or eighteen that constitute the first flight. Singularly enough the first flight of steps does not lead to the platform round the temple, but to a landing above, from which one has to go down to it by means of two smaller staircases, one on the right and another on the left. This being the case with the other three stairways also, the result is that if any one wishes to move round the temple along the platform he has to climb up and down by the four smaller stairways on the four sides of the temple.

If we follow the main stairway after the first flight, we find the steps reduced in breadth. Just where the smaller steps begin there were on two sides the gateways of the covered side-stairs leading down to the floor of the platform. Continuing the ascent along the main stairway and treading over ten of these smaller steps we reach the door of the shrine. It was of massive proportions, and must have produced a striking effect, but only fragments of it now remain. The door as well as the front, back, and sides of the walls of the opening were decorated with Kāla-Makara ornaments, combined with figures of lion, lotus, divine beings *etc.*

The door leads to a chamber about 10 ft. square, the front side being a little longer than the rest. The walls of this room have beautifully decorated panels carved with recalcitrant spirals and rosette-patterns.

Behind this is the main shrine about 23 ft. square, with decorated panels on the walls. It contains an image of Śiva (Pl. XXI), represented as a human figure with four hands. On two sides of the door leading to this shrine are the two guards Nandīśvara and Mahākāla.

So far about the front of the temple. In the case of the other three sides, the stairways lead directly to the chapel. The walls of these chapels are plain except for five projecting courses in the middle. Three of these are decorated successively with palmette, rosette and again a palmette ornament. These are followed by a roll moulding and a plain flat course.

Against the back wall of these chapels are the images of gods, Gaṇeśa, Bhaṭāra-guru, and Durgā in Mahiṣāsuramardinī posture, occupying respectively the western, southern and northern chapels.

The two smaller temples of Brahmā and Viṣṇu need not be described in detail as the general arrangement is the same save that there are no side-chapels, and consequently no stairway except on the front or eastern side. These two temples are of the same size. Each side of the basement measures 17½ yds. of which the projection covers more than 14. The height of the basement is about 10 ft. and the depth of the projection about 5 ft.

The sculptures on the central vertical part of the lower base of the temple (or the upper basement) and the inner side of the balustrade require special mention. As regards the first, the panels in the Brahmā-temple contain a Brāhmaṇa or Ṛṣi between two standing figures, and those in the Viṣṇu temple, a divine figure between two females. A definite explanation of these figures is not yet forthcoming. Van Stein Callenfells has suggested that those in the Viṣṇu temple represent the different incarnations of the God.

As to the sculptures on the inner side of the balustrade, those in the Viṣṇu-temple represented the episodes from the life of Kṛṣṇa some of which can be definitely identified. As regards the Brahmā-temple, nothing exists *in situ*, but detached reliefs containing the last part of the story of Rāmāyaṇa *viz.*, the banishment of Sītā, the birth of Lava and Kuśa *etc.* are found scattered about, and they most probably belonged to this temple. In that case we must presume that the story of Rāmāyaṇa was continued from the balustrade of the Śiva temple to that of the Brahmā temple.

In addition to the principal image of the god in each of these temples, there are against the back wall three smaller representations of the same god. Evidently the four images in each of these temples corresponded to the four images in the Śiva-temple, *viz.*, one in the main shrine and three in the side-chapels. The principal image of Brahmā and one of the smaller have four arms each, while of the other two, one has eight and the other six arms. The attributes in the hands are also different. The principal Viṣṇu image is four-armed. Of the three smaller ones, two represent the Vāmana (dwarf) and Narasiṁha (Man-Lion) incarnations, while the third, a two-armed figure, holds in one hand a four-armed figure of Lakṣmī.

The five other temples within the main enclosure are not only much smaller than, but also different in plan from the three temples in the western row described above. They are square in plan, but the projections on the side occur only on the main body of the temple, and neither on the basement nor on the base of the temple. The decorations also differ a great deal though we come across panels with tree-and-vase motive and lion-niches.

The central temple of the eastern row contains an image of Bull, the rider of Śiva. Against the back wall are the images of Sūrya and Candra, standing on lotus-cushions which rest upon chariots drawn by horses, seven in the case of Sūrya and ten in the case of Candra. Sūrya holds with two hands a lotus flower in front of his body, while Candra holds aloft a soma plant with the right hand and a flag with the left. The latter has a third eye, evidently a Śaivite characteristic.

Among the detached fragments of stone lying scattered about, some contain very short inscriptions, a sort of memorandum for the artist, such as we find in Barabuḍur. The script of these records belongs to later Central-Javanese period. The use of marlstone, and of large pieces of stone (sometimes weighing more than 1000 lbs.) also mark these temples to be of later date. Other technical peculiarities also bear out the late date, and, as has already been remarked above, there are certain features in these temples which characterise the art of Eastern Java. It thus marks the period of transition between the arts of Central and Eastern Java. Dr. Stutterheim, however, thinks that the eastern characteristics are to be attributed to the fact that the founder of the temple was an East-Javanese king[1].

§7. Other localities.

In addition to the monuments described above, there are remains of many other temples in different parts of Central Java, in varying degrees of preservation, Some of them, if not most, were earlier than Lara-Jongrang, but it is not possible to attempt a detailed notice of them all in this work. A brief and rapid review of some of them must suffice for our present purpose.

The temple of Selagriya[2] (Sanskrit Śilāgṛha=stone house?) near Magelang is situated on a spur of the Sumbing hills overlooking a deep ravine. It is a nice little temple of the standard type, though some of the usual mouldings are absent. Its decoration was never completed, but three beautiful

1. B. K. I., Vol. 90 (1933), pp. 267-70.

2. Krom—Kunst, I, pp. 403-407, Pl. 33.

images of Śiva-Guru, Durgā on Mahiṣāsura, and Gaṇeśa adorned the three niches on the projections of the three sides.

The Caṇḍi Setan[1], near Magelang, of which little remains above the foundation, consisted of a group of seven temples in a line, having the main shrine in the centre and three on each side—the whole standing on a rectangular brick floor. It has yielded no less than fourteen stone images of Gaṇeśa and was evidently dedicated to that God. The neighbouring temple of Caṇḍi Reja[2], with a brick foundation, is very remarkable in that it contains, in addition to the images of important gods, also those of the minor gods, specially the Dikpālas such as Yama, Varuṇa, Vāyu *etc.*

The Caṇḍi Asu[3] (also called Añjing) at the western foot of mount Merapi has several striking peculiarities. It is in an unfinished state, and this enhances its value for the study of the Javanese architecture. For here we find an excellent example of what a temple would look like after the architectural part was over and before the sculptors had begun their task of decorating it. Here we find not only the blank panels, pilasters, and walls, but also blocks of stone put in their proper place, awaiting to be converted into antefix, makara, lion and other ornamental designs. It shows the vigour and grandeur of purely constructive design, and, in a negative way, demonstrates the value of decoration when properly applied. It also shows that the Javanese architects correctly understood the well-known artistic principle that decorations must always be subordinated to the architectural design and never allowed to dominate or distort its main features.

The Caṇḍi Asu also shows in several respects the beginnings of those modifications which were afterwards so characteristic of the Eastern style of architecture. The temple stands on

---

1. Krom—Kunst, I, p. 408. 2. Krom—Kunst, I, p. 408.

3. Krom—Kunst, I, pp. 417-422, Pl. 34.

a high basement, but there is not sufficient space round it to serve as a passage of circumambulation. The high basement, the raised base of the temple, and the body of the temple itself, all follow one another in unbroken succession. The staircase from the ground does not lead direct to the basement but to a projection on its front side, and the corners of this projection are visible on two sides of the top of the staircase. This was ultimately developed into two temples at the two angles formed by the staircase with the basement. In details of ornament also we meet with Triśūla-Cakra (Trident and wheel combined) and the lion's head conventionalised into a floral pattern—two characteristic features of the Eastern style. It may be noted that some of these characteristics are also met with in the Lara-Jongrang temples.

Nothing remains of the body of the temple except a portion of one side wall. But the existing ruins give clear indication of a bold conception, vigorous execution, and artistic conception of a high order. If the temple were completed, and stood in a fair state of preservation, it would have easily ranked with the most important monuments of Central Java.

Another remarkable monument is Caṇḍi Merak[1] which lies to the immediate west of Kali Bogor, above nine miles to the north of Klaten in the Surakerta Residency. It was a mass of ruins until the restoration by Perquin in 1925. It resembles the temple of Ngawen, in having in front of the main shrine an elaborate Gopuram, with the doorway in the centre and two sidewalls adorned with niches. There are certain characteristic deviations from the usual classic type. In the first place the base and the temple are both square in plan with a projection only in the east where the Gopuram stands. Although there is no projection, the walls of the temples are adorned with niches in the usual way. Secondly, the roof, consisting of five stages, has more distinctly the

1. O. V., 1927, pp. 154-188, Pll. 24-34. Plans VIII-XIV.

shape of a pyramidal tower. Each stage of the roof has a prominent Caitya-window niche in the centre, with Kāla-Makara decorations. The two corner towers on each side are also of somewhat peculiar shape.

The doorway of the Gopuram (Pl. XI, Fig. 2) is also of remarkable design. The horizontal lintel, supported by two carved vertical posts, and adorned with a Kāla-head in the centre, supports an elaborate framework above it. The top-piece of this framework is a Kāla-head with two elaborate scrolls on two sides, resting on a horizontal bar. The enclosed space is beautifully carved with flying figures, floral design, *etc.* Between the lintel and the horizontal stone bar is another horizontal bar adorned with beautiful seated figures. The sculptures and decorative ornaments indicate a high degree of skill and elegance (Pll. XXIV-V). Among the images is one of Gaṇeśa which shows that it was a Śaiva temple.

A few words must be said about the rock-cut temples in Java. In this respect the Indo-Javanese architects never attained a high degree of success and this is particularly striking in view of the wonderful cave-temples wrought in India and the high degree of artistic excellence displayed therein.

The Batu-rong cave[1] in the Beser hill in the neighbourhood of Magelang is a long chamber with vaulted roof, containing a *liṅga* and *yoni* on a square footstool. There is a niche on the right wall and some carvings on the back wall. The doorway is about 6½ ft. high and 3 ft. broad.

There is a group of caves in Kuta-Arja[2]. Two of these are in the southern side of Gunung Lanang. A portion of the rock has been polished to make the façades. The larger of the two is 6½ ft. high, about 16 ft. broad, and 18 ft. deep. Both contain *liṅga* and *yoni*, formed out of the primitive rock.

1. Krom—Kunst, I, pp. 427-8.

2. Krom—Kunst, I, pp. 428-432.

About half a mile to the north lies the cave of Gunung Tebasan. It consists of a long antechamber, measuring 40 ft. broad, about 10 ft. deep, and 8 ft. high, leading to two small inner chambers containing *liṅga* and *yoni*.

To the south of this is the Batu Layang cave (also called Kali Tepus or Tepus) which also consists of an antechamber leading to the main cell beyond it.

To the west lies the cave of Selagriya or Batu-ruma on Gunung Meranti. The front of this cave is wholly open and it contains a *liṅga* and a *yoni*.

The object which these cave temples were meant to serve is not quite clear. They could not have been possibly designed, like ordinary temples, as public places of regular worship, as they were too far from inhabited localities. Friederich has equated the name Tebasan with 'tapas' and referred to the caves as dwelling places of Śaiva ascetics. As is well-known, the caves in India were also intended for the residence and worship of the ascetics, and Friederich's suggestion appears to be quite reasonable, even apart from the linguistic argument on which it rests.

There is, however, no doubt that some caves were associated with the cremation of dead bodies. An excellent, and perhaps for the present a unique, example is furnished by the Siti Jedog,[1] to the south of the *Desa* Plasareja and to the east of Kademangan, in the district of Blitar (Eastern Java). The large number of funeral vases and urns found in and near the cave leave no doubt about its real character. Perhaps it was a sanctuary consecrated to Yama or Kuvera.

A review of the architectural remains in Central Java shows that they are confined to a limited area, *viz.*, the Subdivision of Wanasaba, the Dieng plateau, the Residencies of Kedu and Jogyakerta, and the adjoining portions of the districts of Semarang and Surakerta. The further we go to the west of this area the less prominent become the products

1. O. V., 1927, pp. 29-31, Pll. 2-6.

of Indo-Javanese art. Only smaller objects, and images mostly removed from Dieng and other holy places, are found, and there can thus be hardly any doubt that although Hindu culture made its influence felt in these regions they were outside the main sphere of that culture.

Some parts of this outer area, notably the districts of Dara in Pekalongan and Tegal further to the west (specially Slavi, Balapulang, Bumi Java, Banjumudal, Bumil-aju and Bantar-kavung) form an exception. Here we meet with stone images of Hindu gods and even remains of temples. But side by side there are rude images of Polynesian character referred to above in connection with the Pre-Hindu antiquities of Sumatra and Java. According to Krom we must presume here a mixture of Hindu and indigenous influences whereas in the rest of the outer area, there was a pure, though weakened, form of Hindu culture and civilisation. Krom[1] further believes that the Hindu element in this mixed culture is to be derived from Central Java and not from the later kingdom of Pajajaran as is generally believed. According to the same scholar this Indo-Javanese-Polynesian culture originated in or shortly after the period of Central Java, and ultimately influenced in its turn the regions further west as far as Suṇḍa.

While the views of Krom appear no doubt quite reasonable in the present state of our knowledge, they cannot be regarded as more than a hypothesis. Attention may be drawn to the recent theories on the origin of New-Javanese literature[2], and a similar explanation may be offered for the mixed culture of a part of Central Java. Besides, the political history of Central Java is too imperfectly known to allow generalisations about the nature and extent of Hindu influence in its different parts, simply on the ground of the existing archaeological remains.

---

1. Krom—Kunst, I, pp. 432-439.

2. Cf. Bk. V, Chap. IV.

CHAPTER II.

SCULPTURE OF CENTRAL JAVA.

§ 1. Dieng.

The Javanese sculpture, like Javanese architecture, presents itself to us in a mature stage, when the artist had mastered the technique and long passed the stage of clumsy primitive efforts.[1] This is, no doubt, due, to a great extent, to the fact that Indian colonists brought with them skilled artists and mature traditions of art.

Following the plan adopted in the case of architecture, we may begin with the sculptures of Dieng[2]. These may be studied under three heads: (1) Decorative or ornamental sculpture; (2) Relief-figures; and (3) Detached images.

1. The decorative sculptures offer comparatively few *motifs* such as garland, lotus-petals, foliage and flame. As already noted, in connection with the temples, they show a simplicity of design and boldness of execution, and on the whole fit in well with the general architectural plan. A sense of dignity and restraint pervades them and indicates an intellectual refinement.

2. The relief-figures include the Kāla-Makara and the human busts within the niches in the roof of Caṇḍi Bima. These latter (Pl. XII. Fig. 2) show a high degree of excellence and form the high-water mark of Indo-Javanese sculpture of the Dieng period.

Fergusson[3] regarded these busts as those of Buddha, and Havell[4] looked upon them as representations of Bhīma, the

1. References given in connection with architecture also include sculpture. Only additional references will be given in this section.

2. For illustrations cf. Cohn-Ind., Pll. 157-160.

3. History of Indian and Eastern Architecture (1910), Vol. II, p. 431.

4. Indian Sculpture and Painting, pp. 142-3, Pl. XLI.

and the top. Beneath the central post was a small niche which contained a detached image of a lion standing on an elephant's head. The space between the niche and the smaller post was decorated with lotus and rosette *motif*.

The mouldings above the wall are wholly lost and can only be guessed from the scattered fragments. It appears that just above the post with recalcitrant spiral was a moulding of palmettes. The many dwarfish Gaṇa-figures which lie on the ground show that there was a band decorated with these figures as is the case at Caṇḍi Kalasan.

We may now turn to the inside of the temple. As already said above, one of the stairways leads directly from the ground to the main shrine, while the three others lead to the side-chapels.

The main stairway begins at a distance of about 8 feet from the projection of the basement. The lowest step is about 7½ ft. broad and so are the remaining seventeen or eighteen that constitute the first flight. Singularly enough the first flight of steps does not lead to the platform round the temple, but to a landing above, from which one has to go down to it by means of two smaller staircases, one on the right and another on the left. This being the case with the other three stairways also, the result is that if any one wishes to move round the temple along the platform he has to climb up and down by the four smaller stairways on the four sides of the temple.

If we follow the main stairway after the first flight, we find the steps reduced in breadth. Just where the smaller steps begin there were on two sides the gateways of the covered side-stairs leading down to the floor of the platform. Continuing the ascent along the main stairway and treading over ten of these smaller steps we reach the door of the shrine. It was of massive proportions, and must have produced a striking effect, but only fragments of it now remain. The door as well as the front, back, and sides of the walls of the opening were decorated with Kāla-Makara ornaments, combined with figures of lion, lotus, divine beings *etc.*

To the same class belongs the image of Durgā[1], found in the same locality. Although inferior to the preceding one in artistic merit, it exhibits an advanced technique and highly developed conception of art. The prostrate buffalo and the sad dejected face of the demon offer a striking contrast to the triumphant smile of the goddess. The representation of the demon just issuing out of the buffalo is also well conceived. It may be noted in passing that the goddess holds in her hands the attributes of Viṣṇu *viz.* conchshell, discus, lotus etc.

§ 2. Barabuḍur[2].

The Javanese sculpture may be studied at its best in the Barabuḍur and the associated temples of Mendut and Pavon. Here we may easily distinguish three different classes of sculpture *viz.* (1) Decorative Relief; (2) Detached images; (3) Narrative relief.

1. Purely ornamental designs, though they are mostly overshadowed by the two other elements, constitute a striking feature of the sculptures of Barabuḍur. A few good specimens are to be seen in the decoration of the gateways and of the posts or pilasters separating the narrative reliefs. A sense of elegance and refinement pervades them all, and we are reminded of the decorative arts of the Gupta period. The rosette and geometrical patterns on the gateways and the intricate floral scroll-work on the posts (dividing the reliefs), sometimes involving the most complex spirals, bear striking

1. Cohn-Ind., Pl. 159.

2. The two big volumes of Plates (cf. p. 193, f. n. 1) give the best and most comprehensive illustrations of the sculptures of Barabuḍur. Readers having no access to them might consult, with advantage, 1. Verneuil—Java, Pll. III-LXV and 2. Cohn—Ind., Pll 147-156.

Some sculptures of Barabuḍur, along with a few from Lara Jongrang and Singhasari, were removed to Bangkok. For an account of these cf. B.K.I., Vol. 73 (285-310), 79 (491-518), 83 (503-13).

resemblance to those found on Dhāmekh Stūpa. The decorated pilasters of Barabuḍur also resemble those of the Gupta period. The floral scrolls, with or without birds and animals, more specially various forms of lotus, are of an exceedingly refined style.

Some of the most favourite decorative motives, illustrated in Pll. XVI, XVIII and XIX, are (a) a series of semicircular garlands alternating with hanging garlands; (b) floral spirals; (c) floral scroll with animals and birds; (d) conventional vase with flowers.

Some of the panels of Barabuḍur, as already observed in course of the description of the monument, have purely decorative reliefs.

2. The detached images of Buddha in Barabuḍur (Pl. XIII), and of Bodhisatvas in Mendut (Pl. XIV) may be regarded as the finest products of Indo-Javanese sculpture. Fine modelling, as far as it is compatible with absence of muscular details, refined elegance of features, tasteful pose, close-fitting smooth robe and a divine spiritual expression of face are the chief characteristics of these figures. The art must have, therefore, been ultimately derived from the classical art of the Gupta period in India. This point, though recognised by some, has not yet been very forcefully brought out, but the more one studies the images of the Barabuḍur group the more is one impressed with the essential characteristics of the Gupta age which they display. The following observations on the Gupta images by a distinguished art critic may be applied, without any qualification, to the Indo-Javanese images of this period.

"In the Gupta period the image has taken its place in architecture; becoming necessary, it loses its importance, and enters into the general decorative scheme, and in this integration acquires delicacy and repose. At the same time technique is perfected, and used as a language without conscious effort, it becomes the medium of conscious and explicit statement of spiritual conceptions. With a new beauty of definition it establishes the classical phase of Indian art, at once serene and energetic, spiritual and voluptuous."[1] "Gupta sculpture, though less ponderous than the ancient types, is still distinguished by its volume; its energy proceeds from within the form, and is static rather than kinetic."[2]

Pl. XIII illustrates one of the long series of very pleasing and remarkable Buddha figures that adorn the niches and the small perforated *stūpas* of Barabuḍur. It has smooth, round, but not attenuated, limbs, and the presence of the robe is indicated by the ends above the wrist. The calm divine expression of the face is brought out in an easy graceful manner, and the whole body seems permeated with a radiant spiritual energy issuing from within. It may be compared with the seated Buddha image from Sāranāth.

3. Narrative reliefs of Barabudur.

It is impossible to deal adequately with the extensive series of narrative reliefs in Barabuḍur in the short compass of this work. The subject-matter of these reliefs, so far as they have been identified, has been briefly explained in connection with the architectural description of the monument. In view of the very large number of reliefs it is not possible to give even a general idea of the different types of artistic work by means of copious illustrations and adequate explanation. All that can be attempted here is a sort of introduction to these wonderful series of sculptured reliefs by means of a few examples selected mainly from the life-story of Gautama Buddha represented by 120 panels on the top of the chief wall of the first gallery. As noted above, the relief-scenes follow very closely the text of Lalita Vistara and may be easily identified.

Pl. XV, Fig. 1 illustrates the descent of the Bodhisatva to earth. The pavilion in the centre on which he sits is being

---

1. Coomaraswamy, p. 71. 2. Ibid, p. 72.

carried down by the gods who hold it on either side. On both sides are escorting gods and *apsaras* with umbrellas, flags, flowers, fly-whisks, and incense-burners. The cloud beneath the pavilion, the hovering attitude of the gods and the backward waving of the flags and fly-whisks are the artistic devices employed to indicate the swift motion through the air.

Pl. XV, Fig. 2 illustrates the selection of Gopā as wife by the Bodhisatva out of a number of Śākya maidens. The servants are seated on the right and the rejected maidens under a pavilion on the left. In the centre Gopā sits kneeling before the Bodhisattva. The scene is thus described in Lalitavistara :

"All the young maidens gathered in the Assembly Hall. One after another they came to the prince and received valuable ornaments, till these were all exhausted. Lastly came Gopā and said : "Prince, what have I done that you despise me ?" The prince replied : "I despise thee not, but thou comest last of all". So saying he took the ring from his finger and gave it to her."

Pl. XVI, Fig. 1 illustrates the famous scene in which the Prince riding out on a chariot meets a sick person. Mark the very realistic picture of the sick and the richly ornamented borders on the three sides.

Pl. XVI, Fig. 2 illustrates another famous scene. After the amusements and festivities prince Gautama finds himself in the apartment where the dancing girls were sleeping—"some with their garments torn away, and others with naked limbs, and mouths awry and squinting eyes......". While gazing at these indecorous women he heard the divine voice : "How canst thou find pleasure herein ? Thou dwellest in the midst of a graveyard". His mind is filled with loathing and he decides upon an ascetic life.

The scene is portrayed with vivid reality, but it is to be noted that there is no obscenity or vulgarity into which an artist describing a scene like this might easily have degenerated.

Pl. XVII, Fig. 1 illustrates the visit of king Bimbisāra to Bodhisatva. On the left is a rocky landscape with trees, animals, and birds. The Bodhisatva is in a cave. King Bimbisāra with one attendant is seated on a rock while his other attendants sit under the trees.

Pl. XVII, Fig, 2 represents Buddha seated with his five ascetic disciples on the Gayā mountain. Mark the rocky landscape with the Nairanjanā river on the right.

Pl. XVIII, Fig. 1 represents Buddha and the gods who request him to take food. Apart from the landscape and the ornamental borders, the individual figures of the gods deserve special notice.

Pl. XVIII, Fig. 2 is a representation of a famous episode in Lalitavistara which may be summed up as follows.

'The Bodhisatva picked up a rag from graveyard and wanted to wash it. Thereupon the gods made to appear first a pond and also a stone on which to wash it. Śakra, the chief of the gods, offered to wash it himself, but the Bodhisatva refused, and after himself washing it got into the pond. Māra caused the sides of the tank to rise high so that the Bodhisatva, weak and exhausted as he was, could not come out. He thereupon requested the goddess of a tree standing near by to bend its branch and with its help came out of the pond.'

The relief shows a beautiful lotus pond with birds. The tree-goddess is kneeling on the left. Śakra is indicated by his chief attendant's headdress, which has the shape of the trunk of an elephant, and the goad in his hand. The naturalistic representation of the lotus bud and leaves is noteworthy.

Pl. XIX, Fig. 1 represents an episode in the story of Sudhanakumāra in Divyāvadāna. The prince Sudhanakumāra, after wandering long in search of his beloved consort Manoharā, arrives at the city where she lives. He sits near a tank and sees a number of girls fetching water. Learning that the water was meant for the bath of his beloved, he calls one of the maids aside and throws his ring into her jug, by which his presence is at last indicated to Manoharā.

The relief shows a lotus pond in the centre with a swan. Altogether there are nine maids with water-jugs. Some of them have already filled their jugs and are going back to the palace depicted on the left. One is shown in the act of filling the jug and others are waiting their turn. To the right the prince sits on a raised seat under a tree, evidently narrating something which a maid in front of him is listening to with rapt attention. The jug is placed on the ground before her. Presumably the prince throws the ring into the jug. According to the text the prince did it without being seen. This is possible in the relief only on the presumption that the maid was too engrossed with the recital to notice the ring being thrown in.

The relief is a fine piece of sculpture. The division of the charming and graceful maidens into two groups on two sides of the pond, the delicate carving of the lotus leaves, buds and the small plants on the edge of the pond, the varying and graceful poses of the maidens, and the prince,—all testify to a high degree of artistic skill. The relief recalls the very familiar and poetic image of village maidens gathered round a pond in the dusk, and this lovely scene serves as a beautiful contrast to the love-sick forlorn prince in the background. The composition must be regarded as a beautiful poetic conception nicely executed, and, taken as a whole, may be regarded as one of the finest reliefs in Barabuḍur.

The reliefs of Barabuḍur are specially designed for illustrating some definite texts. Wherever we have been able to discover this text we find the sculptor making a faithful reproduction of it as far as his limited space permits. In reproducing the story he seldom tries to pick up the crucial event or episode as of special importance, nor does he emphasise in any way the leading movement or action in a theme, relegating accessory details into a subordinate position. But he deals with the whole story in a uniform manner, treating the essential point very much in the same way as its minor detail. In other words, the Barabuḍur reliefs are descriptive and not dramatic. The sculptor avoids excitement or sensationalism of any kind and is content in narrating the story in a colourless form.

In the composition of reliefs we therefore almost always find quite a large number of figures, many of whom play only a very subordinate rôle, and whose absence would very often not only not matter in the least, but would rather help to direct our attention to the main actors and main incidents in the story. There are, of course, exceptions to the rule, but there is no doubt about the general tendency.

In spite of these obvious defects the reliefs have several characteristic merits. In the first place the artist always displays a fine sense of symmetery, harmony and rhythm in grouping his figures. They are skilfully arranged in small groups balancing each other, while the different poses, varying attitudes, and distinct appearances and dresses of figures in the same group serve to remove the aspect of monotony and dullness which would otherwise be inevitable in a scene depicting quite a large number of persons. For example, of the gods and *apsaras* in Pl. XV, Fig. 1, and the women in Pl. XVI, Fig. 2, no two figures have the same attitude or exactly the same dress and appearance.

The artist has further freely made use of trees, plants, animals, and birds to break the dull monotony of his scene. True to Indian traditions, he shows a keen appreciation of the beauties of nature, and delights to depict human beings in surroundings of natural beauty, as far, of course, as his texts would permit. The landscape, specially trees, rocks and rivers, is conventional but finely executed, and the lotus ponds in Pl. XVIII, Fig. 2, and Pl. XIX, Fig. 1 are lovely examples of naturalistic designs. The figures of the trees, birds and animals, and sometimes of pavilions and palaces, and the skilful way in which they are added to a scene to enrich and enliven it, are worthy of the highest praise.

The artist has attained a high degree of success in the representation of human figures. Considering the large area filled by thousands of them, we could hardly expect great beauty of form in individual figures. But if few of them may be regarded as of surpassing beauty, there are fewer still among the thousands of figures, which have fallen below a fairly high average standard, and this, by itself, calls forth our highest admiration and reflects the greatest credit upon the genius and resourcefulness of the artists of Barabuḍur.

In designing the human figures the artist, true to Indian tradition, has aimed at reproducing a type rather than an individual. But he has been very successful in delineating and distinguishing these types. For example, the royal attendants (Pl. XVII, Fig. 1), ascetics (Pl. XVII, Fig. 2), and the gods, (Pl. XVIII, Fig. 1) are clearly marked types distinguished from one another. Yet no two figures of even the same type are exactly the replica of each other, and there are always some shades of difference in their features. Once our eyes are accustomed to a little heaviness and roundness of the figures, which are, no doubt, due to racial physiognomy, we find them possessed of a fair degree of grace and charm. As our eyes wander over the hundreds and thousands of figures, we note with admiration how each of them has been chiselled with great care and skill, so as to bring out the lovely form of the body. The scanty dress, both of the men and the women, made the task infinitely greater, as the artist had to pay attention to all the parts of the body. The figures are seldom made to stand or sit in an erect or rigid attitude, but infinite variety of poses and bends are introduced, giving the artist an opportunity to display his masterly technique and sense of rhythm by delineating them in fine graceful curved lines.

The figures of women are almost always carved with a special care. The round bosom, full thigh and hip, slender waist and the pliant limbs endow many of them with an unspeakable grace and charm. Sometimes we meet with new types of novel beauty ; for example the Kinnaris depicted in Pl. XIX, Fig. 1. The artist has deliberately created a new type to distinguish them from ordinary human beings. The tall slender forms, and the graceful poses of these figures, radiant with life and beauty, mark them as the creation of a master artist with striking ideals of originality of design.

The artist has shown equal powers of carving deformed or ugly creatures. Although generally naturalistic he sometimes grows realistic, as for example in representing the sick man in Pl. XVI, Fig. 1 and some of the courtiers in Pl. XIX, Fig. 3.

The artist has also succeeded well in delineating difficult movements of the body. The dancing scene in Pl. XIX, Fig. 2 is a fair specimen. The posture of the dancing girl in the centre and the position of the arms of the musicians with two parts of the cymbals (or similar instruments), just on the point of striking one another, are particularly noteworthy.

§ 3. Lara-Jongrang[1]

The general disposition of the sculptures in Lara-Jongrang and their subject-matter have been referred to in course of the description of the temple. It is necessary here only to refer to their artistic excellence.

A highly developed aesthetic sense is noticeable in all the sculptures, both decorative ornaments and relief figures. The Kāla-Makara ornament, on the top of the niches in the balustrade, is a pleasant contrast to the usually hideous and distorted monster's face that we meet with elsewhere. But even this was excelled by the beautiful conventional design of the same which we notice above the niches of the basement. Here the face is almost unrecognisable in the graceful curves and the beautiful complex of intertwining spiral, the whole producing a linear design of infinite beauty.

---

1. For illustrations, cf. Cohn—Ind, Pll. 161-164 in addition to the works cited in f. n. 3, p. 212.

The same aesthetic sense has transformed the tree-and-vase motive into a floral bouquet whose charm holds in awe of admiration the two Kinnaras seated on its sides. The Kinnara figures, half-bird, half-human, are very appropriate. To appreciate the beauty of the tree you must have the eyes and heart of a human being but to enjoy it perpetually you must have the wings of a bird. Taken as a whole, the decorative reliefs are very charming and graceful and show a variety of designs.

A high degree of aesthetic sense also pervades the delineaation of human figures. The best seems to be the triple figures in the niches on the outer side of the balustrade. Characterised alike by the elegance of forms and the harmonious grouping, they may be regarded as the best jewels in the ornamentation of the temple.

The figures in the neighbouring panels are less elegant, but full of life and movements, bringing into relief the still beauty of the principal figures. In these attendant figures the artist has shown in a remarkable degree his power of delineating movements of all kinds and infusing life and vivacity in them. The man, for instance, who is playing on the *mṛdanga* (a kind of drum) is depicted as if his whole body is dancing with the tune. The skill with which different postures of the human body are faithfully drawn is also worthy of notice.

All these peculiarities appear again in a still more remarkable degree in the famous series of reliefs representing scenes from the Rāmāyaṇa.[1] There are altogether forty-two panels depicting the story of the Rāmāyaṇa up to the arrival of Rāma

---

1. For a complete illustration and interpretation of reliefs, cf. Kats—Het Rāmāyaṇa, Plates 1-42. For interpretations by Stutterheim, cf. B.K.I. Vol. 84 (1928) pp. 126 ff. Stutterheim believes that the panels are arranged with reference to the course of the sun with whom Rāma is identified. Thus the pictures about the prosperity of Rāma are in the east (rise of the sun) and those of adversity in the west (sun-set) etc, Ibid pp. 118-132.

and his monkey-troops to Laṅkā. It will be beyond our scope to describe all of them, but a few typical scenes may be discussed.

1. The very first panel (Pl. XX, Fig. 1) represents *anantaśayana* of Viṣṇu. The god is seated on serpent *Śeṣa* and the sea below it is indicated by waving lines and aquatic animals such as fishes and crabs. Viṣṇu has four hands. The upper right arm holds the discus and the upper left, the conchshell. The object in the lower right hand is indistinct, while the empty lower left hand is stretched, with palm outside, in the act of greeting the five figures on his left. These represent the gods who have come to request him to be incarnated on earth for killing Rāvaṇa. The foremost of these figures, distinguished from the rest by his peaked beard and peculiar headdress, probably represents Brahmā. He presents an offering (arghya) to Viṣṇu.

Viṣṇu is seated in a peculiar manner. His left leg is doubled up and two ends of a girdle that pass round his body are tied a little below the knee. This method of keeping the body at ease is also noticeable in the sculptures at Sānchi, and Barabuḍur. To the right of Viṣṇu, Garuḍa is seated in a reverential attitude, holding with two hands a lotus with long stalk towards his master.

The theme is delineated with admirable force and simplicity. There is a beautiful harmony in the whole composition, and the artist has shown his sense of symmetery and balance. As in the body of the temple, the decorative ornaments are kept in due subordination. The most remarkable thing is, however, the variety of features and expressions which we notice in the five divine figures. Each of these is graceful in his own way, endowed with different features and imbued with different expressions. Taken separately each would have constituted a charming figure by itself, and this is a rare thing in a composition of this kind. The continuation of the scene, in panel II (Pl. XX, Fig. 2) depicts king Daśaratha with his queen and sons, and probably the sage Viśvāmitra.

2. The panels X, XI, XII, (Pl. XX, Figs. 3-4) delineate the tragic scene of the banishment of Rāma. To the left is a long scene depicting the coronation of Bharata with its attendant joyous ceremonies such as music and dancing. To the right, Rāma and Sītā are being driven in a chariot towards the forest.

In the centre the old King Daśaratha and queen Kauśalyā are seated overwhelmed with grief, the king's head drooping over his left shoulder, and the queen closing her eyes with left hand. The sorrow of the royal couple is reflected in the dejected and somewhat startled faces of the two attendants sitting on the right. The placing of this scene between the other two at once brings into prominence the great tragedy of the whole.

Apart from the masterly setting of the whole scene, the details are worthy of a great artist. The sorrow of the king and queen is shown in a simple but very effective manner. Both of them have their faces turned towards the right but not looking at the departing chariot, a sight too painful for them. The face of Rāma is sad, that of Lakṣmaṇa sadder still, but not so the face of Sītā, in whom the joy of her husband's company seems to outweigh all other considerations.

Remarkable is also the attitude of Bharata and his queen. They look morose and sit apart, in strong contrast to the posture in which loving couples are usually represented. Compare, for example, that of Rāma and Sītā in panel XVI., and of Daśaratha and his queen in panels II and IX. Amid the joyous surroundings of their coronation Bharata and his queen alone are sad and unhappy.

3. The panels XVII—XX. (Pl. XXI, Figs. 1-2) represent the episodes of Sūrpanakhā and Mārīci. Beginning from the left, the first scene represents Rāma seated in his hut, while Sūrpanakhā, with her maid, kneels down before him, offering some presents. The forest is indicated by two trees, under one of which Sītā stands, at a distance, looking at the scene with a jealous eye.

The next scene shows the same two figures—Sūrpanakhā and her attendant—before Lakṣmaṇa. His outstretched left hand with a pointed finger is a warning to them to retire, while an arrow (or a club or some other weapon) in his right hand completes the threat. Poor Sūrpanakhā, frightened and disappointed, bursts into tears. The difference in the attitude of the two brothers is worthy of note.

The next scene represents Sītā seated in her hut, while Lakṣmaṇa, left to guard her, sits below her.

Next we find Rāma in the thick forest just letting oft the arrow which has pierced the golden deer. Above the deer is portrayed the hideous figure of *Rākṣasa* Mārīchi, uttering the fatal cry. The forest is indicated by trees, plants and shrubs, while the figure of Rāma in the act of throwing the arrow is faithfully drawn, his left hand holding the centre of the bow, with right hand stretched back behind his body. The running deer with his head turned back towards his pursuer is also admirably carved.

4. Lastly we may refer to panel XXXIX, (Pl. XXI, Fig. 3) in which Hanumān, on his return from Laṅkā, narrates the story of Sītā to Rāma. The artist has very cleverly depicted the different effects of the story on the different persons present. Rāma is overpowered with emotions, but is evidently fully absorbed with the mental vision of Sītā which the narrator's story has conjured up before him. Lakṣmaṇa, too, is deeply moved, but less absorbed than Rāma. Sugrīva and the seated human figure behind him are visibly affected by the pathos of the story which they are listening to with rapt attention. The two monkeys on the extreme right pay no attention to the story and are making merriments, in strong contrast to the rest.

If we compare the attitude of Rāma with that of Sītā in panel XXXVI, (pl. XXI, Fig. 4) when she hears the news of Rāma from the same Hanumān, we can easily mark the difference in the two characters. Sītā is visibly affected, her whole body leaning forward towards the speaker. But while her emotion is only too visible, Rāma presents, outwardly, a calm placid figure, with a slight twist of the left hand (in common with Sītā) as the only external indication of the deep emotion which is agitating his body and mind. Whereas Sītā is looking eagerly towards Hanumān, Rāma is turning away from him. In Sītā the emotional element reigns supreme, while it is subordinated in Rāma to a strong will-power and intellectual force.

In conclusion we may refer to the detached images of the gods specially those of Brahmā, Viṣṇu and Śiva in the temples. They are beautifully modelled, but the expression lacks the ideal abstraction which is the dominant keynote of Barabuḍur Buddha. The features, though somewhat stiff, are, however, characterised by an elegance and refinement of high order. The image of Mahādeva (Pl. XXII) will serve as an example.

The above review makes it clear that the art of Lara-Jongrang is more naturalistic than that of Barabuḍur and is characterised by a greater feeling for movements and human passions. It is more informed by human life and activity, though not devoid of the graceful charm of idealism. It has brought the divinity of idealism to the earth below, but with less abstraction and more animation than is the case with Barabuḍur. It is dramatic and dynamic while the latter is passive and static. In short, Barabuḍur and Lara-Jongrang represent respectively the Classic and Romantic phases of Indo-Javanese art.

From a strictly technical point of view, the figures of these reliefs perhaps suffer in comparison with the finished products of Barabuḍur. But the artist has shown a very high degree of skill in delineating not only human figures but also apes, aquatic animals, and plants.

§. 4. Other localities.

From the point of view of art in general and sculpture in particular, Dieng, Barabuḍur and Lara-Jongrang constitute three important landmarks in the gradual stages of its development. The period of interval that separates these three is not very long, and all of them were constructed, at the outside limits, between 750 and 950 A.D. Yet we notice distinct characteristic features in them which may be conveniently, if not very accurately, expressed by designing them as primitive, classic, and romantic.

Even at the risk of slight inaccuracies we may very appropriately classify the sculptures in other localities under one or other of these heads. It will be beyond the scope of the present work to undertake a detailed study of these sculptures. After having broadly indicated the nature of the three different schools we shall content ourselves with a brief review of the sculptures of other localities in relation to them.

The sculptures of Pringapus belong to the Dieng school. So far as purely decorative sculptures are concerned those of Pringapus constitute a great advance upon Dieng. Here the sculptures consist mainly of scrolls and spirals interspersed with figures of men, birds and semi-divine beings, a very familiar Indian design which was carried to its highest excellence during the Gupta period. Brandes has given a spiritual interpretation of these sculptures. In his opinion they convey a sense of repose and dignity and inspire the visitors with devotion and spiritualism which it was the manifest object of the temple to invoke. Without going so far, it is easy to recognise that the theme of these sculptures is in full harmony with, and calculated to emphasise the repose, serenity, and natural beauty of the environs of a temple. The Pringapus temple also illustrates the growing importance of decorative sculpture in a temple, but as yet it has not overshadowed the architecture.

The decorative reliefs of Kalasan, Sari, Sevu, Merak, Pavon and Ngawen belong essentially to the Barabuḍur school, and possess the same degree of excellence. But they appear to possess greater attraction simply because they are not subordinated to the narrative reliefs and possess a richer content and variety. A few specimens from Caṇḍi Merak are illustrated in Plates XXIV—XXV.

The decorative reliefs of Caṇḍi Plaosan are more exuberant but less pleasing. They consist mainly of floral spirals and show technical skill of a high order. But they seem to overshadow the architectural designs and there is a sort of monotony unrelieved by human or animal figures such as we find in the cases of Mendut and Pavon.

The fine images of Buddha and Avalokiteśvara in Caṇḍi Mendut (Pl. XIV) are very beautifully modelled and belong to the classical style of Central Java such as we find in Barabuḍur They show the same characteristic features with perhaps a greater degree of refinement and delicacy. Attention may be drawn to the fact that the back frame of the throne on which Avalokiteśvara is seated possesses the same Siṁha-Makara motive as we find in the case of the famous Buddha image of Sārnāth. The halo is, however, different. The Buddha figure may be compared with that in cave no IX at Ajaṇṭā.[1]

The images of Caṇḍi Banon (Pl. XXIII), though Brāhmanical, belong to the school of Barabuḍur rather than that of Lara-Jongrang. Figure (b) is a fine example of elegant modelling. Even the legs and feet which are usually executed in a rough way, are beautifully modelled, and the ornaments of the body are disposed of in such a way as not to obstruct a full view of the whole figure. There is an indescribable charm in every detail, and although the figure is shown as standing erect, its graceful posture offers a striking contrast to the somewhat stiff attitude of the Mahādeva of Lara-Jongrang. The Śiva image of Semarang[2] also shows some of the fine qualities which we notice in those of Banon.

---

1. V.A. Smith—Fine Arts, p. 178, fig. 123
2. T.B.G., Vol. 71 (1931), p. 666, pl. 3.

The Caṇḍi Vurung has also yielded a number of fine images of gods. The relief figures as well as images in the round at Merak also show a graceful charm and freedom of pose (Pll. XXIV-V).

The images of Caṇḍi Plaosan show a definite break from the glorious traditions of Barabuḍur. The images of Bodhisattvas (Pl. XXVI) show a richer decoration, both of the body as well as of the halo, but the modelling is less refined, and the expression and features, less elegant. In this respect they rather resemble the images of Lara-Jongrang.

The images of Caṇḍi Banon and Plaosan clearly demonstrate that the essential principles of art were the characteristics of a particular age and locality, and not determined by the different religious sects in whose service they were employed.

In conclusion we may refer to an image, now in the British Museum, which in the opinion of A. J. Bernet Kempers, probably represents the Dikpāla Nairṛta (the guardian-deity of the south-west) and belonged to Central Java.[1]

---

1. B.K.I., Vol. 88 (1931), pp. 514 ff. and Plate. Stutterheim regards it as a Bodhisatva from Singhasari (B.K.I., Vol. 80, p. 297.)

Chapter III

THE ARCHITECTURE OF EASTERN JAVA

§ 1. Early Monuments

The art of Eastern Java may be regarded as a continuation of that of Central Java, and if we treat it separately, it is merely from geographical and chronological considerations. The monuments of this art belong exclusively to the eastern part of Java, and are, with a few exceptions, posterior to those of Central Java described above, but they illustrate the normal development of the principles which underlay the earlier art. Although characterised by certain definite tendencies which gradually assert themselves prominently and transform the entire nature of Indo-Javanese art, it would be wrong to regard the Eastern art as something radically different from the earlier phase of Indo-Javanese art noticed in Central Java.

It is therefore natural to assume that when for some reason or other (see Bk. III, Ch. II) the political and cultural centre of the Indo-Javanese was shifted from Central Java to the eastern region, the artistic traditions were carried to the new home and underwent there a normal development, though undoubtedly affected by new surroundings and new conditions of life and society.

It must not be forgotten, however, that there are epigraphic evidences to show that temples were built in Eastern Java even during the period before this transition. As until recently no remains of these monuments were known, their relation with those of Central Java and with their successors in Eastern Java during the later period formed an interesting problem. In view of what has been said above regarding the continuity of the art of Central Java in the east, it was presumed that this older phase of Eastern art was either identical with that of Central Java, or that if it were different, it had no effect upon the art of the later period. The recent discoveries at Badut and Besuki establish the soundness of the first presumption, and there is hardly any doubt now that the art of Central Java was really the Indo-Javanese art in general for the eighth and ninth centuries A.D.

The almost total disappearance of the older monuments of Eastern Java offers a striking contrast to the state of things in Central Java, and certainly calls for an explanation. Two reasons may be adduced for this deplorable condition. In the first place the temples were made of brick and were therefore naturally more liable to decay. Secondly, whereas Central Java was left to its fate from the tenth century A.D., Eastern Java was in continued occupation. The consequence was that while the monuments of Central Java were only exposed to process of natural decay, those of Eastern Java were readily replaced by others according to the needs and tastes of new generations of people. Many examples of this phenomena may be quoted from India. To take only one, we may contrast the fate of the Hindu city of Benares with that of the neighbouring Buddhist monasteries at Sāranath. The latter was deserted about the eleventh century A.D. and its monuments were gradually converted into heaps of ruins. But recent researches have unearthed many of the old monuments by removing the debris at the top. In the case of Benares, however, which has been in continuous occupation from at least eighth century B.C., not a single structure exists which can be definitely dated before the Muhammadan period.

This process of destruction does not hold good only in the case of the older monuments of Eastern Java before the tenth century A.D. It has also continued its work in subsequent ages, so that very few monuments exist to-day which may be ascribed to the period anterior to the foundation of the Singhasāri kingdom, although the foundation of many such temples is testified to by epigraphic evidence.

As noted above, the oldest temples in Eastern Java are those of Badut and Besuki.[1] The ruins of the former lie about six miles from Malang in the *desa* Badut, sub-division Dau. The ruins consisted merely of a massive heap of stones, but the Dutch Archæological Department has partially reconstructed the temple from the fragments lying scattered about. There is absolutely no doubt that it was purely Central-Javanese in character. The basement is square in plan but severely plain. The western face of it is intersected by the staircase, the stone curbs of which are richly decorated and end in volutes. The main body of the temple stands on the basement leaving a circumambulating path about 5⅓ft. wide. It is square in plan with a portico on the west side. The base of the temple has the usual profile consisting of a plinth, an ogee and a roll-moulding which projects boldly to the front.

The staircase leads to a portico the door of which is crowned by a Kāla head, the place of Makara on the two lower ends of the jambs being taken by a peculiar decorative piece of stone. The cella is nearly square and fairly big, measuring about 11½ft. by 12ft., as opposed to the small size of the shrines usually met with in Eastern Java. A Yoni and a Linga, now set up there, perhaps also originally belonged to it. The Yoni is divided into fragments, but the Liṅga is in a fair state of preservation.

In the middle of the chamber is a pit of fairly large dimensions. It is about 6½ft. square, the walls being made of stone. Nothing was however found inside. It has been suggested that it originally contained the stone urn which has been discovered amid the ruins. Perhaps someone originally dug up the pit and brought out the urn.

---

1. O.V., 1923 (p. 87); 1925 (pp. 8-10) Pll. 1-4; 1929 (Bijlage H, pp. 245-257, Pll. 16-32, Plans I-VI).

The walls on the north, south, and east have each a niche in the centre. These originally contained images of gods, two of which, Durgā and Guru, were found and have been replaced. There was also a niche on each side of the portico on the western wall. The niches are crowned by Kāla-heads supporting miniature temple-roofs with divine figures flying through clouds on two sides. The walls on the two sides of the niches are divided into panels and decorated with wall-paper designs or *cakra-triśūla.*

Above the walls is a well-defined cornice with richly ornamented antefixae. Practically nothing remains of the roof above. Among the decorative *motifs* may be mentioned trees, vase with lotus, and Kinnaris. The plan, the method of decoration, the images, and the decorative ornaments all belong to the style of Central Java. The temple was enclosed by a wall, remains of which can still be traced for a considerable length.

To the west of the main temple were three small subsidiary temples, of which very little remains. A Nandi and a Linga were found among the ruins and probably occupied two of these temples.

About 1½ miles from Badut was found the missing fragment of the Dinaya stone inscription. It has been suggested by B. De. Haan that the ruins of Badut might belong to the temple mentioned in that inscription, and although he admits that this is a pure conjecture, he ascribes the foundation of the temple to the dynasty of Sañjaya, and during the period when it temporarily sought shelter in the eastern regions *i.e.* between 670-785 Śaka. In any case the temple of Badut must be regarded as one of the oldest in the whole of Java.

A little to the north of Badut we come across the remains of another temple at Besuki within the same sub-division Dau. Only the basement of the temple remains. It is square in plan, each side measuring more than 21 ft. There is a projection on the west side with a staircase, while the walls on the other sides contain three richly decorated panels divided by plain pilasters. There are also two sculptured panels on two sides of the staircase on the western side. The sculptures in the panels are mostly animal figures and vases with lotus. The figures of Durgā, Gaṇeśa, Bhaṭāraguru, and a Linga have been found among the ruins. To the south-west corner of the projection, next the staircase, a *Linga* has been built up into the body of the temple itself. The characteristic feature of the temple is that its plan, the sculpture, *motifs*, and the mode of decoration are purely Central Javanese in character.

The basement of the temple was faced with stone-slabs, but the main structure was made of brick. Some decorative features, *e.g.* the Kala-head over the main entrance and those over the niches were made of stone.

Before the discovery of the temples of Badut and Besuki the Caṇḍi Gunung Gangsir[1] (also called Derma or Keboncaṇḍi), made of brick, was regarded as the oldest monument in Eastern Java. It stands on a very high basement about 13 yds. square, which has a projection only on the front (eastern side), about 13½ ft. broad and 5½ ft. deep. The staircase which commences about 18½ ft. in front of the projection does not lead to the top of the basement, but to a higher landing (about 15½ ft. above the ground level) from which a smaller staircase leads to the cell. Thus only a small part of the projection is visible, that between the curbs of the staircase and the front side of the basement. Instead of being developed into corner temples, this part of the projections follows the outline of the basement as in temples of Central Java, and this proves the antiquity of the structure.

The basement consists of a very high plinth, followed by ogee and roll mouldings, and then, between prominent upper and lower bands, the vertical central part, divided into panels flanked by pilasters. The upper and lower bands are decorated with palmette, and the vertical part with flower-and-vase *motif*.

---

1. Krom—Kunst, II, pp. 27-33.

The upper part of the basement up to the cornice has suffered very much.

The base of the temple looks almost like a second basement, as in Lara-Jongrang. Here, again, there is a central vertical part between decorated upper and lower bands. Pilasters with ornaments at their upper and lower ends, divide this central part in long panels which are decorated with lotus-vases between two sitting naked female figures.

The base of the temple rises immediately behind the basement without leaving sufficient room for a passage. Above the base are the usual ogee, roll and other carved mouldings on which the main body of the temple rests. It is square in plan, with slight projections on three sides. In the centre of the projection is a niche, and there are smaller niches on both sides of it, as well as on the two sides of the doorway of the shrine. The niches stand on a decorated base and their upper part is triangular. The posts at the corner of the walls and of the projection are decorated with a round hole at the bottom in which birds are figured as if in their nests. There are other decorations too, but all belong to the type met with in Central Java.

The first stage of the roof alone exists and it repeats the main features of the temple.

The cella is about 12 ft. square and ends above in a hollow pyramidal cone under the roof somewhat in the style of Kalasan.

A torso riding on a bird is found among the scattered ruins and may be the figure of Viṣṇu or Brahmā, thus indicating the Brāhmanical character of the temple.

On the grounds of technique of architecture, the Caṇḍi Gunung-Gangsir may be regarded as contemporary or even earlier than Lara-Jongrang. To the same period, or perhaps a little later, may be referred the Caṇḍi Sumbernanas[1], to the

---

1. Krom—Kunst, II, pp. 34-35. Stutterheim thinks that it was founded in the period of Balitung (898—910 A.D.); B.K.I, 1930, p. 305.

north of Blitar. It is also made of brick and its lower part, which has alone survived, has the classical profile of Central Java. Images of Bhaṭāra-Guru, Brahmā, and Nandi have been found in the ruins of this temple, and their style, particularly that of the last, approximates very closely to that of Lara-Jongrang.

The earliest dated monument in Eastern Java is the tomb and bathing enclosure known as Jalatuṇḍa.[1] It lies on the western side of Gunung Bekel, one of the four peaks of the mount Penanggungan. An area, 55 ft. long by 44 ft. broad, was surrounded by walls on all sides. The back wall was built against the hill side, and the two side-walls followed the level of the sloping ground by terraced stages. The front wall has entirely disappeared. These walls were crowned by small towers at regular intervals. The water came through three spouts, one in the centre and two others on two sides of the back wall. These spouts were made into decorated figures, set in a niche, and we still find a Nāga-head on the left and Garuḍa-head on the right side. Over the right hand spout a second niche with decorated top still exists. The water from each spout fell into a cistern, over the walls of which there were gargoyles to carry the surplus water. The walls of the middle cistern, the largest of the three, consist of several decorated mouldings.

On the back wall, to the right of the middle cistern the figures 8.9.9 are legibly engraved, and close by, on the southern wall of the same cistern, are the letters 'Udayana'. This is the name of the father of Airlangga who probably built this place as the final resting ground of his remains in the year 899 or 977 A. D.[2]

A few yards below the middle cistern was discovered the royal coffin which is now in the Batavian Museum. It is a square box on a high round lotus cushion, all made up of

1. Krom—Kunst, II, pp. 35-39, pl. 46.

2. See above, Part I, p. 263 fn. 1.

one piece of stone. The box has a pyramidal cover and is divided into nine compartments all of which contained bones and ashes. There were, besides, plates and coins, both of gold and silver. The gold plates were decorated with figures of *nāga* and tortoise with mystic syllables and also inscriptions in honour of Śiva, the lord of *Bhūtas* and Agni, the lord of *Dvijas.*

Two other words have been found inscribed in this structure *viz.* "gempeng", and "Mragayavati". The latter probably stands for Mṛgayāvatī, a female name, but this is not the wife of Udayana as one might expect. The meaning of the other word is not known.

There is a second tomb and bathing enclosure at Belahan[1] on the opposite side of mount Penanggungan. It resembles that of Jalatuṇḍa in many respects and has yielded a number of very beautiful images. The finest of these is a figure of Viṣṇu on Garuḍa (Pl. XXXV). It has been suggested with great probability that this figure of Viṣṇu is a portrait of king Airlangga.

§2. Singhasari Period

The first notable monument in Eastern Java of which enough remains to give us a fair idea of its architectural peculiarities is Caṇḍi Kidal[2] (Pl. XXVII Fig. 1), the cremation-sanctuary of king Anuṣanātha. As this king died in A.D. 1248, the temple must have been built within a few years of that date, before (if the king himself had made it) or after (if it was built by his successor).

The basement of the temple is square in plan with projection in front. It stands on a base consisting of a plinth, a lower band, the broad central part divided into deeply sunken panels between pilasters, an upper band and the cornice. There is no decoration on any part of the base.

1. Krom—Kunst, II, pp. 39-44, Pl. 47.

2. A detailed account is given in 'Publicaties van den Oudheidkundige Dienst in Nederlandsch Indie—Deel I ; for a shorter account cf. Krom—Kunst, II, pp. 53-67, Pl. 49.

The basement proper consists of a plinth, the lower band, an ogee moulding, the broad central part, a second ogee, the upper band, and the cornice. An ogee moulding springing inward from above the cornice leads to a terrace on which the main body of the temple stands, leaving a small open passage all round it. There is no decoration in the basement except the central part. Here, between two projecting upper and lower bands, decorated with curling foliage-motive, the vertical part is divided by pilasters into a number of oblong sunken panels, on which we find sculptured medallions with foliage-*motif* sometimes with the addition of animal figures. The pilasters are decorated with vase-and-foliage *motif*. In the distribution of ornaments between panels and pilasters we find a radical difference from the art of Central Java, where the heavier decorations—like vase—are on the panels and the pilasters are either empty or carry only light vertical decorations. In the four corners of the basement, across the entire breadth of the central part, are four lions, in high relief, sitting on a cushion and looking in front. Similar lions adorn the two corners made by the projections and the staircase. In the middle of the central part (except on the front side) are also figures in high relief depicting a Garuḍa carrying, respectively, on the north, east and southern sides, a seated female figure, a nicely decorated vase with a cover, and a spout in the form of a nāga and three nāgas. These probably refer to the vase of Amṛta carried by Garuḍa, the female figure denoting Lakṣmi. The representation of the Garuḍa conforms remarkably well to that of Belahan and thus Caṇḍi Kidal may be regarded as belonging to the art of the older period.

The main body of the temple stands on a low base which has the same outline as that of the basement. Above this are the walls, a great part of which is covered by the doorway in front, and a large niche on each of the other three sides. The remaining parts of the walls have several plain bands, between the cornice and an ogee above, and the plinth and another ogee below. Immediately under the upper ogee, and also just above the lower one, are several projecting and receding string courses, either plain, or decorated with palmette, garland, spiral or foliage motives. The plain portion of the walls between these has just in the centre a flat horizontal band, decorated with recalcitrant spirals, ending in a triangular piece at each corner of the building. Above and below this central band the plain space is covered by a medallion on each side of the niches.

These niches stand in high relief against the background of the walls, and their upper part consists of a series of square fillets each projecting beyond the lower. These are surmounted by the cornice which has pointed pieces at the two ends, and stands at the same height as the central decorated band of the walls. In front of the niche is a projecting door frame crowned by a Kāla-head which is placed against, and covers the central part of the upper bands of the niches. The cornice supports a framework which may be called the roof of the niche. It is topped by two thick decorated bands above which rises the crowning piece, a broad flat and ornamented block of stone reaching up to the upper ogee of the walls. The posts on two sides of the niche end in a sort of curbs with volute ends which run over the proper base of the temple and intersect it in the middle. The niches are empty.

A staircase in front of the temple leads to the terrace above the basement. The part of the projection adjoining the staircase has a different profile from the rest which follows that of the basement. A second staircase enclosed between curbs with volute ends leads to the doorway of the cella, and obviously this feature is partly imitated in the case of the niches. In almost all respects the front resembles the side walls, if we substitute for the niches the doorway whose ornaments repeat on a large scale those of the niche. There are, however, two notable exceptions. In the first place, the big Kāla-head placed above the doorway covers the entire upper part reaching the first stage of the roof; secondly, there are two small niches on two sides of the doorway, just where we should expect the lower medallions on the analogy of the side-walls. These niches resemble in main features the great ones on the side-walls, and one of them has in front the figure of Mahākāla. The other niche was evidently meant for the other gate-keeper, Nandīśvara.

From the doorway two small steps lead down to the cella. The walls are quite plain and end in the usual vaulted roof by means of a series of projecting layers. The chamber is empty, the Śiva image it once contained having disappeared.

The roof of the temple consists of a number of horizontal stages, each receding only a little from the lower, so that the whole structure must have originally attained to a considerable height. The first two stages, separated by a deep indentation and a plain band, consists of flat bands decorated with branch and foliage motive and intersected by a number of zigzag lines. The third and fourth stages consist of a number of sunken panels flanked by pilasters with a series of lower and uppper bands. The vertical height of these stages offers a striking contrast to the flat horizontal stages bellow. The fifth and sixth stages correspond to the first two, and though the upper part of the roof is ruined, there is hardly any doubt that these alternating double stages were repeated until the space was sufficiently diminished to be covered by a crowning piece.

Just in front of the main staircase is a rectangular terrace, more than a yard high. There is a figure, probably of Viṣṇu, and formerly there were more, on this terrace. Both the temple and the terrace were surrounded by a stone wall more than 1½ ft. high, enclosing an area about 22½ yards square. The temple, however, does not occupy the centre of this area, and there are remains of a second enclosure made of brick. The foundations of three other structures and a bathing-place are to be found in the neighbourhood. It may be noted that the temple is made of stone but brick is used in filling up the interior.

To the north-west of Singhasāri lies the tower-temple known as Caṇḍi Singhasāri[1] (Pl. XXVIII). On a low and broad platform about 46½ ft. square, rises the basement about 11 ft. high. It has a complex profile consisting of the ogee moulding and a number of projecting and receding courses. It is square in shape with deep projections on all sides, thus having the shape of a Greek cross.

The main body of the temple stands on the square basement, its lower parts being surrounded by a stone ring which crowns the basement. It is about 21¼ ft. high and square in shape with a slightly projecting niche on each side. These niches have separate profiles of their own, and a Kāla-head, placed above them, reaches up to the cornice. The roof above it consisted of several stages of which two alone remain. The first stage consisted of several horizontal courses. One of them is decorated with lions' heads, looking front, placed side by side, and another with a pair of lions sitting back to back between a makara on each side. The next stage above it consists of five miniature temples on each side. Nothing remains of the rest of the roof, which evidently consisted of repetitions of the two lower stages.

Two characteristic features distinguish this temple. In the first place, the projections of the basement which cover almost its entire height upto the cornice, do not correspond to any similar projections in the main body of the temple and are developed into separate chapels. These have independent profiles and look like four additional buildings added to the original structure. Four big Kāla-heads which crowned them

1. A comprehensive account of the temple with numerous illustrations is given in Vol. II, of the Archaeologisch Onderzoek op Java en Madura (1909). For a shorter account cf. Krom—Kunst, II, pp. 70-86, Pll. 50-54. References to literature on the Caṇḍi Singhasāri are given in the two books noted above. On the image of Bhairava now at Leiden, which is supposed originally to have belonged to this temple, and important hypotheses derived from this, cf. T.B.G., 1925, pp. 521 ff; 1934, pp. 441 ff.

are still the dominating features of these buildings, but they are badly damaged (Pl. XXXIX, Fig. 2).

Secondly, the cella inside is within the basement, the western side chapel serving as its vestibule. Thus what appears from outside as the main body of the temple is really above the cella and should rather be regarded as its roof.

Like Caṇḍi Asu, the decorative work of the building was left unfinished, though we can judge of its character from a few completed specimens. Thus the posts of the southern niche are decorated with foliage-spiral while the other niches are quite plain, and the blocks of stone under these posts in each of the niches were evidently meant to be carved into some figures. The Kāla-head on the eastern niche was scarcely begun while the others were fully worked. The latter show how the lower part has been conventionalised into foliage patterns though the upper part still betrays the real character of the monster-head.

Of the figures of gods which once adorned the cella, the side-chapels, and the niches, only a damaged figure of Bhaṭāra-guru is now *in situ*, in the southern chapel. Four others, Durgā, Gaṇeśa, Nandīśvara, and Mahākāla are now in the Leiden Museum. These are all remarkable for the rich decoration and the nice execution of details which characterise the Singhasāri school of art.

The presence in the roof of a band with animal motive, particularly that of lion's head and *makara*, led Brandes to formulate a direct Indian influence. This is, however, denied by Krom who attributes the similarity to a common derivation from old Indian art. The absence of these features in Central Java is explained away by assuming peculiar liking of the East-Javanese people for this sort of decoration.

As regards the date of the building opinions differ. Brandes concluded from the difference in style that Caṇḍi Singhasāri was later than Caṇḍi Jago. He further identified it with Caṇḍi Pūrvapatapan, the burial-temple of king Kṛtanagara according to Pararaton. On this assumption he attributed the unfinished character of the temple to the sudden catastrophe which involved Kṛtanagara and his kingdom in a common ruin in A.D. 1292.

Krom, however, points out that the materials at our disposal are insufficient for the assertion, either that Caṇḍi Singhasāri is later than Caṇḍi Jago, or that the former represents the burial-temple of king Kṛtanagara. He, however, accepts Brandes' arguments in so far as it relates to the close relationship, both in style and decoration, between Caṇḍi Jago and Caṇḍi Singhasāri, and relegates both to the Singhasāri period.

Caṇḍi Jago[1], also called Caṇḍi Tumpang, is one of the most important monuments of the Singhasāri period. It is one of the two burial-temples of king Viṣṇuvardhana, the one in which he was represented as a Buddhist god. As king Viṣṇuvardhana died in 1268, the temple must have been erected some years before or after that date.

The temple (Pl. XXVII, Fig. 2) stands on three platforms each of which is not only smaller than the lower, but also considerably set back behind it. This gives the temple a peculiar appearance, like a tower-temple on the back portion of a raised structure.

The first platform is 6½ ft. high and 25½ yds. long. The back part is a square measuring more than 15 yds. each way. In front of it are three successive projections, the first one 13 yds. wide running up to a length of 14 ft., the second 10½ yds. wide and about 9 ft. long, while the third or the last has a width of 8½ yds. and a length of 8 ft. In the angles formed by the first and the second projections there are corner pieces with independent profile, a characteristic of East-Javanese style. In the two angles made by the second and third projections are placed two staircases against the second

1. Vol. I, of the Archaeologisch Onderzoek of Java en Madura (1904) deals with Caṇḍi Jago with copious illustrations. For a shorter account cf. Krom—Kunst, II, pp. 95—136, Pll. 57-63. References to literature on the subject are given in these publications.

projection so that the third one looks almost like a landing or platform between them. The profile of the first platform is of the usual type. Above a high plinth, which nearly covers half the height, we find the usual vertical central part between an ogee moulding and other upper and lower bands. The vertical central part is sculptured with continuous reliefs and projects forward. The ogee moulding and the cornice were decorated respectively with lotus leaves and floral scroll with birds and animals. The birds and animals serve, in the main, merely a decorative rôle, though it appears from some loose fragments that there might have been representations of animal stories.

The second platform may be divided into three parts. Beginning from behind, the first part is a square, each side measuring 30 ft. with slight projections, 18 ft. long, in the middle of all sides except the front, where two notches separate it from the next part which has the same width as the first and a length of more than 15 ft. The third part is a projection from the middle of the second part, having a width of 10 ft. and a depth of $5\frac{1}{2}$ ft. On two sides of the third part the vacant space of the second part is almost covered by the staircases and their heavy stone curbs, beautifully decorated in front and sides by foliage and animal *motif* (Pl. XLI, Fig. 2). As in the case of the first platform, the third or foremost part of the second may be regarded as a landing between the staircases.

The second platform has a very complex profile, consisting, besides the ogee mouldings, of a large number of projecting and receding courses both above and below the central vertical part. The central part, decorated with continuous relief sculptures, is sunk and not projecting like that of the lower platform. The decorations of the ogee mouldings and the cornice resemble those of the first platform, but there are a number of other bands having decorations of a different type such as geometrical patterns or a waving twisted rope with pointed stakes.

The second platform being smaller in size than the first on which it rests, and having a different ground plan, there is naturally a passage of irregular shape round it. On this, close to the plinth, is a stoneband completely encircling the entire second platform. It does not, however, follow the windings of this platform but has a simpler ground plan. From the back line, 11½ yds. wide, the two sides run straight to the front for a distance of 16 yds. Then turning inwards for 3 ft. on each side, the two lines continue for more than 4 ft. where they are joined by the front line, which has thus a reduced width of 9½ yds. This stone band round the second platform is carved with a running frieze of sculptured reliefs.

The third platform is square in shape, each side measuring nearly 23 ft. with slight projections on three sides, 14 ft. broad and 9 inches deep. Ir front a similar projection is covered almost entirely by two staircases, coming up sideways from right and left and thus at right angle to the main axis of the building. Beyond these staircases was placed originally a small terrace, which was, however, later increased in size and hid the exterior of the stone-curbs of the staircases.

The profile of the third platform resembles that of the first, save that the central part, with relief sculptures, is sunk and not projecting, and its upper and lower bands, resemble those of the second platform.

Above these three platforms rises the main body of the temple. In order to bring this temple in a line with others we may regard the first platform as the foot of the basement and the second, as the basement itself, while the third may be regarded as the base of the temple.

The temple is square in plan, each side measuring about 18½ ft., with slight projections on all sides measuring about 11½ ft. broad and 9 inches deep. The projection on the front contains the doorway, while the three others have each a niche 2 ft. 3 inches broad and more than 3 ft. 3 inches deep. The profile of this temple has now mostly disappeared but resembled that of the second platform. The walls had, among other decorations, a frieze of sculptured reliefs, and, in keeping with the style of Eastern Java, we find a decorated band exactly in its centre. Above this band nothing now remains, though it is probable that for the sake of symmetery the decoration of the upper half corresponded with that of the lower half.

The jambs of the doorway and the niches are decorated with foliage *motif* with a lion at the lower ends (Pl. XLI, Fig. 1). The square blocks supporting the jambs and the lintel are all similarly decorated. Four great Kāla heads (Pl. XXXIX, Fig. 1) which crowned the door and the niches have been recovered from the scattered ruins round the temple.

The cella was about 10 ft. square but the floor and the walls are too badly damaged to give any clear idea of the nature of the room. There are several holes on the floor which were probably designed to carry off water.

Reference has already been made to narrative reliefs in various parts of the building (Pl. XLVI, Fig. 1). About their technical character along with that of the decoration in general of the temple, which all betray a typically East-Javanese character, more will be said in a later chapter. It will suffice here to say only a few words about the general contents of these reliefs, so far as they have been definitely identified.

In the first platform we find the animal stories of the Tantri texts and the Jātakas, as well as the beginning of the story of Kuñjarakarṇa. The latter is continued in the stone belt round the second platform. The reliefs in the second platform give the story of Pārthayajña, and those of the third, the story of Arjunavivāha. The little that remains of the reliefs of the body of the temple shows that they dealt with the story of Kṛṣṇa, and the episode of Kālayavana is still traceable.

The main image of the temple, that of Amoghapāśa, representing the features of king Viṣṇuvardhana, was found among the ruins in a very damaged condition. The images of the four followers, who usually accompany the god, have also been found. These are (1) Bharāla Sudhanakumāra (Pl. XXXIII), (2) Śyāmatārā, (3) Bharālī Bhṛkuṭi, and (4) Bharāla Hayagrīva. The names of these deities are written on the stone in purely North-Indian character, which was then not in use and probably also unknown in Java (that of the second has been lost).

Along with these have been found five smaller images, with similar inscriptions, representing Bharāla Akṣobhya, Bharāla Ratnasambhava, Bharālī Māmakī, Bharālī Pāṇḍuravāsinī, and Bharālī Locanā. We have thus in Caṇḍi Jago almost a complete set of the Dhyānī Buddhas and their Śaktis.

The Indian origin of the inscriptions as well as the technical peculiarities of these images led Brandes to the view that they were either directly imported from India or made by Indian artists in Java. Krom, however, disputes both these views. The question will be discussed in a later section.

The Caṇḍi Jago undoubtedly offers one of the most important relics of later Buddhism in Eastern Java. Its sanctity in the eyes of the contemporaries was indeed very great. King Kṛtanagara, son of Viṣṇuvardhana, made bronze plates in which the deities of this temple, referred to above, were united in a group, and five of these bronze replicas have come to light. These contain the names of the gods, the Buddhist formula, and a short record of king Kṛtanagara, all written in the same Indian script as we find on the stone images. The same group was reproduced in stone by the same king and sent to Sumatra where it was formally set up in 1286 A.D.[1] It still exists and is known as the Amoghapāśa of Rambahan.

It may be noted here that an image of Dharmapāla has been found among the ruins of Caṇḍi Jago and a similar image has been found in Sumatra close to the place where the Amoghapāśa image was originally set up.

---

1. See Part I, p. 299.

§3. The Majapahit Period.

In spite of the political convulsions that transferred the seat of authority from Singhasāri to Majapahit there is no corresponding break in the continuity of the art traditions in Eastern Java. This is less to be wondered at when we remember that the royal dynasty of Majapahit derived its claims to rule over Java from that of Singhasāri and tried by every means to keep alive the bond between the two. Naturally the art of Singhasāri continued to develop in a normal way even under the new regime.

The first notable monument of this period is Caṇḍi Javi[1] at the foot of the Velirang. It is the same as temple Jajava which contained the remains of king Kṛtanagara and where the king was represented by the excellent images of Śiva and Buddha. It was begun by king Kṛtanagara himself, but completed, most probably, by his son-in-law Kṛtarājasa Jayavardhana, the first king of Majapahit. The Nāgara-Kṛtāgama, to which we owe this information, also gives an interesting description of the temple when it existed in its full glory. It appears to have been of the shape of a tower-temple and contained an image of Śiva; but an image of Akṣobhya was placed hidden in an upper chamber which, however, subsequently disappeared.

At present nothing exists except the basement. It is square in plan with two successive projections in front, each having a different profile. Against the second projection was laid the staircase and on both sides of it were placed corner buildings in the usual way. The basement had its central part decorated by a long series of relief sculptures divided into panels.

The small temple, rather the model of a temple, at Kotes, to the east of Blitar, known also as Caṇḍi Papoh[2] is important as it gives us a complete representation of an East-Javanese temple, particularly its roof. The temple itself is square in

1. Krom—Kunst II, pp. 138-150. 2. Ibid, pp. 152-7, Pl. 64.

plan, with projections on all sides, containing the door and niches, and the usual structures at the two angles formed by the front projection and the wall of the temple. Each side of the square measures only 34 inches, but the height of the temple is more than 8 feet. The roof looks like a truncated pyramid, consisting of a succession of four receding horizontal stages, square in shape and sharply differentiated from one another by a deeply sunken part. Above the fourth stage is a plain broad square block slightly tapering upwards, which supported the crowning ornament. The three lower stages of the roof were formed of broad horizontal bands decorated with scroll-work and heavy antefix ornaments both in the middle and the corner. The decoration of the fourth stage was somewhat different. The images found among the ruins indicate that the temple was Śaivite in character. The temple is to be dated in 1301 A. D., as this date is inscribed on one of the two altars standing on the same high and broad platform on which the temple stands.

Very little now remains of the palaces and temples that once adorned the city of Majapahit. The most notable monument in the vast area of its ruins is the gateway, like South-Indian Gopuram, at Bajang-ratu[1] (Pl. XXIX, Fig. 1), about 54 ft. high. The central structure, which alone remains in a fair state of preservation, is built on the model of a temple, square in plan with projections on all sides. On the north and south these projections are covered by the doorway while in the other two directions there are the usual niches. The most interesting feature of the building is the roof which has been preserved almost in its entirety. It consists of a succession of fourteen horizontal stages, each only a little smaller than and slightly set back behind the one below, so that the whole structure has a pyramidal shape. The lowest two stages of the roof consist of flat bands with relief. The two above them consist of a series of five moulded

1. Ibid, pp. 190-3, Pl. 68.

balusters on each side, connected by a horizontal decorating band placed on their top. The space between the balusters being empty, the stages containing them offer a sharp contrast to the others. The upper stages merely consist of an alternation of these double stages, on a gradually reduced scale. Above the topmost stage occur three horizontal bands which support the massive top-piece, a square block of stone with slightly tapering walls resting on a lotus band. This top-piece supported the crowning ornament which, however, is missing.

Of the notable monuments in Eastern Java that were erected during the glorious period of the Majapahit empire, a few alone remain to tell the tale of its old grandeur.

The Caṇḍi Jabung[1] (Pl. XXIX, Fig. 2) to the east of Kraksaan in the Residency of Pasuruhan is an excellent example. The basement and the base of the temple are square in plan with projections on all sides, but the main body of the temple is circular in shape with rectangular projections on the four sides. A decorated stone band, on a plain plinth, forms the lower part of the basement. Then follow the decorated ogee mouldings between ornamented upper and lower bands, and a profusely decorated central vertical part, consisting of sculptured panels, divided by decorated pilasters.

The base of the temple also has decorated ogee mouldings and a central part consisting of sculptured panels. The main body of the temple, as already said above, is round. It has a complex profile consisting of a large number of plain courses both above and below. Between them are three ornamented bands, one in the middle and the other two forming respectively the lowest band of the upper moulding and the topmost of the lower one. The rectangular projections are developed into niches with projecting and decorated doorways surmounted by Kāla-Makara. They stand on rectangular bases and have had an absolutely independent profile. The

1. Ibid, pp. 196-203, Pl. 70,

front projection, of course, served as the main doorway leading to the cella about 8½ ft. square. Little now remains of the roof. The present height of the temple is about 52½ ft. The peculiar shape of the temple, *viz.*, a combination of round and angular forms, the skilful design by which the upper circular part was merged into the lower rectangular one, the harmonious adjustment and well-balanced proportion of the different parts, and finally the scheme of decoration, at once vigorous and restrained, all invest this monument with a high degree of importance.

This Buddhist temple was known as Bajrajināp aramitāpura and is probably identical with the temple of Kalayu, referred to in the Nāgara-Kṛtāgama, as the burial temple of a member of the family of king Hayam Wuruk.

Not far from Paree, to the east of Kaḍiri, lie the remains of Caṇḍi Suravana[1] (old Śura-bāṇa), also called Caṇḍi Bloran, which was visited by Hayam Wuruk in A. D. 1361. At present nothing remains save the basement, about 25½ ft. square, with a series of three successively smaller projections on the front *i. e.* western side.

The foot of the basement, about 1½ ft. high, consists of a plain plinth, a decorated cornice, and the central vertical part between a decorated upper and a lower band. The central part consists of projecting sculptured panels, divided by plain flat pilasters. At each corner are dwarfish monster-figures, and in the centre of each side (except the front), a decorated rectangular block of stone, all of which stretch from the plinth to the cornice. Above this, the basement proper really consists of two parts, separated by double ogee mouldings decorated with lotus-leaf *motif.* The lower part is plain, with only a small decorated piece of stone projecting from the centre. The upper part is almost entirely covered on each side by a big oblong sculptured panel, the small margins on its two sides forming two raised and decorated

---

1. Ibid, pp. 209-216, Pl. 71-7 .

pilasters. The sculptures on the big panels illustrate the poem Arjunavivāha. The sculptures on the corner pilasters have been explained by Brandes as the scenes from Rāmāyaṇa, but this is doubted by Krom. Fragments of images found among the ruins indicate the Śaivite character of the temple.

Of the neighbouring temple called Caṇḍi Tigavangi.[1] also the high basement alone remains. It has a large number of decorated mouldings above a plain plinth. The central vertical part is carved with a running frieze representing the scenes of Sudamala. According to Pararaton Caṇḍi Tigavangi was formerly known as Kusumapura and was the burial temple of the Prince of Matahun, Hayam Wuruk's brother-in-law, who died in A. D. 1388.

The Caṇḍi Keḍaton (known earlier as Andungbiru)[2], erected in A.D. 1370, lies to the south of Kraksaan. It is a basement, pure and simple, with no superstructure above it. It is 20 ft. square, with a projection on the north, and offers the characteristic features of an East-Javanese basement. Its panels and pilasters are decorated with relief sculptures illustrating Arjunavivāha. They show, however, considerable variations from the existing text of the poem.

The Caṇḍi Pari[3] (Pl. XXX) to the north-west of Porrong, erected in A.D. 1371, offers a striking contrast to East-Javanese temples and shows many features of the temples of Champā, *e.g.* those of Mison. The roof and the basement are mostly ruined. In the middle of each wall is a small niche with independent profile and a triangular roof. The walls have a large number of plain and decorated bands both above and beneath the niches. Otherwise, the walls of the temples are almost plain, for although there are plain oblong panels they can hardly be distinguished from the equally plain background of the walls. The temple is made of brick and was undoubtedly influenced by examples of Cham temples.

1. Ibid, pp. 216-222, Pl. 73.
2. Ibid, pp. 223-229.
3. Ibid, pp. 229-234, Pl. 74.

Another monument of the same period is the gateway of Jedong[1], erected in A.D. 1385, which has the profile of a temple. Its decoration was left incomplete. The most interesting part of the building is the roof which is fairly preserved up to a great height, and consists alternately of a broad horizontal stage and a vertical one, consisting of a series of moulded balusters.

The greatest and most famous monument in Eastern Java is the temple complex of Panataran[2] (old name Palah), to the north-east of Blitar. Unlike Caṇḍi Sevu the various structures that compose the group of Panataran were not parts of the same plan or design but grew up sporadically around what had come to be regarded as a sacred ground from early times. The building activities can be traced throughout the thirteenth and fourteenth centuries A. D. The great temple which naturally occupies our chief attention belongs probably to the middle of the fourteenth century A.D. during the Regency, while the Peṇḍapa-terrace and a smaller temple, which come next in point of importance, belong to the reign of Hayam Wuruk.

The whole temple area, 196 yds. by 65 yds., was enclosed by a wall with its chief entrance to the west. The enclosed area was again divided into three parts by two cross walls. The main temple occupied the rearmost *i.e.* the eastern part (Pl. XXXI). Three terraces, each smaller than, and having a different ground-plan from the lower, supported the main temple. The temple has, however, disappeared altogether, and the terraces alone remain.

The first terrace is square in plan with projections on each side. The front projection is deeper than the rest, and the walls on its two sides have smaller double projections. Two

---

1. Ibid, pp. 238-243, Pl. 76.

2. Ibid, pp. 244-284 (Pll. 78-87), which also gives, on pp. 283-4, references to literature on the subject. The Rāmāyaṇa reliefs are reproduced in Kats—Het Rāmāyaṇa (Figs 1-106)

staircases, built against these double projections lead from the ground to the first terrace. Together with the projections the first terrace measures about 37 yds. by 33 yds.

The second terrace was placed on the first leaving a passage around it on all sides. It is also almost square in plan, each side measuring about 21 yds. But instead of projections there are recesses in the centre of each face. In front, however, a large part of the recess is covered by a staircase built against a double projection. As the recesses correspond to the projections of the first terrace, a large space was available in this part of the passage, and four small chapels were built here on the four sides. These have, however, utterly perished.

The elevation of the first two terraces is similar and resembles that of the basement of a temple. Its characteristic features were the decorated pilasters at the corners which project in front along the entire height above the plinth, and support a miniature temple above the floor of the terrace. The reliefs on the central part, in the first terrace, consist of a number of medallions, on three superimposed slabs, decorated with reliefs representing an animal amidst foliage. These animals are of great varieties including even some species which are not found in Java. The space between the medallions, resembling flat pilasters, are covered with reliefs representing scenes from the Rāmāyaṇa. In the second terrace, the central part is covered by continuous reliefs illustrating Kṛṣṇāyana. It appears that the version of the poem followed by the artist is somewhat different from the existing text, but there is an agreement about the essential points.

The third terrace is square in plan with triple projections in front against the centre of which the staircase is placed. It stands on the second terrace, leaving a passage all round. It has a very simple elevation, *viz.*, the central part with decorated string courses above and below. The central part is divided into a number of sunken panels flanked by pilasters. The panels are decorated by winged *nāgas* with projecting heads, and the pilasters by winged lions with raised hind legs. The vertical character of the reliefs of the third terrace offers a striking contrast to the horizontal character of those of the first two, and clearly indicates that it was designed to support a structure above it. In other words, the third terrace may be regarded as the base of the temple which it once supported.

Although nothing now remains above the third terrace the scattered fragments give some idea of the walls of the temple which once stood on it. A number of *gaṇa* figures as pilasters, and the panels between them, decorated with animal figures, served as the base. The upper part stood on a number of richly decorated courses, and had a great niche in the centre of each side, with images, respectively, of Brahmā, Viṣṇu, and Śiva, and their *Vāhanas*. There were also decorated panels and images of other gods *e.g.*, Indra, Kārttikeya, Vāyu, Agni, *etc.*, on their proper *Vāhanas.*

The big images of four temple-guards, (Pl. XL, Fig. 1.) about 6½ ft. high, found among the ruins, were originally placed on the two sides of the two staircases of the first terrace. The pedestal on which they stand bears the date A.D. 1347.

As already said above, the temple area was divided into three parts. In addition to the big temple there are remains of a stone and a brick temple in the eastern part.

In the central part are found detached images of *rākṣasas*, temple-guards (dated A.D. 1319), a door-lintel (dated A.D. 1318), and remains of temples, both of brick and stone. But the most remarkable is the stone basement on which has been reconstructed the small Nāga temple.

The elevation of the basement is somewhat complex, consisting of a large number of plain courses and ogee mouldings. On the corners and the middle of the wall of the temple, as well as on two sides of the doorway, are decorated pilasters supporting richly ornamented and well-proportioned human figures, most probably divine beings. Sunken panels between these pilasters are decorated by medallions with animal and foliage reliefs. Waving bodies of serpents, reaching as high as the cornice, and down as far as the top of the panels, surround the temple-walls on all sides, and are supported by the figures on the pilasters. It forms a very characteristic feature of the temple and reminds us of the waving garland motive of the Indian art. The staircase is enclosed between massive stone-rails with spiral ends. These are decorated with triangular reliefs and on two sides of it are the usual corner-structures.

The front or westernmost part of the area contains, besides loose brick ruins, three monuments;—a small temple, dated A.D. 1369, in the axis of the big temple, the Peṇḍapa-terrace dated A.D. 1375, and lastly a terrace in the north-west corner.

The temple belongs to the classical type of East Javanese art and offers a refreshing contrast to the innovations noticed in the big temple and the Nāga temple described above. The basement and the base of the temple are square in plan, and have a very simple elevation consisting of plain courses. The body of the temple is also square in plan, but the continuity of the walls is broken by the niches on three sides and the door-way in front. These have independent elevations, and, with the Kala-heads above their cornices, extend almost over the whole length of the temple-wall from the base to the frieze below the cornice. The remaining portion of the wall consists of a number of plain and richly decorated courses, among the latter being the two ogee-mouldings, the course above the upper ogee, and three courses in the middle part.

The roof has almost entirely disappeared, but as reconstructed in recent times with the help of loose fragments, it shows the usual pyramidal form of East Javanese temples, with alternate double horizontal and double vertical stages.

The Peṇḍapa terrace is a long (north-south) and narrow platform of stone approached by two staircases on the west. The stone rails of the stair-cases are decorated by a triangular ornament above, and a serpent below. The body of the serpent runs beneath the rail, along the entire base of the terrace, forming its lower course. Above this is a panel with continuous reliefs, broken only by the two staircases. Above this frieze of sculptures is the projecting cornice decorated with animal and foliage motive, which also occasionally illustrates some animal fables. The reliefs on the central frieze illustrate, among others, the story of Bubukṣa. As in the case of Barabuḍur there are still remains of short labels, indicating the story to be illustrated, which were no doubt meant for the guidance of the artist. But even these have not enabled the scholars to identify all the reliefs.

The other terrace in the north-west corner is quite plain and does not require any detailed description. Beyond this we come to the main entrance of the big temple area. It is a broad doorway with an opening about 13 ft. wide, and is flanked by two kneeling Rākṣasa figures. The date 1242 (A.D. 1320) engraved on these figures, taken along with the dates found on the monuments of the second part, indicate that the general plan of the temple area was completed in that year, and that some monuments, including the big temple, were merely added later in the vacant spaces. It may be added that the temple complex was dedicated to Śiva.

Beyond the enclosing wall and to the south-east of it are the remains of a bath constructed in A.D. 1415 on a much lower level than the temple area. The oblong cistern is approached by a staircase, and is open to the east. The walls on three other sides are made of brick below supporting a single upper course of blocks of stones carved with reliefs, representing animal-stories[1]. Two plain courses of stones above it are later additions. In front of the side walls are two pilasters, each carved with a human figure on its two visible sides. These figures are clad in very simple style but executed in bold outline.

Caṇḍi Panataran is the last great monument of Eastern Java of which sufficient remains exist to give us some definite

1. The interpretation of Krom is corrected by Crucq in O.V. 1930, p. 221.

idea of its character. Ruins exist everywhere to indicate that the art of temple-building continued to flourish till the last days of Hindu rule in Java, and even later, but unfortunately very little is preserved to enable us to add any new aspect in the delineation of East Javanese art. We shall, therefore, conclude this account by referring to a few more architectural remains which offer some peculiar or striking features.

The Caṇḍi Vringin Brañjang[1], to the south of the Klut hill, is of a unique design. It is made of stone and is nearly square in plan, measuring 14 ft. by 11 ft. It has neither basement nor any base, and the walls rise directly from the ground to a height of 10½ ft. up to the simple mouldings of the cornice. The most characteristic feature is, however, the roof which consists of four slanting sides meeting in a point, like a thatched cottage in Bengal. Another peculiarity is the total absence of decoration.

The Caṇḍi Jadi, on the Vajak or Vali-Kukun hill, is another unique structure. On an ordinary basement, square in plan, with shallow projections, and with usual elevation, stands a similar superstructure, which is, however, soon changed into an octagonal form, supporting a round wall, without any opening.

The inside is also round and there is no trace of a staircase for descending to the interior. Various suggestions have been made regarding this building. It has been supposed to be a prison or an observatory. The latest view is that of Krom who regards it as a sort of 'Tower of Silence' where the Parsis expose their dead bodies for being eaten by vultures. This is, however, contested by Stutterheim who regards the monument as the base of a *stūpa*, the round pit serving as the hidden chamber for relics. The upper part being constructed of perishable materials has altogether vanished[2].

---

1. Krom—Kunst, II, pp. 314-6, Pl. 91.

2. Ibid, pp. 320-21; B.K.I. Vol. 80 (1924), pp. 447 ff and plates; also Vol. 81, pp. 543ff and plates.

The temple-complex of Selakelir[1], on the Penanggungan hill, bears two stones dated A. D. 1434 and 1442, and may thus be regarded as one of the latest products of Majapahit art with definitely known dates. It is in a very ruined condition, but enough remains to show that while the general plan and even the detailed decorations follow the standard model of East Javanese temples, already important modifications have been introduced which were destined slowly to change the style in a new direction. These remarks are specially applicable to the small temple on the north-eastern corner. Here not only the relative proportions of the different parts are markedly changed, such *e. g.*, as the space between lower and middle courses, the size of the corner-piece *etc.*, but *motifs*, well-known in themselves, have been put in places where they did not occur before. A characteristic example of the latter is furnished by the decorations of the door-jambs with waving-rope motive. Similar remarks are applicable also to the sculptures. On the whole it is evident that the style is undergoing a marked change in order to develop in a new direction.

A brief reference should also be made to a few cave temples in East Java. A group of two, known as Selamangleng[2] is found to the west of Blitar, on the north of Vajan or Valikukun hill. One of them is a roughly hewn chamber more than 13 ft. broad, about 10 ft. deep, and 6 ft. high. It is open on the front, and a little more than 2¼ ft. above the floor, the three walls are decorated with continuous reliefs, illustrating the poem Arjunavivāha. A little to the south is a second cave without any decoration, but the rock-wall between the two was once carved with reliefs.

Another cave, also called Selamangleng[3] lies on the hillock Klotak in Wilis mountain, to the west of Kediri. It is not only more complex in design but also more richly

---

1. Ibid, pp. 399—406, Pl. 102.
2. Ibid, pp. 318-19, Pl. 92.
3. Ibid, pp. 329-332.

adorned with decorative sculptures and narrative reliefs. The front wall, looking east, has two entrances. The one to the right has a rectangular doorway leading to a chamber (No. 1) about 13 ft. broad, 6⅓ ft. deep and 5¾ ft. high. Against the back wall is a stone bench with a raised cushion on one side, while a doorway leads to a second chamber (No. 2) further back, nearly octagonal in shape, and measuring about 10 ft. broad, 8½ ft. deep, and 5¼ ft. high. A pedestal placed against the northern wall of this chamber supports a polished stone with a decorated band, evidently the backpiece of the seated image which once occupied the pedestal, with probably two more images on two sides. To the right is a small niche.

The entrance on the left-hand side of the front wall, leads through a somewhat rounded doorway to a chamber (No. 3) about 6½ ft. broad and 5¾ ft. high, with a Nāga head amidst clouds, sculptured on the left-hand or southern wall. This chamber, which communicates with No. I, serves as an antechamber to another (No. 4) on a lower level, measuring 12½ ft. broad, 11 ft. deep, and nearly 6½ ft. high. Against its back wall, in the middle of a raised floor, a seated image, on a pedestal with lotus-cushion, is placed in a niche with cloud-lines, flanked by two smaller niches which no doubt served as lampstands. A small stairway, with 3 steps in the southern wall, leads up to a higher domed chamber (No. 5), 7⅓ ft. broad, 6½ ft. deep, and 6¼ ft. high, against the back wall of which is a seated Buddha in Dharma-cakra mudrā.

The cave complex is no doubt a combination of monastery and chapel as we find in India. Its most characteristic features are the decorative sculptures offering a variety of *motifs*, such as men, animals, birds, trees, hills, clouds, flames *etc.*, and probably also some narrative reliefs illustrating Jātaka stories. The front wall has a niche which probably once contained an image, and by the side of it is an inscription in characters of the eleventh century A.D. The sculptures inside the cave, however, belong to the style of Panataran and thus indicate a later date. A loose fragment of a pedestal found on the site bears the date 1353 (1431 A. D.). It is probable, therefore, that the cave was originally constructed in the eleventh century A. D. but its decoration was added four centuries later. The Buddha image may have belonged to the original cave.

Reference has already been made to the unique cave at Siti Jedog which served as a burial place[1].

§ 4. Post-Majapahit Period

The fall of Majapahit almost coincides with the end of Hindu culture in Java. But still the art traditions survived, and we must therefore briefly touch upon the artistic remains of Java dating from the period after the fall of Majapahit. In view of what has been said above (Part I, pp. 410-11) regarding the last stages of Hindu culture in Java, these remains may be broadly divided into two classes. First, the structures and images on the uplands, notably on mounts Willis, Lavu and Merbabu, where the Hindus, fleeing from the triumphant Muslims, found a last refuge ; secondly, the remains in the eastern corner of Java where the Hindus maintained some sort of political authority up to the eighteenth century A.D.

As regards the first, the most characteristic feature of the structures is a series of terraces on the hill side. A typical example is furnished by Sukuh[2] to the western side of Mount Labu. A number of terraces once existed here, but the upper four alone now remain, and they were surrounded by stone walls. A series of three gateways standing in a right line give access to these terraces. These portals, made of stone, are somewhat singular in design, as their front and back walls as well as those on the sides are not vertical but slant towards each other like Egyptian Pylons. The first

1. see above, p. 229. 2. Krom—Kunst, II, pp. 372-381, Pl. 99.

portal is about 40 ft. broad and 26 ft. high, and its walls are sculptured with reliefs. The passage of the doorway is about 6′-9″ long, 3′-3″ broad, and 7′-6″ high.

The first terrace contained some loose images and relief sculptures, and the second was empty. On the third terrace, however, is found a peculiar structure (Pl. XXXII, Fig. 1), a stepped truncated pyramid, about 19½ ft. high. It was constructed of horizontal stone courses, forming steps, which supported a rectangular platform. The walls of the latter were decorated, but the upper part is quite plain, and never supported any superstructure. The floor of this platform, which contained only a Yoni, was about square in shape, each side measuring a little more than 20 ft., whereas the base of the pyramid was about 50 ft. broad. On the western side of the platform is a projection with a staircase in front, running down the pyramid and enclosed between curbs. Near this main structure were two smaller ones, a basement and an obelisk, and a large number of images. Among these are a Liṅga (6½ ft. high), Śiva, Garuḍa, Durgā and tortoises. Van Stein Callenfels has explained some reliefs as illustrations of Sudamala.[1] On the first terrace were a Liṅga and Yoni very realistically represented. Javanese newly married couples used to pass by these stone figures, to prove that the bride was still a maiden, for otherwise her Sarong would fall down or be torn.

At Penampihan,[2] on the eastern side of Mt. Willis, we find a similar succession of three terraces. On the lowest terrace is an oval structure of stone, with the two ends slightly raised, so that the whole thing had the appearance of a ship. In the centre stood a two-armed figure, richly ornamented, with a serpent as sacred thread and representing a Wajang-type. Among smaller images was one of Gaṇeśa. On the third terrace (the second being empty) stood three

1. Cf. also B.K.I. 1930, pp. 561 ff, 564 ff.

2. Krom-Kunst, II, pp. 366-372.

structures, a big one in the centre between two smaller ones. Of the central structure, the basement alone remains. It has a projection in front, of the shape of the head of a tortoise, on whose back the entire monument is placed. Around the tortoise are two snakes whose hoods serve as the corner pieces.

Among other localities may be mentioned Ceta[1], on the top of the Lavu mountain, which had fourteen terraces. In all these places numerous Śaiva images and sculptured reliefs have been found as at Sukuh. But most of these are roughly worked, and there are many absolutely strange figures, including examples of obscene or obnoxious character. Besides, the inscriptions of both Sukuh and Penampihan are written in alphabets which are related to, but very different from the usual East Javanese type.

On the whole the remains of Sukuh indicate an art very far degenerated from, though not altogether unconnected with, that of Majapahit, and Penampihan belongs to the period of transition between the two. But it may be noted that a few images, notably two of Sukuh (Pl. XXXVII, Fig. 4.), indicate a far higher level of artistic skill than the generality of existing remains would warrant us to presume.

There are also other localities with terraces, where absolutely no traces of Hinduism have been met with. It has been suggested that this terrace-cult was Indonesian in origin, on which Hinduism was engrafted at a later date, mostly during the fifteenth century, when, fleeing before the triumphant Islam, Hinduism found a last refuge on these hill sides.

This view may be supported on grounds of architecture. Fergusson noted long ago the striking resemblance between the remains at Sukuh and the contemporary edifices in Yucatan and Mexico. From this he drew the inference that "the building races of Central America were of the same family

1. Ibid, pp. 381-85; B.K.I. 1930, p. 557.

as the native inhabitants of Java." Although there was no direct communication between these races during the historical period, there is some force in Fergusson's hypothesis that "it was the blood and the old faith and feelings of these two long dissevered branches of one original race that came again to the surface, and produced like effects in far distant lands".[1]

It has been already remarked above that the portals of Sukuh resemble the pylons of ancient Egypt, such for example, as those at Karnak. It may be noted, however, that similar forms, with a still greater resemblance to those of Sukuh, are still in use among the Haussa (or Houssa), a people of the Sudan, who constitute the larger part of the population in Sokoto, Adamawa and Gando. This may be cited in support of Stutterheim's theory[2] of Egyptian influence upon the art of Eastern Java, though such hypotheses must be regarded as very premature.

The wide spread of this common form of architecture among primitive races strengthens the view that the art of Sukuh indicates a revival of the primitive or indigenous element of culture after the downfall of the Hindu civilisation in Java.

While Hindu culture and civilisation maintained a precarious existence in Java proper in isolated hill sides, and were gradually degenerated into primitive cults, things were more favourable in the eastern corner, where, as already said above, petty Hindu states existed up to the eighteenth century. Unfortunately the monuments in these regions were mostly in brick and have thus left little traces behind. But quite a large number of ruined structures, with images of Hindu gods and a large collection of gold, silver and bronze images of Buddhist gods, leave no doubt that the practice of temple-building continued in the north, south and

---

1. Hist. of Ind. and East. Architecture, Vol. II, pp. 439-40.
2. I.A.L. Vol. III, p. 27.

south-eastern parts of Eastern Java. Where some decorations can still be traced, as at Kranjingan, they make a favourable impression about the skill of the artist. It is sad to think that many of these remained in a fair state of preservation even less than hundred years ago, and were allowed to perish for want of proper care. Insignificant in themselves, they might have enabled us to add the last link in the chain of Indo-Javanese art which we have traced from Dieng to Selakelir. Many European visitors have left descriptions of these temples, and we give below a short account of one of them, a temple at Macanputih, called Meru, on the eastern extremity of Java.[1]

A heavy brick wall surrounded the temple, rather a temple-complex or a town. The wall was 12 ft. high, 6 ft. thick, and had a circumference of 2¾ miles.

The temple was made of layers of brick inside, and chalk-stone on the outside. The steps leading to the basement were of the shape of half-moon, while the basement itself was like a monstrous tortoise surrounded by two serpents with heads in front and tails at its back. Some writers, however, differ in their description, mentioning an alligator and two dragons in place of the tortoise and two serpents.

The walls were divided by ornamented projecting courses into eight squares, decorated with floral arabesques. In front of the temple was a terrace or a platform. Among the images are mentioned those of Gaṇeśa, Brahmā, Garuḍa, Nandi and a group of life-size figures of Gopis bending respectfully before Kṛṣṇa.

It may be noted that the general plan of the basement is similar to that of Penampihan, the division of the walls into squares resembles that of Caṇḍi Pasetran, and that the terrace in front of the temple has its counterpart in Caṇḍi Kidal. Thus on the whole the temple preserved old elements, though

---

1. Krom—Kunst, II, pp. 413-417.

perhaps with new modifications. The same conclusion follows from the meagre accounts of the sculptures that we possess. Like those of Selakelir, they show continuity of old traditions with a certain degree of novelty in the method of application. Thus we find the beginnings of a new development whose further course can, however, be traced, not in Java but only in Bali on the other side of the channel.

Chapter IV

SCULPTURE OF EASTERN JAVA

The sculpture of Eastern Java may be studied separately under the following heads.

1. Narrative reliefs.
2. Images of gods in the round.
3. Other images in the round.
4. Decorative work.

1. Narrative reliefs.

The sculptured reliefs representing stories bear a decided stamp of their own and form the most characteristic distinguishing feature of the art of Eastern Java. The chief peculiarities of the style are the following :

(a) The human figures are coarsely executed. They are vulgar and ugly, and sometimes queer and distorted like the puppets of Wayang.

(b) There is no idea of symmetery, rhythm, harmony, or perspective in the composition or grouping, the figures being arranged in a line with trees or other objects interspersed between them.

(c) The figures, lifeless and devoid of expression, usually look like silhouettes.

(d) Exuberance of decorative ornaments such as trees, scrolls, and spirals, generally regarded as cloud-lines.

(e) The busts are always shown in their frontal aspect, even though the head or legs, or both, are turned sideways.

(f) The figures are carved in low relief.

These characteristics are illustrated by the well-known reliefs of Caṇḍi Jago (Pl. XLI, Fig. 1) and Caṇḍi Panataran

(Pl. XXXII, Figs. 2-3). The reliefs of Caṇḍis Suravana, Tigavangi, and Bangli[1] show the same characteristics in more or less marked degree.

Dr Stutterheim has recently drawn attention to the relief-sculptures at Guwa Pasir near Tulung Agung, and in his opinion they are 'works of the highest order'.[2] But in spite of undoubted vigour in the execution they show the degraded features of Eastern Javanese art.

Any one who compares the Rāmāyaṇa reliefs of Panataran (Pl. XXXII, Figs. 2-3) with those of Prambanan (Pl. XXI, Figs. 3-4) where they represent the same episode, can immediately perceive the great gulf that separates the two schools of art. The degradation of one of the best forms of art into one of the lowest is difficult to explain simply by the lapse of time. As a matter of fact, so far as we can judge from the few imperfect reliefs in the bathing enclosure of Jalatuṇḍa, the degradation in a very marked form had already begun in the tenth century A.D. The reason must, therefore, lie in the racial characteristics. In other words, the predominantly Javanese element in the East now asserts itself against the Indianised central region which lost its supreme position in the ninth and tenth centuries A.D.

2. The images of Gods.

Nothing illustrates more forcibly the conservative force of religious traditions than the divine images of Eastern Java. In contrast to the degraded forms of men, and occasionally also of gods, which we meet with in the relief sculptures, the images of gods and goddesses in the round are made in old style.

Take for instance the divine images in Caṇḍi Jago (See pp. 266-7). With the exception of Hayagrīva which is deliberately designed to portray a hideous unnatural figure, all the other images show the characteristic Indian or

---

1. Krom—Kunst, III, Pl. 105.
2. T.B.G., Vol. 73 (1933), pp. 453-68, Pll. 1-6.

Indo-Javanese style which attempts to combine naturalism with divine idealism. The treatment is less satisfactory than that of Central Java, but the continuity of tradition is unmistakable. The standing images of Amoghapāśa, Bhṛkuṭi, Sudhanakumāra (Pl. XXXIII) and Śyāmatārā are profusely decorated with ornaments, and their dress is made of Batik or flowered cloths. The details of clothes and ornaments executed with meticulous care, and natural, not conventional, lotus leaves and stalks on two sides, form a very characteristic mode of decoration in these figures. In spite of all these decorations and a richly elaborated head-dress, the figures are somewhat stiff and rigid, and they lack the elegance of the images of Central Java. The faces are not, however, altogether, devoid of divine expression, and there is a sort of radiant energy issuing from them. On the whole they possess a striking resemblance to the mediaeval Brāhmanical images of India, and were probably executed by specially imported Indian artists, as the Indian character of the short inscriptions (labels) shows.

The images of Akṣobhha and Ratnasambhava are in the usual fashion of a seated Buddha, with close-fitting robe. The head is missing in both, but enough remains to show that the execution is far inferior to that of Central Java.

The three female counter-parts of Buddha, Locanā, Māmakī and Pāṇḍuravāsinī, are all represented as seated cross-legged on a lotus-cushion like the Buddha figures. Locanā has a surprisingly naturalistic expression, and may have been modelled as a portrait. Māmakī has a calm serene expression such as we meet with in Central Javanese figures. The head of the other is damaged. All the three are decorated with ornaments and elaborate head-dress.

The images found at Singhasāri present the same characteristic features as those of Jago, but are on the whole executed with greater artistic skill. The Gaṇeśa[1] is seated on a cushion surrounded by human skulls, and the terrible

1. Another very fine image of Gaṇeśa which was in Singhasari up to 1896 is now in Bangkok; cf. B.K.I., Vol. 79, pp. 511 ff. Pl. 6.

and hideous naked figure of Bhairaba is represented as seated on a jackal with his foot on a similar cushion. The four hands of Bhairaba hold respectively a trident, short dagger, drum, and a pot of wine ; he wears a garland made of human skulls and is decorated with other ornaments. The Mahākāla has a short stout figure armed with club in one hand and mace in another. Durgā strides on the prostrate Mahiṣa and holds various weapons in her six hands. With her left hand she seizes the head of Asura, a dwarfish figure standing on the horn of the buffalo. The Nandīśvara has a more pleasing appearance. The image of Brahmā is a fine example of a benign god, calmly meditating, with his eyes fixed upon a lotus on the palm of his hands, joined in front of his body. The two figures of Nandi are also well executed.

The finest image in the whole series is that of Prajñā-pāramitā, undoubtedly the best specimen of Eastern Javanese sculpture (Pl. XXXIV). Her calm divine expression and serene beauty, recalling the earlier days of Javanese art, have evoked much enthusiastic and perhaps somewhat extravagant praise. A careful examination, however, shows that both in conception and execution the image is inferior to the best images of Central Java. It lacks the vitality and energy and that refined elegance and mystic touch of divinity which distinguish the Buddha images of Barabuḍur. In essence it belongs to the Eastern school, and shows the same external features, *viz.*, rich ornaments, elaborately worked head-dress, minutely decorated clothes, and natural forms of lotus flowers which characterise alike the images of Singhasāri and Jago. Only the effort of a great genius has succeeded in infusing some life and animation which distinguishes it from, and places it above the somewhat stiff and rigid figures of these schools. The hand of the genius may also be traced in the comparative moderation of the decorations and the fine execution of details (including the seat), which add a distinct charm to his lovely image and offer a refreshing contrast to the normal figures in Eastern Java.

An image of Gaṇeśa from Jimbe, now at Bara[1], resembles that of Singhasāri, but is even more profusely decorated. Its back, in particular, is richly carved, the most noticeable element being a Kāla-head covering nearly the upper half.

The images of the Majapahit period show the same general characteristics, but gradually a new element is added, the so-called "garland of rays". To the halo behind the head is added a number of short unequal lines, resembling the conventional representation of the rays of sun, and gradually these surround the whole image. The figure of Pārvatī, with Kārtika and Gaṇeśa on two sides, is a fair example [2].

In addition to the ordinary images of gods we have to note a series of remarkable images of gods which are designed as portraits. In India, and some of her eastern colonies like Champā, the practice prevailed of associating the name of the king (or his relations) with that of the god founded by him (or in his memory), and sometimes also of making the image of the god resemble his own. Evidently the same idea of deifying the king is responsible for these portrait-images of gods.

The Viṣṇu image of Belahan[3] (Pl. XXXV) is one of the finest in this series. The god is seated on a lotus-seat on the head of Garuḍa. The two upper hands hold a *cakra* (discus) and a *śaṁkha* (conch-shell), while the two lower hands are joined on his lap. The left leg is crossed over the right thigh and the right leg is placed on the shoulder of Garuḍa. The latter is represented as a gigantic figure, trampling down two serpents under his feet.

Viṣṇu has a serene majestic face, but the image is not an idealisation of divinity but realistic representation of an individual. There are good grounds to believe that the figure is that of the famous king Airlangga (11th cent. A.D.). The modelling of the image is good and the composition as a whole

---

1. Krom—Kunst, III, Pll. 55-6.
2. Ibid, Pl. 93.
3. Ibid, Pl. 47.

shows skill of high order. It is also probable that the image of Prajñāpāramitā, described above, is a portrait of queen Ḍeḍes. A fine Śiva image, now in the Colonial Museum at Amsterdam, is supposed to represent Anūṣanātha. It is perhaps the finest specimen of figure sculptures of the thirteenth century A.D., combining as it does serenity with ideal beauty[1].

Another fine example is furnished by the Hari-Hara image of Simping[2] (Pl. XXXVI) representing the features of king Kṛtarājasa. Two of his hands hold *śaṁkha* (conch-shell) and *gadā* (club), and two others, *akṣamālā* (rosary) and *triśūla*, attributes respectively of Viṣṇu and Śiva. The features are lovely, and the expression is graceful. The rich ornaments, decorations of the clothes, and the natural lotus-leaves, among others, relegate it to the school of Singhasāri and Jago, and it may be regarded as one of the best productions of this school. An image of Pārvatī, in Caṇḍi Rimbi, is of the same size, and so completely resembles the Hari-Hara figure in point of style and decoration, that Krom has regarded it as a portrait of the chief queen of Kṛtarājasa, the daughter of Kṛtanagara[3]. These images show that the school of art, to which they belong along with the images of Singhasāri and Jago, flourished in the early Majapahit period.

A stone image in the Batavian Museum (No. 288) is supposed to be the portrait of Rājapatnī, Hyam Wuruk's grandmother. But the forms are heavy and inelegant and

---

1. B. K. I., Vol. 89 (1932), pp. 12 ff. and plate. The image is also reproduced in Ars Asiatica, Vol. VIII, Pl. 34.

2. Krom—Kunst, Vol. III, Pl. 65. An Ardhanārī image in the Berlin Museum is regarded by Stutterheim as a portrait of Kṛtanagara. It is a fine piece of sculpture (T.B.G. Vol. 72, pp. 715ff. Figs. 1-3). But J.L. Moens thinks that it was a portrait of Ken Angrok or king Rājasa which was placed in the Śaiva temple at Kagenengan (Ibid Vol. 73, pp. 123 ff.); for further arguments of Stutterheim in support of his view, cf. ibid, pp. 292 ff).

3. Krom—Kunst, II, p. 167.

show a very decadent style.[1] A Viṣṇu image in the Ethnographical Museum at Leiden also appears to be a portrait of some king[2].

Beautiful naturalistic figures, single or in groups, are occasionally met with in the ruins of temples. Their exact meaning and purpose are uncertain, but they show that pure aesthetic ideas were not foreign to Eastern art. The image of a mother and child found at Sikuning (Pl. XXXVII, Fig, 1) is a good example. It may be a representation of the goddess Hārīti or Ṣaṣṭhī (as the halo indicates a divine figure), but the artist has produced a natural, not idealistic figure. In spite of the stiffness and the rigidity of the main figure, it does not altogether lack charm and grace, and the pose of the child in the swing is very fine.

One of the latest specimens of these portrait images is furnished by a figure of Mahādeva[3] found in Majakerta. The face is strongly marked by Chinese and Javanese elements. The fully developed 'garland of rays' marks it as belonging to late Majapahit period.

There is one characteristic detail in the Eastern Javanese stone sculptures which may be noted here. The figures have, beside the ears, the loops of a fillet which is used either merely as an ornament or for holding fast the crown. Sometimes the loop is combined with long floating fillets, while occasionally the last ornament alone occurs. Now this loop and the floating fillets are characteristic features of the Pāla art and were possibly imported into Eastern Java direct from Bengal or Bihar. It may be noted that some other features, *e.g.*, the peculiar head-dress, the wearing of a shawl by a female figure and the presence of attendants in individual figures, betray the influence of the Pāla art[4].

---

1. O. V., 1930, Bijlage F., Pl. 54a.
2. B.K.I., Vol. 89 (1932), pp. 251-2 and Plate.
3. Krom—Kunst, III, pl. 93.
4. Kempers, pp. 50-53, 72.

In conclusion we may briefly refer to the images of semi-divine or mythological beings. Pl. XXXVII, Fig. 2 illustrates the image of Maharṣi Tṛṇavindu found in Singhasāri. It is a heavy, stout, and pot-bellied figure. A monk's garb covers the lower part of the body from waist to ankle, but it is transparent enough to make the legs quite visible. Heavy moustache and long-flown beard, a curious head-dress, and ends of girdle hanging in front are characteristic features of the figure. A trident on the side, a rosary and a kamaṇḍalu in the two hands, and the halo behind the head indicate the semi-divine character. It is an ideal representation of a semi-divine ascetic.

3. Images other than those of gods and semi-divine beings are not uncommon in Eastern Java, and some of them are really good works.

The ruins of Majapahit have yielded several important and interesting sculptures. One of them, the head of a Javanese woman, is illustrated in Pl. XXXVII, Fig 3. The figure is five inches high and is carved in grey stone of a very fine structure. It has a fine realistic touch which we rarely meet with in Indo-Javanese sculptures. Bosch justly regards it as one of the best pieces of sculpture ever found in Java.

A beautiful figure serving as a spout is illustrated in O. V. 1925, p. 16, Pl. II. The head is missing but the trunk is most richly and elaborately carved. The execution is good, though the style is somewhat different from what we usually meet with in Eastern Java.

Far different in style are the two images of Majakerta (Pl. XXXVIII). They, too, once served as spouts, perhaps in some royal bathing enclosure. Their well-proportioned long limbs, graceful poses, moderate but well-designed decorations, and smiling faces offer a striking contrast to the usual type of Javanese figures we have hitherto described. Unfortunately, the number of these images is so few, that it is difficult to say whether we should regard them as products of a new school of art, or works of an eccentric genius who boldly cut himself adrift from the trammels and conventions of his age. In any case these show that the art of Eastern Java had still life and vitality in it, and was not altogether devoid of a feeling for beauty, even in the latest Hindu period.

The spirit did not die out even after the fall of Majapahit. The best in the latest phase of art in Eastern Java, so far at least as the figure sculpture is concerned, is indicated by the human head, found in Sukuh (Pl. XXXVII, Fig. 4). In spite of outlandish decoration of head by horn-ornaments, and the rustic expression, the artist has succeeded in infusing character and individuality in a remarkable degree.

Among the Javanese images two classes are of peculiar character, and fairly common. The first is the series of Kāla-heads that adorn the different temples. Amongst these those of Jago and Singhasāri are reproduced in Pl. XXXIX. Next to them we may refer to the figures of temple-guards, which are often found in front of the main entrance of temples. These are massive, heavily built, stout figures, often with dreadful or repulsive expression. Sometimes they were well decorated. Pl. XL, Fig. 1 illustrates the beautifully decorated relief on the back of the temple-guard at Panataran. The details, particularly the animals, are well executed, and the whole scene shows a good idea of grouping and composition. But this sort of decoration on the back, unconnected with the main image, such as we find also in the case of Gaṇeśa at Bara, is a peculiarity of Eastern Javanese art and scarcely to be met with anywhere else.

4. In spite of the degraded character of the reliefs and images, the purely decorative sculpture of Eastern Java occasionally reaches a fairly high standard. A pedestal illustrated in Pl. XL, Fig. 2 shows a high quality of work with the familiar *motifs* of lotus-scroll and waving garland.

The purely decorative works of Caṇḍi Jago show well-conceived designs, somewhat on the model of Central Java, but the execution is coarser. The floral scroll, with birds and animals, seems to be a favourite motive. Those illustrated in Pl. XLI, and Pl. XLVI, Fig. 1 may be taken as fair specimens of the more successful efforts in this direction. There are endless varieties of scroll *motifs*, which sometimes resemble the waving garland *motifs* of India. These are also met with in Panataran where the execution is sometimes more elegant, (compare *e.g.* the corner pilasters).

The scroll with bird and lotus is also a favourite motive at Singhasāri, and sometimes well executed. An ornamental band made up of a row of Kāla-heads, and another of a succession of lion's head and makara, both carved in very low relief, form unique features in the decoration of roof in Singhasāri.

Well executed figures of animals are also met with in other decorative reliefs. There is a fine spirited representation of a horse in the relief at Singhasāri, depicting the chariot of the sun drawn by a team of seven horses.

After having reviewed the monuments and sculptures of Eastern Java we may point out their distinctive features as compared with those of Central Java.

The first thing that strikes even a casual observer is the lack of symmetery in the general plan of the temple-complex. Unlike Central Java, the main temple does not occupy the central position with subsidiary temples arranged round it in a definite order. Here the temples are arranged pell-mell without any plan or design. Besides, the smaller temples are not replicas of the central big temple, but the different temples have different designs. A conspicuous example of this is furnished by Caṇḍi Panataran.

Secondly, the several parts of the same temple have proportions very different from those of Central Java. The basement is given an undue importance, while the pyramidal roof dominates the whole temple.

Thirdly, the bas-reliefs are executed in an altogether different manner. Instead of naturalistic or realistic reliefs of Central Java we meet with curious Wajang-like figures. There is an eagerness to fill up the vacant space with details which have no relation to the main theme. There is, besides, the inexorable law of frontality. Even in figures carved in profile, while the position of the legs, arms and heads is so designed as to connect the successive figures in a group, the upper part of the body is carved frontally so that both the shoulders remain visible.

Indeed, the whole spirit of the bas-reliefs seems to be different. The texts illustrated in the reliefs had no relation with the nature of the temple itself. Further, while the reliefs in Central Java were epic in character, in Eastern Java they were more dramatic, fastening attention on each episode rather than on the series as a whole.

Fourthly, there are important variations in architectural decorations, the place of the Kāla-Makara ornament, *e.g.*, being taken mostly by the Nāgas. Besides, the ornaments are not generally suited to the architectural parts to which they are applied. They are not only exuberant and excessive, but instead of emphasising the different parts of the structure, they serve to hide them. Far from being subservient to architectural plan they seek to play an independent rôle.

Lastly, as regards sculptures in the round, they are, generally speaking, unnatural, stiff, and rigidly facing front.

In spite of these vital differences it may be held as more or less certain that the Eastern Javanese Art is not an independent growth but a derivation from that of Central Java, though this is denied by Stutterheim. It is held by many scholars that the differences are to be explained by a systematic process of degeneration and degradation. Dr. Stutterheim has,[1] however, successfully demonstrated that we have to reckon with one very important factor in explaining the origin of Eastern Javanese Art. It is the Indonesian spirit proper, which was less dominated by Indian culture in Eastern than in Central Java, and in course of time strongly asserted itself.

1. Djawa, Vol. VII (1927), pp. 177ff. B.K.I. Vol. 79 (1923), pp. 323ff.

Dr. Stutterheim observes that the theory of degeneration applied to Eastern Javanese art is as misleading as when it is applied to post-Gandhāra art in India. In both cases it is a degeneration when compared to classic art. But, really speaking, we notice in both only the gradual predominance of indigenous elements over those imported from abroad, and it can hardly be called degeneration. This analogy is, however, misleading on two grounds. First, the influence of classic art in India was much smaller, and secondly, the post-Gandhāra art in India reached a level of excellence which rivalled the classic,—a position never attained by the art of Eastern Java. Nevertheless, the position taken up by Stutterheim can be clearly understood from the analogy.

Dr. Stutterheim has advanced several arguments to prove his contention that the Eastern Javanese art had an independent growth, and that its peculiar characteristics are to be explained by what may be called Indonesian spirit proper.

He points out that the absence of symmetery in the plan of the temple-complex is also characteristic of the temples of Bali and other Polynesian sanctuaries.

The peculiarities of the bas-reliefs are explained by the theory of magic prevalent among the primitive peoples. According to this theory man is not regarded as a separate entity by himself, but all creations are the results of the presence, in varying degrees, of an all-pervading magic power in them. Fire is a symbol of this magic power and plays a great rôle in East Javanese art. The theory is obviously not conducive to the natural or realistic representation of man. The laws of frontality are deliberately applied mostly to heroes and gods who are magically powerful persons, and the want of perspective is not due to any lack of artistic skill.

The bas-reliefs in different parts of Indonesia exhibit similar characteristics. We can hardly explain them if we regard the Eastern Javanese style as merely a later development from that of Central Java. If, on the other hand, we hold that the Central Javanese style had influenced an existing Indonesian style similar to what we meet with in other islands not influenced by the Hindus, we get a good explanation of the phenomena.

The phallus and the so-called obscene scenes in the East Javanese Art are also the results of 'magic'—a belief that the magic power emanating from these parts of the body and the act of copulation will drive away the evil spirits. These beliefs, confined to the mass in Central Java, did not find an expression in the art of Central Java, but came to the forefront in Eastern Java. Here also we can trace similar phenomena in other islands not influenced by the Hindus. In Java the old ideas are only slightly tinged by Hindu influence.

The magic belief is seen in the Gaṇeśa image of Bara where a Kāla figure is carved on the back to protect it from bad influence.

The stiffness of the statues in E. Java is explained by the following custom current in Indonesia and Further India. The ashes of a deceased king are put in a hole, above which a structure is built. Therein is placed the image of the god who had already been identified with the king during his life-time, and whose figure is modelled after his features. (These structures are properly called Caṇḍi or burial-temples). The image serves as the medium between the new king and the one recently dead. A contact between the world of the living and the dead benefits the prince (or also the people) in a way which is, however, far from clear. Most of the East Javanese temples are of this type, and this explains the difference in the type of divine figures.

Whatever we might think of Stutterheim's theory as a whole, there is hardly any doubt that the gradual assertion of indigenous elements was a very important factor in the development of East Javanese art. We find exactly the same phenomenon in literature. In both cases Indonesian element was superimposed upon the old classic

Indian tradition, and the process of Javanisation grew stronger in the same proportion in which the direct stream of influence from India was gradually weakened. But a strong residuum of the Indian influence remained even when that stream ceased altogether to flow.

Chapter V.

BRONZE SCULPTURES.

Java has yielded quite a large number of bronze figures. These are mostly images of gods, though some were household objects such as lamp-stand, handles, *etc.* These were all cast by the process known as *cire perdue.*

The images of gods cover a wide field from iconographic point of view. They include gods and goddesses, not now known in India, though their existence in ancient times is vouchsafed by *sādhanā* (description in canonical works) or parallel images in Tibet and other countries which derived their religion from India.

Artistically the images follow the stone sculptures and are characterised by a graceful and serene naturalistic representation. The grotesque and the bizarre have been avoided as far as practicable, even where the original conception, as revealed in the text, would have lent itself easily to an ugly and hideous form. The artists, while conforming to the religious texts, have followed their high aesthetic ideal and produced on the whole well-conceived and well-proportioned figures with harmonious and beautiful forms.

In view of the ease with which the small handy bronze figures are liable to be removed to distant places, it is impossible to treat them according to locality. This also makes it difficult to classify them according to style until more detailed research has been carried on in this subject. We shall, therefore, merely give a general review of the bronze figures in Java.

A very large number of bronze figures were discovered in 1913 at Caṇḍiraja[1] near Ngañjuk in Kediri, and about

1. Krom—Kunst, II, pp. 445-6, Pl. 109. For a detailed account cf. Krom's article in Rapporten van den Oudheidkundigen Dienst in Nederlandsch-Indie, 1913. pp. 60 ff.

fifty of them are now in the Museum at Batavia. Only a few of these have been definitely identified, but the rest, though forming parts of a group belonging to the pantheon of Mahāyāna Buddhism, are unlike any other images hitherto known in Java or elsewhere. All the images (Pl. XLII) are seated cross-legged on a double lotus, but they are distinguished from one another by different attributes and postures of hands. The chief figure, larger than the rest, has a back-piece, surmounted by a Kāla-Makara ornament of the shape of a Caitya-window and crowned by an umbrella. The figures are well cast and show that the art of casting in bronze was highly developed.

These and other bronze figures in the Museum at Batavia have been dealt with by Krom and Bosch[1].

The collection of bronze figures in the Royal Ethnographical Museum at Leiden has been described by Dr. A. C. Tobi.[2] Although important from iconographical point of view, these do not call for any special remarks as works of art. The joint figure of Vairocana and Vajradhātvīśvarī is a fairly good specimen[3] (Pl. XLIV, Fig. 1).

The bronze figures in the Swabe collection[4] at Jogyakerta contain some good pieces. The seated Buddha figure in Bhūmisparśa-mudrā (attitude of touching the earth) with flames rising above the head is a fine image with good modelling (Pl. XLIII).

The collection of Lim Ju Choan at Mageland contains a few good pieces[5].

The Resink-collection contains a fine image of the goddess Śrī[6] (Pl. XLIV, Fig. 2) holding an ear of rice in the left hand,

1. O. V., 1923, pp. 138 ff. 2. O. V., 1930, pp. 158 ff. Pll. 50-53.
3. Cat. IV., Vol. V, Pl. XI, Fig. 2.
4. O. V., 1930, pp. 232-3, Pll. 55-6.
5. Rapporten, 1911, Pll. 185-7.
6. Krom—Kunst, II, p. 439, Pl. 108 (left).

and with an oval aureole crowned by an umbrella. In spite of somewhat unusually elongated middle portion it is finely modelled and has a beautiful expression.

The bronze images in the Srivedari Museum[1] at Solo is described by Bosch. It contains some good pieces.

The image of Trailokyavijaya[2] (Pl. XLV) in Jogyakerta is also an excellent specimen of bronze-casting. It has four faces and eight arms, holding various weapons, and strides vigorously across the prostrate bodies of Pārvatī and Śiva's bull. Its strength and vigour are represented very artistically and the whole figure is radiant with energy and movement.

The bronze group of Śiva and Pārvatī, found in Temanggung is a good specimen of bronze art[3] (Pl. XLVI, Fig. 2.).

The bronze bell found in Kalasan[4] (Pl. XLVII, Fig. 1) is a fine work of art. It has the shape of a *stūpa* on a lotus base. Round its centre is a band of decorative sculptures composed of a row of flying parrots forming a sort of garland. On the top is a small lion placed upon a smaller lotus base. There is a ring on the back of the lion by which the bell was suspended.

Bronze images from Java are found scattered about in the European Museums. Two fine Mañjuśrī figures are described and illustrated by Coomaraswamy[5]. One of them has been referred to the ninth century A. D. or a little later on palaeographic evidence and stylistic consideration. It was found near Dieng.

Dr. F. M. Schnitger has described a nicely executed bronze piece, now in Malang (E. Java), depicting Brahmā

1. O. V., 1923, pp. 138-154.

2. Cohn—Ind, Pll. 166-7. The same figure is referred to as Dharmapāla by Havell (Indian Sculpture and Painting, p. 60, Pl. XVII) and its artistic merits are highly extolled.

3 I. A. L., Vol. III (1929), p. 98, Pl. IV.

4. I. A. L. Vol. II, p. 70, Pl. III.

5. J. R. A. S. 1909, p. 290, Pl. II, figs. 4-5.

and Viṣṇu on two sides of a *liṅga*. It undoubtedly refers to the well-known story, related in the Vāyupurāṇa, how neither Brahmā nor Viṣṇu could trace the upper or lower limit of Śiva in the form of a *liṅga*, and therefore acknowledged his superiority. Dr. Schnitger refers the image to the thirteenth or fourteenth century A. D[1].

Quite recently Dr. A. J. Bernet Kempers[2] has made a critical and elaborate study of the Indo-Javanese bronzes with special reference to their relation to the Pāla art in India. After a very careful and painstaking analysis he has come to the conclusion that a limited group of bronze-figures in Eastern Java have been decidedly influenced by the Pāla art, but the Pāla influence had no share in the evolution of Central Javanese art. In other words, "the Hindu-Javanese bronzes in general have not developed from Pāla art, but the Pāla images have enriched the art of Java with a number of motifs and types."[3] These motives and types have affected also the stone sculptures of Eastern Java, and Dr. Kempers particularly lays stress on several Pāla features in their dress and composition, such as 'the loops and ribbons by the ears, the *shawl* of the Bhṛkuṭi image from Caṇḍi Jago, the attendants on the two sides of the main figure, the bodice of the Durgā from Caṇḍi Singhasāri, standing with the legs apart,' *etc.* Some of these, *viz.* the loops and ribbons near the ears, have developed into peculiarities of East-Javanese art. Dr Kempers has further traced the influence of South India, Ceylon, and Further India on some Indo-Javanese bronze images.

Metals other than bronze were also used for making images, though their number is small.

---

1. Tropisch Nederland, 28th June, 1937., p. 75.

2. "The Bronzes of Nalanda and Hindu-Javanese Art"—The article originally appeared in B. K. I. Vol. 90 (1933) pp. 1-88, and has since been published separately at Leiden.

3. Ibid, pp. 73-4.

A fine Manjuśrī statuette in silver is reproduced in Pl. XLVII, Fig. 2. It has been referred to A. D. 800, but the date is uncertain. A number of gold and silver images, along with those of bronze and stone, perished in the disastrous fire that destroyed the Dutch pavilion in the Paris Exhibition on June 28, 1931. Some of these were very beautiful and their loss is to be deplored by all lovers of art. A few of these are reproduced in T. B. G. vol. 71 (1931), pp. 663 ff., Pll. 1-20. Among the more serious losses may be mentioned the Śiva image of Semarang, the image of Tṛṇabindu from Singhasāri, one of the spout-figures from Majakerta, and last, but not the least, the fine bronze Buddha of Kota Bangun (see under Borneo) one of the finest products of Indonesian art.

Chapter VI.

ART IN BALI.[1]

Outside Java, the island of Bali is the most important region in Malayasia from the point of view of the history of art. Although very poor in architectural remains, its sculptures offer a fruitful subject of study. For a chronological study of the artistic remains of Bali, we may distinguish the following broad periods.

I. The Early period, which may be called the Hindu period or Old-Hinduistic Period (eighth-tenth century A. D.).

II. The Early Indo-Balinese period (tenth-thirteenth century)

III. The Middle Indo-Balinese period (thirteenth-fourteenth century)

IV. The modern period (fifteenth century and later)

It would be more convenient to treat architecture and sculpture separately for the whole period of Balinese history.

ARCHITECTURE.

II. The Early Indo-Balinese Period.

Very little remains of the old buildings of Bali, and there is not a single structure which may be positively dated before the eleventh century A. D. Of the monuments which have been tentatively referred to this period two alone deserve detailed consideration, a rock-cut monastery, called Goa Gaja, and the rock-hewn temples of Gunung Kavi.

---

1. Unless otherwise stated, the pages, plates, and figures in the following footnotes refer to "Oudheden Van Bali' by Dr. W. F. Stutterheim (Singaradja, 1929).

The Goa Gaja[1] (=Skr. Guhā—Gaja or Elephant's cave) is a cave situated a little to the south of the road from Pliatan to Bedulu, and on a small rivulet, tributary to the Petanu. The name was explained by Heyting as Elephant cave by regarding the front of the cave as shaped like an elephant. But as Bosch has shown, the figure is really a Kāla-head partly damaged.

The cave was hewn out of a large isolated block of stone. The entrance consists of an almost rectangular opening (slightly slanting upwards) about 3′-3″ wide and 6′-6″ high. Above this is the Kāla-head, with nose and left cheek badly damaged. Its prominent features are protruding eyes, ear-rings (used by females), and fingers of two hands with nails curled inside. The cave itself serves as the body of the monster. On two sides of the head, the front of the rock is carved with the so-called rock-motive, a sort of decoration such as we often find on rocks in Eastern Java. It consists of a series of intricate and intertwining curves (meant for leaves or petals) deeply undercut so as to give a free play to light and shade. In Goa Gaja this *motif* is improved by the addition of small panels depicting men and animals.

The opening runs to a rectangular passage which is at first 6½ ft. broad, and then narrows down to half this width. At the end of the passage, which is about 29½ ft. from the entrance, lies a rectangular chamber at right angles to it, the whole structure thus having the shape of a T. This main chamber has a length of 43′-3″ with breadth of 9 ft. It has eleven niches, seven on the back wall, one on each side wall and one on each side of the passage in front wall. Towards the left end, the floor of the chamber is raised to serve as a step beneath the niche. There are also four other niches, one on each side of both the wider and the narrower passage.

---

1. For a detailed account and illustration of Goa Gaja, cf. Bosch in O.V., 1923, pp. 66ff ; Heyting in O.V., 1925, pp. 94ff. Pl. 23 ; N.I.O.N, 1926, pp. 333ff ; 375ff. Moojen—Bali, pp. 104ff.

All these niches except three are now empty. A Gaṇeśa image is found in one, while another contains a part of the back of a *rākṣasa* which is now placed in front of the cave. The third niche, to the right end of the main chamber, contains three *Liṅgas*, each surrounded by eight smaller ones and encircled by a band at the centre.

Two words are inscribed on two sides of the entrance. The script of one of these may be referred to the eleventh century A. D. to which period the cave also probably belongs.

Next to Goa Gaja we may refer to the rock-hewn temples or Caṇḍis, of Gunung Kavi,[1] near Tampak Siring (Pl. XLVIII, Fig. 1). On the rock walls, on the two sides of the rivulet Pakerisan, have been excavated ten niches—five on each side—with a temple façade within each. These are not really temples, but merely reproduce their forms over the burial places of kings and queens, members of royal family, and one high royal official. The temple façades have all the mouldings, but are not decorated with sculptures or ornaments. The most interesting part is the high conical storeyed roof which perhaps shows a transitional stage between the art of Central and Eastern Java.[2] The detached towers in the temple-roofs of Central Java were, as we have seen, transformed in Eastern Java into a series of successive vertical mouldings between the horizontal bands of the roof. Here at Gunung Kavi, the towers still exist, but they regularly form successive stages in the roof.

According to Stutterheim nine of these temples were built over the burial places of the youngest brother of Erlangga and his eight queens; the tenth, which stands a little apart,

1. Krom—Kunst, II, pp. 52-53, Pl. 48. O.V., 1920, pp. 115-16; 1921, pp. 60ff, pp. 97ff; 1922, pp. 79ff. B.K.I. Vol. 76, p. 483. N.I.O.N., 1926, pp. 264ff, pp. 295ff. Djawa, 1921, Afl. 3. Moojen-Bali, pp. 104ff. Stutterheim, pp. 145ff.

2. This is the view of Krom (Kunst, II, p. 53), but is denied by Stutterheim (p. 147 f.n. 1).

being that of a high royal official.[1] It may be added that there is a small monastery near the temples. The use of the so-called "Kediri-script" in the inscriptions on the temples led Stutterheim to refer their construction to the eleventh century A. D., as an inscription in the same script bears the date 1077 A. D. H. T. Damste has, however, referred the foundation of the group to 959 A. D. on the strength of a Candra-Sengkala record. Stutterheim, however, sticks to the old date, taking 959 A. D. as the date of a natural bursting of the rocks, or of the foundation of the monastery.[2]

A little to the south of Gunung Kavi, at the junction of the Krobokan and Pakerisan rivulets, there is a similar temple-façade within a niche flanked by two other lower chambers serving as monasteries, all hewn out of rock.[3] Similar niche monasteries called Goa-Garba[4] are found in Pura Pengukur not far from Pejeng. All these may be referred to about the same period.

III. Middle Indo-Balinese Period.

An example of a similar rock-hewn Caṇḍi of a later period is furnished by that lying between Pejeng and Tatiapi on the river Kalebotan.[5] But numerous examples of miniature Caṇḍis enable us to form an idea of the changes that came over the temple structures during the thirteenth and fourteenth centuries A. D. Among the more remarkable changes we may note the following[6] :—

(1) The square towers of the roof have been transformed into round vases.

(2) The basement has got an independent profile consisting, like classical Javanese temples, of a plinth, ogee and pointed half-round mouldings above and below the central vertical part, and the cornice.

1. PP. 145-6.
2. B.K.I. Vol. 90, pp. 297ff.
3. PP. 146-7, Fig. 39.
4. PP. 147-8, Fig. 40.
5. PP. 181-2, Fig. 74.
6. Cf. Figs. 69, 71, 73, 75.

(3) The cornice is furnished with ante-fixae ornaments, the fore-runner of what we find in modern Balinese temples. Occasionally we meet with Kāla-Makara ornament.

(4) Sometimes we find a plain vertical block of stone in the middle of the front-side of the basement, and this is perhaps now represented by the decorated piece in sacrificial altars in the modern temples in Bali.

The miniature Caṇḍi from the Pura Desa Pedapdapan at Pejeng shows that sometimes a temple had three subsidiary chapels on the three sides, containing images of gods.[1]

Although we have no example of big structural temples dating from a period before the fifteenth century A. D., their existence can be inferred from the finds of isolated parts of temples resembling those of the miniature Caṇḍis. A stone lintel of a fairly big size has, for example, been found in the neighbourhood of Panataran Sasih,[2] and this undoubtedly proves the existence of a big temple.

Among minor architectural objects may be mentioned the square pillars supporting lotus cushions. The specimen from Pura Santrijan[3] illustrates the early form and that from Pura Desa at Bedulu[4] shows the later development. The Nāga-heads in the later example were transformed into ante-fixae ornaments, and ultimately we have the modern 'Kekocong', hundreds of which can be seen on the corner-pilasters of boundary walls[5].

IV. Modern period

There are many beautiful temples of moderate size in Bali, but all these are subsequent to the period when Javanese settled in large number in Bali after the fall of Majapahit. It would be convenient for a proper understanding of the subject if we give an idea of the general plan of temple-enclosure before describing specific examples.

---

1. P. 181, Fig. 69. 2. P. 181. 3. Fig. 79.
4. Fig. 80. 5. 184.

The temple area is divided into three court-yards (Pl. XLVIII, Fig. 2), separated from one another by low walls with gate. An interesting peculiarity is that these gates are not placed in the same line of axis nor is any of them placed precisely in the centre of the wall.

The first court-yard is usually empty, though occasionally there is either a Balê or an offering-pillar. From the first court-yard one passes through the principal gateway to the second court-yard. Here we usually find a number of Balês and the offering-pillar. The *Balé* is a small square chamber where the offerings are kept. It has usually a stone-foundation which supports wooden posts and rafters carrying a simple pointed roof. The posts and rafters are decorated and the scenes from the Rāmāyaṇa and Mahābhārata are illustrated on the walls. In the Pura Desa (public temple in a locality) there is a special Balê called Balê Agung, a long rectangular chamber, which serves as a prayer hall for the village elders on the new and full-moon days. A seat for the god is placed at one end of the chamber.

A simple doorway leads to the third court, the holy of the holies, which contains a row of temples, sacred altars for offerings, seats of gods made of stone, small houses, offering-pillars, and occasionally also a bell-tower.

Of the temples, those dedicated to Śiva, Viṣṇu and Brahmā, called Meru, are the principal ones. The sanctuaries of Viṣṇu and Brahmā lie respectively to the north and south of that of Śiva. The height of the temple-roof and the number of storeys it contains clearly shows that Śiva occupied the highest place in the Trinity, and Brahmā, the lowest.

Having thus described the general plan of temple we shall now describe the different parts of it in some detail. In essence, the plan of a Meru resembles that of Javanese temples, and rock-hewn Caṇḍis of Bali. A square basement with mouldings, a square chamber constituting the cella, and a conical pyramidal roof consisting of a series of gradually diminishing storeys ending in a finial representing *liṅga* or *ratna*,—these have been the essential features of Balinese temples in all ages. There have been no doubt modifications, mainly due to materials used. At first perhaps the shrine was closed by wooden walls and the roof was made of wooden frame with thatched cover. Gradually stone replaced wood in all these parts. Pl. XLIX illustrates the chief temple of Besakih which preserves the wooden forms. The next stage, when the walls of the sanctuary were made of stone, the roof remaining the same, is illustrated by the temple of Kesiman (Pl. L). The final evolution of a temple completely made in stone is illustrated by the temple at Tonjo (Pl. LII, Fig. 1). It is remarkable how the roof has an altogether different appearance although the essential features remain the same.

Next to the temples, the gateways demand our chief attention. They are either open or closed at the top. The former type is chiefly found in North Bali at the entrance of the first court-yard. It is virtually a large opening flanked by two pilaster-like constructions, having neither doors nor any roof.

There is no doubt that the closed gateway was modelled as a miniature temple, and the chief gateway in North Bali with two side-gates exactly correspond to the three Merus.

Pl. LI illustrates the open and closed types of gateways at Singraja. The beautiful inner gate with a roof of five storeys, exactly resembles a Meru, and shows the scheme of decoration which plays such a prominent part in Balinese temples. The open or split doorway on the right-hand side of the figure is obviously derived from the other type.

The Balinese display their artistic skill in lavishly decorating these gates and sometimes colour is added to heighten the effect.

The smaller adjuncts of the temple such as offering pillar with niches (Pl. LII, Fig. 2), sacred altars for keeping offerings (Pl. LV, Fig. 1), and Bell-towers (Pl. LIII) (see later) are also sometimes done with elaborate details.

SCULPTURE

1. The Hindu Period

The earliest sculptures in Bali are the Buddhist figures engraved in relief on small clay tablets. These are found with small clay stūpas containing small clay seals inscribed with the well-known Buddhist formula '*ye dharmā hetuprabhavā* etc.' The purely Indian alphabet of these inscriptions may be referred to the eighth century A.D. The relief figures of the Buddhas and the Bodhisatvas may also be approximately referred to the same, or perhaps a little later period, and show a purely Indian style. Stutterheim describes this style as 'internationally Buddhistic' and says that such figures could as well have been found in the mountains of Tibet or the hills of China. But he has not adduced any evidence in support of his assertion. The style is, however, predominantly Indian, and these figures might well have been mistaken for Indian sculptures of the late Gupta period. This can only be explained by a predominant Indian element in the population of Bali who had carried their art traditions direct from India, and had not yet been subject to indigenous influence, at least to any considerable degree. The figures were presumably impressed upon clay by means of bronze stamps, and the tablets were perhaps regarded as sacred objects or amulets with magic properties[1].

But the influences of art-traditions of Central Java at about the same period (*c.* eighth to tenth cent. A.D.) are proved by the image of Śiva from Bedulu illustrated in Pl. LIV. Although somewhat damaged, this fine figure is undoubtedly reminiscent of the flourishing period of Central Javanese art. The political influence of Mataram dynasty[2] over Bali may account for

1. See below, Chap. IX. Also cf. T.B.G. 1935, pp. 133-4 for the evidence that the clay-seals were made in Bali and not imported from outside.

2. See above, Vol. I, pp 419ff.

this. Reference may also be made to a remarkable head of a Buddhist (?) image (Pl. LVI, Fig. 1) which shows the peculiar smile of Cambodian figures. Its high cylindrical head-dress contains a lion's head in front, and on the whole it shows striking difference from Javanese style.

To judge from these and other similar sculptures which may all be dated between the eighth and tenth centuries A. D., we must regard this as the earliest period in the evolution of art in Bali during which the Indian influence was dominant and indigenous element was conspicuous by its absence.

II. Early Indo-Balinese Period

During the succeeding period, however, the native element comes to the forefront, and we find a distinctive Balinese style. But gradually this Balinese style is influenced by Javanese, evidently on account of the close political relations subsisting between the two islands.

The earliest specimens of this art are furnished by two groups of images found at Pura Sukavana on the Genung Panulisan[1] (Pl. LV, Fig. 2). Each group consists of two figures, a man and a woman, in one case standing, and in the other case, seated. The standing images wear clothes of variegated patterns, while the seated ones have plain clothes and wear the sacred threads across the upper part of the body. Both groups have a small round object in their hand. The figures appear to be those of a king and a queen, and both groups may represent the identical royal pair. The date 1101 A. D. engraved on the back makes it not unlikely that they were the parents of Airlangga, *viz.*, Udayana and Mahendradattā. This is, however, by no means certain.

About this class of images Stutterheim has observed as follows :—"Some figures of deified kings and queens, very often depicted together standing on one base, show such

1. Figs. 19, 20.

pronounced Indonesian features that no doubt can remain about the drastic departure from Hindu styles. The bodies have no more the slender grace and movement of the Hindu gods. Rigidly closed, they stand like mummies. The hands and feet are heavy and crude and the faces larger than the proportions of nature would allow for".[1]

Stutterheim has very rightly drawn attention to the fact that some of the peculiar features of this style may perhaps be due to the circumstance that the statues were intended to represent deceased kings and queens, and belonged to a special category of art, which may be called the 'art of the dead'.[2] That the Balinese art in this period was capable of producing more graceful figures is proved by the statues found near the cave Goa Gaja, to which we next turn.

The images found in the cave, and those that are now set up in front of it, were evidently brought from some other places in the neighbourhood. Among these are several male and female figures, including an image of Gaṇeśa, which served as water-spouts. The female figure, illustrated in Pl. LV, Fig. 3, is a fine piece of sculpture. The modelling is graceful and shows a developed technique and naturalistic style allied to Indian art. The expression is full of serenity and beauty. Another group, Hāritī surrounded by seven children, though less successful as work of art shows a fair

1. I. A. L., Vol. VI, pp. 2-3.

2. In a recently published work Stutterheim maintains "that almost everything that remains from the ancient art of Bali and Java pertained to this cult of deceased kings. Hardly any of the innumerable images found or excavated ever served for the direct worship of a god in the manner customary in India previously and now.........In brief, nearly all the pieces of any significance, fashioned of natural stone and thus able to resist the wear of ages, belonged in the past to the cult of dead kings." (Indian influences in Old-Balinese Art—pp. 23-4) It is impossible to accept this highly exaggerated value attached to the cult of the dead kings. The absurdity of this view will appear from the account of images given in this Chapter.

degree of skill. Stutterheim has drawn attention to the fact that the style of these works resembles that of Belahan, and he refers them to the reign of Airlangga.[1] To the same group belong other sculptures which have a more pronounced indigenous element.[2]

The third group of images, called Kutri-group, shows the same style as we meet with in Goa Gaja. The best specimen of the group, Durgā-Mahiṣāsuramardinī,[3] found at Kutri, is now very badly damaged, but enough remains to show that it was one of the finest images in Bali. The goddess stands over the buffalo and holds various weapons in her eight hands. A similar figure from Pura Puseh in the neighbourhood offers a strong contrast by its heaviness and lack of grace.[4] Midway between the two stands the figure of the eight-armed Amoghapāśa.[5]

The fourth group of images, called Gunung Kavi group, found over a wide area from Genung Panulisan to the southernmost part of the island, is characterised by the presence of a cursive writing known as Kediri script. There is no uniformity of style in these images. Some of them indicate an independent style, but others resemble more or less that of the Kutri-group. Among the former may be mentioned the fine figure of a young lady found in Pura Sukavana[6] on the Gunung Panulisan. The ornaments are different in character, but simpler and more finely worked. The face is badly damaged, but the features are on the whole graceful. An inscription on the back, dated 999 Śaka, relegates it to the last quarter of the eleventh century A. D.

Before closing the Early Balinese period we may make a few general remarks. As we have seen above, purely Balinese traditions prevailed at the beginning, but these were gradually modified by the art-traditions of Java. This can be easily explained by the close contact between the two islands

1. pp. 123-4. 2. Fig. 23. 3. Fig. 27.
4. Fig. 28. 5. Fig. 29. 6. Fig. 31.

during the period of Airlangga. It is, however, also very probable that the accession of this Balinese prince on the throne of Java introduced Balinese art-traditions in Java, and this may explain the characteristic and distinguishing features of East Javanese art as opposed to that of Central Java. The somewhat sudden growth of a new style of architecture and sculpture in Eastern Java forms an interesting problem, and the possiblity that the Balinese influence might have been an important factor in this transformation cannot altogether be ignored. Unfortunately sufficient data have not yet been collected for the purpose.

III. Middle Indo-Balinese period

From the point of view of art and architecture the two following centuries, the thirteenth and the fourteenth, may be regarded as the Middle Indo-Balinese period. We give below a short description of some of the representative specimens of the period.

(a) Pl. LVI, Fig. 2. illustrates an aristocratic lady. The purely formal representations of dress and the attitude of frontality, together with the coarseness of the legs and hands, show a degraded form of art. The face is, however, vigorously executed, and special attention may be drawn to the terraced head-dress, the long hanging ear-ornaments, the peculiar shape of the halo, and the heavy ornaments.

The figure shows the gradual dominance of Indonesian over Indian element which is also a characteristic feature of late East-Javanese art. As the figure contains a short record, with a date equivalent to 1342 A. D., it is earlier in date than the known Javanese specimens of that style. It is conceivable, therefore, that this assertion of indigenous spirit might have exercised considerable influence in the later development of Javanese art.

Stutterheim thinks that it was a memorial image of a dead queen, perhaps the mother of king Valajayakṛtaningrat.

(b) Several sculptures represent a combination of four figures facing the four directions. A good example is furnished by Pl. LVI, Fig. 3. The head-dress and the ornaments resemble those of the preceding one. Each figure has got four hands and a third eye, and holds a *śaṁkha* (conch-shell) and a book in the upper hands. It seems therefore that each figure represents the Hindu Trinity, the third eye, the *śaṁkha*, and the book being respectively the attributes of Śiva, Viṣṇu and Brahmā.

(c) A horrid but vigorously executed example of the above type is furnished by Fig. 1, Pl. LVII. It illustrates four dancing figures with masks in the form of shields covering their faces.

(d) Sometimes the sculptures are realistic and even characterised by individuality, as we find in the Sukuh-group in Eastern Java. The best specimen is furnished by the figure of a man with child serving as a spout.[1] Another good specimen is the figure of the so-called ascetic Arjuna serving as a spout.[2] The features are fairly modelled, and the dress and ornaments are of the simplest kind.

(e) The fanciful and bizarre figures like those of Eastern Java are also not wanting[3].

(f) A composite scene is depicted on a sacred water-pot found in Pura Puser at Pejeng[4] (Pl. LVII, Fig. 2). It is about 2½ ft. high, drum-shaped, and open at the top. The whole outer surface is minutely carved. The principal figures are those of eight snakes in four pairs on four sides. The hoods of each pair are interwined and crowned by a Śivaliṅga. The tail of each snake is interlaced with that of the neighbouring snake in the next group, and the two ends of each pair of tails support a lotus cushion on which a god is seated. The body of the snake is carried by gods, richly dressed, and bending under the heavy burden. They are

1. Fig. 64.
2. Fig. 61.
3. Fig. 62.
4. Pp. 169 ff. Figs. 57-60.

evidently running over the sea, the representation of which covers the lower part. The upper part is filled with landscape, plants, trees and birds, and a few figures. The upper and lower rims are covered respectively with lotus petals and conventional floral designs.

The whole scene is overcrowded with details and indicates a degraded form of art such as we meet with in Eastern Java. It has undoubtedly a mythological import, the exact nature of which is, however, difficult to understand. There is a short record of date in Candra Sengkala. It has been interpreted by Stutterheim as 1251 (=1329 A. D.) but the reading is doubtful.

But by far the most notable monument of the period is found at Jeh Pulu[1] less than a mile to the south of Desa Bedulu. It is a chamber hewn out of the side of a small hillock. The front is open, but there were three pilasters of which one has disappeared. This chamber probably once served as a monastery, but is now empty. The most interesting part of the monument is a long series of reliefs on the left covering a space of more than 80 ft. along the hill-side. The height of the reliefs varies, but may be roughly taken as 6′-6″.

This series of sculptured reliefs (Pll. LVIII-LIX) is undoubtedly the best so far discovered in Bali, and in point of grouping, composition and phonetic value, occupies a very high place indeed in any critical estimate of Indonesian art outside Central Java. A clear conception of the subject-matter, concentration on essential features avoiding unnecessary details, absence of over-crowding, and a general sense of rhythm, symmetery, and harmony are the chief characteristics of these reliefs. The execution of the individual figures also sometimes reaches a high level. The pose, modelling, and expression of the first three figures on the left indicate a high artistic skill, while the spirited hunting scene in the centre, and the figures of a horse and rider on the extreme right show that the artists

1. O. V., 1925, pp. 96-8, Pll. 24-27.

were equally capable of executing vigorous and animated movements. Among the scenes illustrated is a representation of a dwelling house, with a female figure standing near the doorway. The house closely resembles an ordinary thatched cottage in Bengal, with four triangular roofs meeting in a point at the top. On both sides of the door the walls have sculptured decorative motives such as scroll, and reel and bead border. The so-called rock-motives, used to fill the vacant space, are somewhat different in design, and have served as a clue to the dating of this record. Dr. Bosch concludes that the sculptures should be referred to the Majapahit period.

Before we conclude the study of sculptures we may refer to two characteristic specimens which cannot be definitely referred to any specific period. The first is a Śivaliṅga surrounded by eight busts and eight seated figures in two rows.[1] The upper row of busts is enclosed within lotus petals, and the figures in the lower row are seated on lotus cushions.

The next is a representation of Narasiṁha incarnation (Pl. LX, Fig. 1). The styl is very peculiar, almost baroque in character.[2]

IV. Modern Period

The sculpture of the latest period is best seen in the decoration of the hundreds of temples scattered over the island. The Balinese, not rich or resourceful enough to raise imposing structures, lavished their skill and energy in the exuberant and excessive decoration of temples, specially their gates and walls, by means of sculpture and painting. Among purely decorative elements we find a rich variety of foliage, flowers and geometrical patterns, besides birds, legendary animals, Kāla heads, and figures, which are often of grotesque, fantastic and demoniac character. Reliefs, depicting stories from old Hindu scriptures, adorn the walls. Among the

1. Fig. 85. 2. Fig. 86.

figures in the round we have not only images of benevolent gods and mythical beings such as Garuḍa and Kinnara, but also gods of terrific appearance, dreadful dvārapālas (temple-guards), and various types of demons and monsters. In spite of high technical skill and some amount of graceful beauty, the art is marked by a highly conventionalised style and the general tendency seems to be a leaning towards the representation of the weird, the grotesque, and the terrible in a somewhat Baroque style. This will be best illustrated by Pll. LIII, LV (Fig. 1), and LX. It must be remembered, however, that the weird and grotesque representations are dictated by religious considerations, and used for the definite purpose of warding off evil spirits who are continually threatening the sacred places with destruction. The modern Balinese art is a living one, and an adequate idea of its nature and varied character can only be given by a large number of illustrations which are impossible within the present scope of this work.

Conclusion.

A general review of the architecture and sculpture in Bali enables us to mark several well-defined stages in the evolution of its art. At first it was dominated by purely Indian traditions. From the tenth century A. D. the art was gradually modified by the working of indigenous element, and it was further subjected to influence from Java. The result was that during the same period we find different styles and levels of excellence in proportion to the presence or absence of Indian and Indo-Javanese tradition and influence. This may be called the truly Balinese period as distinguished from the purely Indian period preceding it. Following Stutterheim's classification we have divided this period into Early Indo-Balinese and Middle Indo-Balinese periods. In general it is not always easy to distinguish between the two, though on the whole the later period is marked by a gradual lessening of Indian influence, the growing influence of late East-Javanese style, the marked dominance of Tāntrik ideas, a predilection for the bizarre, fanciful, repulsive, and uncouth figures, the exuberance of ornaments, and some peculiarities in dress, head-gear, and ear-ornaments.

The final Javanese conquest of the island of Bali in the fourteenth century A. D. led to a sudden end of the normal evolution of art in that island. For some time the artistic instinct lay dormant, and it appeared as if it vanished altogether as it did in Java after the Muslim conquest. But with the infusion of new blood as a result of the large-scale immigration of the Javanese into the island we find a gradual revival of art, specially temple-architecture. Thus was ushered in the modern period of Balinese art which continued down to the Dutch conquest of the island. Although considerably influenced by the Javanese ideas, the modern art is based on the traditions of the earlier Balinese art. Whether it would continue to flourish under the present conditions is more than can be said at present.

Chapter VII

ART IN SUMATRA

The archaeological remains in Sumatra are very poor, and it is not possible to write a connected history of its architecture and sculpture. The most convenient way of dealing with the extant remains is to treat them separately according to some well-defined regions.

I. Palembang (Śrī-Vijaya)[1]

We may begin with Palembang, generally identified with the capital of the far-famed kingdom of Śrī-Vijaya.[2] It is a matter of considerable surprise that it has not yet yielded any architectural remains of any importance. A brick terrace or floor of a Buddhist foundation on the Seguntang hill outside the city of Palembang, and similar ruins at Caṇḍi Angsoka within the city itself practically exhaust the list. Dr. Bosch has truly observed that "unless we presume that only perishable materials were used or that there has been a general subsidence of the soil, we must conclude that the extant remains give no support to the view that the capital of Śrī-Vijaya occupied the site of the present Kota Palembang.[3]"

We are, however, more fortunate in regard to sculptures. For, although their number is not very large, they are of considerable interest.

---

1. The account is based on the following :—

Perquin in O. V., 1928, pp. 123ff. Bosch in O. V., 1930, pp. 152ff. Krom in A. B. I. A., 1931, pp. 29-33.

As regards the origin of the art of Śrī-Vijaya I have discussed the question in an article in the Journal of the Indian Society of Oriental Art, June, 1935. The article also contains a detailed discussion of the sculptures of Palembang, referred to below.

2. On this point, see Part I., pp. 209ff. 3. O. V., 1930, pp. 155-6.

A Buddha statue found on the Seguntang Hill (Pll. LXI-LXII) may be regarded as belonging to the earliest period of Śrī-Vijayān art.[1] The most striking feature of the figure is the drapery with prominently marked fold-lines. It is unlike anything hitherto discovered in Sumatra and Java, and must be traced directly to Indian influence. Originally a Gandhāra origin was postulated, but the nature of the fold-lines and the threefold vertical border at the back definitely militate against this view. In a recent article Krom traces its origin not to Gandhāra school but to 'some Indian school of art in which the Graeco-Buddhist principles are found in a modified and Indianized form *e.g.* that of Amarāvatī."[2] This is more acceptable, although we need not confine our attention exclusively to Amarāvatī school. For drapery like this was current in Mathura, and the Mathura school exerted its influence all over Northern India. Similar drapery is found in images as far apart as Bihar and Ceylon.

Another remarkable stone statue is that of Avalokiteśvara found near the village of Bingin in the Palembang Sub-division[3] (Pl. LXXI, fig. 1). Its vigorous expression gives it a peculiar stamp of originality and indicates a high degree of technical skill. A torso found at Mangkubumi, and the fragment of a Bodhisatva head found at Seguntang are also good specimens of art[4].

Special importance attaches to three bronze images, found in course of dredging the river Komering, about 1100 yds. from the place where it flows into the river Musi. According to Bosch these finds indicate it to be the probable site of the old

---

1. By piecing together the loose fragments which were found on the Seguntang Hill it was possible to reconstruct the torso only. For illustration cf. A. B. I. A., 1931 Pl. XI, a, b. The Head of the statue was subsequently traced by Schnitger in the Museum at Batavia (Oudheidkundige vondsten in Palembang-Bijlage B, 1st Ed., p. 4, 2nd Ed., (Palembang, 1935) pp. 1, 4.

2. A. B. I. A., 1931, p. 32.

3. Ibid, Pl. XII, d.

4. Schnitger, op. cit, pp. 5, 6, 10.

capital city, which thus lay to the south of modern Palembang in a territory now fully covered by morass.

The images (Pl. LXIII, figs. c, d, e) are those of Avalokiteś-vara, Buddha, and Maitreya.[1] The most striking feature of these figures is the style. It is difficult to agree with Krom that these 'might easily be taken for Javanese Bronzes'.[2] As Bosch has already observed, the style is very different from that of the stone Buddhist images of pure Central-Javanese type found at Bukit Seguntang. The same scholar has further remarked that these images furnish the only known specimens in Śrī-Vijaya of a style most closely related to the Śailendra art of Java[3].

In my opinion these images bear a far closer affinity to Indian art. The style of the bronze image of Buddha is clearly reminiscent of the Gupta period, and that of Maitreya probably belongs to the same school. The fine image of Avalokiteśvara probably represents a later stage of the same art. These three images may be regarded as the best specimens of sculpture discovered in Sumatra. Taking them along with the Buddha image of Seguntang we may infer that a direct stream of artistic influence flowed from India to Śrī-Vijaya down to the sixth and seventh centuries A. D.[4].

Reference may be made to a peculiar bronze head of Buddha.[5] (Pl. LXIII, figs. a-b.). A fillet, decorated with rosettes, surrounds the head,—a feature not met with elsewhere. In this case also we cannot postulate a Javanese origin.

The high degree of development of bronze sculpture in Sumatra is also evidenced by the images of Buddha and Vairocana[6] described by Schnitger, and a very fine bronze elephant with a female driver and a man sitting behind her (Pl. LXIV) which was found in the river by Kg. Penja-

---

1. Illustrated in O. V., 1930, Pl, 45. A. B. I. A., 1931, Pl. X, c. d. e.
2. A. B. I. A., 1931, p. 31.
3. O. V., 1930, p. 156.
4. Cf. my article referred to in f. n. I, p. 323.
5. A. B. I. A., 1931, Pl. X. a-b.
6. Op. cit. pp. 7-9.

bungan, in the Mandabilang Sub-division.[1] A bronze image of Śiva, of the style of Central Java, and three others of Śiva, Viṣṇu and Brahmā of the fourteenth century have been found near Kota Palembang. The latter stand on their riders, lion, Garuḍa and swan[2].

II. Jambi (Malayu).

Next to Palembang we may refer to Jambi, the capital of the famous kingdom of Malayu. The most important ruins in this region are those of Solok to the west of Jambi. A big structure must have once stood there. Nothing now remains of it except a standing Buddha image and four great Makaras [3] (Pl. LXV, Fig. 1) which no doubt served as the decorative ornaments of stair-curbs. Ruins of temples and a few images have also been found in other localities in the neighbourhood. One of the Makaras at Solok bears a date 986 (=1064 A.D.), and in style resembles the Javanese. This is somewhat perplexing as the political domination of Java over Jambi dates only from the thirteenth century A. D. It appears that Jambi imbibed the culture of Java more than other parts of Sumatra.

The Javanised art of Jambi spread all over the ancient kingdom of Malayu, as far as the Padang Highlands[4]. It must be noted, however, that the four Makaras at Solok offer rich varieties of style, and differ, in many respects, from that of Central Java. These Makaras display a high

---

1. O. V., 1920, p. 62, Pl. facing p. 64.

2. Jaarboek, Vol II, 1934 (published by Royal Batavian Society) Pll. 2-3. A stone image of a princess in the Majapahit style is figured in Pll. 5-6.

3 Dr. C. J. Neeb describes and illustrates the four Makara heads found near Jambi in T. B. G. Vol. 45 (1902), pp. 120-27. Dr. Brandes (Ibid. pp. 128ff) gives a critical description of the Makara heads and indicates their great difference from the Central Javanese art. He also gives a list of some other antiquities of Jambi.

4. A. B. I. A., 1931, p. 30.

degree of technical power and are fairly good specimens of Sumatran art. It is possible that the art of Jambi was an Indo-Sumatran art subjected to considerable influence from Java.

III. The Tapanuli region.

Almost all the old structures of Sumatra have been so completely ruined that it is not possible to discuss their architectural style. The one structure of importance, that is in a fair state of preservation is Biaro (Bihāra) Bahal I in Padang Lawas (Tapanuli)[1] (Pl. LXV, Fig. 2., Pl. LXVI). It stands on two square basements, and is itself square in shape with shallow projections on each side. The basements have a number of sunken panels decorated by sculptures. The body of the temple is intersected by a number of horizontal courses. A domical *stūpa* stands on the square roof of the temple and forms its śikhara, as it were. A garland-decoration surrounds its central part.

The Buddhist character of the temple is indicated by an image of Bohisattva inside it, and the remains of a *stūpa* (Pl. LXIX, Fig. 1), and of a pillar of the form of an elongated stūpa in the neighbourhood.

A second temple, Biaro Bahal II,[2] (Pl. LXVII) had probably the same general features, though the stūpa-śikhara is missing, and only the lower part now survives. It contained an image of Heruka, and there were also three heads of Buddha (Pl. LXVIII).

Remains of other temples have also been found in Padang Lawas, notably Biaro Si Topajan[3] and Biaro Si

1. O. V., 1920, p. 68 ; 1925, p. 15, Pl. 5 ; 1926, pp. 26, 142 ; 1930, pp. 136ff. Pll. 32-36. Plans VI-XIV.

2. O. V., 1930, p. 139, Pll. 40-42.

3. O. V., 1920, p. 65 ; 1925, p. 11 ; 1926, pp. 25ff ; 1930, p. 135, Pll. 29ff, Plans I-V. On p. 243 (Corrigenda et Addenda) of O. V. 1930, Goris suggests that the second inscription contains a date Śaka 1157 which then must be the date of the temples, at least of Si Topajan.

Mangambat[1], but they are too ruined for any general description. Their ruins have, however, furnished important clues for the origin and antiquity of the Sumatran art.

The date of the structures can be approximately ascertained from epigraphic data. An inscription in the Biaro Si Topajan bears the date 1157 Śaka=1235 A.D. The Biaro Bahal I and II may also be ascribed to the same period[2].

The sculptures of Biaro Bahal I such as the dancing rākṣasa figures (Pl. LXVI, Fig. 2), the crouching lions, the temple watchers, and the Makara ornament do not belong to any primitive school of art, but show a high degree of technical power. But their artistic conception cannot be regarded as very high. The same thing may be said of the decorative motives.

As regards sculptures in the round, the stone image of Bajrasatva[3] and the Bronze female figure[4] in Biaro Bahal I deserve special attention (Pl. LXIX, Figs. 2, 3). Longhurst regarded the former as being in the same style as an image he found at Salihundan in the Ganjam district, not far from the old port of Kalingapatam, and belonging to the sixth century A. D. Bosch rejects this view and regards it as belonging to the Pāla school of sculpture. The latter seems to be the right view. The bronze female figure is undoubtedly of south Indian character. Longhurst referred it to the fifteenth century A.D., but Bosch places it about five centuries earlier. Here again we are inclined to agree with the Dutch scholar. Prof. K. A. N. Sastṛi is inclined to refer the image to a still earlier period, about seventh century A. D. [5].

The Heruka image[6] in Biaro Bahal II (Pl. LXVIII, Fig. 2) is very important from iconographical point of view, as it

1. O. V., 1930, p. 134, Pl. 29a. According to Bosch the ruins clearly betray the influence of Central Java, and the temple probably belongs to the Śailendra period.

2. Bosch at first assigned somewhat later date but changed his view on the correct reading of the date of Si Topajan Inscription.

3. O. V., 1930, Pl. 37a.

4. O. V., 1930, Pl. 38.

5. J. G. I. S., Vol. III, pp. 104ff.

6. O. V., 1930, Pl. 41.

closely corresponds to the Indian representation of the same figure, which is very rare. It is badly damaged and calls for no special remark from artistic point of view.

It is obviously risky to form any general conclusion about the art of Sumatra from such incomplete data. Dr. Bosch, who has studied the question more thoroughly than others, has, however, drawn some general conclusions from a critical study of the temples. The following observations sum up his views on the subject[1].

"The history of Buddhism in Tapanuli begins with the well-known bronze image of Bhaṭāra Lokanātha of the year 1024. As Krom has remarked, the scripts resemble the Old-Javanese alphabets of Central Java, and the style is closely related to that of Central Java.

"In later times a Buddhist art developed in Padang Lawas, which is sharply differentiated from Indo-Javanese by many characteristics. This may be attributed to foreign influence, particularly that of South India, which is proved by the inscription of Porlak Dolok and the bronze female figure in South Indian style found within the enclosure of Biaro Bahal I. But a closer examination negatives this theory. For neither the architectural nor the sculptural style of South India is reflected in the remains so far discovered in Padang Lawas. Thus a direct influence of South India falls to the ground. On a closer comparison of the Biaros with the Indo-Javanese temples, it appears that both have the same essential plan, and the differences are merely due to the different manners of execution. The essential elements of Bahal I and II,—the square basement with passage for circumambulation and balustrade, the stair-curbs ending in makaras, the square body of the temple with projections on the sides, the square roof with octagonal upper part and niches (Bahal II) ending in the Stūpa-form Śikhara,—all these belong to Central Java, though they have undergone in Batakland more or less radical changes

1. O. V., 1930, pp. 144ff.

and transformations, which give an altogether different appearance to these temples. The stone is replaced by brick. The relations of the lower parts to one another and to the whole are different. Ornaments, though using the same motive, make an impress of a different character; cf. *e.g.* the style of the Siṁha and the Rākṣasa figures in Bahal I. It is notable that although the main parts of the Biaros are essentially Central-Javanese in character, there are additional elements which seem to be derived from the East-Javanese art. Take for instance (1) the unsystematic plan of the complex, in which the principal temple indeed occupies a central position in respect of the surrounding wall, but the other structures are irregularly distributed in the temple area; (2) the absence of semi-circular and ogee mouldings in the basement where the rectangular courses in the base and the cornice correspond to each other; (3) the placing of temple-guards to the two sides of the entrance of the main temple; and (4) lastly, the standing position, the dress (Kain Pandjang) and the raised left fore-finger of these figures. The common characteristics of the Biaros and the Indo-Javanese architecture—which may be still multiplied—strengthen the view resulting from the absence of South Indian characteristics, *viz.* that the development of the art in Lawang Padas is not to be attributed to external influence. This art must have developed in or shortly after the Śailendra period (before the Lokanātha image of 1024 A. D.) during which an art tradition was formed directly or indirectly under the Central Javanese influence. This tradition was maintained in the following centuries with an additional influence from East Java, and subjected to a strong native influence. Thus was produced an art which clearly betrayed its Javanese origin, but nevertheless presents special character of its own."

The general conclusions of Bosch do not, however, carry immediate conviction. The peculiar characteristics of the Sumatran art, as distinguished from Indo-Javanese, entitle us to regard them as Indo-Sumatran, and many of the resemblances between the two may be attributed to their common origin from Indian art tradition. We need not necessarily look to South India as the home of the parent style,—an obsession which accounts for much misconception and confusion of ideas—but we may hold that the Indo-Sumatran style owed its origin to Indian colonists who settled in this region of Sumatra. It is the result of Indian art traditions modified in Sumatra, and perhaps to some extent influenced by Java.

Krom has expressed this view in connection with the ruins of Muara Takus, on the upper Kampar river, and Tanjung Medan (Lubuk Sikaping)[1]. There are remains of six brick monuments in the former place, including three *stūpas.* One of these, a high, slender, towerlike structure is a fairly good specimen of Sumatran art. The *stūpa* at Tanjung Medan is similar in design. Krom regards these as well as the Biaro Bahal described above as originating from Indian colonists who settled along the rivers Kampar, Rokan, Panei, and Barumun which flow to the sea on the eastern coast of Sumatra.

Indirect evidences of the settlement of Indian colonists in these regions are not altogether wanting. One of the *stūpas* at Muara Takus contained, in its relic-chamber, a golden plate and a piece of stone, both engraved with Vajra and the mystic syllables in Indian scripts. A golden plate at Tanjong Medan also contained the mystic syllables and the names of Dhyānī Buddhas written in Indian script. Inscriptions in similar scripts have also been discovered in the Karimun islands, not far from the mouth of the Kampar river.

Krom is inclined to associate these ruins and inscriptions with the Śailendras. He is no doubt largely influenced by the prevalent belief that Śrī-Vijaya was the chief seat of Śailendra power. Bosch refers the inscriptions of Muara

1. Geschiedenis[2]—pp. 132-3; Kunst—II, pp. 422-3. T. B. G. Vol. 35 (1893) pp. 48-74.

Takus, and also the *stūpas*, to a period not earlier than the twelfth century A. D.[1]. But whatever the date may be, these inscriptions indicate a direct stream of colonisation from India and the architectural remains also seem independently to bear the same testimony.

In conclusion it is interesting to note that we possess the name of at least one great sculptor in Sumatra. This is Sūrya, the master-artist who carved the image of Lokanātha in A. D. 1024[2].

---

1. O. V., 1930, pp. 148-9.
2. Not. Bat. Gen., 1887, pp. 176-178.

Chapter VIII

ART IN BORNEO

No remains of old architecture have survived in Borneo, but we have a few specimens of sculpture which enable us to form a fair idea of its artistic achievements. Reference has already been made to the Mukhaliṅga of Sepauk and the sandstone image of Sanggau[1].

The stone image of Mañjuśri[2] (Pl. LXX, Fig 1) excavated between Gunung Kupang and Karang Intan, District Martapura, Residency of South and East Borneo, shows a purely Indian style. The modelling is rather rough, at least appears to be so from the present damaged condition.

But by far the most important specimens of sculpture in Borneo are the images found in Genung Kombeng, to which reference has been made above[3].

The images may be divided into two groups: (I) Śaiva and (II) Buddhist.

I. The largest figure is that of Mahādeva[4] (Pl. LXX, Fig. 2). The god stands on a lotus cushion and has four hands. The upper right hand holds a rosary, the lower a Triśūla, the upper left hand, a flywhisk, and the other is empty. A high *mukuṭa*, necklace, a heavy *upavīta*, a band round the upper abdomen, girdles, armlets, and anklets decorate the body. The thin transparent cloth ends just above the anklet, and its waving edges are seen on both sides. The other figures[5]

---

1. For these and other images, cf. Bk. I, Chapter VIII.

2. O. V., 1925, Pl. 10(a).

3. Bk. I, Chap. VIII. For a detailed account with illustrations, cf. O. V., 1925, pp. 132ff, Pl. 29-34; also cf. "Midden-oost Borneo Expeditie, 1925, specially the concluding chapter.

4. Ibid, pl. 31-a.

5. Ibid, pl. 31, b, c, d, 32a.

are those of Guru, Nandīśvara, Mahākāla, Kārtikeya and Gaṇeśa. It appears from analogous examples, that the temple containing these was dedicated to Śiva, whose figure occupied the shrine, and there were five niches for Guru, Gaṇeśa, Durgā (not found), Mahākāla, and Nandīśvara. The figure of Kārtikeya was probably placed in the wall. The presence of a head of Brahmā shows that there was also a temple dedicated to that god, and it is a natural inference that a Viṣṇu temple completed the group.

II. The Buddhist figures (Pl. LXX, Figs. 3-4) are marked by a high head-dress, having the shape of a truncated cone, and resembling a *stūpa* or a *śikhara.* Among these figures only one[1], with the right hand in Varamudrā, and the left hand holding an *utpala* surmounted by a *vajra,* may be definitely identified as Vajrapāṇi. The four-armed figure[2] having *cāmara* in the right back hand, *cakra* in the left, the right forearm in *varamudrā,* the left fore-arm on the knee holding the stem of a lotus which rises high above the shoulder, decorated with armlets, bangles, heavy ear-ornaments, necklaces, girdles, and sacred cord, and seated on a double lotus cushion, is evidently a Dhyānī-Bodhisatva (Sambhoga-kāya), emanating from a Dhyānī Buddha—probably Amitābha.

The four-armed female figure[3] has both fore-hands on the knee holding lotus ; the right rear-hand holds a long book ; and the left rear-hand a very peculiar object—a long pole supporting a ball-like thing, crowned by an umbrella or a disc, with a knob at the top.

From an iconographic point of view the Buddhist figures offer a puzzle. With one exception, they differ from any example of a Buddhist deity known elsewhere. We must, therefore, suppose either (a) that they are forms of Buddhist god which by an accident have been preserved only in Borneo, or (b) that the attributes are wrongly mixed up by the artist

1. Ibid, pl. 33-a.
2. Ibid, pl. 33-c.
3. Ibid, pl. 33-d.

who worked from memory or oral instructions, ill understood, or (c) that a new combination of forms and attributes was evolved in Borneo.

From an artistic point of view the few images indicate a highly developed school of sculpture in Borneo. The image of Mahādeva is perhaps the best. The pose and modelling of this graceful figure, with the calm placid smiling face which combines the dispassionate abstraction and the benevolence of the great god, reminds us of the figure of the same deity at Lara-Jongrang. The same qualities mark, in a less degree, the two four-armed Buddhist gods, a male and a female, though here the features are a little heavy and less graceful. The heads of two other figures[1] are also remarkable pieces of sculpture.

Other figures are much inferior in conception and execution. The most notable instance is that of Gaṇeśa, a lifeless figure of very poor specimen. There is hardly any doubt that the images found in the cave of mount Kombeng belong to different ages and are productions of different schools.

Several other objects, excavated at Muara Kaman, now form part of the regalia belonging to the Sultanate of Kutei. Among these may be specifically mentioned a small golden figure of Viṣṇu[2], worn by the crown-prince on ceremonial occasions, and a golden figure of tortoise[3]. Viṣṇu is four-armed, holding a discus, conch-shell, and mace in three hands, while the fourth, the lower right hand, is in *vara-mudrā*. The workmanship is of primitive character.

The most beautiful metal-work discovered in Borneo is the fine bronze Buddha, found at Kota Bangun, near Muara Kaman. It was deposited in the Batavia Museum[4], but perished in the disastrous fire that destroyed the Dutch pavilion in the Paris Exhibition of 1931.

1. Ibid, Pl. 33-b, 34-c.
2. Ibid, Pl. 35-a.
3. Ibid, Pl. 35-c.
4. Ibid, Pl. 36; also, A. B. I. A., 1926, Pl. XI.

The Buddha (Pl. LXXI, Fig. 3) stands erect with the right knee slightly bent forward. He wears a transparent, close-fitting dress, whose edges are seen above the anklets and then passing over his left arm fall in folds. The garment passes over the left shoulder leaving the right uncovered. There is no *urṇā* but the *uṣṇīṣa* is unusually high. This was perhaps due to the existence of an umbrella over his head. It has now disappeared, but there is a socket on the back for fixing it.

A monk's bowl is placed on the palm of the left hand. The right hand is in the *Vitarka-mudrā*, and on its palm are engraved several signs,—two concentric circles, and several dots and curved lines. These are usually regarded as *jāla*, one of the signs of Mahāpuruṣa. Foucher explains the term as a number of regular signs on the palm of the hand, whereas the previous explanation of the term was a net-work or spider's web[1].

Another characteristic feature of the palms of the figure is that something like a skin covers their entire backs up to the point where the fingers begin. In the Gandhāra sculptures, there is a similar covering up to the middle of the fingers. It was regarded as a *jāla* (spider's web), but this interpretation is unacceptable, inasmuch as this phenomenon is observed only when the hands of a Buddha figure are outstretched, and not when they are placed on the lap or otherwise connected with the body. It is thus obvious that the covering was intended to protect the fingers from damage, as the small pointed pieces of stone could otherwise be easily broken. But this original purpose being lost sight of, it not only came to be applied to bronze statues where it was unnecessary, but was also confined to the back of the palm below the fingers where it could be of no use.

The bronze Buddha of Kota Bangun is the only figure in Malayasia which shows this characteristic, and we must,

1. Foucher—L'art Greco-Bouddhique du Gandhāra Vol. II, pp. 304ff.

therefore, suppose that the artist must have received his inspiration direct from India.

Dr. Bosch traces this influence to Gandhāra, but neither the dress nor the general style are in favour of this supposition. It may be noted that an image of Buddha found at Mankuwār, near Allahabad, shows the same characteristic feature[1].

From an artistic point of view the bronze Buddha must be given a very high place in the art of Malayasia. The modelling of the figure, though highly creditable, is not certainly at its very best, but the artist has succeeded in infusing into his creation an admirable expression of divine grace and pious benevolence. The inexpressible and ineffaceable smile, betokening good-will and blessings to the whole world, and the calm placidity of the face, even while the hands indicate a mood of discussion, raise this figure to a high class of art, and it deserves to be ranked with the Buddha figures of Barabuḍur with which it shows great stylistic resemblance.

The relation of the art of Borneo to Indian art is obvious, and the only question for determination is whether its origin is to be traced direct to India or through Java.

Discussing the figures found at Kumbeng, Dr Bosch negatives the former idea chiefly on the following grounds.

1. The grouping of the Śaiva figures agrees with that frequently met with in Java, whereas in India, preference is given to other combinations (maṇḍala).

2. The image of Kārtikeya possesses typically Indo-Javanese characteristics.

3. The style is closely related with that of Hindu-Javanese art.

At the same time Bosch points out that certain features strikingly differentiate these images from Indo-Javanese. Among these he refers specially to (1) the chiselling of the stone round the Triśūla ; (2) the flat form of the Kamaṇḍalu

1. V. A. Smith—Fine Art in India and Ceylon, fig. 119 (p. 173).

(water-pot) of the Guru; and (3) the representation of the elephant-head of Gaṇeśa.

Dr. Bosch is, therefore, unwilling to attribute the images of Kutei to Indo-Javanese artists. According to his view the people who made these images were either Indo-Javanese colonists in Borneo who had been out of touch with the motherland for a long time, or indigenous Dayaks who had imbibed the culture and civilisation of the Indo-Javanese.

Any view expressed by such a competent authority as Dr. Bosch deserves a very serious consideration. At the same time we must point out that his argument about the grouping of Śaiva figures is not quite intelligible. The figures were not actually found grouped in any particular manner, and their hypothetical grouping is made on the analogy of Javanese temples. To use this as an argument for Indo-Javanese origin is, therefore, very illogical.

As regards the style, there are both resemblances and differences even when we consider the Śaiva group of images. But the Buddhist figures of Kombeng are very unlike those found in Java, both from iconographic and artistic point of view. In particular we must postulate a direct Indian influence in the case of the bronze Buddha figure of Kota Bangun and the figure of Gaṇeśa at Serawak.[1] All these considerations would rather incline us to the belief that the Hindu colonists of Borneo developed independently an art which was perhaps influenced to a certain extent by the Indo-Javanese.

1. J. Str. Br. R. A. S., Vol. 85 (1922), pp. 210ff.

Chapter IX

ART IN MALAY PENINSULA

The old sanctuaries and sculptures in Malay Peninsula[1], dating from the period prior to its conquest by the Siamese, are not many. Even of the few so far discovered it is not easy to form an accurate idea in the absence of a scientific archaeological publication giving full details and illustrations. This is all the more regrettable, as the few specimens, already known to us, invest this region with a peculiar interest, and raise interesting problems which we are not in a position to solve at present.

We may begin with sculptures (Pl. LXXI, Fig. 2, Pll. LXXII, LXXIII). These are both Brāhmanical and Buddhist. Among the former we may refer to the fine images of Viṣṇu and other deities near Takua Pa, at Pra Narai hill and Phru No,[2] those of Viṣṇu at Vieng Sra[3] and at Srivisay hill[4] between Bandon and Surat, those of Gaṇeśa and Naṭarāja Śiva[5] whose place of origin is unknown, and a second Viṣṇu and a Śiva Bhairava[6] from Vieng Sra.

Most of the Buddhist images—Buddha and Lokeśvara—come from Caiya, to which we may add two *in situ* in the cave

---

1. The most important publications, on which the following account is mainly based, are the following (referred to in the following footnotes by the Roman letters).

   A. Lajonquierre—B. C. A. I., 1909, pp. 188ff.

   B. Do. —B. C. A. I., 1912, pp. 125ff.

   C. G. Coedès —I. A. L., Vol. I, pp. 57-72.

   D. Dr. H. G. Quaritch Wales—I. A. L., Vol. IX, No. I.

   E. Ars Asiatica, Vol. V.

2. A, pp 233-4, figs 25-6. D, Pll. II, IV.
3. C, PL. XIV.
4. Ibid, Pl. XV.
5. A, Pl. IV. Fig. II.
6. C, Pll. V-VI.

of Phu Khao Ngu.[1] Two bronze images now in Bangkok also originally belonged to Caiya[2].

G. Coedès has divided the images into three classes according to the style, *viz.*, (1) Indo-Javanese, (2) Indian, and (3) Local.

Under the first heading he includes the two bronze images of Caiya, but evidently with some amount of hesitation. It appears to me that there is not sufficient reason to attribute their workmanship to Javanese or Sumatran influence rather than to a direct influence from India. As a matter of fact, the images of Śiva, Bhairava, and Viṣṇu (No. 2) from Vieng Sra which Coedès places in the second category—'very much approaching the Indian prototype'—are less Indian than the two bronze images. I would, therefore, prefer to group the first two categories of Coedès as Indian and recognise only two classes, *viz.* (1) Indian, and (2) Local.

Some images in Class I, belong distinctly to the Gupta school of Art, *e.g.* the fine sandstone figure of Buddha from Vieng Sra[3] (Pl. LXXIV, Fig. 1), the bronze Buddha from Rambutan, and the very beautiful standing bronze Buddha found at Pengkalan near Ipoh, in Perak State.[4] In this class there are certain images of a very high order of artistic merit. The Viṣṇu image from Vieng Sra (Pl. LXXIII, Fig. 1) has not only a fine modelling but an individuality and strength which easily rank it as one of the best specimens in the whole of Indo-China. The general treatment undoubtedly indicates the influence of Gupta traditions. Its peculiar head-dress, similar to a modern Fez, is found in later Khmer art, and it is reasonable to hold that this element was introduced there through the influence of the art of Malay Peninsula. The image of Phru No[5] hill (Pl. LXXI, Fig. 2) also belongs to the same style and is of excellent workmanship

1. A, pp. 226, 228; Figs 19, 21-23.
2. E, pp. 17, 56; Pl. 47. C, Pll. III-IV.
3. D, Pl. V-1.
4. Winstedt—History of Perak, p. 4.
5. D, Pl. II, 1.

Lojonquiere even goes so far as to say that it is far superior to any sculpture hitherto discovered in Indo-China.

The two bronze images of Lokeśvara at Caiya testify to the high level which was attained not only by the art of bronze-casting, but also by the sculpture of the Peninsula in general. The naturalistic treatment, with graceful modelling, and a serene expression are characteristics of these images. The same may be said of the three Brahmanical images found at Phra Narai hill, Takua Pa[1] (Pl. LXXII). All these would rank as some of the best artistic achievements of Indian colonists.

The second Viṣṇu image and the Bhairaba from Vieng Sra (Pl. LXXIII, Figs. 3-4) although Indian in inspiration and style, already indicate by their rigidity and facial expressions the influence of local factors which led to the growth of an indigenous school of art.

A comparison of the three images of Caiya, belonging to this local school[2], with the two bronze images of the same god found in the same locality, would convey an adequate idea of the influence of local development upon what was originally an Indian style. Rigid formalism takes the place of modelling, and we miss the grace and serenity in the expression. Occasionally, however, the artist succeeds, in spite of his limitations, in infusing something of the old spirit.

As regards architecture we have two most important sanctuaries in Caiya, *viz.*, Vat Phra That and Vat Keo.

The Vat Phra That[3], a brick temple (Pl. LXXIV, Fig. 2), stands on a square basement, with sides regularly oriented. The basement, about 6 ft. high, with each side measuring more than 20½ ft., has flat mouldings intersected by eight pilasters on each side.

---

1. Good illustrations of these are to be found in D, Pl. IV.

2. C, Pll. 7-9.

3. A, Pl. II. fig. 7, Pl. III. fig. 8. D. Pl. VI-1, B. E. F. E. O., Vol. XXXI, p. 378, Pl. XXXIX, fig. 41.

The main temple occupies the centre of the basement, at each corner of which is a small detached *stūpa*. The temple is likewise square in plan with deep projections on sides, that of the east constituting the ante-chamber to the cella. The cella is nearly 3 ft. square, and its walls are plain.

Externally the walls stand on a moulded base and support a heavy cornice. The projections have also flat mouldings, and heavy cornice supporting a tympanum. The roof consists of three gradually decreasing stories, each of which is a miniature of the main temple including the corner *stūpas*. Above the third storey is a conventional lotus bud, surrounded by eight *stūpas* and supporting the tall spire encircled by rings.

There is an exuberance of Stucco decorations, but they are mostly later additions. Parmentier has already noted that Vat Phra That represents a type of construction which is carved on the bas-reliefs of Barabuḍur.[1] But this is true only of the general plan, not of the decorations.

The Vat Keo[2] is also a brick sanctuary, but it is in a much more dilapidated condition. The cella is square and approached by an ante-chamber in the east. Corresponding to this ante-chamber there are three chapels on three other sides. As Mr. Coedès has observed, its plan resembles that of Caṇḍi Kalasan. But its architecture "recalls closely the cubic art of Champā and the (Pre-Khmer of archaic type) Prasāt Krahām of Phnom Kulen (Cambodia)." "Thus we have the surprising phenomenon appearing here so unexpectedly of a single building combining some of the basic characteristics of the early buildings of Cham, Pre-Khmer and Javanese styles." Dr. H. G. Wales has justly emphasised the fact that the buildings to which Vat Keo bears strong points of resemblance are among the earliest of Indian colonial types,

1. Etudes Asiatiques Vol. II, p. 210.

2. D, Pl. VI-3. B. E. F. E. O., Vol. XXXI, pp. 380-4. Pl. XL-XLIV, figs. 42-4.

and that we have in Caiya the survival of very early non-specialized types of Indian colonial architecture[1]

On the northern extremity of the Peninsula, at Pechaburi, there is a group of temples called Vat Kampheng Leng[2] built in Kāmboja style. Inside an enclosure are three temples in a line, north to south, with two *Gopurams* on the two sides of the central temple. The temples were originally Brāhmanical, but now contain images of Buddha, though images of Viṣṇu or Garuḍa are still met with.

By far the most imposing structure in the Peninsula is the Vat Phra That in Nakhon Śrī-Thammarat (Ligor).[3] It consists of a group of buildings within an enclosed area. The central structure is a *stūpa* of the type known in Siam as Phra Cheidi. A square base, measuring 33 yds. each way, supports a number of circular mouldings upon which rests the bell-shaped body of the *stūpa*. Above it is a square box supporting a high conical structure consisting of a large number of discs gradually decreasing in size, corresponding, no doubt, to the umbrellas.

The base of this central *stūpa* is surrounded by a covered gallery on all sides. In front of the staircase which gives access to the top of the base is a rectangular treasure-chamber.

The *stūpa* is situated in a large court-yard 142 yds. long (north-south) and 87½ yds. broad (east-west). In this court-yard are arranged in several lines hundreds of smaller *stūpas* of the same shape as the central one.

There are 171 seated Buddha statues in the court-yard. The walls of the galleries which surround the *stūpa* and the courtyard, as well as those of the treasure-chamber, are carved with relief sculptures. These have been covered by thick layers of plaster. There are also two other smaller structures inside the court-yard. On the whole the Vat Phra That has a splendid and imposing appearance.

---

1. D, p. 21, C, p. 65. 2. A, pp. 208ff., Pl. I, figs. 3-5.

3. A, pp. 229ff., figs. 16, 24; B. pp. 148ff. fig. 34. D, p. 22.

Though the central shrine is undoubtedly Siamese in style, there is a small building in the court-yard (Pl. LXXIV, Fig. 3) which M. Claeys regards as a miniature reproduction of the original shrine. M. Claeys has demonstrated the wide-spread custom that when an old shrine was substituted by a new one, a small miniature of it was preserved in the precincts. M. Claeys has also drawn attention to the fact that the style of this small building recalls the architecture of Caṇḍi Kalasan in Java and the temples of Dong Duong and Mison in Champā. This will appear from the plan and elevation[1].

There are a few Brāhmanical temples in Nakhon Sri Thammarat. One of them, Ho Phra Isuon, has been described by Dr. H. G. Quaritch Wales and M. Claeys, both of whom emphasise the strong Indo-Javanese style of the building. Dr. Wales thinks that the style is even more primitive than anything found on the Dieng Plateau in Java, and remarks: "But just as the little colony of Brahmans, who trace their descent from India, exist in this great centre of Buddhism as a survival from an earlier order, so they have preserved in their little temples the memory of an early Indian colonial type of architecture[2]." Unfortunately, the photograph of the temple, as published by Dr. Wales, does not give sufficient details for an archæological description.

1. B. E. F. E. O., Vol. XXXI, pp. 373ff. For plan see fig. 40. For Elevation, fig. 39 and Pl. XXXVIII. Cf. also D, Pl. VI-2.

2. D, pp. 22-3, Pl. VII. B. E. F. E. O., Vol. XXXI, pp. 373ff.

Chapter X

ART IN OTHER ISLANDS

1. The Philippines

That the influence of Indian art penetrated even into the Philippine islands is proved by two images. One of them, a Śiva image of copper, was found on the Sibu island in 1820. It is a little more than three inches high, and shows features of Indian or Indo-Javanese art.

The second is a golden figure of a female deity (?) (Pl. LXXV, Figs. 1-2) seated cross-legged. It was found in a ravine on the left bank of the Wawa river near the town of Esperanza, Agusan Province, Mindanao. It is made of 21 karat gold, and weighs nearly 4 lbs. The figure has a richly decorated head-dress and many ornaments in arms and other parts of the body. It is presumably the image of a goddess, but in the absence of any attributes it is difficult to identify her. Although it cannot be regarded as very beautiful, the sharp features of the image show that the art technique was developed far beyond the primitive stage.[1]

2. The Island of Celebes.

The island of Celebes has yielded a fine bronze image of Buddha (Pl. LXXV, Fig. 3). It was found on the western coast, on the bank of the Karama river, about six miles inland. The most characteristic features of the figure are the fold-lines of the upper garment which passes over the left shoulder and leaves the right one bare. The fold-lines are neat and schematic, and so also are the small ringlets formed by the

1. O. V., 1920, p. 101 and plates.

hair. The hands and legs are broken. The Buddha has a full oval face with thick lips and heavy features.

Artistically the image must be distinguished from the usual Indo-Javanese and Indo-Sumatran type, and its style is derived directly from India. Dr. Bosch traces it to the Amarāvatī school of sculpture. Perhaps it is safer to regard the style as of the early Gupta period without special reference to any locality.[1]

The presence of a similar bronze Buddha figure at Dong-Duong (Annam) shows the wide spread of the Gupta style of art over the whole region denoted by the term Far East.

---

1. T. B. G., Vol. 73 (1933), pp. 495-513 and plates.

Chapter XI

GENERAL REVIEW OF THE ART OF SUVARNADVĪPA.

A broad review of the art of the different regions which we have sketched above leads to some conclusions of a general nature.

In the first place we find a general affinity in architecture and sculpture of these regions, an affinity which is undoubtedly to be explained by the fact that they had directly or indirectly derived their art from one common source.

This common source is the Gupta art of India. By this expression I do not mean the art of any particular locality, but rather the classical phase of Indian art which is designated by that name, and which distinguishes itself easily from the ancient and mediaeval art of India, whether of the north or of the south.

This statement will perhaps meet with a general acceptance in case of sculpture. Indeed this has been hinted at—though not worked out in detail—by eminent art critics, like Coomaraswamy. We have seen above that some images of Buddha in Malay Peninsula and Sumatra are unmistakably Gupta in character, and that those of Barabuḍur in Java are also to be ultimately traced to the same source.

This is indeed what could be normally expected. The Hindu colonies in Malayasia can be definitely traced from about the fourth or fifth century A. D. The people who left India about that period, or even during the next two centuries, carried with them living traditions of the Gupta art, and these blossomed in their new homes, modified in varying degrees by the new influences and environments to which they were subjected.

As regards architecture this view has not found any general expression so far. This is undoubtedly to be explained by the fact that we have no definite idea of the Gupta architecture, as very few important sanctuaries of that age have survived in a clearly recognisable shape. Still the proof is not altogether lacking that in architecture, too, the fundamental characteristics were already evolved in the Gupta age.

In judging of the style of architecture we should primarily keep three things in view, *viz.*, (1) plan of the temple, (2) its roof, and (3) the decorative scheme.

As regards the plan of temples we have seen above that the system almost universally adopted was that of a square chamber with projections on all sides, that in the front (generally East) serving as entrance.

That this general plan characterised the temples of the Gupta period is amply evidenced by the temple of Bhitārgāon[1] which has exactly the same plan. Bhitārgāon is a village about 20 miles south of Cawnpore in U. P. Its brick temple is described by Vogel as a unique specimen of the architecture of the early Gupta period. The Gupta temple at Nachna[2] in Bundelkhand and at Deogarh[3] on the Betwa have also a similar plan.

The roof of the Bhitārgāon temple consists of a series of receding stages—each a replica of the main temple—with a hollow cone inside. As we have seen above, this forms the characteristic feature of the roof of the early temples of Java. That this method was generally adopted in constructing the roof of the Gupta temples is further evidenced by the extant portions of the roof of the Deogarh temple and the illustration of temple-roofs used as decorative devices in Gupta sculptures

1. Cunningham in A. S. R., Vol. XI, pp. 40ff., Pll. XIV-XVI. Vogel in Ann. Rep. Arch. Surv. I. 1908-9, pp. 8-18 and plates.

2. Progr. Rep. Arch, Surv. W. Circle, 1918-19, Pl. XVI. A. S. R. Vol. XXI, Pl. XXV.

3. A. S. R., Vol. X, pp. 100ff, Pll. XXXIV-XXXVI.

of Sārnāth[1]. A careful examination of these will convince everybody that the principles of roof-construction which we find in Malayasia were based on the Gupta style. Dr. Coomaraswamy has rightly observed that the "Nāgara spire (*i. e.* śikhara of Northern India), however elaborately developed, really represents a piling up of many super-imposed storeys or roofs, much compressed[2]."

To the same Gupta style also belongs the general plan of decoration, such as carved panels and pilasters, arched niches with figures, scroll-work with figures of birds and animals, the Makaras etc. Even the most characteristic feature of the Javanese decorative art—the ubiquitous Kāla-Makara—has its prototype in the Gupta art[3]. I may add that the general plan of the mouldings of the Javanese temples has its counterpart in Gupta style[4].

Dr. Vogel has already remarked that "the spire of the Bhitārgāon temple with its rows of heads peeping, as it were, out of so many dormer-windows, bears a curious resemblance to some of the so-called Raths at Māmallapuranm near Madras, and also to the Caṇḍi Bima on the Dieng plateau in Central Java. ...Another Javanese temple which exhibits the same peculiarity...is the Gunung Gangsir...a brick temple

1. D. R. Sahni—Catalogue of the Museum of Archaeology at Sarnath, Pll. XXV-XXVIII. The Daśa-Avatāra temple at Mārkaṇḍa, 90 miles S. E. of Nagpur, offers a developed type of similar roof (A. S. R., Vol. IX, pp. 142ff. Pl. XXVIII).

2. Coomaraswamy, p. 83. Cf his remarks on p. 94 about the resemblance of the roof of Sirpur temple with that of Caṇḍi Bima.

3. The Kāla-Makara is undoubtedly derived from Indian Kīrtimukha. Cf. *e.g.* the following illustrations ; Memoirs A. S. I. No. 44, Pl. VIII-fig. 3 ; Bhattasali (see f. n. 2 p. 351) Pll. 26, 34, 63, 64, 66) ; Indian Sculpture by Stella Kramrisch, fig. 96.; Banerjee—Mediaeval Sculpture, Pll. XXXIII, XXXV ; J. G. I. S. Vol. II, pp. 38ff.

4. Cf. *e.g.* mouldings of a pedestal in a temple at Khoh (A. S. R. Vol. IX, Pl. III) and Paraoli (Vol. XX, Pl. XXIII). For a developed form at Pathāri, cf. Vol. VII, Pl. XI.

on the border of the residencies of Surabaya and Pasaruan. It is the oldest temple known to exist in Eastern Java." It is, perhaps, not a mere accident that the oldest temples, both in Eastern and Central Java, should exhibit the characteristic Gupta style of decoration.

Dr. Vogel's reference to Mamallapuram deserves more than a passing notice. It has been too common a fashion to trace the architecture and sculpture of Java to a South Indian origin, as there are certain resemblances between the two. But it is seldom recognised that these south Indian specimens are themselves derived from the Gupta art, and that therefore such resemblances as we find may be explained very easily by the common parentage of the two. At the same time there are vital objections to the theory of South Indian origin. From the earliest to the latest period, pillars form a very prominent feature of the south Indian architecture, but they are conspicuous by their absence in temples of Java, which agree in this respect with north Indian architecture.

All the evidences that we possess seem to indicate, that down to the seventh century A. D. the regular sea-port in India, which served as the port of embarkation for Malayasia, was Paloura near Ganjam, or Tāmralipti in Bengal. I-tsing definitely says about Tāmralipti that "this is the place where we embark when returning to China[1]." Again we know from the same author, that the royal marine of Śrī-Vijaya plied regularly between that port and Tāmralipti, touching Malay Peninsula on their way[2]. Besides, the famous monastery at Nālandā had grown into an international centre of Buddhism, and through it Indian culture spread to the Far East, where Śrī-Vijaya seems to have been the most important centre of Mahāyāna Buddhism. It is, therefore, no mere accident, that precisely in Sumatra and Malay Peninsula we find sculptures which exhibit clear Gupta influence. Through these regions traditions of Gupta art,

1. P. XXXIV. 2. P. XXX.

mainly of Eastern India, must have reached the regions in the interior including Java[1]. Both Dr. Bosch and Dr. Krom have justly remarked that South India exercised no influence of any importance on the art of Sumatra. This may be regarded as generally true of Malayasia, until the tenth or eleventh century A. D., when the Colas established an intimate and direct contact between South India and the Far East. Until then the main inspiration of Indian culture flowed from Eastern India rather than Southern. The influence of the latter was carried to a certain extent only indirectly through Ceylon.

The successive phases in the evolution of art in India must have also exercised great influence over the development of art in Malayasia. It is beyond the scope of the present work to enter into a minute and detailed discussion of this point, but a few broad facts may be stated.

In sculpture the influence of Mediaeval Indian art introduced similar transformation in Java. In particular the influence of the Pāla school is to be clearly noted, and similar influences of other local schools may be detected on a closer scrutiny.

In architecture, the recent discovery of the temple of Pāhārpur shows how a complex plan like that of the central temple at Sevu has its Indian prototype. In the miniature roof illustrated in Bengali sculptures of the Pāla period, we get an Indian prototype of the storied roofs in Java, Bali, and Pagan[2].

Lastly, we may notice the thoroughly Indian character of the conception and execution of art in Malayasia before it was modified by the local influence. The general grace and charm of the naturalistic figures, and the emphasis on their inner spirituality, make us feel at every step that they were direct offshoots of the art of India, which transcended all

---

1. Cf. the views of Dr. H. G. Q. Wales, as given on p. 344.

2. Iconography of Buddhist and Brahmanical sculptures in the Dacca Museum by Dr. N. K. Bhattasali, pp. XIIff. Pll. XIV, XLVIII.

geographical limitations in its natural expansion and development. It has already been noted above that the fauna and flora represented in Javanese art are purely Indian, and there is absolutely no trace of local peculiarity in these respects.

In course of time, owing to various causes, the direct contact with India grew less and less. It resulted in a gradual assertion of the local Indonesian element which ultimately dominated over the Indian. There was also a great decadence in the art of India, and the fountain having dried up, the stream that was fed by it ultimately ceased to flow. Thus the Indian period of art was succeeded by what may be called the Indonesian period. Nowhere can the nature and progress of this change be so clearly traced step by step as in Java, but we find exactly the same phenomena in other parts of Malayasia.

In Java the two periods are roughly represented by the art of Central and Eastern Java. We may, therefore, conclude this general review by a recapitulation of the main features of the art of Eastern Java.

While there is no doubt that it shows continuation of the old traditions of Central Java, there is equally little doubt that it indicates a gradual assertion of indigenous spirit over the purely Indian elements that dominated the earlier art. In sculpture, this gradual process of Javanisation is clear and unmistakable, and even he who runs may read it in the grotesque, clumsy, vulgar, and coarse reliefs in Caṇḍis Jago, Suravana, and Panataran. The divine images of Singhasāri, Jago, and other places, and some rare specimens of decorative sculpture indicate, however, that either the Indian influence had not died out altogether, or it was revivified from time to time by fresh immigration of artists from India. It also appears that the profane hands of the neo-artists did not yet dare to soil the figures of divinities. In architecture the influence of indigenous spirit is manifest from the absence of any symmetrical plan of a temple-complex. It is noticed also

INDEX

INDEX

INDEX

INDEX

INDEX